# Institutions for the Earth

**Global Environmental Accords Series**
Nazli Choucri, editor

*Global Accord: Environmental Challenges and International Responses*
Nazli Choucri, editor

*Institutions for the Earth: Sources of Effective International Environmental Protection*
Peter M. Haas, Robert O. Keohane, and Marc A. Levy, editors

# Institutions for the Earth
## Sources of Effective International Environmental Protection

edited by Peter M. Haas, Robert O. Keohane,
and Marc A. Levy

The MIT Press
Cambridge, Massachusetts
London, England

Second printing, 1994
© 1993 Massachusetts Institute of Technology

This book was set in Sabon by Asco Trade Typesetting Ltd., Hong Kong and was printed and bound in the United States of America.

Library of Congress Cataloging-in-Publication Data

Institutions for the earth : sources of effective international
  environmental protection / edited by Peter M. Haas, Robert O.
  Keohane, and Marc A. Levy.
    p.   cm.—(Global environmental accords)
  Includes bibliographical references and index.
  ISBN 0-262-08218-7.—ISBN 0-262-58119-1 (pbk.)
  1. Environmental protection—International cooperation.
2. International agencies.  I. Haas, Peter M.  II. Keohane, Robert
O. (Robert Owen), 1941–   . III. Levy, Marc A.  IV. Series.
TD170.2.I556  1993
363.7'0526—dc20                                       92-34908
                                                           CIP

# Contents

## IV Conclusion

# Series Foreword

A new recognition of profound interconnections between social and natural systems is challenging conventional constructs as well as the policy predispositions informed by them. Our current intellectual challenge is to develop the analytical and theoretical underpinnings crucial to our understanding of the relationships between the two systems. Our policy challenge is to identify and implement effective decision-making approaches to managing the global environment.

The Series on Global Environmental Accords adopts an integrated perspective on national, international, cross-border, and cross-jurisdictional problems, priorities, and purposes. It examines the sources and consequences of social transactions as these relate to environmental conditions and concerns. Our goal is to make a contribution to both the intellectual and the policy endeavors.

# Foreword

Global environmental threats have attained a prominent position on the international agenda. These transnational problems cannot be managed by one country acting alone. Policymakers need effective institutions to facilitate cooperation across borders and to organize political energies for environmental policy change. In the rapidly evolving world of international environment policy—particularly in the post–Cold War period—how have institutions fared, what functions have they performed well, and how can they be improved in the future?

International environmental institutions have proliferated since the 1972 United Nations Conference on the Human Environment. Over sixty multilateral environmental treaties have been signed, and new regimes have been established for the protection of stratospheric ozone, the protection of many regional seas from pollution, the regulation of oil pollution from tankers, the control of European acid rain, regulation of trade in potentially hazardous farm chemicals, and many others. Still, we do not know how effective existing institutions are at accommodating the challenges to governance posed by environmental issues.

Social science should have a role to play in answering these questions. Yet most scholarly analysis of international environmental policy has understated the institutional dimensions. Policy content has been stressed at the expense of policy process, and little or no systematic attention has been paid to the international institutions that must shape that process. This project began with questions about the effectiveness of existing international institutional efforts to protect the environment and a concern for making social scientists' understanding about international institutions meaningful for the 1992 United Nations Conference on Environment and Development (UNCED).

For thirty-five years, Harvard's Center for International Affairs (CFIA) has been concerned with exactly this type of policy-relevant basic research. Thus in 1990, Robert Paarlberg, Peter Haas, and Robert Keohane drafted a proposal that the Rockefeller Brothers Fund supported. Marc Levy later joined as coeditor. A team was assembled from the broader CFIA community, and an organizational conference was held in December 1990 to develop common approaches for each of the case studies. The project benefited at that organizational meeting from the constructive and informed contributions of Peter Thacher and Oran Young. The final papers were subjected to critical review at a second conference in December 1991.

The contributors found an important role for international environmental institutions in promoting international cooperation. By performing three major functions—what Haas, Keohane, and Levy call the three Cs: increasing governmental concern, enhancing the contractual environment, and increasing national capacity—international environmental institutions have contributed to more effective national efforts to protect the quality of the global environment. Effective international environmental institutions thus helped to overcome some of the typical national bottlenecks that hinder coordinated measures to reverse the frightening trends of global environmental degradation and improve the possibility of sustainable development of our planet.

International institutions are not static. They are best understood in a dynamic context. Environmental protection is a process, and institutions have contributed to the development of more stringent measures for environmental protection over time. By targeting attention on an issue, and helping to generate public commitments by governments, institutions contributed to an evolving process of environmental protection. National groups, such as environmental NGOs (nongovernmental organizations), and also private corporations, have then been able to hold their governments accountable for their public commitments. There is a division of labor here. Institutions help to establish a baseline which other bodies in society then supervise.

These papers went through at least three drafts, with extensive comments by the editors on contributors' drafts—including those of contributors who also served as editors. The editors are grateful to all the contributors for their intelligent and prompt responses to criticisms, their energy, and their lack of defensiveness.

The contributors, and the Center for International Affairs, are grateful above all to the Rockefeller Brothers Fund for its generous support of this project. We especially thank Colin Campbell, president of the Fund and William F. McCalpin, who worked with Professors Haas, Keohane and Paarlberg on behalf of the Fund in developing the proposal. The contributors also thank the staff of the Center for International Affairs, especially Christopher R. Briggs-Hale, who provided logistic support for the conferences and for the volume. Madeline Sunley, acquisitions editor at MIT Press, quickly secured four very helpful anonymous reviews of our manuscript, and played a key role in facilitating arrangements for publication by the Press.

Thanks are due to so many people for their comments that we hesitate to mention individuals by name. The authors of the papers have, in separate acknowledgments, indicated their greatest intellectual and editorial debts. Here, it is important particularly to recognize the encouragement, criticisms and suggestions of William Clark of the Kennedy School of Government at Harvard, and the commentaries of Antonia Chayes and David Fairman at a seminar at the Kennedy School in February, 1992, at which Robert Keohane presented the main outline of the project. The editors are also thankful for constructive suggestions to participants at seminars at the Stanford University Department of Political Science and the International Institutions Program of the Center for International Affairs at Harvard, where Robert Keohane made presentations, and to participants at the Second World Structures Convocation in Washington, D.C., where Peter Haas presented the draft conclusion.

The rewards of intellectual labor come not merely in the product, but in the process of discovery and the stimulating discussions associated with any coherently designed joint work. The contributors all regard themselves as having been enriched by these interactions, and hope that the result, presented here, will make a contribution, however modest, to protecting the environment of the earth.

Joseph S. Nye, Jr., Director
Center for International Affairs
April 13, 1992

# I

# Introduction

# 1

# The Effectiveness of International Environmental Institutions

Robert O. Keohane, Peter M. Haas, and Marc A. Levy

The United Nations Conference on Environment and Development (UNCED) constituted the world's most comprehensive organized response to international environmental degradation. UNCED sought to adopt conventions on greenhouse gases and biodiversity; enunciated principles by which humans should conduct themselves relative to the environment (the Earth Charter); adopted a program of action to implement the Earth Charter (Agenda 21); and debated a set of institutional and financial arrangements to support such measures.

It is common to find expressions of profound skepticism regarding the ability of the nation-state system to solve the problems on UNCED's agenda. Because states are ultimately concerned with protecting national security and maintaining economic growth, they may be incapable of adequately addressing the fundamental problems which have given rise to environmental issues. As long as governments protect national interests and refuse to grant significant powers to supranational authorities, these critics argue, the survival of the planet is in jeopardy. In the words of one such critic, "our accepted definition of the limits of national sovereignty as coinciding with national borders is obsolete."[1]

We are grateful to Antonia Chayes, Barbara Crane, Ernst B. Haas, Robert Paarlberg, M. J. Peterson and David Victor for written comments on earlier drafts.
1. Jessica Tuchman Mathews, "Redefining Security" *Foreign Affairs* 68, 2 (Spring 1989): 174. Writing in 1990, Lynton K. Caldwell cited the following assessment approvingly: "There are many problems that call for institutional management of a global character, but we do not believe that it lies within the capacity of the present system of states to alter to this extent the attitudes, values, and sources of support necessary for such a transformation. . . ." *International Environmental Policy: Emergence and Dimensions*, 2nd revised edition

The skeptics are surely right to warn that the planet's ecosystem is in danger and that its protection will require modifications in traditional interpretations of state sovereignty. Yet world government is not around the corner: organized international responses to shared environmental problems will occur through cooperation among states, not through the imposition of government over them. Before becoming depressed by this prospect, we should note that interstate cooperation has achieved major successes with problems that earlier seemed as daunting as UNCED's agenda does today. Cholera, which formerly ravaged populations in regular cycles, was virtually eliminated through international cooperation. Slavery has all but disappeared, also with the help of international conventions. Atmospheric testing of nuclear weapons has been banned under the auspices of an international treaty. Human activities for which the rates of anthropogenic releases to the environment have decelerated since 1955—of sulfur, lead, and carbon tetrachloride—are all areas in which international environmental institutions were developed and applied.[2]

The international community's ability to preserve the quality of the planet for future generations depends upon international cooperation. Successful cooperation, in turn, requires effective international institutions to guide international behavior along a path of sustainable development. By "institutions" we mean persistent and connected sets of

(Durham: Duke University Press, 1990), citing Cyril Black and Richard Falk, "Introduction: The Structure of the International Environment," *The Future of the International Legal Order*, vol. 4 (Princeton: Princeton University Press, 1972), ix. See also David Newsom, "The New Diplomatic Agenda: Are Governments Ready?" *International Affairs* 65, 1 (Winter 1988–1989). Such skepticism, which runs deeply through much writing on the international environment, was starkly reflected in discussions in 1989 concerning the possible creation of a new organization, Globe, which would have been given the power to initiate and enforce environmental agreements (*Financial Times*, 13 March 1989).

2. Tragically, cholera has recently reemerged in Latin America. For data on long-term human-induced environmental degradation see B. L. Turner II, William C. Clark, Robert W. Kates, John F. Richards, Jessica T. Mathews, and William B. Meyer (eds.) *The Earth as Transformed by Human Action* (Cambridge: Cambridge University Press, 1990). The data mentioned come from Robert W. Kates, B. L. Turner II, and William C. Clark, "The Great Transformation," 8. See also James Gustave Speth, "Environmental Pollution," in National Geographic Society, *Earth '88: Changing Geographic Perspectives* (Washington, D.C.: National Geographic Society, 1988).

rules and practices that prescribe behavioral roles, constrain activity, and shape expectations. They may take the form of bureaucratic organizations, regimes (rule-structures that do not necessarily have organizations attached), or conventions (informal practices). The institutions on which we focus in this volume include both organizations and sets of rules, codified in conventions and protocols that have been formally accepted by states. It is convenient to use the word "institutions" to cover both organizations and rules, since clusters of rules are typically linked to organizations, and it is often difficult to disentangle their effects. On issues such as ozone depletion and acid rain in Europe, rather sweeping commitments are coupled with very small organizational structures, whereas on some other issues such as population, many organizations exist without much agreement on the rules that should govern issues such as support for family planning programs. Each case study has a slightly different emphasis, on rules or organizations. When we refer to both rules and organizations together, we use the more general term, institutions. The broad question we ask is whether international institutions, thus defined, promote change in national behavior that is substantial enough to have a positive impact, eventually, on the quality of the natural environment. In focusing on this question, we by no means assume that the impact of international institutions is necessarily positive. Often, for effective global action to be taken to improve the environment, international institutions are necessary; but they are certainly not sufficient. Indeed, if the rules and practices of international institutions are inconsistent with realities of power or ecology, they may become meaningless; and if their content creates perverse incentives, they may do more harm than good. None of the institutions discussed here seems to have been harmful on balance; but the possibility surely should be recognized.

Maurice Strong, Secretary General of UNCED, has argued that:

The need for international cooperation is inescapable, and growing almost exponentially. This in turn has focused renewed attention on the principal instruments through which such cooperation is carried out. Most notable are the United Nations and its system of agencies, organizations, and programs.... These organizations ... provide the indispensable structure and fora on which international cooperation depends. They are the newest, least understood, least appreciated, and least supported of all the levels of our hierarchy of governance—and the most removed from the people they serve. They represent not the precursors of world government but the basic framework for a world system of governance which is imperative to the effective functioning of our global society.[3]

Maurice Strong's emphasis on the centrality of international institutions is well placed, but nonetheless constitutes a puzzle. How can international institutions, which necessarily respect the principle of state sovereignty, contribute to the solution of difficult global problems? What are the sources of effectiveness for institutions which lack enforcement power? Answers to these questions are not only intrinsically important; they could help the current generation of world leaders to design more effective international environmental institutions.

Today's environmental diplomats, however, have few rigorously argued studies to guide their activities. Most international environmental institutions are of relatively recent origin, and academic research has lagged even further behind. Transboundary and commons environmental problems did not receive extensive international attention until the 1960s, and the environment really only became a subject of international policy and academic study with the 1972 United Nations Conference on the Human Environment (UNCHE). Over half of the 140 multilateral environmental treaties that have been adopted since 1921 were concluded since 1973. This volume is an effort to apply some of the accumulated academic insights to this recent history of environmental cooperation.

The contributors to this volume ask whether, and through what mechanisms, international institutions can be effective in making the environment more conducive to a healthy life for natural species, including but not limited to human beings. The contributors analyze the factors influencing organized responses to seven international environmental problems: oil pollution from tankers, acid rain, stratospheric ozone depletion, pollution of the Baltic and North seas, mismanagement of fisheries, overpopulation, and misuse of farm chemicals. They identify the roles played by international environmental institutions in attempting to solve these problems. Their analysis is largely informed with concepts and methods drawn from political science.

3. Maurice Strong, "What Place Will the Environment Have in the Next Century—and at What Price?" *International Environmental Affairs* 2, 3 (Summer 1990): 211–212.

The contributors focus on institutional effectiveness: Is the quality of the environment or resource better because of the institution? That is, without the institution would things be worse? This does not mean that problems are solved, merely that the international institutions had a positive contribution on the treatment of shared problems. Many environmental threats are caused by such factors as population pressures, unequal resource demands, and reliance on fossil fuel and chemical products which degrade the environment while also providing real social benefits to large numbers of people, as exemplified by agrochemicals. We ask whether institutions can help retard the rate of environmental decline, even if they fail to confront the underlying causes of such decline. We are pragmatists.

Truly effective international environmental institutions would improve the quality of the global environment. Much of this activity, however, is relatively new, and on none of the issues discussed in this book do we yet have good data about changes in environmental quality as a result of international institutional action. So we must focus on observable political effects of institutions rather than directly on environmental impact.[4]

Institutions can be important factors in protecting the environment. While environmental degradation is ultimately the result of aggregated individual decisions and choices, individual choices are responses to incentives and other forms of guidance from governments and other national institutions via laws, taxes, and even normative pronouncements.[5] Governments, too, respond to incentives and pressures from international institutions. Even on environmental issues which primarily affect and are caused by individuals in developing countries, national actions are guided by international institutional pressures.

4. This operationalization is meant to be compatible with that of Marc A. Levy, Gail Osherenko and Oran R. Young, "The Effectiveness of International Regimes: A Design for Large-Scale Collaborative Research," unpublished paper, Institute for Arctic Studies, Dartmouth College, 4 December 1991.
5. A pioneering study of a decade ago by Kay and Jacobson also focused on the functions of international organizations and their political effects. See David A. Kay and Harold K. Jacobson, eds., *Environmental Protection: The International Dimension* (Totowa, NJ: Allanheld, Osmun, for the American Society of International Law, 1983). See Chapters 2, 4, 7, and 8, this volume, for examples of how corporate and individual decisions reflect the incentives offered by public policy.

In this regard, we can reformulate the old adage to read Think Locally, Act Globally.

Effective institutions can affect the political process at three key points in the sequence of environmental policy making and policy implementation: (1) They can contribute to more appropriate agendas, reflecting the convergence of political and technical consensus about the nature of environmental threats; (2) they can contribute to more comprehensive and specific international policies, agreed upon through a political process whose core is intergovernmental bargaining; and (3) they can contribute to national policy responses which directly control sources of environmental degradation. Effectiveness in agenda setting and international policy formulation are facilitating conditions. National policy responses, because they directly affect the behavior of actors relevant to the environment, constitute a necessary condition for improvement in environmental quality. None of these conditions are logically sufficient, however; the best laid plans may prove inadequate. In the absence of good data on environmental effects, understanding how institutions affected these phases of policy activity enables us at least to undertake a preliminary analysis of whether international environmental institutions may be helping to protect an endangered earth.

## The Research Presented in This Volume

We have chosen seven environmental issues which have sufficiently long histories to enable us to make some preliminary judgments about the effectiveness of international institutions. We have tried to illustrate a range of comparable experiences, rather than select cases of either success or failure or simply focus on familiar topics that are widely regarded as important but which lack common analytic features. Our issue areas correspond to much of the substantive concern at UNCED: greenhouse gases and climate change (ozone protection); genetic diversity and resource management (fisheries management); and more general concerns with pollution control (Baltic and North Sea, acid rain, oil pollution from tankers, chemical regulation). Most transboundary and commons issues are regional. The population case is not simply an environmental problem, but, along with economic development, it is crucially important in all issues of environmental quality. Thus we believe that our range of cases is fairly representative of broader classes of problems confronting the international community.

These issues fall into two discrete classes. In the first, discussed in part I, harm is directly transmitted from one set of countries to another, via a physical or biological medium. Such direct transmission occurs in commons and transboundary problems, because the consequences of activities in one country are felt in another (transboundary) or affect a resource which is outside the jurisdiction of any one country (a commons problem). While there are many different types of transboundary and commons problems, we have chosen cases that are sufficiently similar to permit comparative conclusions. Stratospheric ozone depletion, European acid rain, marine oil pollution, Baltic and North Sea pollution, and most fishery problems are all cases in which the sets of countries who cause the problem and those who suffer from it overlap significantly. Therefore the politics of reaching solutions to these problems all took the form of seeking agreement on rules specifying mutual restraints. The chapters in part I are presented roughly in descending order of the promptness and effectiveness of international action.

A second class of issues involves environmental problems in which direct harm is felt only within national borders, and therefore mutual restraint is not the focus of political bargaining. Such problems, such as soil erosion and dwindling sources of safe drinking water, enter the international political agenda because one set of states wishes to promote national solutions within another set of countries. In broad terms, what is required for these problems to be solved is the development of concern within the countries where they occur, and the development of the domestic political and administrative capacity to implement solutions. International institutions can provide information, skills, resources and persuasion to boost both concern and capacity. The cases examined in part II include safe use of pesticides in the developing world, and population policies.

Both types of problems threaten human survival. Commons and transboundary problems affect the long-term sustainability of the planet's ecosystems, perhaps none more starkly than the threat of global climate change. But national problems may affect more individuals in the near future, especially in the developing world.

The two classes of problems often overlap in actual practice, and the distinction is not meant to be rigid. Solutions to national problems are often justified in terms of broader commons resources; population policies are justified in part by their role in reducing stress on the earth's atmosphere, for example. Often the solution to transboundary and commons problems will entail the transfer of concern and capacity to states which lack it, for example to Eastern European governments regarding acid rain. We apply our classification, therefore, in a way that is sensitive to the varying dynamics that may exist within a single issue area. Its utility lies in enabling us to be precise in analyzing the nature of institutional effects we observe.

We seek to uncover such institutional effects through a three-step analysis. First, the authors portray specific environmental problems, their causes and possible solutions, within a particular issue area. What were the configurations of interests and the areas of actual or potential conflict and cooperation? Second, we identify and describe efforts to respond to these problems, focusing on agenda setting, international policy formulation, and national policy development. We seek to describe patterns of activity for each sequence in each issue area in a way that highlights important similarities and variations, both across sequences within each issue area and across issue areas. Throughout our analysis, we look not simply at types and levels of international action in each issue area at each point in time, but at the pattern of change over time. Are agendas, policies, procedures, actions and impacts changing—and if so, in what directions? Since our conception of effectiveness is dynamic, it is particularly important to see whether positive change has occurred. Finally, the authors assess the precise role that international institutions had in contributing to the outcomes described in step two.

This final step requires reconstruction of causal mechanisms linking institutional characteristics with behavioral outcomes. Each author seeks to imagine how policies would have changed in his or her issue area in the absence of multilateral institutions, in the hope that such an analysis will yield valuable insights about the degree to which international institutions have been effective forces for environmental improvement, and the conditions under which particular strategies are more or less likely to succeed. To focus the analysis of the chapters and make them comparable with one another, each author explores the impact of international institutions on the three conditions that we claim are essential for effective action on environmental problems: high levels of *governmental concern*, a hospitable *contractual environment* in which agreements can be made and kept, and sufficient *political and administrative capacity* in national governments. Thus each chapter is organized descriptively around our three phases of activity—agenda setting, international policies, and national policy responses—and analytically around the categories of concern, the contractual environment, and political and administrative capacity.

### Descriptive Analysis: Three Phases of Policy Activity

Our approach is to analyze each issue area according to separate sequences of action, beginning with an initial bargaining situation and leading to a pattern of policy change. These sequences range from one or two years to two decades in length. They are defined not arbitrarily by a length of time, but by the analyst's judgment of the period during which the international policy process for the issue remained similar in fundamental ways, with the same crucial actors, similar conceptions of interest, and institutional continuity. Breaks between sequences imply discontinuities in some fundamental aspect of the political process. There is a great range from failure to change policy or improve the environment (early oil pollution regime; early fisheries cases) to considerable success, in terms of policy and of prospective impact on the environment (ozone negotiations). Quite a number of cases show ambiguous patterns, in which substantial changes in policy agendas, scientific research, and regulatory policies have been observed, but in which the extent of impact on the environment is contested or not yet clear (acid rain in 1980s, Baltic and North Sea since 1987, population since 1984); or in which impressive agenda setting and interorganizational collaboration still encounters huge obstacles in affecting ultimate environmental goals (chemical pesticides).

Within each sequence, we examine three distinct phases of action: agenda setting, international policy formulation, and national policy development. These are analytically distinct phases, but often overlap in time. There is often feedback from one to the other, as agendas are modified in light of governments' experiences with international and national policy actions, and as international and national policy actions are modified to reflect new scientific understandings about environmental problems and solutions and new agenda items.

### Agenda Setting

Countries must first identify problems for collective response. Hence, we first look at the agenda-setting phase. What problems are recognized as requiring action? Are evaluations of new problems accurate, and do they promptly reach the political agenda once having been identified?

Institutionalized agenda setting is an untidy process. Environmental monitoring is seldom conducted regularly, and authorities are often in conflict regarding who is responsible for such monitoring. Monitoring supported by governments or international organizations is subject to budgetary whims, while scientists often lack the resources to conduct necessary monitoring on their own. Many decision makers lack sufficient scientific input to make well-informed judgments.[6] Governments and interest groups that face high costs of environmental regulation or are unfazed by environmental threats may block expansion of the international agenda.

With respect to agenda setting, there is variation in the sources of pressure for institutional action. Powerful governments lead the way in some areas, pressed by concerned publics under the influence of perceived environmental crises. Such was the case, for instance, with respect to oil pollution from tankers, population policies, ozone depletion after 1985, the Baltic and North seas after 1987, and acid rain in Europe during the 1980s. In the 1970s, however, scientists raised the issue of ozone depletion in the absence of strong public or governmental concern; and nongovernmental organizations (NGOs) have taken the lead in raising the issue of chemical pesticides. Many regional seas programs were initiated after scientific revelations of regional contamination. Most issues appear to have received political attention following some sort of well-publicized shock or disaster. Some agendas for action

6. Viktor Sebek, "Bridging the Gap Between Environmental Science and Policy-Making: Why Public Policy Often Fails to Reflect Current Scientific Knowledge," *AMBIO* 12, 2: 118–120; Martin W. Holdgate, "The Environmental Information Needs of the Decision-Maker," *Nature and Resources* 18, 1 (January–March 1982).

were very ambitious, as in the population area during the 1960s, when large-scale delivery of family planning services was envisaged, or in the ozone negotiations of the 1980s, which moved quickly toward proposals for full phase-out of chlorofluorocarbon (CFC) production. Others, however, were modest, as in activities to control oil pollution at sea, to establish fisheries commissions, or to reduce acid rain in the 1980s.

**International Policies**
Agendas must be converted into policies or other measures for collective application. Significant action is often necessary to stem environmental threats. The pace of action is important: Did countries quickly act to convert the agenda to meaningful measures for environmental protection? We are especially concerned with the form of action. Did the conference or international organization merely make normative pronouncements; did it develop monitoring programs, sponsor scientific research or build national administrative capability; or did it establish specific regulatory standards? International population institutions, acid rain and ozone depletion negotiations in the 1970s, and collaboration between the United Nations Environment Program (UNEP) and the Food and Agriculture Organization (FAO) on chemical pesticides in the 1980s, all stressed scientific research or building national political and administrative capacity, often within stringent budgetary limitations. On the other hand, international regulatory institutions were developed to deal with marine oil pollution, the Baltic and North Seas, acid rain, and ozone depletion in the 1980s.

Concerning the negotiation of regulations specifying mutual restraints, decision making took place, in general, through multilateral conference diplomacy. Such processes are often highly conflictual, with governments seeking to avoid measures that will force their firms to lose any competitive advantage. Bargaining dynamics at this stage often involve leader states, who have already developed relatively stringent and forward-looking measures, and laggard states, who have relatively meager environmental measures and avoid international agreements involving more stringent measures.

In most of the sequences we examined, international decisions were taken by consensus. Only in some fisheries commissions and in recent ozone discussions were decisions taken by majority vote. Even in those cases, because of the need to preserve the appearance of universal support, maintaining consensus played a strong role. Governments always had the option of choosing not to participate in an agreement if they could not accept the emerging consensus; thus they could protect their sovereignty.[7] Such a least-common-denominator system frequently confers great blocking power to laggard states. Thus we look at institutional features involving voting rights, participation, frequency of meetings, and the like, which condition the way leaders and laggards interact.

However, the most important sources of variation in decision making across our cases do not derive from variations in formal rules, but from variations in the degree of political pressure brought to bear on the issue by governments responding to domestic political agitation. Indeed, without public and governmental pressure, effective action is unlikely to take place. Some international movement is possible simply from publicity generated by scientists or NGOs, and significant improvement in international policies has followed the participation of experts and scientists in influential international organizations and in government agencies of influential governments. Yet, there is discernibly more movement once most governments are subject to domestic pressure and there is a push from strong governments. The inability of international institutions to effectuate significant policy change without such pressure is suggested by the analysis with respect to Baltic and North seas, chemical pesticides, fisheries and population cases. *If there is one key variable accounting for policy change, it is the degree of domestic environmentalist pressure in major industrialized democracies, not the decision-making rules of the relevant international institution.* However, we do find that the institutions that have given rise to the most dramatic changes in collective policy making are those that were able to apply constructive channels for such domestic pressure to reach governments.

For national environmental issues, as discussed in Part II of this volume, the key political dynamics center not around the negotiation of mutual restraints but around the adoption of common norms and the development of political and administrative capacity to imple-

---

7. In the Conclusion to this volume (Chapter 8) we explore in more depth the implications for state sovereignty of international environmental institutions.

ment domestic policies on behalf of such norms. Therefore collective decision-making procedures are of less relevance than procedures aimed at promoting higher levels of concern and boosting capacity. Such procedures are commonly more operational in nature than those aimed at generating regulatory decisions. Scientific review panels are established, technical assistance teams are dispatched, financial aid programs are implemented. We find that through such programs institutions can succeed at spreading concern and capacity. Success is much more pronounced within the developed countries than the developing countries, however, which does not bode well for international negotiations involving North and South. We find evidence, for example, that Western European states became more concerned about acid rain through the operation of institutional activities, and that developed countries became more concerned about stratospheric ozone depletion due to activities connected to the Montreal Protocol. But with respect to the safe use of pesticides and population control, we find little increase in concern or capacity in the Third World that can be attributed to international institutions.

International institutions do not operate independently; on the contrary, they interact with one another. Institutions may come into conflict when conceptions of mission differ but jurisdictions overlap. The politics of issues in which several institutions operate may be quite different from those that have not been organized, or that are monopolized by a single international agency with its own clearly demarcated regime. In light of all that has been written about jurisdictional conflicts in the United Nations system, it is somewhat surprising, but heartening, to discover that in our cases, cooperation among agencies is more salient than interinstitutional conflict. With respect to chemical pesticides, UNEP managed to collaborate with the FAO, making the latter institution more "green" and less dirty. Coalitions of international institutions were also evident with respect to the UN Regional Seas Programme, coordinated by UNEP, and preliminary measures to implement resolutions on the phaseout of CFCs. UNEP's small size may be an advantage, forcing it to coordinate with larger agencies with greater administrative capabilities.

Governments are often caught by such organizational webs, and develop a stronger proclivity for effective environmental cooperation because more domestic groups are linked in an environmental coalition due to the possible rewards available from multiple organizations. Moreover, the crosscutting legal obligations assumed by governments toward multiple organizations make it harder for governments to withdraw from ongoing discussions and to renege on commitments.

Effective international policies for transboundary and commons problems require measures for monitoring countries' actions. We find that monitoring makes a big difference in institutional effectiveness, for reasons discussed in greater detail in the Conclusion.

## National Policy Responses

Ultimately, it is national decisions that affect environmental quality, even though international measures may have been necessary to overcome national reluctance to act and to reach harmonized national measures. Thus, we pay close attention to the extent to which national policy efforts actually comply with new international obligations. The authors look at actual and nominal national measures for environmental protection: what laws are passed, what new policies adopted, the extent of their enforcement, and what funds are invested.

Our studies reveal four types of national policy efforts. Some countries simply avoid international obligations by failing to sign treaty commitments. Others accept commitments but fail to live up to them. A third group accepts commitments and achieves compliance. Finally, a fourth group goes significantly further than explicit obligations require. Effective institutions nudge countries further along this path.

Countries that fall into the first two categories we call "laggards." Laggards typically possess much weaker environmental measures than others. The economic costs of increasing these measures may be high, and noncompliant laggards may have agreed to regulation only reluctantly. Many laggard countries also have supported collective policies knowing that they would not have the scientific, technical or administrative capacity to implement the rules, but hoping that "joining the club" would entitle them to assistance. Rich laggards (such as Britain with respect to acid rain) may also respond to political embarrassment or pressure from their own scientists or publics. Poor ones may require financial aid. In fact, in some areas such as the Baltic Sea, regulations were means of setting priorities for investment, which required funding either from public authorities in the wealthier countries of the region, or by private investors. Implementation of environmental policies is seldom simply a matter of compliance with legally binding standards imposed on governments by international institutions. Rather, it more commonly involves a combination of binding international law and public exposure of noncompliance (often by less inhibited nongovernmental organizations), normative persuasion, scientific argument, technical assistance, and investment.

"Leaders," on the other hand, willingly sign and comply with treaty commitments, and often go further than these commitments require. Leaders commonly possess a more advanced domestic environmental policy apparatus, and often are subject to more intense domestic political pressure than other countries. Domestic pressure, for example, led to U.S. leadership on marine oil pollution in the 1970s and ozone in the 1980's. Leaders are often motivated by being the first to suffer environmental damage; being first often means being most severely affected as well. Thus Sweden and Norway were leaders in acid rain, Britain in marine oil pollution. Domestic pressure, advanced policies, and disproportionate damage all give leaders higher levels of concern and capacity than others. In our cases these differences prompted leaders to promote institutional solutions to environmental problems.[8]

## Causal Analysis: Institutional Effectiveness

If some critics of the international system go too far in dismissing the potential of conventional diplomacy to yield productive responses to global problems, it would be equally foolish to have blind faith in international treaties. There are good reasons for healthy skepticism regarding the ability of international institutions to solve environmental problems. States maintain control; the institutions themselves are typically quite weak. Furthermore, our studies may paint too optimistic a pic-

8. For a more general discussion of leadership, see Oran R. Young, "Political Leadership and Regime Formation: On the Development of Institutions in International Society," *International Organization* 45, 3 (Summer 1991): 281–308. Young hypothesizes that the empirical regularity we observe constitutes a necessary condition, that "institutional bargaining cannot yield agreement concerning the provisions of constitutional contracts in the absence of leadership" (p. 302).

ture, since we have selected existing institutions, focusing only on issues where cooperation took place. So even though international institutions have responded in some form to all of the environmental issues discussed in our study, complacency is not in order. Even in the cases we examine we cannot assume that altered national activity alone proves impact. Policies might have changed as a result of shifts in domestic politics or scientific discoveries not occasioned by international action. Since we want to use our knowledge of the past to offer advice to designers and leaders of international organizations, as well as to help solve our analytical puzzles, it is essential for us to try to understand precisely how international institutions make a difference.

We carefully heed the warning that institutions are strongly affected by state power and interests as well as by other political forces. When states refuse to cooperate, as in the cases of farm chemicals, population, and many fisheries, institutions can play at best a marginal role. Such an understanding requires that we formulate and support a causal argument connecting regime characteristics and activities with the processes and outcomes described in our chapters.

We are sensitive to the possibility that sometimes institutions will play meager roles not due to unfortunate circumstance, but by design. Environmental politics is replete with symbolic action, aimed at pacifying aroused publics and injured neighbors without imposing severe costs on domestic industrial or agricultural interests. Politics within international institutions are also often highly symbolic: governments can vote one way and act another, on issues ranging from economic development to arms control. The environmental rabbit that is pulled at the last minute from an organizational hat may turn out to be illusory or ephemeral.

With these reservations in mind, we can nevertheless make some exploratory attempts to assess what factors may help to account for national policy change, and to ascertain degrees of, and conditions for, institutional effectiveness. Each author also asks whether the institutional process is sustainable, that is, whether it is capable of responding to future problems as they emerge.

The key to this assessment is an exercise in hypothetical counterfactual analysis, found in each chapter. Having described changes in agendas, in international policy, and in national policy, each author asks the question: suppose it had been impossible to construct a multilateral institution to cope with this problem—how would policies actually affecting the environment have been different? That is, each author imagines a situation with the same governmental policies, resources devoted to the problem, and scientific knowledge (except insofar as these factors were affected by international institutions). Then he or she asks what environmentally relevant policies would have emerged from such a situation, and how different they would have been from those that are observed. Some of the authors also explore another hypothetical question: what politically and economically feasible international institutional arrangements could be imagined that would have produced more effective policies in the area under review?

Rigorous answers to these counterfactual questions require the construction of causal pathways, supported with empirical evidence. Such pathways provide concrete mechanisms by which international institutions can alter the behavior of state actors, and in turn improve environmental quality. We argue that, at the level of international society, effective management of environmental problems requires three fundamental conditions to be met. First, governmental concern must be sufficiently high to prompt states to devote scarce resources to solving the problem. Since concern is typically generated by political action within societies, it is unlikely to be sufficient without active networks of individuals and groups, linked to the political system, pointing out environmental hazards and demanding action on them.

Second, transboundary and commons problems cannot be effectively resolved without a hospitable contractual environment. By this phrase we mean that states must be able to make credible commitments, to enact joint rules with reasonable ease, and to monitor each other's behavior at moderate cost so that strategies of reciprocity can be followed. In short, it must be feasible for governments to make and keep agreements that incorporate jointly enacted rules, without debilitating fear of free-riding or cheating by others.[9]

9. For discussions of the general issue that we are grouping under the label, "improving the contractual environment," see Robert O. Keohane, *After Hegemony: Cooperation and Discord in the World Political Economy* (Princeton: Princeton University Press, 1984), especially Chapters 5 and 6; Kenneth A. Oye (ed.), *Cooperation Under Anarchy* (Princeton: Princeton University Press,

Finally, states must possess the political and administrative capacity to make the domestic adjustments necessary for the implementation of international norms, principles, or rules. By political and administrative capacity we refer not only to the ability of governments to make and enforce laws and regulations, but also to the broader ability of actors in civil society to play an effective role in policy making and implementation. On the side of the state, the issue is broadly political as well as administrative, since the legitimacy of governments, and the degree to which they receive loyalty from their subjects and honest service from their own officials, are often open to question.[10] Civil society, for its part, must be capable of generating discussion and criticism of governmental action and inaction, and of participating in finding and carrying out policies that respond to environmental problems. Developing countries and the governments of Eastern Europe have typically lacked adequate capacity on both the governmental and societal dimensions—governments have often been unable either to understand or to regulate the impact of their citizens and industrial enterprises on the natural environment; and groups within civil society that could have been the source of information and criticism either do not exist or have been repressed.

Any particular international environmental issue will emerge onto the international political agenda with given values of concern, the contractual environment, and capacity—what we label "the three Cs." Any

---

1986). With respect to environmental issues, these questions are discussed in Elinor Ostrom, *Governing the Commons: The Evolution of Institutions for Collective Action* (Cambridge: Cambridge University Press, 1990); and Oran R. Young, *International Cooperation: Building Regimes for Natural Resources and the Environment* (Ithaca: Cornell University Press, 1989).

10. Myron Weiner and Samuel Huntington (eds.) *Understanding Political Development* (Boston: Little Brown, 1987); H. Jeffrey Leonard (ed.), *Divesting Nature's Capital: The Political Economy of Environmental Abuse in Developing Countries* (New York: Holmes & Meier, 1985); H. Jeffrey Leonard and contributors, *Environment and the Poor: Development Strategies for a Common Agenda* (New Brunswick, N.J.: Transaction Publishers, 1989); Theodore H. Moran (ed.), *Multinational Corporations: The Political Economy of Foreign Direct Investment* (Lexington, Mass.: Lexington Books, 1985); Theodore H. Moran and contributors, *Investing in Development: New Roles for Private Capital?* (New Brunswick, N.J.: Transaction Books, 1986); Charles S. Pearson (ed.), *Multinational Corporations, Environment, and the Third World* (Durham, N.C.: Duke University Press, 1987).

effective action of international institutions with respect to the global environment is likely to follow a path that increases concern or capacity, or improves the contractual environment. Since we are interested in the impact of international institutions on environmental quality, we are able to focus our analysis by emphasizing how international institutions affect the values of the three Cs. If governmental concern, the quality of the contractual environment, or political and administrative capacity are low, action on environmental problems will suffer.[11]

In fortuitous cases, concern, capacity, and the contractual environment are all favorable to effective management, and international institutions either are not needed or can succeed with minimal effort. This was probably the case in the 1911 Fur Seal Treaty discussed in Chapter 6 by M. J. Peterson. In most other cases, however, conditions are not initially ripe for successful joint management. Institutional effectiveness, in such cases, can be assessed by judging the extent to which they perform functions that boost the three Cs.

Institutions can offer rewards or punishments contingent on state policy in order to increase governmental concern, and government preferences may change in response to the resulting shifts in material incentives. For example, international population institutions have sought to alter government policies by providing technical and financial assistance to national family planning programs, and the Montreal Protocol contained provisions calling for trade sanctions against non-signatories.[12] Institutions can also generate new information that alters states' perception of the consequences of their actions. Institutional responses to the acid rain problem caused a number of states to redefine their views concerning the atmospheric transport and ecological effects of sulfur dioxide. That perceptual shift helps account for much of the change in policies witnessed in Europe.[13] Sometimes such a process of

11. Occasionally national problems of international importance (such as population control) will not require regulatory rules and therefore will not be constrained unduly by poor contractual environments. It is possible, however, that facilitating rules are of importance even for national problems (see Chapter 7 on pesticide trade). Our limited set of cases does not permit us to draw from generalizations.
12. Barbara Crane, Chapter 8, this volume; Edward Parson, Chapter 2, this volume.
13. Marc A. Levy, Chapter 3, this volume.

redefinition of interest occurs through the interaction of institutional activity and networks of scientists and experts known as epistemic communities.[14]

Institutions can also heighten state concern by magnifying public pressure on recalcitrant states. Peter Haas and Marc Levy find, for example, that public exposure in high-level meetings concerning the North Sea and acid rain, respectively, engendered political responses within the United Kingdom that contributed directly to policy changes there (see Chapters 3 and 4). Institutions can shape domestic politics by providing information that is useful to particular domestic factions, by helping bureaucracies fight turf battles, and by generating salient public commitments around which political actors can focus domestic debates. International institutions can interact with nongovernmental organizations (NGOs) and environmental movements to increase public concern, either through cooperative programs or as a result of public criticism of the international institutions and national policies by NGOs leading environmental movements. Robert Paarlberg, in Chapter 7, finds evidence for these effects within developing countries, which helps explain changes in their behavior toward pesticide imports.[15] NGOs and environmental movements are often important sources of governmental concern about the natural environment.

In seeking to improve the contractual environment in order to enhance the ability to make and keep agreements, institutions have a variety of means at their disposal. They can reduce the costs of negotiating agreements by generating information about potential zones of agreement and providing a forum for bargaining. Edward Parson finds that international institutions had this effect in the case of stratospheric ozone depletion, making it possible to advance negotiations in response to rapidly changing—and increasingly frightening—scientific findings.[16] The monitoring activities of international institutions can also be vital to the ability of states to make and keep agreements. Wherever states have reason to fear the consequences of being cheated, monitoring can help reassure them that such cheating will be detected in time to make

14. Peter M. Haas, *Saving the Mediterranean* (New York: Columbia University Press, 1990).
15. Robert Paarlberg, Chapter 7, this volume.
16. Parson, Chapter 2, this volume.

appropriate adjustments. Monitoring makes state commitments more credible, thereby increasing the value of such commitments. In addition, international environmental institutions can create timetables for action, regular policy reviews, and other mechanisms that call for states to demonstrate repeatedly their commitment to solving the problem at hand. Such regular interactions may encourage a process of reciprocity by creating more opportunities for revealing intentions and responding to the actions of others.

Finally, in seeking to augment political and administrative capacity, institutions can foster the transfer of information, skills, and expertise necessary for effective domestic programs. This is the central goal for population institutions and the revised prior informed consent process governing pesticide trade.[17] In addition to these direct information-dissemination and training activities, institutions can build coalitions with development banks and foreign aid agencies in order to funnel major quantities of aid toward projects that will help weak states increase their administrative capacity. Institutions can also help build capacity by providing a public commitment to a set of norms and principles, which domestic proponents of adjustment measures can use in attempting to overcome their opponents in funding and turf battles.

## Lessons and Conclusions

We conclude the book with analytical observations and some modest suggestions for improving international governance of environmental issues. We find evidence for institutional effectiveness operating through all three roles—boosting concern, building capacity, and facilitating agreement. Often a single institution affects behavior in all three ways. It is important, therefore, for both analysts and practitioners not to presume that international environmental institutions only perform one family of tasks when they study past institutions and create new ones. The most effective institutions tailor their interventions to political situations they face.

In answering the puzzle of effectiveness, we show that state sovereign-

17. Chapters by Barbara Crane, Chapter 8, and Robert Paarlberg, Chapter 7, this volume.

ty is not incompatible with international progress in solving difficult problems. Institutions do not need enforcement powers to succeed, and it is unrealistic to hope that governments will grant them such powers. But at the same time that institutions must respect the legal integrity of the nation-state, we conclude that the most effective institutions penetrate the state politically to a high degree. Such penetration often makes use of political allies outside the formal institutional apparatus. Indeed, intergovernmental organizations can be expected to be more effective as catalysts for transnational networks of nongovernmental organizations and transgovernmental linkages among sympathetic governmental bureaucracies, than as independent actors. For instance, nongovernmental organizations, interacting with UNEP and the FAO, have played a critical role (using the media) in putting issues of chemical pesticides on the international agenda, even in the absence of strong pressure to do so from powerful governments.

International institutions do not supersede or overshadow states. They lack resources to enforce their edicts. To be effective, they must create networks over, around, and within states that generate the means and the incentives for effective cooperation among those states. In this volume we seek to show how contemporary international environmental institutions have attempted to construct such networks. We try to ascertain the conditions under which they have been more or less effective in so doing. In the conclusion, we seek systematically to summarize our findings in order to illuminate some common patterns that will help us to understand the international politics of environmental institutions in the 1990s, and some ways in which collective management may be improved.

# II

## Transboundary and Commons Problems

# 2

# Protecting the Ozone Layer

Edward A. Parson

Ozone in the stratosphere, the atmospheric layer between 10 and 50 kilometers above the earth's surface, protects life on earth by absorbing most of the incoming damaging ultraviolet-B (UV-B) radiation from the sun. It was first proposed in 1973 that chlorofluorocarbons (CFCs), an exceedingly useful and versatile class of industrial chemicals, could break down in the stratosphere and release catalysts that destroy ozone. Ozone destruction permits increased levels of UV-B radiation to reach the earth's surface and causes increases in skin cancers and other health and environmental damages.

While several countries acted unilaterally to restrict use of CFCs, particularly in aerosol spray cans, no international control action was taken until the mid-1980s. Then, a series of treaties were signed that included pledges to eliminate CFCs by 2000, and to help developing countries do so through financial and technical assistance. More than seventy countries have joined, and CFC use has declined more than 20 percent since 1986.

The ozone treaty is widely cited as the most successful example of international environmental cooperation to date and the best model for progress on such issues as climate change. Some argue, though, that ozone was an easy issue—that strong scientific evidence, the lack of coherent industry opposition, and the availability of alternatives meant that CFCs would have been eliminated with or without effective international institutions.

This chapter examines the evolution of the ozone issue, asking whether and how international negotiations and institutions made a difference in the outcome. It argues that the international institutions—negotiating bodies, the U.N. Environment Program (UNEP) acting as secretariat, expert scientific bodies, and recently created implementing bodies—were necessary for controlling CFCs. Ongoing negotiations provided a forum for persuasion, for coordination of proposed control measures, for building representatives' confidence that costly controls undertaken by their countries would be reciprocated, and for putting pressure on the reluctant. Institutions established in the 1985 and 1987 agreements empowered activist nations and the secretariat to advance the agenda and restricted the use of spurious scientific disagreement as an obstructionist tactic. Treaty control measures adopted in 1987 and 1990 brought about larger and faster national CFC reductions than would have occurred otherwise. New implementing institutions have built capacity to reduce CFCs in developing countries and in user industries.

The chapter first discusses the CFC industry and the development of scientific concern about ozone loss. It then traces the history of international action on the ozone layer and national ratifications and responses, and analyzes the determinants of the international agenda and action, in particular the influence of international institutions on the outcomes. The chapter ends with an overall assessment.

### Setting the Agenda: CFCs and the Development of Scientific Concern

Long thought to be completely safe, CFCs were charged in the early 1970s with damaging the ozone layer and threatening health and environmental risks by allowing increased amounts of ultraviolet (UV) light to reach the earth's surface. Since the first statement of scientific concern in 1973, stratospheric ozone science has gone through two broad stages: about ten years of confusion and concern, with newly discovered information frequently revising estimated risks both up and down; then, since 1985, a period of convergence in the basic science, coupled with new observations that give steadily increasing grounds for concern.

CFCs were invented in 1928 by DuPont and General Motors chemists seeking a nontoxic heat transfer fluid for refrigeration. The simple stable molecules, derivatives of methane and ethane with chlorine and fluorine added, came to be used in a wide variety of applications. Aside from refrigeration and air-conditioning, they were used for blowing foams, as solvents, sterilants, freezing agents, surface treatment agents, and propellants for aerosol spray cans. Major new uses were found for CFCs each decade, and world production doubled roughly every five years through 1970. Halons, related chemicals containing bromine, are effective, nontoxic, noncorrosive fire extinguishers.

CFC production is concentrated in a few countries. In the 1970s, the United States produced about half the world total, and DuPont about half the U.S. total.[1] The United Kingdom, France, Germany, Italy, and the Netherlands each had one or two major producers, while Japan had five smaller producers and there were a few plants in Spain, Greece, the USSR, and several developing countries.[2] Aerosol sprays were 50 to 60 percent of consumption in the United States and worldwide. Most CFCs are used to produce other goods, and user firms are numerous, diverse, and typically much smaller than CFC producers.

For 40 years after their invention, CFCs were thought completely benign. Then, in the early 1970s, concern arose that they could lead to destruction of ozone in the stratosphere, resulting in increased levels of UV radiation at the earth's surface and thereby causing increases in skin cancer, cataracts, and immune disorders as well as damage to crops and ecosystems. The proposed mechanism, published in 1974, was as follows. Because CFCs are so chemically stable, they persist long enough in the lower atmosphere to diffuse across the boundary to the stratosphere. There, they are broken apart by solar UV radiation and release chlorine atoms, which act as catalysts to convert ozone into molecular oxygen. Although ozone is also continually re-created from oxygen by UV radiation, the presence of chlorine speeds up ozone destruction but not ozone creation, thereby reducing the equilibrium level of ozone. With less UV being absorbed by ozone in the stratosphere, more penetrates to the lower atmosphere.[3] Ozone loss of 1 percent causes about 2

1. DuPont CFC revenues were about $600 million, or 2 percent of total revenues.
2. Geigel, M., 1985, "CEH Product Review: Fluorocarbons," *Chemical Economics Handbook*, SRI International.
3. The basic chemistry of ozone creation and destruction in the stratosphere was explained in Chapman, S., 1930, "On Ozone and Atomic Oxygen in the Upper Atmosphere," *Philosophical Magazine and Journal of Science* 10 (September): 369–83. Modern controversy over ozone loss first concerned nitrogen oxides (NOx) in the exhaust of the supersonic transport (SST), as

percent increase in surface UV, which in turn causes somewhat more than 2 percent increase in skin cancers.[4]

While evidence supporting several pieces of the CFC–ozone depletion hypothesis was gathered by 1977, continuing discoveries concerning other, related stratospheric reactions caused total estimates of ozone loss to fluctuate markedly until 1985. As an indication of the variation, successive National Academy of Sciences (NAS) reports gave estimated total ozone losses of 7 percent, 16.5 percent, 5 to 9 percent, and 2 to 4 percent.[5] Through this entire period, however, there was always pro-

---

presented in Crutzen, Paul J., 1970, "The Influence of Nitrogen Oxides on the Atmospheric Ozone Content," *Quarterly Journal of the Royal Meteorological Society* 96:320–25, and Johnston, H., 1971, "Reduction of Stratospheric Ozone by Nitrogen Oxide Catalysts from Supersonic Transport," *Science* 173:517. The SST-ozone controversy may have had two significant impacts on the CFC-ozone controversy: first, it spawned a major environmental impact study that built up the capacity of U.S. stratospheric science: Grobecker, A., S. Coroniti, and R. Cannon, 1974, *The Report of Findings: The Effects of Stratospheric Pollution by Aircraft*, U.S. Department of Transportation, DOT-TST-75-50; Glantz, M. H., J. Robinson, and M. Krenz, 1985, "Recent Assessments," in Kates et al., eds., *Climate Impact Assessment*, New York: Wiley, 565–98. Second, related U.S. discouragement of the Anglo-French Concorde may have generated suspicion among European technical communities that U.S. officials exaggerate environmental risks: Morrisette, Peter M., 1989, "The Evolution of Policy Responses to Stratospheric Ozone Depletion," *Natural Resources Journal* 29 (Summer):803; Downing, T. E. and R. W. Kates, 1982. "The International Response to the Threat of Chlorofluorocarbons to Atmospheric Ozone," *American Economic Review* 72(2):267–72; Benedick, Richard E., 1991, *Ozone Diplomacy: New Directions in Safeguarding the Planet*, Cambridge: Harvard University Press, 32–33. The risk of chlorine catalysis was first raised by Stolarski, R. S., and R. J. Cicerone, 1974, "Stratospheric Chlorine: a Possible Sink for Ozone," *Canadian Journal of Chemistry* 52:1610–15. Measurements of CFCs in remote regions, suggesting the absence of tropospheric sinks, were provided by Lovelock, J. E., R. J. Maggs, and R. J. Wade, 1973, "Halogenated Hydrocarbons in and over the Atlantic," *Nature* 241:194–96. The landmark paper identifying CFCs as the main source of stratospheric chlorine, independently presenting the mechanism for chlorine catalysis of ozone destruction, was Molina, M., and F. S. Rowland, 1974, "Stratospheric Sink for Chlorofluoromethanes: Chlorine Atom–Catalyzed Destruction of Ozone," *Nature* 249:810–12. Wofsy, S. C., M. B. McElroy, and Y. L. Yung, 1975, "The Chemistry of Atmospheric Bromine," *Geophysical Research Letters* 2:215–18, proposed a similar reaction cycle for bromine.
4. Titus, J., ed., 1986, *Effect of Changes in Stratospheric Ozone and Global Climate*, Washington, D.C.: Environmental Protection Agency.
5. National Research Council, 1976. *Halocarbons: Effects on Stratospheric Ozone*. Washington, D.C.: National Academy Press; National Research Council, 1979, *Stratospheric Ozone Depletion by Halocarbons: Chemistry and*

jected a large ozone loss in the upper stratosphere, compensated to a varying degree by ozone creation in the lower stratosphere. The early 1980s also saw serious dispute over whether ground-based measurements already showed global ozone declines, and whether CFC consumption would start growing again. Around 1984 a theory called the "chlorine catastrophe" generated intense but short-lived concern by proposing that large CFC increases could produce extreme ozone loss.[6]

Following this period of fluctuating concern, ozone science since 1985 has proceeded steadily in the direction of increased concern. The first landmark was the May 1985 publication of the "ozone hole" paper by members of the British Antarctic Survey. This group had maintained a small research station in Halley Bay, Antarctica, for 25 years, and had seen large ozone losses each austral spring since September 1982. Though they had delayed publication of their findings, suspecting instrument errors, the 40 percent loss they saw in September and October 1984, along with corroboration from a second station several hundred miles further north, moved them to announce their results.[7] NASA's Nimbus 7 satellite, in polar orbit since 1978, had also recorded the ozone loss, but release of the data had been delayed while it was checked for instrument error.[8] When released, the satellite data showed a region of severe ozone loss as big as the continental United States, originating

---

*Transport.* Washington, D.C.: National Academy Press; National Research Council, 1982, *Causes and Effects of Stratospheric Ozone Reduction: An Update.* Washington, D.C.: National Academy Press; National Research Council, 1984, *Causes and Effects of Changes in Stratospheric Ozone: Update 1983.* Washington, D.C.: National Academy Press. The estimates are equilibrium ozone losses in steady-state, giving continued emissions at early 1980s levels.

6. The catastrophe arose in one-dimensional models, which showed highly non-linear increases in ozone loss above a certain chlorine concentration. Two- and three-dimensional models failed to reproduce the result because of horizontal transport, and concern faded. Prather, M. F., M. B. McElroy, and S. C. Wofsy, 1984, "Reductions in Ozone at High Concentrations of Stratospheric Halogens," *Nature* 312 (15 November):227–31; Sand, Peter H., 1985, "The Vienna Convention is Adopted," *Environment* 27, 5 (June 1985).

7. Farman J. C., B. G. Gardiner, and J. D. Shanklin, 1985, "Large Losses of Total Ozone in Antarctica Reveal Seasonal ClOx/NOx Interaction," *Nature* 315 (June):207–10.

8. Early news reports suggested that NASA's data filters had simply discarded the low observations. NASA officials deny this in correspondence reproduced in Pukelsheim, Friedrich, 1990, "Robustness of Statistical Gossip and the Antarctic Ozone Hole," *The IMS Bulletin* 19, 4:540–42.

around 1980. No available theory explained the loss but three were soon advanced, one of which blamed chlorine from CFCs.[9]

The ozone hole paper was published just as a comprehensive international assessment of ozone science was about to go to press, so the report simply noted the measurements and reported that further analysis was under way. Released in January 1986 and cosponsored by seven agencies under the lead of the World Meteorological Organization (WMO), the report compared all major ozone models and presented several scenarios for global ozone loss: 9 percent with emissions of CFCs and other relevant gases constant at 1980 levels; substantially higher losses with increased CFC consumption; and no loss when constant CFC emissions are offset by growth in emissions of carbon dioxide, methane, and other gases.[10]

Also in 1986, analyses of satellite ozone measurements seemed to show global ozone losses as high as 4 percent. The measurement was highly controversial because the instrument's performance was degrading and it was not certain that analysts had adequately corrected the resultant drift in measurements. In response to this controversy, NASA organized an international team of scientists called the Ozone Trends Panel (OTP) to review all ozone measurements available, both satellite and surface, and determine whether a global change was occurring.

Large NASA-sponsored scientific groups went to Antarctica in September of 1986 and 1987 to look for the cause of the hole. Evidence from ground and balloon observations in the 1986 expedition favored the chlorine hypothesis but was inconclusive.[11] The 1987 expedition, though, flew instruments on high-altitude aircraft into the hole and found striking, almost definitive confirmation of the CFC-based theory, as well as ozone loss as high as 95 percent in the lower stratosphere.[12]

9. Special supplement issue, *Geophysical Research Letters* 13 (November, 1986).

10. WMO, 1986, *Atmospheric Ozone: 1985*, WMO Global Ozone Research and Monitoring Project, Report No. 16. The sponsoring organizations were NASA, NOAA, and FAA in the United States; UNEP and WMO; the EC Commission; and the German Ministry of Science and Technology.

11. *Geophysical Research Letters* 13, 1986:1191–1362. Special supplement on causes of the Antarctic ozone hole, compiled before the reports of results from the first NOZE expedition.

12. Anderson, J. G., W. H. Brune, and M. J. Proffitt, 1989, "Ozone Destruction by Chlorine Radicals within the Antarctic Vortex: The Spatial and Tem-

Over the next few months theorists worked out the detailed mechanism for Antarctic ozone destruction. Reactions that occur on the surfaces of the polar stratospheric clouds (PSCs) that form in the extremely cold Antarctic night release highly reactive species of chlorine and bromine. These species accumulate in the area confined by the polar vortex, until the sun rises in the spring. Under sunlight and low temperatures, they break apart to release chlorine and bromine catalysts, which rapidly destroy ozone. The process stops when the temperature rises and the vortex breaks up.[13] Some contend that the heterogeneous chemistry that forms reactive species on PSC surfaces could occur on other surfaces too, such as the different kinds of PSCs that form in the Arctic winter, or sulfate aerosols that occur naturally in the stratosphere from volcanic eruptions.

On 15 March 1988, the Executive Summary of the Ozone Trends Panel was released. The analysts had exhaustively reviewed the record of ozone observations from ground stations, calibrating them and removing known sources of natural variation. They found significant ozone losses only in the north temperate latitudes: 2 to 3 percent in summer, and 2 to 6 percent in winter from 1969 and 1986, two to three times greater than the losses predicted by models.[14] Five separate groups, including one sponsored by CFC manufacturers, reanalyzed the data and confirmed the results.[15]

Following the Antarctic results, there was concern that similar ozone destruction may be happening in the Arctic. NASA-led studies in 1988 and 1989 found highly perturbed stratospheric chemistry similar to that

poral Evolution of ClO-$O_3$ anticorrelation based on in situ ER-2 data," *Journal of Geophysical Research* 94:11465–79.

13. McElroy, Michael B., R. J. Salawitch, S. C. Wofsy, and J. A. Logan, 1986, "Reductions of Antarctic Ozone due to Synergistic Interactions of Chlorine and Bromine," *Nature* 321:759–62; Molina, L. T., and M. J. Molina, "Production of $Cl_2O_2$ from the Self Reaction of the ClO Radical," *Journal of Physical Chemistry* 91:433–36; McElroy, Michael B., and R. J. Salawitch, 1989, "Changing Composition of the Global Stratosphere," *Science* 243:763–70.

14. National Aeronautics and Space Administration, 1988, "Executive Summary of the Ozone Trends Panel," Washington, D.C., 15 March 1988. The full OTP report was not published until January 1991.

15. WMO, 1989, *Scientific Assessment of Stratospheric Ozone: 1989*, WMO Global Ozone Research and Monitoring Project, Report No. 20, ix.

in the Antarctic, but no ozone hole.[16] Although the Arctic should be less vulnerable than the Antarctic, because it is warmer and because its vortex usually collapses before sunrise, the expeditions found risk of a future Arctic ozone hole, depending on weather conditions from year to year as well as chlorine levels.

Recent observations continue to show increased ozone losses globally, in the Arctic, and in the Antarctic. The Antarctic ozone holes of 1990 and 1991 were the most severe so far in both intensity and duration.[17] In December 1990, NASA scientists presented corrected satellite measurements that showed global average ozone loss of 3 percent over twelve years, and 9 percent in mid-northern winter. These losses are two to three times greater than predicted by homogeneous models.[18] Significant temperate-latitude losses in spring and summer have recently been reported for the first time.[19]

### International Policies: History of Negotiations and Decisions[20]

#### 1977 to 1985: Washington to Vienna

Following the 1974 charge that CFCs could destroy the ozone layer, an intense three-year debate in the United States focused specifically on aerosol sprays, regarded by many as a frivolous and expendable use. The debate was marked by high public and media attention, enactment of several state-level CFC restrictions, two petitions by the Natural Resources Defense Council (NRDC) to the Consumer Product Safety Commission requesting CFC bans, and a hard-fought industry campaign led by DuPont, arguing that the science was too speculative and

16. *Geophysical Research Letters* 17, 1990:313–564. Supplement on the Airborne Arctic Stratospheric Expedition, 17 March.
17. UNEP, 1991, "Executive Summary, Scientific Assessment of Stratospheric Ozone, 1991," 22 October 1991.
18. National Aeronautics and Space Administration, 1991, "Statement by Dr. Robert T. Watson and Dr. Richard S. Stolarski," testimony to Subcommittee on Science, Technology, and Space of Committee on Commerce, Science, and Transportation, United States Senate, 16 April 1991, 3.
19. UNEP, 1991, "Scientific Assessment of Stratospheric Ozone."
20. In addition to published sources and United Nations documents, this discussion of the international negotiating history is based extensively on two sources: interviews with members of national delegations, industry officials, and representatives of environmental groups; and meeting notes and briefing materials prepared by members of a national delegation.

uncertain to justify regulation. In the course of this debate DuPont officials, in newspaper advertisements and before congressional committees, stated that if "reputable evidence" showed CFCs to cause a health hazard through ozone depletion, they would stop producing them.[21] Although the science remained confused through this period, U.S. regulators decided in early 1977 to ban CFC aerosols except for a few "essential" uses.

As this U.S. decision was in train, the first significant international initiative on ozone took place: a UNEP-sponsored Washington meeting in March 1977, with representatives from thirty-three nations and the Commission of the European Community (EC). The meeting heard a series of research papers and summaries of national research programs, and drafted the "World Plan of Action on the Ozone Layer," a program of recommended international cooperation in research on atmospheric chemistry and modeling, ozone and radiation trends, health and environmental effects, and emission trends of ozone-affecting substances. The plan was to be implemented by a broad set of institutions— national governments, UN agencies, and intergovernmental and nongovernmental organizations—with UNEP playing a "coordinating and catalytic" role.[22]

The Washington meeting also recommended creating a "Coordinating Committee on the Ozone Layer" (CCOL), composed of experts from agencies and NGOs participating in the Plan of Action. UNEP's Governing Council created the CCOL and adopted the Plan of Action in May of the same year. The CCOL was to coordinate research undertaken by national and international agencies. The Washington meeting, the Plan of Action, and the CCOL all were highly scientific in character.[23] The CCOL met annually from 1977 to 1985, preparing reports that summarized recent research for policymakers and prioritized research needs. The chemical industry, which was sponsoring a few

21. McCarthy, Raymond, 1976, Testimony to the Subcommittee on the Upper Atmosphere, U.S. Senate Committee on Aeronautics and Space Science.
22. UNEP, 1977, Report of the UNEP Meeting of Experts Designated by Governments, Intergovernmental and Nongovernmental Organizations on the Ozone Layer, UNEP/WG.7/25, 8 March 1977.
23. Biswas, Asit K., 1979. *The Ozone Layer*, Proceedings of the UNEP Meeting of Experts, Washington, D.C., 1–9 March 1977. Oxford: Pergamon; UNEP, Report of the UNEP Meeting of Experts.

million dollars of ozone research per year, participated actively. Until January 1982, the CCOL was the only formal international body considering the ozone layer.

CFC production in the United States dropped by half following the aerosol ban, world production by about 25 percent.[24] Three U.S. producers each closed one plant, and one producer left the market. Fearing restrictions on other applications, producers began research into CFC substitutes; DuPont spent $3 to $4 million per year through the late 1970s.[25] American regulators had planned to go beyond aerosol controls, and the Environmental Protection Agency (EPA) issued a proposal for comprehensive CFC controls in 1980. Two new factors prevented further U.S. restrictions, though. First, in summer 1980, U.S. producer and user industries formed a new lobby group, the Alliance for Responsible CFC Policy, which waged a strong antiregulatory campaign.[26] Second, the Reagan administration's new EPA officials were skeptical of the need for CFC controls. Consequently, the pursuit of further CFC controls essentially stopped, as did industry research into substitutes. But the early fight in the United States had created three institutional forces that significantly affected later international debate: a politically sophisticated community of atmospheric scientists; expertise and commitment on CFCs within NRDC; and the Alliance for Responsible CFC Policy.

Three other countries also restricted CFC aerosols in the late 1970s. Sweden and Norway, importers of CFCs, banned "nonessential" aerosols as had the United States, thereby cutting aerosol use by 95 to 98 percent. Canada, a small producer, instead banned CFCs in the three

24. Chemical Manufacturer's Association, 1988, "Production, Sales, and Calculated Release of CFC-11 and CFC-12 Through 1987," December.
25. Reinhardt, Forest, 1989, "DuPont Freon Products Division," Case Number 8-389-112, Harvard Business School, prepared for the National Wildlife Federation, 12.
26. The Alliance had about 400 members, dominated numerically by user industry but principally formed at the instigation of producer industry. The Alliance's principal goal was to prevent regulators from dividing and conquering the industry through a sector-by-sector approach to regulation. Its three founding principles were that any CFC controls should be based on science; should be international, not unilateral; and should apply equitably to all CFC applications. Interview with Kevin Fay, 16 January 1992.

largest applications, hair spray, deodorant, and antiperspirant, cutting use by about 80 percent.

Through the late 1970s, the Nordics pushed repeatedly for authorization of a body to discuss international regulations. They succeeded in April 1981, when UNEP's Governing Council approved a Swedish motion to establish a working group to negotiate an international convention on the ozone layer. The working group first met in Stockholm in January 1982, with the CCOL designated as its scientific and technical advisory body.[27] The Nordic countries, led by Sweden, introduced a proposal for strong control measures which received little support. With scientific concern declining at the time and CFC consumption reduced by the recession and national aerosol bans, nobody but the Nordics considered strong international controls worth the effort. The U.S. delegation arrived unprepared and unwilling to engage in substantive discussions;[28] Europe and Japan were uninterested in any discussions of international controls. The closest the meeting came to controls was a hypothetical discussion of what kind of "triggers" a convention should incorporate—pre-agreed warning signals that, if observed, would indicate a need for action.[29]

The working group met seven times over the following three years, with UNEP providing moral and limited secretarial support. Negotiations moved very slowly, against vehement European opposition. Relations between governments and national producers in Europe and Japan were close, and industry representatives served officially on national delegations through the entire process. The Nordics relaxed their proposal somewhat, to a ban on CFCs 11 and 12 in nonessential aerosols, with

27. In 1980 and 1981, the CCOL reports moved from science summaries toward cautious calls for international regulatory action. Once the Working Group was created, CCOL returned more to the character of a purely scientific advisory body—although its numerical estimates of predicted ozone depletion continued to have strong policy implications.
28. Notes of meeting participant.
29. German Bundestag, 1989, *Protecting the Earth's Atmosphere: An International Challenge*, Interim report of the Study Commission of the 11th German Bundestag, English translation, Bonn: Bonner Universitats Buchdruckerei, 257; Meeting summary in participant's briefing note, 22 December 1981. The state of understanding of the issue at this time was such that several countries had responded to UNEP's data request by saying that they did not use CFCs, so "their ozone layer" was not threatened.

unspecified limits on other CFC uses.[30] The United States, participating somewhat more actively after April 1983 following EPA's leadership change, proposed a control clause similar to U.S. domestic legislation, while Canada proposed one similar to Canadian legislation. The advocates of controls—the United States, Canada, the Nordics, Austria, and Switzerland—finally came together informally in September 1984 to form the "Toronto Group," and endorsed a draft Control Article.[31] The article did not contain a single control measure, but a "multi-options" approach; it listed several possible forms of controls yielding similar overall reductions, of which parties would choose one. Most of the options involved large aerosol cuts, and each one mirrored the existing domestic regulations of one of the measure's sponsors.

Canada presented the Toronto Group's package to a working group meeting in October and met with strenuous objections from EC representatives, who argued that no controls were justified.[32] Under pressure, EC representatives eventually responded with a draft protocol that mirrored their own 1980 measures: 30 percent aerosol reductions from peak 1970s levels, and no expansion of CFCs 11 and 12 production facilities. (Neither of these constraints was binding for the EC in 1984.) The EC representatives argued that only a production capacity cap would guarantee that growth in other uses would not swamp the effect of an aerosol ban. Moreover, they pointed out that allowing trading nations to select different forms of limited control under the "multi-options" approach could permit unlimited global production expansion.[33] Industry representatives on both sides encouraged this deadlock.[34]

30. Participant's meeting notes, April 1983.
31. The group called themselves the "Friends of the Protocol," but were called the Toronto Group by their opponents, and the name stuck. Sponsors of record of the proposed protocol were Sweden, Norway, Finland, Canada, and the United States. Austria, Denmark, Switzerland, and Australia also participated and expressed support "in principle." Meeting notes.
32. January 1984 meeting notes.
33. Commission of the European Communities, 1985, "Observations on the Alternative Control Measures Proposed for Article 2," 27 February 1985. The EC argument invoked the then-current "chlorine catastrophe" to argue that present production levels were innocuous but large increases, which would in principle be possible under the Toronto Group proposal but not under theirs, were potentially catastrophic.
34. Interviews with national and industry officials.

Through this period there was also sharp disagreement over how fast future CFC markets would grow, with industry arguing that markets were largely saturated and others projecting growth as high as 5 or 6 percent per year. In fact, strong growth and promotion of new application markets, particularly foams and solvents, had reversed the declines that followed the aerosol bans. U.S. and world production surpassed their pre-ban peak levels in 1984, and several new investments in production capacity were announced between 1982 and 1986.[35] In November 1984, as advocates of international CFC controls pressed their case, NRDC sued EPA for failing to regulate CFC production. NRDC delayed the lawsuit a few months due to concern that it might obstruct sensitive negotiations, but proceeded when they decided no international controls were likely to come from the March 1985 Vienna meeting.

None did. Early in the discussions, the Nordics had proposed that controls be a central part of the treaty. When participants settled on a "Convention and Protocol" approach, the Nordics consented to move the bitterly contested control provisions first to an annex, then to a separate (but simultaneously signed) protocol. Ultimately, the EC and the Toronto Group could not bridge their differences in time for the ministers' meeting in Vienna, and only the Convention was signed. In it, nations pledged to cooperate in research and monitoring, to share information on CFC production and emissions, to pass control protocols if and when warranted, and to participate in a nonbinding dispute resolution process. Twenty nations plus the EC Commission signed the Vienna Convention. Except for two contentious elements, the dispute resolution process and the voting status and competency of the EC, participants could have agreed to these innocuous measures eight years earlier, for they were all contained in the 1977 World Plan of Action.[36] Even so, a last-minute, ideologically motivated conflict within the State

35. Hammitt, J. K., et al., 1986, "Product Uses and Market Trends for Potential Ozone-Depleting Substances, 1985–2000," Rand report R-3386-EPA.
36. As finally agreed, the dispute resolution process permitted parties to opt in to compulsory participation in dispute resolution by either arbitration or the International Court of Justice, though the decisions of these bodies were nonbinding.

Department over whether the U.S. delegation should sign the Convention had to be resolved by a decision of the Secretary of State.[37]

For those advocating CFC controls, the failure of Vienna was mitigated by one small but ultimately important victory. In return for the Toronto Group's giving up immediate control measures, a resolution was appended to the Convention empowering UNEP immediately to convene working group negotiations for a protocol, to be signed if possible in 1987.[38] This did not reflect formal designation of UNEP as secretariat for the Convention; WMO also wanted the job, and there was division among delegations, with (roughly speaking) scientists favoring WMO and diplomats UNEP. The appointment of a secretariat was deferred to the first meeting of the parties.[39]

### 1985 to 1987: Vienna to Montreal

Following Vienna, UNEP first organized two informal technical workshops, in Rome in May 1986 and jointly with EPA in Leesburg, Virginia in September. The Leesburg workshop on regulatory strategies represented several firsts: environmental NGOs (nongovernmental organizations) participated in the international negotiating process for the first time; the USSR presented CFC production data for the first time; and several novel regulatory approaches were presented. The Canadian delegation presented an innovative proposal to restructure the debate over CFC controls by considering all CFCs comprehensively, deciding on an acceptable global emissions limit, and allocating this limit to countries according to population and GNP in shares to be negotiated.[40] Though the proposal was not adopted, many participants

37. Benedick, *Ozone Diplomacy*, 46; interviews with current and former EPA and Department of State officials.
38. "Resolution on a Protocol Concerning Chlorofluorocarbons," Final Act of the Conference of Plenipotentiaries on the Protection of the Ozone Layer.
39. WMO harmed its own case when, while presenting a bid to be Secretariat at the 1984 Governing Council meeting, WMO's deputy secretary-general stated that present scientific knowledge did not warrant controls and that the Convention should be largely confined to promoting further research. Several delegations objected strenuously to this breach of policy neutrality by a scientific advisory body. Interviews with national officials; meeting notes.
40. Environment Canada, 1986, "A Canadian Contribution to the Consideration of Strategies for Protecting the Ozone Layer," presentation to UNEP Workshop on Economic Issues Related to Control of CFCs, Leesburg, Va., 8–12 September 1986.

credit it with refocusing the control debate more broadly and breaking the long-standing deadlock between the EC and the Toronto Group.[41] An EPA report at Leesburg was the first to shift focus from ozone depletion to chlorine concentration, arguing that stabilizing present chlorine levels would require an 85 percent cut in CFC emissions.

During 1986, the United States assumed a strong leadership role in the negotiations for the first time. In early fall, Administrator Lee Thomas initiated an EPA position advocating full phaseouts of CFCs. In November, following a low-level interagency review, the official U.S. negotiating position was announced: an immediate freeze in CFC consumption, followed by phased reductions to essentially zero (nominally, 95 percent reduction), with interim scientific reviews to determine whether the continued cuts were necessary.

1986 also saw a split in the formerly united front of U.S. and European producers. Previously, both sides held that stratospheric science was too uncertain, and that several years of research were needed to tell whether further CFC controls were justified. The first movement was in March, when a DuPont official announced that substitutes could be available in five years if market conditions warranted the development effort, and that research into substitutes had stopped in the early 1980s.[42] In August the board of the Alliance for Responsible CFC Policy held an all-day workshop to review the recent science assessment report and CFC growth projections, and decided to endorse international controls on the rate of CFC growth.[43] One week after the Alliance announcement, DuPont went slightly further and endorsed international controls on the *level* of CFC production.[44]

DuPont also returned in late 1986 to research into substitute chemicals, spending $5 million in 1986, $10 million in 1987, and $30 million in 1988.[45] The company investigated two classes of closely related chemical substitutes for CFCs: hydrochlorofluorocarbons (HCFCs) and hydrofluorocarbons (HFCs). Both classes are harder to manufacture

41. Interviews with national officials.
42. Strobach, Donald, 1986, presentation to EPA domestic workshop on trends in CFC production and consumption, Washington D.C., March 1986.
43. Barnett, Richard, 1986, press conference, Washington D.C., 16 September.
44. Glas, Joseph P., 1986, "DuPont Position Statement on the Chlorofluoro-carbon-Ozone-Greenhouse Issues," *Environmental Conservation* 13:363–64.
45. Reinhardt, "DuPont Freon Products Division," 12.

than CFCs and cost two to five times as much. HCFCs contain hydrogen, making them more reactive in the lower atmosphere than CFCs and hence only 1 to 6 percent as ozone-depleting as CFC 11.[46] HFCs contain no chlorine and cause no ozone depletion, but both HCFCs and HFCs are greenhouse gases, contributing to the separate problem of global climate change.[47]

Three rounds of formal negotiations followed the workshops, in December 1986 and in February and April 1987. In the opening round, the United States proposed phased consumption reductions of CFCs and halons to near zero; the Europeans proposed a production freeze on CFCs 11 and 12;[48] the Nordics proposed an immediate 25 percent reduction in consumption of CFCs 11 and 12; and Canada reiterated its Leesburg proposal. Progress was very slow in December and February, with some delegates expressing concern that the process would have to go ahead without European participation.[49]

In March and April, several breakthroughs occurred. At the March meeting of the Council of Environment Ministers, the EC moved to a position of 20 percent production cuts. Several observers contend that it was sometime between September 1986 and April 1987 that European industry lost control of national delegations; by April, the Japanese industry representative no longer sat on the national delegation.[50] In April, UNEP sponsored an international scientific meeting in Wurzburg, Germany, where atmospheric modelers from several countries ran their

46. WMO, *Scientific Assessment of Stratospheric Ozone: 1989*, xxx.
47. DuPont's estimate of how present CFC demand will be met in 2000 has changed sharply in the last two years. In 1989 they estimated 30 percent HCFCs, 9 percent HFCs, 32 percent non-fluorocarbons, and 29 percent conservation. In 1991 this was revised to 24 percent HCFCs, 17 percent HFCs, 47 percent non-fluorocarbons, and only 12 percent conservation. Vogelsburg, F.A., 1991, "An Industry Perspective on Phaseout of Chlorofluorocarbons," DuPont presentation to National Academy of Engineering conference, 22–25 April.
48. The Europeans first refused to present or discuss any control proposals, as the delegation had received only "the vaguest of mandates." After the delegations caucused, they presented the production freeze, calling it a "non-proposal" for discussion purposes only. They argued that they were unable seriously to negotiate until after a Council of Environment Ministers' meeting in March, and attempted to block the tabling of a consolidated draft text for future negotiations, and delay the second meeting. Meeting notes; interviews with meeting participants.
49. Briefing note, March 1987; interviews.
50. Interview with national official.

models on common emission scenarios and found they agreed that some ozone depletion would occur with any of the control schemes being proposed. At the April negotiations, UNEP Executive Director Mostafa Tolba participated for the first time, and stated in his opening remarks that the Wurzburg results made it "no longer possible to oppose action to regulate CFC release on the grounds of scientific dissent."[51] Tolba organized closed-door negotiating sessions with ten key countries, which produced a single draft text called "the Chairman's personal text." Although this text became the basis for subsequent negotiations, several key points were settled only at the last minute in Montreal.

Through early 1987, U.S. supporters of controls campaigned actively to build international support for a treaty. U.S. negotiators, EPA officials, and scientists met extensively with foreign officials and scientists, and conducted live video discussions via satellite. Representatives of American environmental NGOs also traveled, encouraging European and Japanese NGOs to become active in the issue.[52] Friends of the Earth U.K. ran an aggressive campaign through 1987, culminating in a boycott threat against twenty specific CFC-aerosol products.[53] The U.S. delegation was pushed domestically by both the NRDC lawsuit and Congress. The lawsuit settlement had called for new interim regulations by May 1987 and final ones by November, subsequently extended for six months.[54] Bills introduced during 1987 called for unilateral CFC cuts by the United States, accompanied by trade restrictions against countries who do not reciprocate.[55]

Still, strong opponents in the U.S. government felt they had not had their say in developing the negotiating position, and succeeded in establishing a high-level interagency process to reconsider all aspects of the U.S. negotiating position. This bitterly contested process, conducted

51. UNEP, 1987, "Report of the Ad Hoc Working Group on the Work of its Third Session," UNEP/WG.172/2.
52. Benedick, *Ozone Diplomacy*, 28, 39.
53. Cook, Elizabeth A., 1990, "Global Environmental Advocacy: Citizen Activism in Protecting the Ozone Layer," *Ambio* 19, 6–7 (October):334–38.
54. Doniger, David D., 1988, "Politics of the Ozone Layer," *Issues in Science and Technology*, Spring, 86–92.
55. Shimberg, Steven J., 1992, "Stratospheric Ozone and Climate Protection: Domestic Legislation and the International Process," forthcoming in *Environmental Law*.

under the Domestic Policy Council and chaired by the Office of Management and Budget (OMB), consisted of twice-weekly meetings from five o'clock P.M. until after midnight for four months. The meetings reviewed all scientific, technical, economic, and policy aspects of CFC control. Leaks from this process asserted that Interior Department officials were advocating "personal protection"—meaning hats, sunglasses, and sunscreen, instead of CFC controls—and seriously embarrassed the administration. The dispute was finally resolved in a cabinet meeting on 18 June, when the president reaffirmed the original U.S. negotiating position.[56]

International negotiations proceeded to the last minute in Montreal in September 1987. The final agreement, worked out in post-midnight ministerial discussions, enacted 50 percent cuts from 1986 levels of production and consumption of the five principal CFCs (11, 12, 113, 114, and 115) by 1999,[57] with interim controls consisting of a freeze in 1990 and a 20 percent cut in 1994. Three halons were frozen at 1986 levels beginning in 1993. Total production and consumption of CFCs and halons were calculated by weighting each chemical by its ozone-depletion potential (ODP), so that countries could choose on which particular chemicals to concentrate their controls. There were a few exceptions to these control measures: those developing countries whose annual consumption is less than 0.3 kg per capita receive a ten-year grace period, while other nations may exceed production limits by up to 10 percent for export to meet these countries' "basic domestic needs"; nations producing less than 25,000 metric tons per year may transfer their production quotas to other parties for purposes of industrial rationalization; and the Soviet Union may count one plant under construction in its baseline. The Montreal Protocol would enter into force when it received eleven ratifications representing at least two-thirds of 1986 global CFC consumption.[58]

The Protocol included several restrictions on trade with non-parties: bulk imports of restricted substances from non-parties were prohibited

56. Benedick, *Ozone Diplomacy*, 58–67.
57. Consumption was defined as production plus imports minus exports, as in the Canadian proposal presented in Leesburg.
58. Montreal Protocol, Final Act, 16 September 1987.

in 1990; bulk exports were prohibited from 1993;[59] imports from non-parties of products containing controlled substances were banned (with the possibility of opting out by formal objection) from 1992; and parties agreed to study the feasibility of banning imports of products made with controlled substances, even though not containing them.[60] Some delegations were concerned that these measures would violate the General Agreement on Tariffs and Trade (GATT), but GATT officials said the discriminatory sanctions would be acceptable if they were clearly related to environmental protection. The Protocol accommodated trade concerns by exempting from the import bans those non-parties who undertake the same controls and data-reporting requirements as parties.

Parties also agreed to provide data on their production and consumption, to share technical information, and to promote technical assistance to help developing countries comply with the protocol. Regional Economic Integration Organizations (REIOs—a set whose only member at present is the EC) are permitted to meet the consumption limits (but not their production limits) jointly rather than country by country. An important innovation was a formal commitment to periodic review. Parties were to meet in 1990 and at least every four years thereafter to determine whether the control measures should be changed. Before each review, expert panels would be formed to assess recent scientific, technical, environmental, and economic developments, and report to the parties. The executive director of UNEP was empowered to advance the first meeting from 1990 to 1989 if one-third of the parties agreed.

## 1987 to 1991: Montreal to London and Beyond

Strong Antarctic evidence against CFCs arrived within weeks of the signing in Montreal, and the first evidence of global decline (the Ozone Trends Panel) within six months. Tolba proposed in November 1987 to

59. Curiously, bulk exports were only prohibited from developing country parties. Others could export after 1993, but could not deduct these exports from their calculated domestic consumption—i.e., exporting to non-parties required reducing domestic consumption.
60. Montreal Protocol, Article 4. This category could include many electronic goods. The stakes are much higher and the detection problems much more severe on this category of goods than on any of the others in Article 4.

exercise his power to advance the first meeting of the parties to 1989. Obtaining the required ratifications was the first priority, for without the treaty in force there could be no review process. The protocol entered into force on schedule on 1 January 1989, with thirty parties (including the EC) representing 83 percent of global consumption.

Though both American and European producers had finally endorsed the Protocol, their position was that the science only justified a freeze, so 50 percent cuts represented a large safety margin. But DuPont again moved ahead of the other producers in March 1988. In late February, DuPont's CEO had written to three senators stating that the scientific evidence against CFCs was not yet clear enough to call forth DuPont's old promise to stop making them. Forced to reconsider just two weeks later when the OTP Executive Summary was released, DuPont announced on 23 March that it would stop producing CFCs and halons by 1999, and endorsed a global phaseout.[61] Other producers, not as exposed as DuPont, awaited the industry-sponsored review of OTP's analysis. In summer 1988, when the completed analysis supported the OTP conclusions, the Alliance, the European industry council (CEFIC), the Imperial Chemical Industries (ICI), and the EPA all announced within a few days that they endorsed a phaseout.[62]

It was also summer 1988 that additional chemicals, methyl chloroform (MC) and carbon tetrachloride (CT) were proposed for controls because of their ozone-depletion risks. CT, which is highly toxic, had been banned for many years in most industrial countries but was still widely used in developing countries and the Soviet Union. MC is a versatile solvent of very low toxicity and reactivity, widely used for metal degreasing.[63] These proposed controls involved a group of producers not previously experienced with the international ozone process. Only ICI is a major producer of both CFCs and MC. The other major producers are Dow with about half the world market, PPG Industries, and Vulcan. American producers and users formed the Halogenated Sol-

61. Shabecoff, Philip, 1988, "DuPont to Halt Chemicals that Peril Ozone," *New York Times*, 25 March.
62. Interviews with national and industry officials.
63. Hammitt, J. K. et al., "Product Uses and Market Trends," 78.
64. UNEP, 1989, "Report of the First Meeting of the Parties to the Montreal Protocol on Substances that Deplete the Ozone Layer," UNEP/OzL.Pro.1/5, 6 May 1989.

vents Industry Association in September 1988, and have subsequently lobbied both domestically and internationally.

The first step in treaty review was to establish the expert panels. UNEP called a meeting in The Hague in October 1988 to define their mandates: a science panel to report projected ozone losses under various emission scenarios; a technology panel to report the availability of substitutes and the feasibility of larger cuts; an environmental effects panel; and an economics panel. The panels worked through the first half of 1989.

While the panels were working, there were important changes in national positions. In March the EC Council, with the United Kingdom now joining the activists, agreed to a full phaseout of all CFCs, "as soon as possible, but not later than 2000." Immediately afterward, at a London conference called "Saving the Ozone Layer," more than a hundred nations endorsed phaseouts and major developing countries first asserted strongly their need for major technical and financial assistance to phase out CFCs.

The first meeting of the parties took place in May 1989 in Helsinki. Here, eighty nations signed a declaration that endorsed phaseouts of CFCs by 2000 and of halons as soon as possible, and somewhat vaguely endorsed financial and technical transfers to less developed countries (LDCs).[64] The Helsinki meeting also fixed budgets for the small secretariats at UNEP headquarters in Nairobi that serve the Protocol and the Vienna Convention (about $1.2 million per year for both, including meeting expenses). It was not possible to amend the treaty at the Helsinki meeting because of notice requirements, but the parties heard interim reports from the panels and authorized UNEP to convene a working group to hear the final panel reports and negotiate Protocol amendments, which would be finalized at the second meeting of parties, in London in June 1990.

The reports of the science and technology panels were strong and influential. Citing major gaps in the models used to predict ozone loss, the science panel moved one step back along the causal chain, projecting future time paths of stratospheric chlorine concentrations, rather than ozone depletion, for various CFC emission scenarios.[65] The ozone hole

65. The chlorine-loading approach was first presented by U.S. EPA at the Lees-

first appeared when stratospheric chlorine was about 1.5 to 2.0 parts per billion (ppb) compared to the present 3.3 ppb. If all processes are reversible, the hole should fill when chlorine returns to below 2 ppb. The panel studied four scenarios, ranging from a freeze to full phaseouts of CFCs, halons, CT, and MC by 2000. They found that even with a global phaseout, chlorine will continue increasing to about 4.5 ppb around 2010, and will not return to 2 ppb until 2060.[66]

The technology panel was organized into sectoral subpanels, each of which consisted mostly of user industry experts financed by their companies. Panelists traveled intensively, visiting plants and laboratories, observing and sharing information on detailed technical solutions to highly specific applications, and spontaneously problem-solving with their hosts. This process generated new knowledge and new commercial opportunities in CFC reduction, and generated an inventory of existing knowledge. The panel report said CFC cuts of at least 95 percent were feasible by 2000, and that substitutes presently exist for 90 to 95 percent of methyl chloroform uses and for "a majority" of carbon tetrachloride uses. Most aspects of the technology panel's work are uniformly praised; the exception is MC, which many contend was added late and received weak treatment.[67] In contrast to the technology and science panels, the economics and impacts panels presented reports that endorsed tighter controls, but were weakly argued and of little influence.[68]

The working group received the panel reports in September 1989, and began negotiating amendments. In their seven sessions through late 1989 and early 1990, they agreed relatively easily to phase out CFCs and halons, and focused most on the terms of the proposed financial and technology transfer mechanisms for developing countries. These discussions derailed briefly in April when the United States apparently

burg workshop, September 1986, UNEP/WG.148.3, Annex 1, 5 and UNEP/WG.148/3, Paper 13; time paths of chlorine concentration first appeared in Hoffman, John S., and M. J. Gibbs, 1988, *Future Concentrations of Stratospheric Chlorine and Bromine*, Washington, D.C.: Environmental Protection Agency, EPA 400/1-88/005, July.
66. WMO, 1989, *Scientific Assessment*, vii.
67. Interviews with panel members and industry officials. The panel was divided on the maximum feasible reduction of halons, with positions ranging from a technology-forcing full phaseout, to no reduction.
68. Interviews with panel members and national officials.

went back on a prior understanding that new funding would be required; but a subsequent U.S. "clarification" put them back on track.[69] Both environmental and industry groups participated actively in these negotiations. While only France continued to send industry officials as national negotiators, some nations now included environmental NGOs as "advisers" on their delegation, in order to fund them to attend meetings.[70]

As in 1987, negotiations continued to the last minute. Finally, the second meeting of the parties, in London in June 1990, established the following revised control measures: all fully halogenated CFCs to be phased out in 2000, with interim reductions of 85 percent in 1997 and 50 percent in 1995;[71] the original three halons also to be phased out in 2000, with an interim reduction of 50 percent in 1995; carbon tetrachloride to be eliminated by 2000 with an 85 percent reduction in 1995; methyl chloroform to be eliminated by 2005, with reductions of 30 percent in 1995 and 70 percent in 2000; and nonbinding resolutions on other halons and on HCFCs.[72]

Several other measures fine-tuned the Montreal Protocol and made it more equitable. Permission to transfer production quotas for industrial rationalization was extended to any parties, not just those below 25 kilotons (kt) per year. Two measures that discriminated against LDCs, weighted voting and the prohibition of non-party exports from developing countries only, were revised; now adjustment of the Protocol requires a two-thirds majority overall, with simple majorities of industrial and developing country parties, and no party may export in bulk to non-parties. Finally, the EC was permitted to report their consumption, import, and export data aggregated.

The most important innovations, though, and the most contentious, were the financial and technology transfer provisions. For financing, a fund was created to pay the incremental costs of developing country

69. Of the outcry that followed the first U.S. announcement, officials report that the one decisive element was a letter from Prime Minister Thatcher to President Bush, implicitly threatening to scuttle the Houston G-7 summit if the U.S. ruined the London meeting.
70. Interviews with environmental NGO representatives and national officials.
71. The 50 percent reduction applies only to the original five CFCs.
72. The resolution on HCFCs calls for phaseouts by 2040, "if possible by 2020."

parties in meeting their control obligations. A specific list of permitted categories of incremental costs is covered. Industrial country parties contribute to the fund according to the UN scale of assessment, and their contributions must be in addition to other funding (although bilateral and regional aid can count as a contribution under certain conditions). The ultimate size of the fund has not been precisely determined, but an interim fund for the three years prior to entry into force was set at $160 to $240 million.[73] Preambular language, inserted at the insistence of the United States, says that the mechanisms adopted in this case are "without prejudice" for measures that might be undertaken for other issues such as climate change.

In addition to the fund, there are two important provisions on technology transfer. First, parties pledge to ensure that the technology necessary to meet control obligations is available to developing country parties on "fair and most favorable terms"—a compromise with the traditional Group of 77 (G-77) position of "preferential and noncommercial." Second, a carefully worded passage states that LDC parties' "capacity to fulfill" the control obligations "will depend upon the effective implementation of the financial co-operation . . . and transfer of technology." One delegate described the intent of this provision as "to acknowledge that they are not required to do the impossible, without permitting a unilateral assessment that they haven't been given enough."[74]

The fund is governed by a fourteen-member Executive Committee of the parties, seven from industrial and seven from developing countries. Each group allocates its seats informally.[75] The Executive Committee has the authority to approve the budget for the fund, develop criteria for project eligibility, and approve proposed expenditures of over

73. The lower figure is without India and China. Each country's joining increases the fund by $40 million.
74. Interview with national official.
75. The donor countries used a system of regional representation whose effect is to give the U.S. a permanent seat (U.S. is an entire region). The other initial members are Canada, West Germany, Finland, Netherlands, Japan, USSR, Brazil, Egypt, Ghana, Jordan, Malaysia, Mexico, and Venezuela. Finland is chair the first year, Mexico vice-chair. The Article 5 countries did not establish a formal procedure for allocating their seats, and at the 1991 Meeting of the Parties had much difficulty designating a successor for one country that wished to step down. Author's observations at 1991 meeting of the parties.

$500,000. If consensus should fail, the committee's decisions follow the same voting rule as adjustment of the treaty: two-thirds overall, with simple majorities among both groups. The committee has a secretariat resident in Montreal, with a three-year operating budget of $7.6 million (drawn from the fund), and nine professional staff. The committee meets roughly quarterly, and participants from both groups of countries describe its work as businesslike, and its working relations as good. In June 1991 it was decided that NGOs will be admitted to future committee meetings except when the committee explicitly decides to exclude them.

The committee does its actual work—promoting CFC phaseout in developing countries—by subcontracting with "implementing agencies," presently the World Bank, UNEP, and the UN Development Program (UNDP). The functions of each are not precisely defined. At the London meeting, it was suggested that UNDP would perform country feasibility studies, the World Bank would administer investment projects, and UNEP would act as treasurer for the fund and perform "clearinghouse functions"—workshops and technical training for developing countries, which have now been assigned to UNEP's Industry and Environment Office in Paris. But in April 1991 the three agencies submitted work plans suggesting that all are bidding to expand their mandates. All three work plans included country studies, training, and pilot or demonstration-scale investment projects. The 1991 budget funded the World Bank at $5 million, UNDP at $1.3 million, and UNEP at $1.7 million (the requests in their proposed 1991 work plans had been $9.5, $5.5, and $2.5 million respectively).[76] The Bank will manage its own projects within its $1 billion Global Environmental Facility, but (after some pressure from the Executive Committee) within a separate ozone trust fund under the authority of the Executive Committee. There are also proposals to work with other implementing agencies—regional development banks, the U.N. Industrial Development Organization (UNIDO), or special national-level agencies created for the purpose.[77] UNIDO,

76. Executive Committee report presented to third Meeting of the Parties, June 1991.
77. This proposal is viewed with skepticism by Executive Committee members, who are concerned about loss of accountability of the implementing agencies to the Parties. Interviews.

for example, proposed a $250,000 project to study CFC disposal and recycling options in three African countries.

There are still major implementation issues to be settled. Detailed preinvestment studies were completed for some countries in 1991, with investment to begin in 1992. The interim fund must be replaced by the permanent one in 1994, and the parties must decide its size and terms of reference. Perhaps most contentious of all, parties must decide what the technology transfer provisions mean in practice. Though the implementation process is not yet fully mature, two important policy decisions are already clear: first, the attempt to retain policy-making power in the parties via the Executive Committee; and second, the implementation process at this stage seems to have some of the character of contracting out with competitive bidding.

The parties' ability to retain control over the objectives of the fund is not yet tested. The test will be in the fully developed relationship with the World Bank as an implementing agency, with its vastly larger resources and different governance structure. The Bank's Global Environmental Facility is ten times the size of the interim multilateral fund, and protecting stratospheric ozone is but one of its four global environmental goals. If other international environmental funds are created, the Bank may well be an implementing agency to them as well. Under these conditions, the Executive Committee may find its control over the objectives and use of the fund diminished.

The decision to contract tasks competitively to implementing agencies is an important innovation and one that may help the parties retain control, even though the competition thus far has not been particularly keen. Aside from the potential efficiencies available, this innovation holds the promise of resolving an old contradiction in international governance: how to do important new international jobs while keeping sovereign authority in the parties who agree on the jobs—that is, how to create new international institutional capacity without creating new international bureaucracies. The early work looks promising, but it is too soon to judge either the effectiveness of implementation on this problem, or the suitability of the new structure as a model for other international environmental issues.

Other than the fund, current implementation issues include difficulties with reporting required data and specification of a noncompliance procedure. On data, the Montreal Protocol requires each party to report their total production, imports, and exports of each controlled substance for 1986, 1989, and annually thereafter. Most parties have now reported 1986 data,[78] but only 28 parties have yet reported for 1989 and many are reporting difficulty with providing the data. Their difficulties are various, but many concern insufficiently fine distinctions in statistical reporting systems. The Harmonized Commodity System does not distinguish ozone-depleting controlled substances from other halogenated hydrocarbons, and the parties have asked the Customs Cooperation Council to revise the system accordingly. An ad hoc group of experts has been established to consider countries' difficulties in reporting data, and technical assistance will be available. Many of the nonreporting countries are low-consumption developing countries for which using UNEP estimates may be a reasonable solution; some, though, are substantial producers such as Italy and Greece.[79]

The noncompliance issue also remains unresolved. An ad hoc group of legal experts created to develop noncompliance procedures presented its recommendations to the London meeting: create an Implementation Committee to discuss instances of supposed noncompliance and report to the parties. The ad hoc group was asked to continue working and develop more specific procedures. They are now developing procedures with a consultative, ameliorative flavor, and will report to the parties in 1992.

Parties are also now considering whether to advance the phaseout schedules and further broaden coverage. The second round of Assessment Panels delivered reports at the end of 1991. A working group will receive the panel reports and deliberate through 1992, with possible amendments to be decided by the parties in August. Many participants expect a phaseout advance to about 1995 or 1997 and agreement on eventual phaseout of HCFCs. More chemicals may also be controlled, particularly methyl bromide.

With CFCs and halons to be phased out, the producer industry's regulatory concerns now center on the treatment of HCFC and CFC

78. Seventeen parties have either not responded or reported that no data is available.
79. UNEP 1991, "Report of the Secretariat on the Reporting of Data", UNEP/OzL.Pro.3/5 and Add.1, 23 May and 19–21 June 1991.

substitutes. Patents are pending on several synthesis routes, and a few plants are in commercial production,[80] but industry representatives estimate that only about 10 percent of the investment required to make the transition away from CFCs is yet committed. Some industry officials say they are awaiting clear signals that they will be permitted adequate returns before making major investment decisions. There are two producer positions. American producers advocate preannounced phaseout dates for HCFCs (possibly in the range of 2020 to 2050), with earlier phaseouts for those with longer atmospheric lifetimes and no regulation prior to phaseout. ICI is advocating a cap on total ozone depletion from all chemicals, with firms free to allocate their production and consumption within the cap.[81]

Environmental NGOs are now shifting resources away from stratospheric ozone to focus more on global warming. Their present positions on the two issues are closely linked. Greenpeace argues that only substitutes with zero ozone depletion and zero global warming potentials should be permitted; such substitutes are presently known for some applications but not for others such as refrigerants in existing equipment. Other groups distinguish among substitutes, arguing for prohibiting any with more than 2 percent of the ozone depletion potential of CFC 11.[82]

## National Policy Responses: Ratification and Implementation

The Vienna Convention entered into force in September 1988 with 20 ratifications, and in March 1992 there were 80. The Montreal Protocol entered into force in January 1989 with 30 ratifications, and in March 1992 there were 74. All major industrial countries ratified Montreal before entry into force, as did Egypt, Kenya, Mexico, and Nigeria among the major developing countries. Brazil ratified in March 1990, as negotiations were underway for the London amendments. At London, both

80. DuPont has commercial-scale plants producing HFC 134a (a CFC 12 replacement), HCFC 123 (a CFC 11 replacement), and dimethyl ether, a nonCFC aerosol propellant.
81. Interviews with industry officials.
82. Greenpeace International, 1991, "Accelerating the Phaseout of all Ozone-Depleting Substances, Including HCFCs," 19 June; Environmental NGOs, 1991, "Crucial Next Steps to Protect the Ozone Layer", statement to the third Meeting of the Parties, 19 June; Interviews.

China and India announced their intention to ratify. India has since ratified the Convention but not the Protocol, and asserts it cannot ratify the amended Protocol until the amendments enter into force. China is less squeamish and announced its ratification at the June 1991 meeting of the parties, as did the Soviet Union. The London amendments narrowly missed the 20 ratifications required for entry into force in January 1992 on schedule, but by March there were 19 ratifications completed and many others in train. Those completed included six EC member states, Japan, the United States, Canada, the Russian Federation, China, and Mexico.[83]

The only national action the Vienna Convention demands is data reporting. But when reports were first required in 1990, the secretariat (interpreting a long, vague list in the Convention of items to be reported) produced an impossibly intrusive form requesting much data of questionable value. The Vienna parties agreed in 1991 to reduce data-reporting requirements, probably by folding them into the more specific and focused Montreal reporting format. With this decision, the Vienna Convention will be reduced to an instrument imposing no specific obligations on its parties.

The Protocol requires national legislation or regulations to implement the control provisions, and most industrial country parties have established such programs. Indeed, all Organization for Economic Cooperation and Development (OECD) nations except Australia have already passed programs implementing the 1990 amendments.[84] They are highly disparate in the legal forms of implementation (legislation, regulations, negotiated agreements with industry) and in the policy instruments used (quotas, tradable permits, taxes, direct use regulation). All except Japan overcomply in some way. Some of the overcompliance is minor: for example, the 1990 U.S. Clean Air Act advances interim CFC and halon phaseout goals by a few years, advances MC phaseout from 2005 to 2002, and includes HCFC controls after 2015 (which the Protocol will likely add next year, but does not contain yet).[85] Some of the overcompliance is extreme: Germany's legislation eliminates CFCs by

83. Personal communication, UN Treaty Office, 9 March 1992.
84. As of summer 1991, Australia's legislation was only delayed by a long legislative queue. Interview with Australian official.
85. U.S. Public Law 101-549, Section 605.

1993, halons by 1996, HCFC 22 by 2000, and CT and MC by 1992. Most programs also include immediate provisions for limiting emissions through recovery, recycling, and destruction; the Protocol presently contains only hortatory language on these, and no explicit obligations, although one ad hoc working group promotes cooperation and the dissemination of information.

For developing country parties, the first control obligation is a freeze in 2000, but some have still announced control programs. Both Brazil and Mexico have announced that they intend to meet the same control schedules as the industrial countries, renouncing the ten-year grace period that the Protocol offers them. Officials say the motivation is primarily commercial, to keep up with their trading partners. At least two non-parties, Taiwan and South Korea, are implementing controls to avoid trade sanctions. Other developing countries are performing studies, either with the help of one of the implementing agencies for the fund or through bilateral arrangements, to determine how to accomplish the phaseouts.

National CFC consumption data for 1986 and 1989 is shown in Table 2.1 for those countries that have reported complete data. As the first control requirement is that industrial countries' CFC consumption in 1989 be no higher than in 1986, the table shows that most countries are far ahead of requirements.

Industry, including both producers and users, is moving ahead of regulations to reduce CFC use in many sectors. Among producers, DuPont has now announced that it will stop manufacturing CFCs in 1996 and halons in 1994.[86] An international producer group is jointly performing assessments of environmental impact and toxicity of HCFCs and HFCs.[87] In Japan, an industry cooperative is working with national regulators to implement a comprehensive system of CFC use limits.

User industry, in part inspired by the variety of innovations publicized by the Technology Panel, has been particularly active in seeking ways to conserve, recover, and avoid CFCs. Many former CFC uses,

86. International Environment Reporter 14, 591.
87. The two studies are the Alternative Fluorocarbon Environmental Acceptability Study (AFEAS) Report, published as Volume 2 of WMO, 1989, *Scientific Assessment*; and the Program on Alternative Fluorocarbon Toxicity (PAFT).

**Table 2.1**  ODP-weighted CFC consumption, 1986 and 1989: tons

| Country | 1986 | 1989 | Change |
|---|---|---|---|
| Austria | 7,760 | 5,860 | −24.5 |
| Canada | 19,958 | 18,843 | −5.6 |
| Finland | 3,301 | 1,886 | −42.9 |
| East Germany | 15,393 | 12,471 | −19.0 |
| Hungary | 5,468 | 4,848 | −11.3 |
| Japan | 118,134 | 109,971 | −6.9 |
| New Zealand | 2,088 | 1,005 | −51.9 |
| Norway | 1,313 | 908 | −30.9 |
| Switzerland | 7,960 | 4,023 | −49.5 |
| United States | 305,963 | 231,083 | −24.5 |
| European Community | 301,679 | 225,985 | −25.1 |
| Jordan | 302 | 257 | −14.9 |
| Malaysia | 2,190 | 3,444 | +57.3 |
| Singapore | 4,052 | 679 | −83.2 |
| Thailand | 2,300 | 4,595 | +99.8 |
| Venezuela | 3,879 | 3,450 | −11.1 |
| All countries reporting | 801.740 | 629,334 | −21.5 |

Source: UNEP/OzL.Pro.3/5 and Add. 1. European Community excludes Eastern Germany.

particularly in cleaning circuit boards and blowing foams, can now be supplanted with unrelated, non-ozone-depleting chemicals or with non-chemical approaches. One group of high-volume solvent users, principally made up of electronics and aerospace firms, has established a cooperative to share freely new techniques in conservation, recycling, and substitutes, including a free computer network to exchange technical information.[88] While finding halon substitutes was, until recently, thought to pose serious difficulties, recent investigation suggests that better management of the existing bank of halons will allow full production phaseouts within a few years.[89]

88. International Environment Reporter 14, 649; Interviews.
89. UNEP, 1991, *Montreal Protocol: 1991 Assessment*, report of the technology and economic assessment panel, December, 2–15.

## Analysis

This section reviews with an analytic perspective the institutional history outlined above, first by asking what determined the negotiating agenda and the international policy decisions at each stage of the process; and second, by focusing on the crucial output of the process—national action. It then asks whether the international processes mattered in determining the outcome observed—or, alternatively, whether it is plausible to imagine reaching the same point through aggressive leadership by one or a few nations—and concludes that international processes have been of decisive importance.

### Determinants of Agenda and International Decisions
**Prior to Vienna**   The early international agenda was limited to forms of cooperation on research and data, the structure of an agreement (Convention and Protocols), the question of whether or not to control CFCs through international measures, and (for only a short time before Vienna and over EC objections) the question of various forms of control. At the earliest stage, it was largely science and scientists that raised concern about the issue and set the agenda. The Washington meeting and CCOL were both predominantly scientific groups whose agendas focused on research. The Convention and Protocol structure was first proposed by a meeting of international legal experts in November 1981 in Montevideo, whose participants were impressed by the success of the approach in UNEP's Regional Seas Program.[90]

Though a few prominent atmospheric scientists remained convinced of the seriousness of ozone depletion throughout the period of apparently declining concern, the Nordics who tried to push a control agenda through this period were thwarted—prior to 1982 by the lack of an authorized international body to consider controls, and through 1984 by other delegations' perception that the Nordics did not understand the current science.[91] Others first advocated only "trigger" controls or no controls, but by 1984 joined the Nordics in the "Toronto Group" proposals. These proposals represented both a softening of

90. Briefing note, 31 December 1981.
91. Participant's notes, working group meeting and advisory committee meeting, 20 November 1981.

earlier Nordic demands, and a recognition by other participants (principally the United States and Canada) that international controls mirroring their own domestic measures could only benefit them.

The deadlock that resulted at Vienna between the conflicting positions of the EC and the Toronto Group seems, in retrospect, completely predictable. Each side proposed international measures that required action on the part of others but not themselves, and indeed in some instances defended their proposals at home by pointing out that they would cost their own industries nothing.[92] Each side presented valid environmental criticisms of the other's proposals, but presented those criticisms in terms suggesting that only these two options were possible and that either one, once enacted, would endure unchanged for decades.[93]

As a result of the deadlock the Vienna Convention contains, with two exceptions, only innocuous measures on which all major parties had agreed since 1977. On the one hand, it includes no control measures because of the persistent, uncomprehended gap between the two control approaches; on the other hand, the Convention itself did not come about earlier because several delegations continued to push for their preferred form of controls, thinking it important and possible to include them in the first negotiated agreement.

**Vienna to Montreal**   Following the Vienna Convention, several factors pushed the agenda forward quickly. The resolution passed at Vienna gave UNEP and its executive director more power to force the agenda— power they exploited effectively by calling two broad, informal workshops prior to resuming negotiations. Discovery of the Antarctic ozone hole, even though CFCs were but one of three proposed causes, kept public and media attention on the issue. Finally, NGO activity increased, first in the United States with the NRDC lawsuit, and later in Europe. Science continued to define several key elements of the negotiating agenda: considering all CFCs, trading them off according to ozone-depletion equivalence, and including halons.

92. Briefing notes.
93. Commission of the European Communities, 1985, "Observations on Alternative Control Measures"; U.S. Department of State, 1985, Public Information Series, 21 January.

Perhaps most importantly, the United States started to provide strong leadership on the issue from early 1986, and many items—some emerging from the science, some not—first appeared on the international agenda as elements of the new, aggressive American negotiating position. A near phaseout of all ozone-depleting substances was the American position from November 1986;[94] in February 1987 the Americans submitted an article proposing control of trade with non-parties; and in May they proposed weighting substances according to ozone-depletion potentials.[95]

It was not science but bargaining that determined the decisions adopted in Montreal. The 50 percent cut that was agreed to had no particular scientific prominence. Indeed, the expert opinion at the time seemed strongly divided. If CFCs were not causing the Antarctic hole, then the 1986 WMO report reflected the prevailing science, justifying at most a CFC production freeze. If CFCs *were* causing the hole, then much more stringent controls than a 50 percent cut were justified—possibly on the order of the 85 percent cuts EPA had calculated would be required to stabilize atmospheric chlorine concentrations. The 50 percent cuts adopted were hence either much too strong or much too weak, depending on how one views the then-partial Antarctic evidence. Cutting by half was essentially a bargained outcome between the EC's proposed freeze and the United States' 95 percent cuts. Where the EC had advocated controlling production and the United States, controlling consumption, it was agreed to do both.

The trade and LDC issues seem to have garnered broad agreement by the time Montreal approached. So had the important provisions for Assessment Panels and periodic review. This measure enjoyed strong scientific support in a time of rapidly developing science while allowing both the activist and the reluctant nations to accept a somewhat uncomfortable control protocol in the hope that subsequent review would jus-

94. While one can read the vaguely worded Nordic proposals as early as 1982 to advocate full phaseouts, the proponents seemed unwilling to say so clearly without a larger coalition supporting them.
95. Ozone-depletion potentials first appear in Miller, Alan S., and I. M. Mintzer, 1986, *The Sky is the Limit: Strategies for Protecting the Ozone Layer*, World Resources Institute Research Report #3 (November), Washington, D.C., where they were referenced to "preliminary estimates, Office of Air and Radiation, EPA, Oct. 86."

tify moving to a more favorable one. Periodic reviews of some form had been elements of the original American, EC, Canadian, and Nordic proposals.

The final Protocol has a fairly strong American flavor, as one would expect from the strength of U.S. negotiating leadership from 1986 and the extent to which the U.S. delegation was pushed by Congress and the NRDC lawsuit. Some European participants contend they were bullied into an agreement that unfairly favored U.S. industry, calling the 1987 agreement "The DuPont Protocol," but the argument is weak. Their only specific claim of unfairness in the Protocol concerns the article on industrial rationalization, which effectively permits rationalization in North America but not Europe; this item, though, was a Canadian proposal.[96]

**Montreal to London**   The three essential elements of the post-Montreal agenda were tightening the control schedule to full phaseouts, broadening the set of chemicals covered, and putting stronger LDC assistance measures in place. With regard to controls, scientific news and results continued to raise public and political concern, and the provision for periodic review once again gave UNEP the power to advance the negotiations relatively quickly when scientific concern called for it. In contrast to earlier confusion and reversals, the science since 1985, and particularly since 1987, has consistently moved toward greater concern.

Scientists' influence has increased since 1987 with the institutionalization of their roles in the Assessment Panels. These panels have provided a channel for science to feed directly into the negotiation process from a forum with the stamp of international objectivity and authoritativeness. All was not sweetness and light in the creation of the panels; many participants describe them as having a U.S. bias, and some report a systematic program of excluding employees of producer industries from the Technology Panel. But even the critics acknowledge that the science and technology reports were of high quality and that the leaders of the process "played fair."

Consequently, particularly due to the strong results they had to report, scientists' influence over the negotiations has advanced beyond

96. Interview with industry, American, and Canadian officials.

their prior agenda-setting role to the exercise of substantial influence over certain aspects of the negotiated decisions. Tolba's earlier statement that it was not possible to oppose controls on the basis of scientific dissent was hyperbolic when he made it in April 1987, but became true in 1989 and 1990. Not all participants in the 1990 negotiations accepted that the science justified full phaseouts, but those who did not were isolated and unable to block global agreement.

Of course, a full CFC phaseout would have been immediately on the post-Montreal agenda in any case, since it had been the prior position of one of the major participants. But when the science panel reported that even full phaseouts would not restore the ozone hole before 2060, and the technology panel reported that viable substitutes for essentially all applications would be available in ten years, it became impossible to mount serious opposition to phaseouts. Negotiators agreed on phaseouts relatively easily.

The science panel's graphs of changes in stratospheric chlorine concentration over time, presented to the working group in November 1989, had impact beyond making the case for a CFC phaseout. They also focused attention on *all* chlorine, thereby requiring consideration of MC, CT, and the HCFCs and suggested a regulatory approach that discriminates according to atmospheric lifetimes.[97] The scenarios' treatment of HCFCs was limited, though, by difficulty in projecting the extent of substitution. Parties could not agree on treatment of HCFCs, and settled for a nonbinding resolution.

Evidence for the panels' influence over decisions is perhaps clearest in the one case where their work was contested. The solvents industry claimed that MC was added late to the technology panel's agenda, and the panel concluded 90 percent substitute availability by mistakenly assuming that MC substitution would be the same as CFC 113 substitution.[98] A different group from CFC producers and new to the process, the solvents industry was caught unprepared. They commis-

97. MC and CT had been mentioned on a CCOL report as early as 1980, but first came to wide attention with Miller and Mintzer, *Sky is the Limit*, in November 1986.
98. In fact, MC was the preferred substitute for CFC 113 in many applications. At the time, very little research on MC substitutes was available. Interviews with panel members and industry officials.

sioned consultant studies and presented their claims to a subsequent meeting of the negotiating group, but found that these were received with suspicion and had little impact.

The environmental argument over MC turned on different interpretations of its short atmospheric life (6.3 years).[99] After three or four lifetimes, the atmospheric concentration of a gas drops to nearly zero. Consequently, to control the date at which stratospheric chlorine drops below 2 ppb, one need only consider MC emissions within three lifetimes of that date, or after 2040 for a 2060 target date. On the other hand, cutting MC now will have the fastest effect on atmospheric concentrations and will shave the most off the peak chlorine concentration that follows a phaseout.

A second-order outcome of the panel's shifting its focus from ozone depletion to chlorine loading was to open up the scenario-modeling field to anyone with a powerful desktop computer.[100] Those who played with scenarios quickly discovered that over several decades, full participation by developing countries would be essential to limiting chlorine levels. This realization drove the discussions of finance and technology transfer, for realizing unanimous participation requires meeting everyone's needs. Representatives of the major developing countries pressed their case very strongly. The details of the financial mechanism and technology transfer articles were bargained outcomes. The United States, the most cautious participant in the financial discussions, was weakened by its temporary reversal in April.

These articles were fought out against the broader backdrop of general LDC equity claims and northern attempts to avoid strong redistributive precedents. With LDC leverage increased by the need for a full global phaseout, and some LDC representatives pressing for very broad claims, the risk of a classic North-South confrontation was real. On the technology transfer language, that both sides now say they gave up too much suggests successful negotiation. Many participants attribute the successful negotiation to a high level of shared concern; surely it was

99. WMO, 1989, *Scientific Assessment*, xxx.
100. Ozone-depletion models, particularly multi-dimensional ones, require supercomputers.

also helpful that estimated costs turned out to be low, declining from billions to hundreds of millions by spring 1990.[101]

**Altering State Behavior: What Did the Institutions Do?**
How much credit do international institutions deserve for the reductions now occurring in ozone-depleting substances? One might argue that the present treaty or an equivalent outcome was determined simply by the eventually decisive science and the intensity of national interests in protecting the ozone layer, and that industry would eventually have acquiesced to a control regime.

Clearly at a couple of points, and arguably at others, institutions advanced the process by building concern and by improving the contractual environment. Their effect is clearest at later stages and more arguable earlier. Since 1987, and especially since 1990, international institutions have also developed capacity to cut CFCs where it did not formerly exist.

Any continuing multilateral negotiation can raise concern and facilitate contracting. Talking about the problem can allow delegations informally to share information, observations, and research and to try to persuade others of the gravity of the problem. Talking about proposed measures gives the opportunity to coordinate their details, identify ways to make them more effective and less costly, and put subtle pressure on the reluctant. In this case, negotiations at least kept the ozone issue in public view and moved some laggard states to stay abreast of the science and to present justifications for their positions. Moreover, it seems that the suasive force of even the earliest negotiations was increased by their being formally authorized by UNEP's Governing Council, rather than arranged ad hoc by the activist nations. There are two pieces of evidence: first, those nations who opposed a treaty also opposed the original authorization of negotiations, and subsequently tried once in 1984 to have the authorization revoked prematurely; second, even those nations who most strongly opposed a treaty continued to attend the negotiations throughout.

101. Reports of third and fourth Working Group meetings, 9–11 May 1990, Geneva, and 20–29 June, London.

Up to 1985, though, few of the potential effects of negotiations were realized. Participants held sharply differing degrees of concern, bolstered in part by differences in national scientific assessments, which showed no sign of being reconciled. Activists succeeded neither in coordinating among themselves nor in persuading the resistant.

Following the 1985 Convention, there were two new institutional factors: the first official international scientific assessment; and the UNEP secretariat, authorized to convene workshops and negotiations with a 1987 deadline. Tolba, exploiting UNEP's enhanced position as secretariat, began pushing aggressively for an effective treaty. The 1986 WMO report, though not officially linked to the negotiations, marked the first time that an international scientific report was able to move the focus of factual dispute out of the main negotiating forum. The WMO report and the 1987 Wurzburg meeting of modelers, though neither presented any new science, authenticated the view that the issue was serious, and delimited the range of possible disagreements that could credibly be attributed to differing scientific opinion.

In late 1986 and 1987, negotiations became more serious and focused. Many participants report feeling increasing concern and an increasing sense of the activist nations' commitment, beginning at the Rome and Leesburg workshops and proceeding through 1988—and report that they subsequently attempted to persuade colleagues at home. During this period, activists first succeeded in coordinating details of proposed control measures, albeit under U.S. leadership. They also began finding ways to modify controls to lower the cost to participants (such as ODP-weighting), and increase the cost to non-participants (such as trade restrictions). The result was a set of more persuasive, more carefully developed control provisions on the table.

But the institutions and accelerated agenda were not all that changed between 1985 and 1987. Other factors favoring controls included strong negotiating leadership by the United States, pushed domestically by Congress and the NRDC lawsuit; U.S. industry's acknowledgement that chemical substitutes were possible; increased German pressure within the EC; and the observation (though without determination of cause) of the Antarctic ozone hole. Institutional factors clearly were not sufficient to bring about the 1987 agreement, but they did advance the process by limiting spurious scientific disagreement as a tactic to obstruct negotiations; increasing the general level of concern and urgency; and providing formal standing for Tolba, enabling him to exercise strong personal leadership.

Since 1987, more institutional factors are present and their effects are clearer. These included first the measures for CFC cuts and accompanying trade restrictions enacted in the Montreal Protocol, and second, the provisions for regular meetings of the parties with periodic expert assessment and treaty review. The control measures enacted in 1987 and 1990 clearly increased everyone's willingness to undertake national controls. Even the activists were willing to go further with the confidence that their measures would be reciprocated. Not even the most activist governments made serious, costly reductions until the treaty was signed. (The early aerosol bans followed movement away from CFCs by consumers and producers, and turned out to be essentially costless.)[102] Since the treaty, all have enacted national controls, many exceeding the provisions of the treaty.

One might argue that this national overcompliance is evidence against the significance of the treaty control measures: if nations overcomply, then the treaty is not a binding constraint and so must not be determining their actions. This argument has two major weaknesses, however. First, not every country overcomplies; even moving only the few major nations who comply precisely counts as a significant accomplishment. Second, in a dynamic process of negotiation and renegotiation, overcompliance does not necessarily indicate action that would have occurred without the treaty. Overcompliance, particularly by an activist nation, can be an attempt to push the treaty further. This is a particularly reasonable explanation for overcompliance since 1990 by nations that unsuccessfully sought advanced phaseouts in 1990 and are now proposing them for the 1992 meeting.

For nations that formerly resisted the treaty, the enactment of formal controls also gives incentives to join: the confidence that they will not be placed at a competitive disadvantage by joining, and the desire to avoid trade sanctions and isolation. That the intent of the drafters was

102. Substitutes for CFC aerosols were cheaper and about as good. Estimated 1983 U.S. savings from the aerosol ban were $165 million. Most substitutes were inflammable, though, and in a few applications they performed worse, so there was some cost and risk imposed that is not counted in these savings.

for unanimous participation is clear from the early, focused attention they devoted to sanctions against non-parties, as compared with the relatively late and less careful consideration given compliance measures. The effectiveness of the treaty in providing incentives to laggards is evident both in the assertions by some delegates that trade sanctions were decisive in their countries' decisions to join, and in the energetic compliance by non-parties Taiwan and South Korea. Such incentives likely grow stronger as the treaty moves toward full participation. With moderate participation, one can imagine a two-regime equilibrium, with a separate international economy of non-parties producing and trading CFCs and related equipment only with each other. But as the number of parties grows, technical progress, economies of scale, commercial standards, and confidence and experience with implementation all act to increase the motivation to join. It seems clear that movement away from CFCs has already proceeded so far that the stable equilibrium will be full participation. That several major developing countries are not taking their ten-year grace period supports this idea, for they would bear no explicit sanctions for proceeding more slowly. While their decisions could reflect attempts to move to the head of the queue for payments, they more likely indicate a "critical mass" effect, wherein the commercial advantage is in abandoning CFCs rapidly if enough countries are doing so.

The cluster of institutional changes enacted in 1987 concerning meetings, expert assessment, and treaty review were of decisive importance for realizing stronger controls in 1990. Establishing the panels moved a broader set of questions—including the feasibility of different phaseout schedules as well as their consequences for the stratosphere—out of the main negotiating forum. Empowering the secretariat to convene such panels, and to call meetings of the parties to review their results, grants it extremely strong power (in cooperation with some of the parties) to force the agenda. There is a delicate balance between the procedural, agenda-forcing power spun off to expert groups and the secretariat, and the substantive power that remains in the parties. That balance is in part maintained through frequent meetings of the parties. The parties in effect have bound themselves to undertake serious review of scientific and technical events, while retaining their ultimate legitimate authority over the decisions enacted.

Following the 1987 and especially the 1990 agreements, institutions have been established whose job is to help implement decisions already negotiated, rather than to facilitate negotiations. These institutions have built capacity to reduce CFC use, develop and implement alternatives, and solve related problems. In some cases, this capacity-building has been intentional. Several small groups have been created to assist parties with implementation, either by disseminating information or by solving widely shared problems.[103] Moreover, the explicit mandate of the fund, executive committee, and implementing agencies is to provide the technical information, planning, and financial support necessary for developing countries to eliminate CFCs. In other cases, the capacity-building has been fortuitous. The technology panels were created to assist negotiations by answering questions about how fast various CFC uses could be phased out. They had the additional effect, though, of bringing together key international groups of technical experts able to develop new non-CFC solutions in specific applications. The result has been recognition of new technical solutions and new business opportunities, which in turn generate substantial new capacity in the private sector.

In summary, international ozone institutions have had increasing effect on national actions over time. The treaty control measures adopted in 1987 and 1990 brought about national controls in countries where weaker controls or none would have occurred otherwise. In negotiations for the 1990 amendments, the institutional combination of assessment panels, periodic treaty review by meetings of the parties, and a strong secretariat was a necessary condition for achieving prompt agreement on phaseouts. The multilateral fund and associated institutions have now begun to make CFC phaseouts possible in countries where they were not previously so.

### National Leadership: Would It Have Been Sufficient?

Though international institutions facilitated the present outcome at many points, and have been necessary at certain points, they were not sufficient conditions to bring about the treaty and national CFC con-

---

103. For example, expert groups have been established on data-reporting difficulties and on destruction technologies.

trols; strong leadership from activist nations was also necessary. Individual nations led by taking the initiative to get negotiating bodies authorized, preparing draft proposals, sponsoring research, and pressuring and persuading the reluctant. They also accepted disproportionate cost burdens in the 1987 Protocol, for the uniform 50 percent CFC cuts imposed substantially higher costs on the leaders—who had already banned aerosols—than on the laggards, for whom aerosol cuts could achieve the 50 percent reduction at no cost.

To argue, though, that international institutions had no significant effect on the outcome, one must claim that equivalently strong action could have come about through national initiatives alone, given the same scientific knowledge and interests. Could CFCs have been phased out without the Vienna Convention? Two counterfactual scenarios can help illuminate this question. First, one might argue that the United States alone could have passed tough domestic regulations accompanied by sanctions, thereby bringing about the equivalent of the treaty through a series of bilateral negotiations. Alternatively, one might argue that a small group of activist nations could have brought about the equivalent of the treaty by each enacting strong domestic controls, then making a collective agreement to formalize and coordinate their controls and provide strong enough incentives for others to join.

The first scenario, that the United States could have dragged the world, has superficial plausibility. EPA's 1988 risk assessment lends it some support, for the assessment found U.S. benefits so huge that extrapolation suggests it would be advantageous even for America to bear the entire cost of global CFC phaseouts.[104] This would presumably happen through enactment of comprehensive domestic CFC regulations including trade restrictions on CFCs and related products from countries that do not follow, along the lines of Senate legislation proposed in 1987.

However, there are several serious difficulties with this scenario. First,

104. The estimated benefits of the 50 percent Montreal controls were $6.4 trillion, mostly from avoided early cancer deaths in the U.S. population born before 2075. Estimated costs were $27 billion. Simple extrapolations suggest that U.S. benefits from a global phaseout may exceed world costs. Environmental Protection Agency, 1986, "Regulatory Impact Analysis: Protection of Stratospheric Ozone."

the resultant controls would not likely have been as well designed as those that emerged in 1987. The United States remained committed to some form of aerosol control through 1985, and though they led the push for more rational controls in 1986–87, most of the innovative features that made the 1987 controls so effective were not originally U.S. proposals. The U.S. delegation introduced the trade measures and ODP-weighting; other delegations introduced the consumption control formula, the inclusion of halons, and the treatment of developing countries.

Second, it is not plausible that the United States acting alone could provide sufficient incentives to persuade the rest of the world to adopt its regulations. It is highly unlikely that the U.S. political system could generate billion-dollar bribes to subsidize the required new investment in the EC, Japan, and the Soviet Union. As for the threat of sanctions, it seems unlikely that broad sanctions would be enacted for this issue alone, or that restrictions narrowly targeted on CFCs would be effective, since American trade in CFCs was small. Congressional bills in 1986 and 1987 did include trade restrictions on CFCs and related products, but it is more reasonable to interpret these as nudges to the international negotiations than as expressions of willingness to act alone.

The most decisive weakness of this scenario, though, is that even the United States commitment to international CFC control was highly uneven. Despite U.S. leadership in the 1970s and at certain crucial stages of the negotiations, U.S. support for consummation of the agreement was threatened by domestic backlash at all three stages: the last-minute attempt by State Department officials to reject the 1985 Convention; the counterattack through the Domestic Policy Council in Spring 1987; and the Spring 1990 attempt, originating in the office of White House Chief of Staff John Sununu, to scuttle the delicate negotiations on a financial agreement. To imagine that U.S. commitment to a global control regime could be sustained against such powerful and ideological domestic opposition without the energy, interests, and reputations involved in a strong international process, is to imagine much greater domestic consistency and unanimity than ever existed on U.S. policy making on this issue. For the United States, and indeed for all activists, a continuing international process provided the momentum needed to smooth over uneven commitment and attention at the national level.

In the second scenario a group of activist nations would coordinate, after enacting their own controls, to coerce others to join. The weakness of this scenario is that a successful control regime requires uniformity in details, for reasons of trade, technical standards, and consistency of obligations imposed on others. Matching the details requires early, detailed coordination among the activists. The failed "multi-option approach" of the Toronto Group in 1984–85 indicates precisely the problem of seeking to accommodate disparate domestic control measures in a post-hoc international agreement. Without coordination from the start, domestic interests in existing regulations can thwart international collaboration.

**Overall Assessment: The Right Measures, but Too Late?**

To this point, I have argued for the effectiveness of international ozone institutions in narrow terms: they brought about stronger measures to protect the ozone layer than would have happened in their absence. In this final section, I evaluate the institutions and negotiations using a different standard: how do the measures adopted compare to what is apparently needed to protect the ozone layer? I close with some speculative observations on whether and how the present control measures could have been brought about earlier.

The Montreal Protocol is widely praised as a model for future environmental agreements. Relative to prior experience with international environmental cooperation, the praise is richly deserved; in many important respects, the agreement is unprecedented, and it is clear that international action achieved more than could have been realized nationally. But relative to what is likely required to protect the ozone layer, serious reservations are appropriate. One reservation is simply that a great deal more work remains to be done. Because CFCs have such long atmospheric lifetimes, parties worldwide must maintain their commitments—to reducing emissions, recovering and destroying existing stocks, enforcing production and consumption controls, and con-

trolling potential new ozone-depleting substances—for more than fifty years. Parties must also decide how to treat the less damaging, but still harmful, transitional substances, and settle remaining implementation questions on financial and technical measures for developing countries.

The more serious reservation, though, is that the Protocol probably represents the right measures enacted too late. Present projections of chlorine-loading show the Antarctic ozone hole not being restored until about 2060. Moreover, recent observations continue to show ozone losses greater than predicted and greater than can be explained by conventional models; consequently, the ultimate extent of ozone loss remains unknown. The risk remains open that even the seemingly rapid international progress achieved will be insufficient to avert serious global ozone loss. From the perspective of 1992, what was done in 1987 should have been done several years earlier.

Could it have been? It is not likely that the 1987 Protocol could have been negotiated any faster than it was; its negotiation, ratification, implementation, and amendment all took place with remarkable speed—particularly given that significant opposition to controls persisted until 1987. But the 1985 Convention, whose only innovations beyond the 1977 declaration were a dispute resolution process and the status of the EC, took eight years to negotiate.[105] Roughly speaking, opponents of international controls blocked the authorization of a negotiating body for four years, then advocates and opponents of controls deadlocked for four years.

The first four-year delay naturally suggests two questions that I have not addressed in this study: why the opponents were able to delay authorization for so long; and whether some other negotiating forum, either ad hoc or under a body other than UNEP, could have led to either a declaratory agreement or international controls earlier than they occurred. The character of the second four-year delay suggests that earlier agreement could have been achieved, had there been better, more persuasive control measures on the table. While confused science through 1985 put the advocates at a disadvantage, there remained some

---

105. Participants argue that these two innovations, particularly the treatment of the EC, were both significant and necessary for future controls, and that negotiating them alone accounted for roughly one year's work. Interviews with current and former national officials.

scientific concern throughout the period, and even by 1981 it was clear that substantial cuts could be achieved (by those who had not already cut) at low cost. But the long-maintained self-serving position of the advocates that others should duplicate their own aerosol controls, followed by the disorganized "multi-options" proposal, were easy for opponents to reject on the soundest of grounds. Had some member of the Toronto Group exercised the leadership necessary to pull the group together around a single well-crafted proposal, one that would necessarily have imposed costs on its proponents as well as on others, it is at least arguable that the deadlock could have been broken and controls enacted in 1985 or even earlier.

# 3

# European Acid Rain: The Power of Tote-Board Diplomacy

Marc A. Levy

In Europe about half the air pollution crosses borders, and much of that kills fish and trees and corrodes buildings and monuments. Governments have responded by collaborating within the Long-Range Transboundary Air Pollution (LRTAP) Convention, as well as by taking measures within the European Community and at the national level. Because of its connections to dtente and the Helsinki process, all the appropriate states are members of LRTAP and participate actively in LRTAP's joint research programs. The joint research is valued by governments and appears to have helped resolve many scientific disputes. When LRTAP was created only two of its thirty members thought acid rain was a serious environmental problem. Now all do, and they are in the midst of an ambitious work plan to develop strict regulatory protocols. If the work plan is followed out successfully, it will result in one of the world's most innovative institutional responses to international environmental hazards.

LRTAP's policy outputs have consisted of coordinated scientific research programs, regular meetings to review research and national policies and to negotiate reduction strategies, and a series of regulatory protocols commiting signatories to reduction targets and timetables. Pro-

I am grateful to Sonja Boehmer-Christiansen, Abram Chayes, Antonia Chayes, William Clark, Peter M. Haas, Michael Hatch, Robert Keohane, Ron Mitchell, M. J. Peterson, Peter Sand, Gudrun Schwarzer, Detlef Sprinz, David Victor and Jørgen Wettestad for comments on earlier drafts. Detlef Sprinz shared invaluable information on the 1991 VOC protocol. I thank Romney Resney for research assistance. For financial assistance I thank Harvard University's MacArthur Committee on International Security, Center for International Affairs, and Center for European Studies; and the Institute for the Study of World Politics.

tocols have been signed covering sulfur dioxide ($SO_2$), nitrogen oxides (NOx), and volatile organic compounds (VOCs). The consequences of these policy outputs on actual national emissions have varied across countries. The poorest European countries show the least effect; they simply failed to reduce emissions. The hard-core environmentalist countries (Norway, Sweden, Germany) reduced significantly, but well in advance of international rules; they would have undertaken reductions in the absence of LRTAP. Some countries reduced emissions but only coincidentally, by virtue of changing energy policies. We do not know what effect LRTAP would have had on these countries if, like the others, they had faced more costly adjustment. In two other sets of countries, however, LRTAP had clearly observable effects on emissions. In one group LRTAP's joint scientific programs led to the development of knowledge of domestic acidification damage that these countries would otherwise not have realized. This new knowledge led these countries to reevaluate their opposition to sulfur dioxide reductions, and they each joined the leaders in seeking steep cuts. Another group was affected by LRTAP by virtue of LRTAP's facilitating a linkage between acid rain and other foreign policy issues. These countries were not concerned about domestic damage, but reduced emissions in order to achieve other foreign policy goals.

LRTAP achieved its successes through consensus building and rule making, but one cannot understand what happened if one examines these activities independently. LRTAP worked because of the way it has integrated the two functions. LRTAP was established as a weak institution, initially oriented only toward scientific research and ambiguous principles. Out of weakness came strength, however. Weak rules permitted strong consensus-building powers, whereas strong rules would have generated hostility on the part of governments. Government opposition was always a threat because, although European governments were willing to make symbolic pledges for the environment, they were (with only two exceptions) loathe at the beginning to take concrete action to prevent acid rain. These skeptical governments felt unthreatened by LRTAP even as its scientific working groups resolved the uncertainties in favor of taking action. Today these governments embrace what they once fought and accept the need for action.

The regulatory rules were weak but not irrelevant. They served a vital role in magnifying pressure on recalcitrant states, in keeping the consensus-building activities high on governments' agendas, and in assisting domestic environmental proponents of action. Rules serve these functions in a process I call "tote-board diplomacy."[1] Protocols were not designed to establish binding rules based on the principle of mutual adjustment toward a pareto optimum (as one observes in trade or arms control negotiations, for example). If mutual adjustment toward joint gains is the goal, one needs strong rules that are complied with. But in a process of tote-board diplomacy weak rules can work quite well, and noncompliance can be part of a successful strategy. In the case of LRTAP, regulatory protocols served as a normative register, indicating both what behavior was considered legitimate and which countries had accepted such a standard as a guide to national policy. The protocols were tote-boards showing who was responsible and who was not. Countries which remained off the tote-board were subject to external pressure and internal pressure; this pressure promoted investigation of domestic damage and facilitated linkage strategies on the part of motivated actors. The same held for countries who registered themselves on the tote-board but failed to comply—they invited external and internal pressure. Tote-board diplomacy proved to be an effective instrument; only the poor countries of eastern and southern Europe, along with Ireland, escaped its effects.

To support the above argument, I first describe the environmental problem posed by acid rain, and the primary international institutional response, LRTAP. I then elaborate the international policy responses which LRTAP has promulgated, and assess the institution's role in shaping the international diplomatic and scientific agenda. I then review the national responses which LRTAP has evoked, and present evidence as to which of these responses LRTAP can legitimately claim credit for. In this last, crucial, step I make use of process-level evidence for indi-

---

1. Tote-boards are devices used to record fund-raising drives and spur greater participation. For example, a university effort to solicit employee contributions to a charity such as the United Way might erect a large sign with different schools listed. Each school would be assigned a target contribution of what is expected, with these targets outlined on the sign in the form of thermometers. As contributions are received, the thermometers are painted in, hoping to induce employees to make enough contributions to fill in their school's thermometers all the way.

vidual countries and illustrate my conclusions with the counterfactual case of what European acid rain politics would have looked like if LRTAP had not been created.

## Creation and Structure of LRTAP

### The Problem

Sulfur dioxide and oxides of nitrogen are released into the air when coal and oil are burned. They can be carried many hundreds of miles by wind currents before being deposited, either dissolved in precipitation or in dry form. Oxides of sulfur and nitrogen form acids, which can damage materials and aquatic and terrestrial ecosystems. The term "acid rain" refers commonly to both dry and wet deposition. Although sulfur dioxide and nitrogen oxides are both also potent causes of respiratory diseases in humans, they are usually safe to humans in the diffuse concentrations that persist over long-range transport. Acid rain becomes a problem when its steady deposition over time eventually exhausts the ability of a receptor (whether a cathedral in Chartres, a forest in Germany, or a lake in Norway) to counteract the acid's effect. Occasionally these long-term effects can generate negative consequences for human health, as when heavy metals are leached into drinking water supplies.[2]

It has been known for over a century that emissions from combustion of coal and oil could generate acidic precipitation. Robert Angus Smith, a Scottish chemist, discovered in the 1850s that sulfuric acid levels in Manchester were correlated with coal burning. Smith worked out the chemical mechanisms involved in an 1872 book, where he coined the term "acid rain."[3] This scientific discovery failed to develop much political salience in light of more immediate air pollution concerns. The British alkali industry was spewing hydrochloric acid into the air with far graver consequences than the sulfur dioxide given off in coal burning.

---

2. Viewers of the Swedish film *My Life as a Dog* will recall the phenomenon of green hair, caused by copper leached into household wells by acid deposition.
3. Robert Angus Smith, *Air and Rain: The Beginnings of a Chemical Climatology* (London: Longmans, Green, and Company, 1872). Smith's work subsequently went unnoticed until 1981, when a National Academy of Sciences report resurrected it. Ellis Cowling, "Acid Precipitation in Historical Perspective," *Environmental Science and Technology* 16 (February 1982), 111A.

Britain regulated the alkali industry successfully, and, along with other industrializing countries, dealt with coal burning as a local health problem. Most countries also followed the British lead in building taller smokestacks to disperse toxic pollutants over a wider area. As these much more serious and immediate problems dominated regulatory politics, Smith's work on acid rain became forgotten.

Swedish researchers, however, began monitoring freshwater acidity levels in the 1940s, and over the 1950s and 1960s began noticing significant increases. In 1968 a Swedish scientist published a paper arguing that Swedish acidification was attributable in large part to long-range transport of airborne pollutants, especially from the United Kingdom and central Europe.[4]

Governments in both Norway and Sweden became concerned, because valuable fish stocks were threatened. They focused attention on the problem at the 1972 UN Conference on the Human Environment in Stockholm. At Stockholm (and in years of prior preparatory meetings) they presented the results of their acidification research and sought international cooperation to reduce sulfur emissions. Other European countries were skeptical of the claim that their emissions were harming Scandinavian ecosystems; the conference did agree to the principle that nations have "the responsibility to ensure that activities within their jurisdiction or control do not cause damage to the environment of other states."[5] The Soviet Union and Eastern Europe did not formally accede to this principle because they boycotted the Stockholm conference over a dispute concerning recognition of East Germany.

Today, there is very little disagreement with the core of the initial Scandinavian claims. The resolution of the scientific disputes was far from even, however. Different countries accepted the claims at different times, and, at a consensus level, different components of the Scandina-

4. Svante Odén, "The Acidification of Air and Precipitation and its Consequences in the Natural Environment," Ecology Committee Bulletin No. 1 (Stockholm: Swedish National Science Research Council, 1968). Cowling attributes Odén with achieving "the first major unification of knowledge about acid precipitation in the fields of limnology, agriculture, and atmospheric chemistry." Cowling, "Acid Precipitation in Historical Perspective," 114A.
5. Quoted in Gregory Wetstone and Armin Rosencranz, *Acid Rain in Europe and North America: National Responses to an International Problem* (Washington, D.C.: Environmental Law Institute, 1983), 134.

vian argument were accepted at different times. The Scandinavian claims can be disaggregated into four logically distinct debates: (1) Did sulfur dioxide travel long distances? (2) Did airborne deposition of sulfur dioxide harm rivers and lakes? (3) Did airborne deposition of sulfur dioxide harm forests and crops? (4) Would proposed domestic abatement measures bring comparable improvements in foreign environmental effects?

The transport debate proved easiest to settle. Immediately after the 1972 Stockholm Conference, the Organization for Economic Cooperation and Development (OECD) launched a study to measure long-range transport of air pollution. The OECD program established a network of monitoring stations, which in 1978 was given institutional status independent of the OECD as the Cooperative Program for Monitoring and Evaluation of the Long-Range Transmission of Air Pollutants in Europe (EMEP). In 1977 the OECD published findings indicating that air pollution did travel long distances and that five of the eleven European countries participating in the study received more pollution from abroad than from domestic sources.[6] EMEP collects three sets of measurements to determine international pollution flows: measurements of air pollutant levels provided by monitoring stations, national emission levels provided by governments, and metereological data. With this information EMEP can generate a table allocating national responsibility for each country's pollution deposition.

In terms of understanding pollution flows to Scandinavia, EMEP should have included participation of both northwestern and Eastern Europe. It initially omitted the countries of Eastern Europe, however, because they were not OECD members. Nevertheless, the full participation of relevant Western Europeans must be counted as a significant success. Most did not accept the Scandinavian premise that pollution traveled long distances when EMEP began, and Britain (the biggest Western European exporter) was especially resistant. EMEP eventually

6. Organization for Economic Cooperation and Development, *The OECD Programme on Long Range Transport of Air Pollutants: Summary Report* (1977). Austria, Finland, Norway, Sweden, and Switzerland received more foreign than domestic pollution; Belgium, Denmark, France, West Germany, the Netherlands, and the United Kingdom received more domestic than foreign.

convinced all of them that long-range transport did indeed occur; by the early 1980s that debate was over.

The Scandinavians had a tougher time gaining acceptance of their claim that long-range transport causes ecological damage and that such damage could be prevented in a cost-effective manner by emission reduction measures at the source. These issues were debated intensely under the auspices of the 1979 Convention on Long-Range Transboundary Air Pollution (LRTAP).

**Creation of LRTAP**

Though charged with solving an environmental problem, LRTAP was a creature of high politics. Following the 1975 Helsinki Conference on Security and Cooperation in Europe (CSCE), the Soviet Union proposed a high-level East-West meeting to discuss environment, energy, or transport issues. The Soviet Union's primary motivation was apparently to continue the process of détente in a policy realm other than human rights or arms control. The task of considering specific options fell to the United Nations Economic Commission for Europe (ECE).[7] The ECE is one of five UN regional economic commissions concerned with collecting and disseminating information as well as facilitating collaboration on a variety of regulatory issues. It contained virtually the same membership as the CSCE (thirty-four parties including the United States and Canada), but unlike the CSCE, the ECE has an organizational infrastructure (based in Geneva).

The ECE studied the options during 1977 and 1978, and settled on the environment as the best candidate for an East-West conference. The transport and energy sectors were too sensitive for the West to let the East participate in multilateral negotiations on them. The ECE considered eleven different environmental issues, and produced a short list consisting of long-range transport of air pollution and "low- and non-

7. Evgeny M. Chossudovsky, *East-West Diplomacy for Environment in the United Nations* (New York: UNITAR, n.d. 1989?), 23–25. The Soviet initiative was announced in a 9 December 1975 speech by Brezhnev, and followed up with a request to the ECE secretariat to discuss the matter at the Commission's spring 1976 meeting. Chossudovsky speculates that one reason the Soviets may have taken the issue to the ECE is that it was scheduled to meet considerably sooner than the next CSCE follow-up meeting.

waste technology and reutilization and recycling of wastes." The ECE finally decided that of these two, only air pollution merited the sort of legally binding international convention desired by the East bloc.[8] The convention was negotiated in ECE working groups over 1978 and 1979.

The Nordic and East bloc countries shared an interest in having the proposed air pollution convention contain binding reduction commitments, the Nordics for environmental reasons and the East bloc for reasons of high politics.[9] Other Western European countries were opposed. None of them had any domestic acidification problem (to their knowledge) and they were skeptical of the claims that their emissions caused damage in Scandinavia. Because the East bloc had little substantive interests in the terms of the convention, the core bargaining was between the Nordics and other West Europeans.[10]

Agreement was made possible when the Nordics dropped their demand that the convention include regulations requiring reductions of sulfur emissions. The others then split, with most either seeing no harm in joining (Britain) or feeling a desire to further détente (France). Germany stood out as the chief remaining opponent of the convention, apparently afraid that LRTAP might create principles that would cause countries to be held liable for future claims of damage in Scandinavia. Germany finally caved in to a united front, and a convention was signed in November 1979 by thirty-three states. The United States and Canada, as members of the ECE, signed LRTAP even though their emissions are irrelevant to European acid rain.[11]

8. Thus sparing a generation of environmental scholars the task of trying to pronounce LNWTRRW.
9. Chossudovsky, *East-West Diplomacy*, 73.
10. The only thorough account of the negotiations is Chossudovsky, *East-West Diplomacy*. See also Wetstone and Rosencranz, *Acid Rain in Europe and North America*, 140–45; and C. Ian Jackson, "A Tenth Anniversary Review of the ECE Convention on Long-Range Transboundary Air Pollution," *International Environmental Affairs* 2, 3 (Summer 1990):217–26.
11. The United States and Canada have remained active participants in LRTAP, despite the lack of substantive connections, for three reasons: inertia growing out of the CSCE process, benefits from scientific collaboration, and symbolic links to the bilateral conflict between them (participation helps Canada put pressure on the United States to reduce sulfur emissions; U.S. withdrawal would constitute an embarrassing escalation of the conflict with Canada). Following the 1990 amendments to the U.S. Clean Air Act and 1991 Air Quality

In terms of rules, the convention can fairly be described as a "least common denominator" compromise. No country accepted any explicit commitment it felt to be significantly costly. The convention establishes the principle that transborder air pollution should be reduced as much as is economically feasible, and creates a mechanism for collecting and disseminating information on air pollution flows, national reduction strategies, abatement technologies, and other items. The principles embodied in LRTAP are very similar to those exposed in earlier OECD guidelines and in the 1972 Stockholm Declaration.

LRTAP did represent two important advances. First, it marked acceptance by Eastern Europe and the Soviet Union of prior western norms concerning transborder air pollution, as well as their participation in ongoing Western monitoring and reporting programs.[12] Second, LRTAP was a framework convention that created an institutional apparatus for performing the information functions and for facilitating the negotiation of subsequent reduction protocols.

### Structure of LRTAP

LRTAP's membership includes all important European states (including the USSR), as well as the United States and Canada.[13] The vast membership is probably a sign of the convention's perceived role in further-

---

Agreement between the United States and Canada, the bilateral conflict has all but disappeared. Perhaps serendipitously, in the last two years researchers have actually discovered a substantive reason for linking North America and Europe. Persistent organic compounds (such as pesticides) travel northward from North America and Europe, and threaten wildlife in the Arctic; LRTAP negotiators are considering a possible protocol.

12. LRTAP almost certainly contributed nothing to broader East-West relations, however; thus it failed to achieve the initial Soviet objectives. The ink was barely dry on the convention when the USSR invaded Afghanistan, effectively knocking détente off the political agenda. If spillover effects went unrealized, though, LRTAP can be credited with keeping East-West cooperation alive within a very limited sphere throughout the 1980s.

13. Although the United States and Canada are parties to LRTAP and have signed regulatory protocols, this chapter does not analyze LRTAP's effects on them. For the pollutants regulated so far under LRTAP, the North American environmental conflict is entirely separate from the European. In North America, bilateral diplomacy has been much more important than LRTAP. See Don Munton and Geoffrey Castle, "Reducing Acid Rain, 1990," in Don Munton and John Kirton, eds., *Canadian Foreign Policy: Selected Cases* (Scarborough, Ontario: Prentice Hall, 1992), 367–81.

ing détente. Of the thirty-three parties to the convention, only Norway and Sweden thought acid rain was a serious problem when they signed. An additional factor is the prior involvement of many West Europeans in the OECD monitoring program. When the convention was being negotiated over 1978–1979 the long-range transport issue was still hotly contested by many states. LRTAP was seen as an extension of the OECD work, in which these states were already deeply involved. In the words of one British official, "EMEP drew us into the 1979 convention."[14]

LRTAP secretariat functions are provided by the Air Pollution Unit of the ECE's Environment and Human Settlements Division. The Air Pollution Unit has remained rather small since its creation, with five professional staff members. The staff's primary responsibility is to organize the various meetings held under the auspices of LRTAP, which have grown considerably in number since LRTAP was signed (there were only nine in 1985, for example, and forty-five in 1990). The rapidly growing workload leaves the staff with little time to do anything else but keep the meetings running smoothly. Virtually the entire Air Pollution Unit's budget is taken up by meetings and salaries. There are no funds for staff travel, and very little for outside consultants.[15] Because the staff is small, overworked, and underfunded, virtually all substantive work is done by government officials of LRTAP signatories.

Since LRTAP entered into force in March 1983, policy-making power has been vested in an Executive Body (EB). Even before entry into force, an Interim Executive Body, created by separate resolution, operated in a similar manner.[16] The EB is comprised of government officials from signatory countries, and meets once a year. The EB has various subsidiary working groups, also all comprised of government officials. These working groups are responsible for drafting regulatory protocols and

14. Interview with U.K. Department of Environment official, Geneva, 28 August 1990.
15. Interviews with ECE officials, July 1991.
16. The importance of interim operation of LRTAP, and of treaties in general, is underscored by Peter H. Sand, *Lessons Learned in Global Environmental Governance* (Washington, D.C., World Resources Institute, 1990), 14–15. By contrast, consider the lengthy ratification delays that plagued the International Maritime Organization's oil pollution regulations (discussed in Chapter 5 of this volume).

overseeing the management of collaborative research projects. Most working groups meet about once a year. Participation in the EB and working groups is open to all signatories to the convention; each elects a smaller Bureau to set agendas and deal with matters requiring action between meetings. Bureaus, consisting of chairmen and two or three vice chairmen, are always chosen with an eye toward maintaining a balance between Eastern and Western participation.

Beneath the working groups are the various cooperative research programs as well as task forces charged with carrying out specific activities deemed necessary by LRTAP's decision-making bodies. These action-oriented bodies are open to all willing to participate in the research or other joint tasks. Unlike the EB and working groups, there is much less attention to geopolitical balancing. With the exception of an EMEP center in Moscow, all action-oriented bodies are headed by Western countries.

In addition to the EB and its subsidiary bodies, there is a parallel set of bodies within the ECE which report directly to the Senior Advisers to ECE Governments on Environment and Water Problems, which predates the LRTAP convention. Under the Senior Advisers is a Working Party on Air Pollution Problems, with four task forces relevant to LRTAP. In practice, the government agencies and personnel active in the Senior Advisers' Working Party on Air Pollution Problems are the same as those active in the EB and its bodies; the two groups coordinate their work to avoid redundancy. A Norwegian proposal to streamline the organization in order to clarify lines of responsibility and reduce meeting-attendance burdens on national officials, circulated at the end of 1986, floundered for several years. In late 1991 the organizational design finally was streamlined considerably, largely because the changes in Eastern Europe and the Soviet Union had broken earlier diplomatic logjams over turf.

The EB is constituted "within the framework" of the ECE's Senior Advisers on Environmental Problems, yet is formally independent of the ECE. Because virtually no decisions are made by a secretariat, but rather by national officials representing their governments, LRTAP has been accurately called a "permanent negotiating process."[17]

17. Paul Fauteux, "Percentage Reductions Versus Critical Loads in the Interna-

LRTAP bodies make decisions by consensus. Because adherence to LRTAP decisions is strictly voluntary, however, not everyone exercises veto power in practice; some opponents simply do not participate. The most important decisions are made among a subset of convention parties who wish to be able to participate. In recent protocols the most environmentalist countries have set the agenda and entered into negotiations with more reluctant countries. The environmentalist countries must choose between offering compromises in order to obtain greater participation and holding out for a better protocol while continuing efforts at persuasion. The convention requires sixteen ratifications to enter into force, out of thirty-three convention parties. Negotiators settled on sixteen as a number that was small enough to prevent small groups from blocking protocols, but large enough to ensure that the aggregate effect would be meaningful. Countries opposed to protocols only exercise veto control in practice if their participation is deemed crucial by the activist countries; otherwise they simply do not participate.

LRTAP meetings are open to nongovernmental organizations (NGOs), industry groups, and intergovernment organizations (IGOs). Among the NGOs the active participants have been the British branches of Greenpeace and Friends of the Earth, the International Union for the Conservation of Nature, the International Council on Environmental Law and the International Institute for Applied Systems Analysis (IIASA). The only industry groups involved have been UNIPEDE (International Union of Producers and Distributors of Electrical Energy) and CONCAWE (Oil Companies European Organization for Environmental and Health Protection). Active IGOs include the World Metereological Organization (WMO), World Health Organization, UN Environment Program (UNEP), the Food and Agricultural Organization, OECD, and the International Energy Association. European regional organizations, including the European Community (EC) and European Free Trade Association, also attend regularly.

Except for IIASA, none of these groups have much direct influence over LRTAP decision making. The influence of NGOs comes mainly via

---

tional Legal Battle Against Air Pollution: A Canadian Perspective," paper presented to a symposium on Environmental Protection and International Law (Vienna, 11–12 October 1990), 6.

activities inside countries, usually publicizing governmental actions within LRTAP. British groups routinely criticize the government for failing to accept international controls on sulfur emissions, for example. In 1988, when a protocol calling for a freeze in emissions of nitrogen oxides was signed, NGOs successfully lobbied environmentalist delegates to sign a separate pledge to reduce nitrogen oxides emissions by 30 percent, though the pledge has no legal status.

The special case of IIASA stems from the organization's expertise in collective decision-making aspects of the transborder air pollution problem. IIASA has developed an interactive simulation (RAINS) which runs on a personal computer, and which permits the user to evaluate the economic costs and environmental benefits of various regulatory options. The RAINS model has been of increasing utility to LRTAP participants in recent years.[18]

## International Policies

LRTAP's primary functions have been to to coordinate national research programs so that they generate the knowledge needed to negotiate and implement pollution reduction protocols, to negotiate these protocols, to monitor emission levels and transport flows, and to monitor national air pollution reduction strategies. Below, these functions will be described in the context of the international policy measures adopted to further them. Subsequent sections will analyze the institution's role in setting the international policy agenda and in promoting changes in national behavior in accord with these policies.

### Coordination of National Research Programs

Coordination of national research programs can be considered the bedrock of all LRTAP's activity. One reason coordination is important is

18. The model is described in Joseph Alcamo, Roderick Shaw, and Leen Hordijk, eds., *The RAINS Model of Acidification: Science and Strategies in Europe* (Dordecht: Kluwer Academic, 1990). The model has been central in recent thinking about how to devise a protocol based on critical loads, as discussed below. There are two other computer models linking regulatory policies and environmental effects, but these have been developed in national laboratories in the United Kingdom and Germany. IIASA's is the only private model which has gained significant use.

that it ensures comparability of results across Europe. Without standardization of data collection, measurement, and analysis procedures, even those countries with an active interest in acidification would be unable to pool their results. With harmonized research methods it is possible to make comparative assessments of environmental quality, and to make better assessments of changes over time. It also enhances the credibility of national research in foreign capitals; Swedish and Norwegian research is better received in Britain today, for example, than it was before LRTAP.

Another benefit of collective research programs is that they foster research efforts in countries that might not otherwise undertake them. In Eastern Europe, acidification researchers were better able to acquire government funding by arguing that the research was part of a treaty commitment. British researchers report the same phenomenon.[19] Poland and Czechoslovakia maintained active research efforts throughout the 1980s, even though they were unwilling to take any significant pollution reduction measures.

The largest coordinated research program is the extensive monitoring program, EMEP, with a 1989 budget of about $1 million. EMEP came under LRTAP's purview shortly after the convention was signed, and is managed by a Steering Body that reports to the EB. EMEP measures pollutant levels in about ninety stations throughout Europe. In addition, national governments report emission levels to EMEP. EMEP combines these two sources of information with meteorological data supplied by the WMO, and produces a matrix showing emission trajectories. With such matrices, it is possible to identify where a country's deposition originates and where its emissions finally end up.

EMEP plays a dual role as both a scientific research effort and a monitoring body which can ascertain compliance with reduction protocols. Monitoring of compliance is therefore performed, coincidentally to the transport research, through a highly sophisticated operation. As one observer has remarked, "Few other international agreements can be said to come equipped with verification instruments of this caliber."[20]

19. Interviews with acid rain researchers in Czechoslovakia and United Kingdom, July–August, 1991.
20. Peter H. Sand, "Regional Approaches to Transboundary Air Pollution," in

Perhaps partly because of such verification procedures, there has never been any suspicion that nations cheat on their emissions reports. Sulfur dioxide emissions would be especially hard to doctor, because it is a fairly simply exercise to convert fuel consumption (for which there are reliable statistics) into sulfur emissions. EMEP considers itself to have too few monitoring stations in southern Europe, and to be hindered by the failure of some countries to report emissions. EMEP estimates emissions using other data sources for nonreporting countries. Reporting records are indicated in table 3.5. Countries are asked to supply emissions data every May for sulfur and (since 1988) nitrogen oxides.

EMEP data is processed in two synthesizing centers, an eastern center in Moscow and a western center in Oslo. The Oslo center produces the Europe-wide maps, and is considered to be technically superior to the Moscow center. These centers were initially funded by their host countries, but under a 1984 EMEP protocol are funded by all LRTAP parties according to a formula based on a "global assessment scale" developed by the UN which uses GNP, population and geographic criteria.

Another series of research programs is overseen by the Working Group on Effects. Each International Cooperative Program (ICP) is operated by a lead country on a voluntary basis. Current ICPs (and their lead countries) are forests (Germany), freshwaters (Norway), materials (Sweden) and crops (United Kingdom). ICPs are created when a country already conducting research in a particular area proposes Europe-wide research in that area under LRTAP's auspices. The EB grants authorization upon recommendation by the Working Group on Effects, and national governments participate voluntarily. The ICPs for forests, materials, and freshwaters were created in 1985, and the crops ICP was established in 1987. A Pilot Program on Integrated Monitoring, essentially similar to an ICP, was established in 1987 with Sweden as lead country.

Currently the coordinating expenses of these research programs are provided by the lead countries, and participating governments pay their own research costs. The forest program is somewhat of an exception: UNEP provided initial coordinating funds during 1986 through 1990,

---

John L. Helm, ed., *Energy: Production, Consumption, and Consequences* (Washington, D.C.: National Academy Press, 1990), 259.

and a group of about a dozen countries agreed subsequently to provide funding voluntarily. The Bureau of the EB has recommended a protocol to formalize cost-sharing responsibilities for research programs, along lines similar to the 1984 EMEP protocol. A very rough estimate indicated that in 1991 coordinating expenses for the five programs altogether would be about $1.6 million.

An important element of research coordination took place outside of LRTAP. Since 1984, government officials have met annually in an informal body called the Meeting of Acidification Research Coordinators (MARC).[21] MARC's first meeting was called to review Dutch plans for a new acidification research program, so that Dutch researchers could benefit from ongoing research elsewhere. It lived on for two reasons. Research coordinators benefited from observing each other's projects directly, and they benefited from the ability to exchange information in more informal settings than the highly bureaucratic LRTAP meetings. One participant calls it an "informal international review process." Sometimes information would be politically sensitive and impossible to raise in other settings. Because MARC has always focused on exchange of information about cutting-edge research, it has only included countries with top research programs; Eastern European, Soviet and southern European countries have never participated.

### Reporting on National Policy Measures

LRTAP also calls on states to submit reports on the efforts they are undertaking to reduce transborder pollution flows. Major reviews of national policies and strategies are conducted every four years, and updates are provided annually.[22] The reports are reviewed at each meeting of the Executive Body. The EB asks states to follow a common format, including emissions of sulfur dioxide, nitrogen oxides, volatile organic compounds (VOCs), ammonia, and carbon dioxide; forecasts of future emissions; and regulatory standards for air quality, fuel quality, and

21. Information in this paragraph comes from discussions with several regular participants in MARC. Countries most active include Canada, Finland, Germany, the Netherlands, Norway, Sweden, the United Kingdom, and the United States; France has become involved recently.
22. Major reviews have been published as ECE/EB.AIR/27 (1991) and ECE/EB.AIR/14 (1987); annual updates have appeared in ECE/EB.AIR/22 (1989) and ECE/EB.AIR/25 (1990).

emissions. In addition, states are invited to describe national strategies and specific policy measures of more general relevance to transborder air pollution.

Strategy and policy reviews are not interpreted; they are simply collated and published. There is no effort to ascertain whose measures place them in compliance with either specific protocols or broader norms. Nor is there any effort to fill in missing information or to correct misleading information. In fact, there is a conscious attempt on the part of the secretariat not to embarrass parties in these reports. Thus the efforts of states as divergent in fact as Poland and Sweden appear in print to have a lot in common. This is not to say that the reports are not taken seriously. Although there are states who routinely fail to submit reports on time and others who submit highly vague and general reports, many approach them with great seriousness. Although no one is ever "cross-examined," states frequently make oral statements offering clarifications and emphasizing major points at EB meetings. In 1986, when the United Kingdom was under great pressure to sign the 1985 sulfur dioxide protocol, it submitted a lengthy report detailing its regulation of air pollution. The report provided explicit policy targets for sulfur reductions, a justification for those targets, and a description of the means under way to achieve them.[23]

### Negotiation of Regulatory Protocols

Three regulatory protocols have been negotiated under LRTAP auspices. A sulfur dioxide protocol was signed in 1985, a nitrogen oxides protocol in 1988, and a volatile organic compounds protocol in 1991. The nitrogen protocol is in the process of scheduled revisions, and a replacement for the sulfur protocol, set to lapse in 1993, is being negotiated. There is discussion underway concerning possible protocols for heavy metals and persistent organic pollutants.

**The 1985 Sulfur Protocol**    The Scandinavians had sought a sulfur protocol during the LRTAP negotiations in 1978, and immediately pushed for one after LRTAP was signed. They sought a commitment to reduce

23. UN ECE Convention on Long-Range Transboundary Air Pollution, Review of Strategies and Policies of the Contracting Parties to the Convention, United Kingdom Response (1986) typescript, 13 pages.

sulfur dioxide emissions by 30 percent from their 1980 levels. This objective was not scientifically determined—it was considered an arbitrary first step.

The East bloc, though willing to sign a protocol in 1978, weakened slightly over the early 1980s. The Soviet Union was willing to sign if it could be bound to regulate transborder flows rather than total emissions; with prevailing winds blowing east, the Soviet Union did not want to take on a commitment to reduce emissions that did not cross borders. Poland was unwilling to sign the protocol, whether regulating fluxes or emissions, because it knew it could not comply. Poland unsuccessfully sought a multitiered protocol in which it might commit to a smaller reduction or a freeze.[24] Hungary was willing to sign a 30 percent protocol and hoped to comply with it. Hungary was not interested in transborder flows, however. Foreign affairs officials wanted to sign in order to further cooperation with the West, and environment officials wanted to sign in order to promote domestic air quality standards for public health reasons.[25] Czechoslovakia essentially deferred to the Soviet Union and was willing to sign the protocol even though there were no plans to reduce sulfur emissions. Policy decisions were made by foreign affairs officials with little input from environmental experts.[26] East Germany exhibited behavior consistent with the Czechoslovakian position.

Sweden hosted a "1982 Stockholm Conference on Acidification of the Environment" to review scientific evidence concerning the causes and effects of acid deposition. Along with data showing a rising number of affected lakes, the conference presented information for the first time that forest ecosystems may be at risk as well. The forest data, presented by German biochemist Bernhard Ulrich, was considered "the most start-

24. Interview with former Polish LRTAP negotiator, Warsaw, 25 June 1991. Ironically, Poland was forced to remain outside the sulfur protocol because it had the most serious commitment to reducing emissions in the East bloc. Its environment officials had set ambitious goals and studied implementation options; they knew that 30 percent reductions were not possible and were unwilling to make a promise they could not keep.
25. Discussions with official in Department for Air Pollution Abatement, Hungarian Institute for Environmental Protection (Geneva, 29 January–1 February 1991).
26. Interviews with Czechoslovakian environment officials, January 1991 (Geneva) and June–July 1991 (Prague).

ling evidence."[27] Ulrich reported that one million hectares of forests in central Europe were at risk, with 100,000 hectares already dying. The forest death, or *waldsterben*, was especially pronounced in Germany's Black Forest.

Government-appointed experts issued a set of conference conclusions that urged states to reduce air pollution and acid rain and to install desulfurization equipment on new power plants.[28] Germany announced that it had joined Sweden and Norway in seeking Europe-wide reduction in sulfur emissions, proposing a 50 percent reduction by 1985.[29]

The German switch caught the other EC member states by surprise and splintered their formerly united opposition to reductions. In 1984 France also declared support for reductions, not because it was concerned about acid rain, but because it had calculated that its nuclear program would reduce its sulfur dioxide emissions considerably.

When LRTAP entered into force in 1983, a proposed sulfur protocol dominated the Executive Body's agenda. In March 1983 the governments of Finland, Norway, and Sweden submitted a proposal calling for a protocol reducing emissions by 30 percent by 1993, using 1980 as a base year. A parallel proposal was submitted by West Germany, Austria, and Switzerland, calling for adoption of a joint strategy "based on the obligation to reduce emissions at source by applying the best available technology which is economically feasible."[30] The central European proposal made specific reference to the Nordic proposal, which it "fully endorsed." The Executive Body was unable to agree on a draft protocol, however, because too few governments supported either alternative.

The diplomatic momentum for a protocol grew through 1984, when interministerial conferences were held in 1984 in Munich and Ottawa. These conferences were high-level rallies designed to pressure laggards into accepting reduction measures. In Ottawa a number of governments announced acceptance of the Scandinavian proposal for 30 percent re-

27. Don Hinrichsen, "Acid Indigestion in Stockholm," *Ambio* 11, 5 (1982): 320–21.
28. Armin Rosenkranz, "The Stockholm Conference: 1982" *Acid News* (1982): 4–8.
29. *ENDS Report* 90 (July 1982), 22–23.
30. ENV/EB/R.10, as cited in Chossudovsky, *East-West Diplomacy*, 155.

ductions, giving birth to the "30 percent club." The 30 percent club was a central component of tote-board diplomacy, putting normative pressure on reluctant states. In June 1983 nine governments were in favor of 30 percent cuts; the number had grown to eleven in March 1984, eighteen in June, and twenty by year's end.[31] In effect, the eleven governments that did not consider sulfur dioxide reductions to be in their interest in 1983 changed their minds once the question became highly public and connected to normative principles.

At Norway's initiative, a draft protocol was circulated in late 1984 calling for 30 percent reductions. The EB approved a version of the protocol as the basis for negotiations and held final talks at its July 1985 meeting, held in Helsinki to commemorate the tenth anniversary of the Helsinki Final Act. Twenty-one parties signed the protocol at Helsinki.

The largest polluters who refused to sign the protocol were the United Kingdom, Poland, and Spain. These three accounted for 23 percent of Europe's 1980 sulfur emissions. The United Kingdom and Poland burned large amounts of dirty coal, and were upwind from the very sensitive ecosystems in Scandinavia. The United States, in a rebuff to Canadian entreaties, also refused to sign the sulfur protocol.

**The 1988 Nitrogen Oxides Protocol**    Nitrogen oxides come from both power plants and automobile emissions. They are responsible for some acid deposition, and also contribute to the formation of ground-level ozone, a gas that is toxic to humans and harmful to vegetation. The scientific consensus now is that ozone is just as harmful to forests and agricultural crops as sulfur deposition. It also is a public health problem in many urban areas. All this was accepted during the negotiations of the nitrogen protocol. There was dispute over the magnitude of the damage, though.

The Scandinavians began seeking a nitrogen oxides protocol in 1985, immediately following the successful adoption of the sulfur protocol. Like the sulfur protocol, a nitrogen protocol would provide target reductions at the national level, but leave each country free to determine how to achieve them.

There was also a vigorous technical debate over how best to reduce

31. Chossudovsky, *East-West Diplomacy*, 180–83.

auto emissions (the principal source of nitrogen oxide emissions). Germany, at one extreme, argued that catalytic converters were required. Britain, at the other, argued that converters were not appropriate for most cars (due to their small engines), but that a "lean burn" engine employing more efficient carburetion was superior. This technical debate was still going on when the question became moot after EC auto directives in 1989 and 1990; each side still thinks it was right.[32]

Of the large Western countries, Germany supported a protocol, while the United Kingdom, France, and Italy opposed it. Nitrogen oxide reductions of any significant magnitude would require strict automobile emission standards. British, French, and Italian automakers lobbied their governments strenuously against such standards. For several reasons their German counterparts did not. German car firms were already required under 1983 legislation to adopt catalytic converters; while firms sought delays in implementation, they accepted the final goal as a given. German carmakers produce a fleet with a much larger average engine size, which can accommodate catalytic converters with a lower increase in marginal cost than the smaller fleets produced in France, Italy, and Britain. In addition, Germany had a major comparative advantage in producing much of the equipment needed to meet strict standards, such as fuel injectors and catalytic converters. Eastern Europe and the USSR were opposed to reductions. They were producing growing quantities of nitrogen oxides. The prospect of reducing auto emissions was especially difficult. In addition to having tiny cars using obsolete technology, the East bloc countries were experiencing rapid growth in automobile production.

In 1987 Europe was split into three camps, as indicated in table 3.1.

The negotiation of the nitrogen oxides protocol was similar in form to the sulfur dioxide protocol. Rather than seeking out compromises aimed at obtaining joint gains, tote-board diplomacy was again the order of the day. In this case, however, the decision was made to settle for a protocol calling only for a freeze. There was special concern that any protocol include a number of East bloc countries, all of whom

32. The vehicle emissions debate is covered in Sonja Boehmer-Christiansen, "The Regulation of Vehicle Emissions in Europe," *Energy and Environment* 1, 1 (1990).

**Table 3.1**  National preferences for nitrogen protocol, September 1987

*30% reductions on 1985 levels by 1995*

Austria
Netherlands
Sweden
Switzerland
West Germany

*Freeze on current levels*

Denmark
Finland
France
Norway
Spain
United Kingdom

*Increases in current levels*

Bulgaria
Czechoslovakia
East Germany
Italy
Poland
USSR

Source:  World Wildlife Fund memo, 3 September 1987; *ENDS* Report 152 (September 1987), 24.

opposed anything beyond a freeze. The protocol was signed in Sofia in November 1988 by twenty-seven parties including the United States and Canada. It entered into force on 14 February 1991, following the six-teenth ratification. The protocol calls on countries to freeze their nit-rogen oxides emissions at 1987 levels by 1995. It is too early to have raw compliance data on the nitrogen oxides protocol.

In conjunction with the signing ceremony, twelve countries an-nounced public pledges to reduce nitrogen oxides emissions by 30 percent by 1998. Most of these countries had opposed the inclusion of 30 percent cuts in the protocol. The precise wording of the declaration permits greater latitude than the draft protocols: it adopts a later dead-line and permits signatories to choose any base year they wish between 1980 and 1986.

**Table 3.2**   Signatories to 1988 protocol on NOx emissions

*Countries signing protocol only*

Canada
Czechoslovakia
Greece
Hungary
Ireland
Luxembourg
Poland
Spain
USSR
United Kingdom
United States

*Countries signing protocol and 30% pledge*

Austria
Belgium
Denmark
Finland
France
West Germany
Italy
Liechtenstein
Netherlands
Norway
Sweden
Switzerland

Source: EB.AIR/R.62 (9 September 1991); "Declaration on the 30 Per Cent Reduction of Nitrogen Oxides Emissions," Sofia, 31 October 1988. See also *International Environment Reporter* (November 1988), 581.

Although the nitrogen protocol has been criticized for not going beyond a freeze,[33] it contains several innovations compared to the sulfur protocol.

First, it contains a commitment to promote transfer of technology used in reduction of nitrogen oxides emissions. The technology transfer

33. For example, in Christer Ågren, "Europe's Nitrogen Policy—Able But Still Hesitant (Air)" *Acid/Enviro Magazine* 9 (June 1990): 6–7.

commitment is rather vague; it is difficult to imagine how a country could fail to comply with it even if that country were inclined toward noncompliance. Nevertheless, increased attention has been paid to technology transfer issues in LRTAP. Shortly after the protocol was signed, Finland volunteered to head a task force on the exchange of technology, and several technical meetings have been held to promote transfer of expertise.

Second, the protocol contains a commitment to apply emission standards based on the "best available technologies which are economically feasible," and specifies these technologies in a nonbinding technical annex. It also requires parties to make unleaded gasoline available on major highways to facilitate the adoption of catalytic converters. Catalytic converters, the primary means for reducing nitrogen oxides emissions from vehicles, require unleaded fuel.

And finally, the protocol requires that negotiations on further reductions begin within six months of the protocol's entry into force. These further reductions are to take into account "the best available scientific and technological developments, internationally accepted critical loads, and other elements resulting from the work programme undertaken under article 6 [of the protocol]."[34] Therefore the requirements of the nitrogen oxides protocol could evolve rather quickly beyond "merely" a freeze to much steeper reductions. If the best available technology were applied throughout Europe, reductions of 60 percent would be possible; critical loads require reductions of at least that amount.[35] Negotiations are just now beginning to undertake the revisions in the nitrogen protocol. The technical annex listing best available technology will be updated regularly, although explicit reduction commitments are not scheduled to be revised until 1994 when the current protocol lapses. Therefore the direct impact of the 1988 protocol will depend on how

34. Protocol to the 1979 Convention on Long-Range Transboundary Air Pollution Concerning the Control of Emissions of Nitrogen Oxides or their Transboundary Fluxes, ECE/EB.AIR/18.
35. A IIASA report estimates that 60 percent reductions by 2000 are possible if vehicle catalytic converters, power plant denitrification technology, and other available techniques are adopted throughout Europe. Precise reduction requirements to meet critical loads have not been calculated, but they are estimated to be in excess of what is technically or economically feasible. Interviews with LRTAP negotiators involved in establishing critical loads, August 1990 and August 1991.

seriously states treat the role of the legally nonbinding technical annex. By fixing a shorter life span than the sulfur protocol and mandating an immediate renegotiation process based on critical loads, the long-term impact is potentially large, though impossible to predict.

**Volatile Organic Compounds** Volatile organic compounds (VOCs), including fuels, solvents, cleaners, and a variety of other chemicals, are precursors of ground-level ozone.[36] That they contribute significantly to European ozone formation, and should therefore be regulated, is not disputed. Following the nitrogen protocol, negotiations began in 1989 on a protocol to regulate VOCs.

The novel scientific problem that VOCs present for LRTAP is that VOCs are comprised of a large number of chemicals which behave in very different ways. They interact differently with meteorological and topographical conditions, in complex ways not yet fully understood, so that their ozone-creating potential varies widely. The United Kingdom wants to devise regulations that take into account these differences, and has assigned ozone-creating potential values to some sixty-nine compounds (much the way the Montreal Protocol assigns ozone-depleting potentials to CFCs). Other countries are dubious of the reliability of these estimates, however; in early 1991 countries decided not to use ozone-creating potentials in the current protocol.[37]

Because VOCs encompass so many different compounds used in a variety of diverse economic activities (from dry cleaning to fuel combustion to industrial solvents), there is little information on how much is actually being released. As of mid-1991, only five countries had conducted thorough inventories of their VOC emissions.

The VOC negotiations elicited three broad sets of national positions. The majority of countries were willing to sign an across-the-board 30 percent reduction protocol. Countries with low ozone problems due to meteorological and geographical conditions, however, wanted to commit only to reducing VOCs in regions responsible for transborder fluxes. This group includes the USSR, Norway, and Canada. The new regimes of Eastern Europe wanted to commit only to a freeze. The East-

---

36. Ozone is toxic to humans in the lower atmosphere, although the same compound in the stratosphere is highly beneficial.
37. *Volatile Organic Compounds Newsletter* (The Hague, February 1992).

ern European behavior recalls the experience with the nitrogen oxides protocol, but this case was entirely different. Czechoslovakia, Hungary, and Poland were all committed to undertaking serious measures to reduce VOCs. (The Czech and Slovak government was willing to accept a binding commitment to employ best available technology on all new sites.) However, none of these countries had any idea what their reductions would add up to, nor how pending economic change would affect emissions. Some Eastern Europeans estimated that their reductions might total on the order of 20 percent, but they did not want to sign anything they could not be sure of complying with.[38]

Negotiations proceeded much as in the other two protocols. There was an attempt to include most of the parties, but little attempt to strike joint-gain bargains. In November 1991, twenty-one parties signed a protocol which was a rather awkward pastiche that merely listed three entirely different forms of regulation (based on the three sets of interests listed above). Countries were permitted to select their own base year; five different base years were chosen, ranging from 1984 to 1990. It is difficult to imagine negotiators doing things much differently. Even if there had been a consensus on adopting stricter targets based on critical loads, the science had not advanced sufficiently by the end of 1991 to establish such loads. The protocol attempts to compensate for least-common-denominator targets and base years by following the lead of the nitrogen oxides protocol—it includes a nonbinding technical annex and mandating quick revisions based on critical loads.

**Future Plans**

The EB has adopted a rapidly expanding work plan for the coming years. Central to this growing work load is the plan to base future protocols on critical loads. If successful, the adoption of critical loads as the basis of LRTAP protocols would constitute a revolution in the management of transborder pollutants. The outcome will not be known for several years; the first protocol that could use critical loads is not scheduled for signing until 1993.

A critical load is defined as "a quantitative estimate of an exposure to

38. Interviews with Czech, Hungarian, and Polish negotiators, Geneva, January–February 1991.

**Table 3.3**   Signatories to 1991 protocol on volatile organic compounds

*States selecting 30% reduction as commitment*

Austria
Belgium
Denmark
Finland
France
Germany
Italy
Liechtenstein
Luxembourg
Netherlands
Spain
Sweden
Switzerland
United Kingdom
United States

*States selecting freeze as commitment*

Bulgaria
Greece
Hungary

*States selecting 30% reductions in specified areas as commitment*

Canada
Norway

Note:  Commitments are to be met by 1999.

Owing to the events of August 1991, the delegations from the former Soviet Union found themselves unable to function effectively. Although four months earlier the Soviet Union had been a staunch supporter of the protocol, only Ukraine was able to sign. Ukraine was unable, however, to indicate which specific commitment it was binding itself to.

Source:  "Note" (unofficial), Legal Liaison Office, United Nations, Geneva, 20 November 1991.

one or more pollutants below which significantly harmful effects on specified sensitive elements of the environment do not occur according to present knowledge."[39] In the mid-1980s Scandinavians began promoting critical loads, a management tool developed in Canada, as a superior alternative to the flat rate reductions now in LRTAP protocols. Flat rate reductions present numerous difficulties. The reduction figures themselves are arbitrary and present the opportunity for unproductive haggling. They necessitate the selection of a base year, which generates very difficult fairness problems owing to varying degrees of prior reductions. And they leave negotiators unsure of how much environmental benefit they will obtain. Critical loads, by contrast, focus negotiators' attention on scientific issues. While no one is so naive as to think politics will disappear, there is the hope that the process will be more productive because critical loads will reduce much of the arbitrariness and uncertainty.

The Working Group on Effects is coordinating a massive effort to prepare critical load maps for Europe. Using dose-response data on soils, vegetation, and freshwaters, national focal centers are preparing critical load maps for sulfur, nitrogen, and total acidity. Critical loads vary a great deal across Europe, because ecological sensitivity is highly dependent on local geology and weather conditions. By examining critical load maps and EMEP's transfer matrices, one can compare how alternative regulatory regimes compare with respect to environmental improvements. If one adds in abatement cost information, it becomes possible for the first time, in theory, to select the most cost-effective regulatory regime. IIASA's RAINS model integrates critical loads, transfer matrices, and cost functions; and other models are in development as well. It is proving very difficult to gain consensus on the cost functions because there are so many ways of achieving reductions, and because abatement strategies generate second-order economic effects which are difficult to estimate.[40]

39. Jan Nilsson and Peringe Grennfelt, eds., "Critical Loads for Sulphur and Nitrogen." Report from a Workshop held at Skokloster, Sweden (19–24 March 1988), 1.
40. For a discussion of critical loads, see K. R. Bull, "The Critical Loads/Levels Approach to Gaseous Pollutant Emission Control," *Environmental Pollution* 69 (1991): 105–23. The most comprehensive maps to date have been published in

There is little practical experience with using critical loads. Only the Netherlands and Canada have actually used critical loads in setting regulations, and only Norway, Sweden, and the United Kingdom have definite plans to do so for future regulations. It is precisely because of this lack of extensive national experience that the possibility LRTAP will use them is potentially so important. It would mark a major change in the nature of reduction protocols because, for the first time in LRTAP's history, countries would be engaging in substantive negotiation over how to regulate emissions. They would be setting policies interdependently; rather than recording the status quo in static protocols, they would be adjusting national policies in accord with negotiated norms.

Of course, it is not certain that LRTAP will base future protocols on critical loads. There is some opposition to basing future protocols on critical loads. While country positions have not yet been staked out (the very first, rather tentative talks on the 1993 sulfur protocol took place in July 1991), one hears skepticism. The chief alternative—what is sometimes called the German approach—would be to base future protocols on applications of "best available technology" (BAT). Use of BAT would be justified in part, and only indirectly, by the sensitivity maps. Ultimately, justification of BAT rests on the precautionary principle, which entails a prima facie commitment to reduce emissions as far as is economically feasible, even if there is not full knowledge of environmental benefits.[41] Although there are these criticisms, critical loads are already dominating LRTAP's agenda, all major countries are participating in the mapping exercises, and there is widespread support for the concept.

Because ecological sensitivity varies so widely across Europe, negotiators are presuming that the 1993 sulfur dioxide protocol will call for

Jean-Paul Hetteling, Robert J. Downing, and Peter A. M. de Smet, eds., *Mapping Critical Loads for Europe: CCE Technical Report No. 1*, RIVM Report No. 259101001 (Bilthoven: LRTAP Coordinating Center for Effects, Netherlands National Institute of Public Health and Environmental Protection, July 1991).

41. For a critique of the critical loads approach, see Lothar Gündling, "Protection of the Environment by International Law: Air Pollution," paper presented at symposium on Environmental Protection and International Law, Vienna, 11–12 October 1990.

**Table 3.4**  Extra national abatement costs and reductions required for hypothetical sulfur protocol based on critical loads and minimum total costs, with no burden sharing (as compared to present policies)

| Country | Additional abatement costs (DM millions) | Additional reductions required (% of planned policies) |
|---|---|---|
| USSR | 9198 | 62% |
| Poland | 4267 | 69% |
| West Germany | 3607 | 23% |
| United Kingdom | 3445 | 76% |
| East Germany | 3189 | 86% |
| Yugoslavia | 3096 | 77% |
| Italy | 2476 | 63% |
| France | 2410 | 71% |
| Czechoslovakia | 2399 | 73% |
| Belgium | 1403 | 86% |
| Romania | 930 | 53% |
| Netherlands | 722 | 68% |
| Hungary | 683 | 65% |
| Spain | 662 | 34% |
| Greece | 493 | 75% |
| Denmark | 385 | 68% |
| Ireland | 170 | 60% |
| Austria | 75 | 12% |
| Luxembourg | 38 | 40% |
| Switzerland | 17 | 8% |
| Turkey | 0 | 0% |
| Albania | 0 | 0% |
| Portugal | 0 | 0% |
| Norway | −200 | −106% |
| Finland | −257 | −51% |
| Bulgaria | −416 | −62% |
| Sweden | −477 | −120% |

Source: Based on IIASA simulation, as reported in "Economic Principles for Allocating the Costs of Reducing Sulphur Emissions in Europe," in *Air Pollution Studies No. 7* (1991), 63–80; UN ECE/EB.AIR/26, p. 78.

states to adopt varying reduction targets. Moreover, abatement costs also vary widely, and some of the countries with lowest costs are directly upwind from the most sensitive ecosystems in Europe. Poland and Czechoslovakia contribute a large percentage of Norway and Sweden's acidification, and face abatement costs as much as 80 percent less than in the west. Calculations made by IIASA provide a scenario, shown in table 3.4, for how emissions reductions and abatement costs would be distributed across countries under a sulfur protocol which sought to attain critical loads at the lowest total cost.

To cope with the uneven distribution of effort likely to be required by a future sulfur protocol, Sweden proposed in 1989 that LRTAP operate an environmental fund, to add a burden-sharing element to a critical loads-based protocol. There is not widespread support for such a fund, however. Today even Sweden no longer supports it, but prefers to direct existing flows of multilateral assistance toward sulfur and nitrogen reduction projects. Sweden has had good results with the Baltic Task Force, which coordinates multilateral assistance aimed at enabling Eastern Europe and the Soviet Union to honor their commitments to the 1974 Helsinki Convention for the Protection of the Baltic Sea.[42]

There is also talk of issuing tradable emission permits to help balance costs and benefits. Permits would be tradable at varying exchange rates, determined by the ecological effects in the ultimate receptors of a given site's emissions. Work on such schemes is under way, though few negotiators consider it likely they will be adopted in the next few years.[43]

The Executive Body is also considering protocols to control heavy metals and persistent organic pollutants, based on recent evidence that those substances travel long distances with serious adverse effects.

42. Interview with Lars Björkbom, Swedish Environmental Protection Agency, Geneva, 1 February 1991. One Swedish concern is to avoid creating additional international bodies where existing ones will suffice. A Swedish Environmental Protection Agency review found 180 international environmental bodies requiring active participation. See Chapter 4 of this volume for more details on the Baltic Task Force.
43. Interview with LRTAP officials, July 1991. Receptor-based marketable permits are vastly more complex than simple emissions permits, and one review considered them to be unworkable in practice. Tom Tietenberg, *Emissions Trading* (Washington, D.C.: Resources for the Future, 1985).

**Interaction with Other International Institutions**
LRTAP operates in an increasingly dense network of international institutions, and the convention must be evaluated on how well it manages this interaction. In addition, those other institutions must be considered part of the international response to the problem of acid rain.

LRTAP has a fairly precise division of labor with the OECD. Following the creation of LRTAP in 1979, the OECD concentrated on collecting and disseminating information. It has not operated monitoring programs in competition with EMEP, nor has it sought to initiate collective regulations. The OECD regularly participates in LRTAP working groups, which in turn routinely utilize OECD information.

The Nordic Council is active in environmental issues, but a high degree of convergence of national interests among Nordic Council members means that it has not had to establish very specific transborder regulations. Instead, similarly strict national regulations are undergirded by rather diffuse regional norms. This situation presents little need for coordination with LRTAP. The European Free Trade Association (EFTA) similarly presents little need for coordination, though EFTA has less environmental content to its work than the Nordic Council. The Eastern Europeans have not had significant regional environmental bodies to contend with.

The European Community (EC) presents the greatest challenge for coordination, because it constitutes the institution which has done the most, besides LRTAP, in the field of acid rain. The EC has a much more diverse membership than the Nordic Council, with very active environmentalist members such as the Netherlands and Germany, as well as members much further behind, such as Greece, Spain, and Portugal. Therefore there almost always are internal environmental struggles going on within the EC, and often these are directly within LRTAP's purview.

In terms of research, the European Community has been expanding its environmental research capacity recently. It now operates an air pollution monitoring program, CORINAIR, which collects some of the same data EMEP does. LRTAP and EC officials have worked out harmonized data collection procedures so that EC members will have to conduct only one set of calculations to meet the requirements of both programs. In 1990 the EC decided to establish a European Environmental Agency to get even more involved in environmental research, primarily at the level of monitoring. The agency has not yet been established because it has been held hostage to a broader fight among member states concerning the seat of the European Parliament. Once the European Environmental Agency begins operations, it will potentially be a serious competitor with LRTAP's working groups, especially since the EC has decided to permit non–EC members to participate in the agency. Eastern European, Nordic Council and EFTA countries have all expressed strong interest in participating in the agency. There has been no precise division of labor worked out with the ECE and LRTAP, analogous to the division between LRTAP and the OECD. To date, however, there have not been any coordination problems concerning the EC's air pollution research.

Regarding regulatory protocols, there is no explicit coordination between LRTAP and the European Community. The most direct overlap has occurred in the case of the EC's Large Combustion Plant Directive (LCPD), which sets nitrogen and sulfur emission standards for large power plants. The LCPD was negotiated over 1983 to 1988, overlapping with much of the negotiations in LRTAP over the sulfur dioxide and nitrogen oxides protocols. The LCPD negotiations were launched when Germany converted to the side of the Scandinavians in 1982 and adopted strict power plant emission standards. It almost immediately proposed that similar standards be adopted European Community–wide. The negotiations within the EC were very tough, eventually pitting the United Kingdom and Spain against everyone else. The directive was finally passed in 1988 after a series of last-minute compromises. The directive specifies reduction requirements for sulfur and nitrogen for 1993, 1998 and 2003 for power plants larger than 50 megawatts. Each country is assigned its own targets for these three years. The initial proposals had single targets applying across the Community, but individual concessions were necessary to obtain agreement.[44]

The European Community also sets standards for vehicle emissions, a major source of nitrogen oxides emissions. A series of directives passed between 1987 and 1990 call for adoption of catalytic converters by

44. A negotiating history of the LCPD can be found in Sonja Boehmer-Christiansen and Jim Skea, *Acid Politics: Environmental and Energy Policies in Britain and Germany* (London: Belhaven Press, 1991), 234–46.

1992. These negotiations were just as difficult as the LCPD, with Germany and some environmentalist allies pitted against Italy, France, and the United Kingdom, all manufacturers of small cars. (Catalytic converters exert proportionally larger increases in price and reductions in power on small cars as compared to large cars.)

Neither the power plant directive nor the vehicle emissions directives were motivated by transboundary concerns. In both cases Germany adopted strict national standards out of concern for its own forests, and sought to extend those standards to other members to equalize the terms of economic competition. Debates within the EC over these measures focused not on environmental effects or on transboundary flows, but on economic costs. This reflects the EC's primary mission, to remove barriers to trade among members.

The EC, then, has taken on the task of regulating the two sectors responsible for the bulk of sulfur dioxide and nitrogen oxides emissions—power plants and automobiles. This stands in contrast to LRTAP protocols, which provide national emission targets but do not specify the means to obtain them (except for the nonbinding annex in the nitrogen protocol). This can be attributed to the EC's role in promoting the common market, which is seen as requiring harmonized environmental standards. Until 1987, when the Single European Act incorporated an environmental basis for EC decision making, the EC could not have adopted national emission targets because such targets would not have had a role in achieving the common market. Now, however, the revised EC treaty permits purely environmental directives. In fact, the recent EC decision setting emission targets for carbon dioxide is similar in form to the LRTAP protocols, though precise national targets have not yet been negotiated.[45]

Unlike LRTAP, European Community negotiations frequently get beyond least-common-denominator politics. This can be attributed to the fact that EC member states are negotiating numerous issues, and have grown accustomed to practicing give and take in order to facilitate

45. On 30 October 1990 the EC's Environment Council adopted a decision to stabilize carbon dioxide emissions at 1990 levels by 2000. Countries with growing energy requirements (such as Spain, Portugal, and Greece) are expected to be permitted to increase emissions while others reduce. The United Kingdom will be permitted to stabilize by 2005.

agreements. Governments are used to losing on some issues and winning on others. Another contributing factor is that governments must contend with the European Commission (which is considerably larger than the ECE and much more independent) and the European Parliament. The vehicle emissions directives were pushed forward by Parliament during a period of rising public environmental sentiment. The Single European Act permits directives deemed to be directly connected to the achievement of the common market to be passed by qualified majority; a 1987 vehicle emissions directive was the first directive to be passed under qualified majority. Finally, decisions in the EC are frequently made by environment ministers meeting informally. Whereas LRTAP decisions are made over the course of months and years in a series of meetings attended mainly by lower officials, EC decisions often are made quickly by officials with cabinet status who are more comfortable with changing positions. When issues are of high political salience, it is not uncommon for meetings to drag on at length as competing positions are argued, then move rapidly toward resolution away from the least common denominator.[46]

One final note regarding the EC and LRTAP: the EC is a signatory to the LRTAP convention, as well as the EMEP protocol. The Commission had hoped to sign the sulfur protocol as well, and would have been able to if one of the earlier LCPD draft directives had passed; the final version falls short of achieving 30 percent reductions by 1993.

**Agenda Setting**

This section analyzes the role of LRTAP in shaping the international agenda concerning long-range air pollution. Did LRTAP influence the international agenda, and if so, how well did it perform this task? To conduct such an analysis one must first characterize the international agenda in terms of clear criteria, then ask the counterfactual question of what the agenda would have looked like if LRTAP had not been

---

46. At one meeting to decide how extensively to phase out CFCs, the most extreme position going into the meeting had been for 95 percent reductions, with many governments hoping for less; the meeting nonetheless agreed on 95 percent, then quickly agreed to go all the way to 100 percent, whereupon one participant joked, "Does anyone bid 105 percent?"

adopted in 1979. The central characteristics of the European acid rain agenda have been (1) a commitment to seeking solutions in a pan-European context rather than by smaller regions; (2) a broad emphasis on all airborne pollutants and all ecological damage, rather than individual pollutants and individual ecosystems; and (3) a rapid inclusion of new scientific knowledge into the diplomatic process. I argue that LRTAP contributed positively to these characteristics of the international agenda, though it cannot claim sole credit.

It is easiest to demonstrate that LRTAP contributed to the fact that solutions were consistently sought in a pan-European context. Despite the presence of rather efficient (by comparison) policy-making apparatuses in the Nordic Council and Euorpean Community, and the difficulty of engaging in East-West negotiations during the 1980s, acid rain talks always retained a strong East-West focus. Whether this was of any substantive consequence is addressed below. In terms of the international agenda, though, it is clear that LRTAP's origins in the Helsinki process kept Eastern and Western governments discussing acid rain with each other when they otherwise would have found it difficult or undesirable.[47]

LRTAP's agenda has been consistently science- and ecosystem-driven, as opposed to pollutant- or source-driven. It stands in marked contrast to the agenda of the European Community, where governments regulate standards for individual sources of pollution and spend relatively little time preparing joint assessments of environmental damage. As a result, although LRTAP was created primarily because of a political crisis over Scandinavian lakes and sulfur, it has evolved into a forum for coordinating research and policies toward a variety of pollutants (many not thought to present transboundary problems in 1979) which threaten a variety of receptors also not thought to be at risk in 1979 (forests, buildings, wildlife, marshes). LRTAP's decision-making structure is designed to achieve precisely this result. Working groups are organized around potential environmental damage rather than specific emission sources. When these groups turn up evidence that appears to warrant negotiated reductions of a specific pollutant, they pass their recom-

47. Chossudovsky considers this one of LRTAP's greatest accomplishments. *East-West Diplomacy.*

mendations on to the Bureau, usually accompanied by a recommendation to establish a working group on the topic. This process permits any pollutant that crosses borders and harms ecosystems to enter the diplomatic agenda. This accounts for the ease with which VOCs entered the agenda, as well as for the current investigations into mercury and persistent organic compounds.

Consider the international agenda if LRTAP did not exist. Each scientific discovery that warranted negotiated reductions would require either that new pan-European instruments be negotiated from scratch, or that nations limit themselves to working within existing regional bodies. The major contender, the European Community, until very recently did not permit environmental decisions by anything but unanimity. It is not surprising that LRTAP's agenda in the past 10 years has moved faster than the EC's. The EC has no regulations governing VOC reductions, and has no plans to investigate critical loads.

Although it is clear that LRTAP made positive contributions to the international agenda, this assessment must be tempered by the realization that first Norway and Sweden, and later Germany, were highly motivated actors anxious to obtain an international solution to the problem of acid rain. Norway and Sweden had succeeded in obtaining a global commitment to the principle of reducing transboundary air pollution at Stockholm in 1972, and in getting a major research program off the ground shortly thereafter in the OECD. That they succeeded with no other allies indicates both that they placed a high priority on the issue and that it was possible to achieve results in the absence of the facilitating agenda-setting mechanisms of LRTAP. If the Scandinavians had not had LRTAP, they would surely have kept trying with at least some significant successes, especially after gaining the support of Germany in 1982. Under such a counterfactual scenario, Sweden would have held the 1982 Stockholm conference, attracting a significant number of delegates. Scientific experts from governments had been motivated to attend in order to keep abreast of late-breaking science, even if their governments had been less concerned about acid rain. The Meeting of Acidification Research Coordinators would have been formed anyway, forging transnational links in the absence of LRTAP. What would probably not have happened in the absence of LRTAP is serious coordination of acid rain research and monitoring with Eastern Europe

**Table 3.5**    National participation in LRTAP research programs (as of October 1990) ranked by number of coordinating/synthesizing centers and number of task force memberships

| Country | Number of task force member-ships | Number of research sites/labs | Number of EMEP emission reports, 1980–1989 | Number of coordinating/ synthesizing centers |
|---|---|---|---|---|
| Norway | 6 | 12 | 14 | 4 |
| West Germany | 6 | 26 | 12 | 2 |
| Czechoslovakia | 5 | 10 | 10 | 2 |
| United Kingdom | 5 | 14 | 16 | 2 |
| Netherla `ds | 6 | 9 | 11 | 1 |
| Sweden | 6 | 15 | 11 | 1 |
| Finland | 6 | 12 | 11 | 1 |
| USSR | 5 | 23 | 15 | 1 |
| Denmark | 5 | 7 | 13 | |
| Italy | 5 | 10 | 9 | |
| Belgium | 4 | 3 | 13 | |
| France | 4 | 4 | 12 | |
| Hungary | 4 | 3 | 8 | |
| Ireland | 4 | 3 | 10 | |
| Poland | 4 | 5 | 12 | |
| Portugal | 4 | 4 | 4 | |
| Spain | 4 | 8 | 6 | |
| Austria | 3 | 3 | 9 | |
| East Germany | 3 | 3 | 7 | |
| Switzerland | 3 | 3 | 9 | |
| Yugoslavia | 3 | 7 | 10 | |
| Buglaria | 3 | 0 | 7 | |
| Greece | 3 | 2 | 2 | |
| Liechtenstein | 2 | 0 | 0 | |
| Luxembourg | 2 | 0 | 2 | |
| Turkey | 2 | 0 | 3 | |
| Holy See | 1 | 0 | 0 | |
| Iceland | 1 | 2 | 4 | |
| Romania | 0 | 6 | 1 | |
| San Marino | 0 | 0 | 0 | |

Source: UN ECE EB./AIR/R.48/Add.1 (October 1990), 28; EMEP/MSC-W Report 2/90 (August 1990), 8.

and the Soviet Union. Without the link to the Helsinki process and détente, these governments would have had little incentive to engage in such activity (whose substantive importance they continued to denigrate at home).

## National Policy Responses

LRTAP calls on members both to participate in joint research and monitoring activities and to meet specific reduction requirements in accord with regulatory protocols.

### Participation in LRTAP Research Programs

A rough measure of national participation in LRTAP research efforts is indicated in table 3.5. The more detailed information from which this measure is derived is attached as an Appendix to this chapter. Countries are ranked here first by operation of of coordinating or synthesizing centers; these are the most extensive form of participation, and require that a country both take the initiative to organize a center and provide funding for coordinating expenses. The list is also ranked by task force memberships. Task forces include ICP Forests, ICP Freshwaters, ICP Materials, ICP Crops, and the Pilot Program on Integrated Monitoring. Membership in the task forces requires that research be conducted at a national level and that this research be harmonized and shared with other participants. Finally, from 1980 through 1989 LRTAP parties were asked to submit a total of seventeen emission reports to EMEP; the number of reports actually submitted is another indicator of the extent of participation in LRTAP's research programs.

### Compliance with Regulatory Protocols

Because EMEP collects reliable emission statistics, it is possible to get a fairly clear picture of national compliance with LRTAP protocols. The most recent official data cover the period through 1989, making it possible to evaluate only the sulfur protocol reliably. Emission levels and percentage reductions are indicated in table 3.6, for both signatories and non-signatories.

The fifth column in table 3.6 shows projections for 1993 emissions for states which have provided them to the LRTAP secretariat. The pro-

**Table 3.6**  Sulfur dioxide emissions, 1980–1989 (as 1000 tons of sulfur), non-signers and signers of 1985 protocol

| Country | 1980 | 1989 | Percent change | Official forecast of % change by 1993 |
|---|---|---|---|---|
| Non-signers | | | | |
| United Kingdom | 2424 | 1776 | −27 | −27 |
| Portugal | 133 | 102 | −23 | 2 |
| Ireland | 110 | 91 | −17 | −22 |
| Greece | 200 | 180 | −10 | |
| Poland | 2050 | 1955 | −5 | 0 |
| Spain | 1625 | 1559 | −4 | |
| Albania | 25 | 25 | 0 | |
| Iceland | 3 | 3 | 0 | |
| Romania | 100 | 100 | 0 | |
| Turkey | 138 | 177 | 28 | |
| Yugoslavia | 588 | 825 | 40 | |
| TOTAL | 7396 | 6793 | −8 | |
| Signers | | | | |
| Austria | 173 | 62 | −64 | −78 |
| Sweden | 251 | 102 | −59 | −63 |
| France | 1755 | 760 | −57 | |
| West Germany | 1600 | 720 | −55 | |
| Luxembourg | 12 | 6 | −50 | |
| Belgium | 414 | 207 | −50 | −48 |
| Norway | 71 | 37 | −48 | −51 |
| Finland | 292 | 156 | −47 | |
| Denmark | 225 | 121 | −46 | −58 |
| Switzerland | 63 | 34 | −46 | −54 |
| Netherlands | 232 | 135 | −42 | |
| Italy | 1900 | 1205 | −37 | |
| USSR | 6400 | 4659 | −27 | −29 |
| Hungary | 817 | 609 | −25 | −30 |
| Czechoslovakia | 1550 | 1387 | −11 | |
| Bulgaria | 517 | 515 | −0 | −25 |
| East Germany | 2500 | 2605 | 4 | |
| TOTAL | 18772 | 13320 | −29 | |

Source: EMEP/MSC-W Report 2/90 (August 1990); ECE/EB.AIR 27 (1991).

jections are an indication of the extent of these countries' commitment to reducing acid rain.

## Effectiveness

As pointed out in the Introduction to this volume, national policy responses tell only part of the effectiveness story. It is necessary to go one step further and ask, what causal role did the institution play in bringing about the national responses we observe? In doing so it is useful to perform the heuristic exercise of imagining the counterfactual case of a similar situation lacking an institutional response.

### Research and Monitoring Programs

As with agenda setting, LRTAP's biggest effect on national research and monitoring programs has been in the East bloc. Without the motivation to further the goals of the Helsinki process, it is difficult to imagine that the Soviet Union, Czechoslovakia, East Germany and Hungary would have participated as actively and as consistently as they did in the research programs coordinated by LRTAP. All of these governments were seeking to *suppress* knowledge of environmental damage, yet were lured into *creating* it because of their entanglement in LRTAP. Eastern European researchers collecting domestic acidification data were routinely blocked from publishing such data directly in their home countries. But if they supplied data to LRTAP working groups, which then published the data in UN publications, it became much easier to publish the data domestically. LRTAP was a moderately high political priority for all of Eastern Europe, and it would have been difficult to censor LRTAP publications. LRTAP research programs permitted East European researchers to refute their governments' claims that they were not suffering significant pollution, without being prosecuted.[48]

The same is probably true for the southern European countries ranked in the middle of table 3.5, as well as for the United Kingdom. None of these countries had significant indigenous constituencies for acid rain research. Yet all joined, to a significant extent, in the research

---

48. Interviews with researchers in Poland and Czechoslovakia, June–July 1991. Czech researchers would often publish EMEP data as soon as they were released by LRTAP, writing small articles as vehicles in domestic journals.

programs of LRTAP. All participated in forest surveys, even though there was little domestic concern for forest health, and in freshwater studies, even though there was little concern for lake acidification.

The hard-core environmentalist countries, especially Norway, Sweden, Germany, and the Netherlands probably did not engage in any serious research because of LRTAP that they would not have undertaken anyway. For them, LRTAP's research programs were a vehicle for persuading other states to take action and a mechanism for collecting regional scientific data for their own use.[49]

**Emission Reductions**

LRTAP's ultimate goal is not the creation of knowledge, but the elimination of pollution. How effective has the institution been at reducing emissions of compounds that damage ecosystems? This analysis relies on sulfur emissions data, because only for sulfur have countries had enough time (since the 1985 protocol) to indicate whether they are responding to international policy measures.

It is readily apparent from table 3.6 that signatories are reducing emissions much more than nonsignatories, and that even with some noncompliance the signatories are likely to meet an overall 30 percent reduction target. This is often pointed to as evidence that the protocol has been effective.[50] Of course, reductions are not by themselves evidence of effectiveness, any more than sunrises are evidence of Chanticleer the Rooster's omnipotence. To measure the effectiveness of the sulfur protocol, one must estimate the reductions that would have taken place even in the absence of a protocol. One rough way to calculate this is to examine official forecasts of sulfur emissions made before the protocol, and compare them with actual emissions after the protocol. This comparison is made in table 3.7. Unfortunately, only thirteen European states made forecasts in 1981, and the states that made

---

49. Dutch environmental researchers report that they are eager to volunteer to serve as research coordinators because it gives them free access to other countries' data.

50. For example: "The SO$_2$ Protocol has achieved real reductions. There has been a decline in SO$_2$ emissions since 1980, and this downward trend is expected to continue." Amy A. Fraenkel, "The Convention on Long-Range Transboundary Air Pollution: Meeting the Challenge of International Cooperation," *Harvard International Law Journal* 30, 2 (Spring 1989): 471.

**Table 3.7**  Comparison of forecast and actual emissions of sulfur dioxide (as 1000 tons of sulfur)

|  | 1981 projection of 1990 emissions | 1989 actual emissions | Percentage difference |
|---|---|---|---|
| Signers |  |  |  |
| Austria | 203 | 62 | −70 |
| Czechoslovakia | 1625 | 1387 | −15 |
| Denmark[1] | 232 | 121 | −48 |
| Germany, FR | 1825 | 720 | −61 |
| Finland | 288 | 156 | −46 |
| Hungary | 925 | 609 | −34 |
| Norway | 67 | 37 | −45 |
| Sweden | 150 | 102 | −32 |
| Switzerland | 54 | 34 | −37 |
| USSR | 13250 | 4659 | −65 |
| TOTAL | 18619 | 7887 | −58 |
| Non-signers |  |  |  |
| Poland[2] | 2000 | 1955 | −2 |
| Romania | 100 | 100 | 0 |
| United Kingdom | 2539 | 1776 | −30 |
| TOTAL | 4639 | 3831 | −17 |

Note:  Where range given in forecasts, mid-point selected. 1. 1995 projection 2. 1988 projection

Source:  1981 forecasts from ENV/IEB/R.13 (20 August 1981), 11. 1989 actual emissions from EMEP, EMEP/MSC-W Report 2/90 (August 1990).

forecasts were those that took their LRTAP commitments more seriously. Few of them did not sign the 1985 protocol, therefore this comparison is not as complete as one would like.

This evidence in favor of the conventional wisdom that the sulfur protocol has been effective is still far from complete, however. Especially significant is that, as table 3.6 indicates, the bulk of the complying countries have reduced significantly more than the protocol requires. This suggests that it was not the protocol that induced the reductions but other factors. In fact, most of the reducers have adopted explicit re-

**Table 3.8**  SO$_2$ protocol compliers and their national reduction goals

| Country | 1980–1989 reductions, percent | Declared reduction targets (percent as of 1989) |
|---|---|---|
| National targets exceed protocol: | | |
| Austria | 64 | 70 by 1995 |
| Sweden | 59 | 68 by 1995 |
| France | 57 | 50 by 1990 |
| West Germany | 55 | 65 by 1993 |
| Luxembourg | 50 | 58 by 1990 |
| Belgium | 50 | 50 by 1995 |
| Norway | 48 | 50 by 1994 |
| Finland | 47 | 50 by 1993 |
| Denmark | 46 | 50 by 1995 |
| Switzerland | 46 | 57 by 1995 |
| Netherlands | 42 | 63 by 1994; 78 by 2000 |
| No national targets above protocol: | | |
| Italy | 37 | |
| USSR | 27 | |
| Hungary | 25 | |

Source: Emission reductions from EMEP/MSC-W Report 2/90. National Targets from *Acid Magazine* 8 (September 1989), 5; and Netherlands *National Environmental Policy Plan*, 1989.

duction targets in excess of 30 percent. These pronouncements (as of 1989) are recorded in table 3.8.

The sulfur protocol did not serve as a guide to regulatory policy. But the protocol was never designed to play such a role. Rather, it served as a normative register in a multifaceted strategy of tote-board diplomacy. It was an instrument for increasing concern and capacity. Therefore we must examine LRTAP's effects on sulfur emissions more broadly, looking for a variety of possible mechanisms by which LRTAP may have influenced national responses.

A review of process-level evidence indicates that the 1985 sulfur protocol had a significant causal impact on emission reductions in seven countries. The analysis behind this conclusion is summarized in table 3.9.

**Table 3.9**   Effect of LRTAP on member states' $SO_2$ emissions

| LRTAP did not affect emissions because . . . | | | LRTAP Affected emissions by . . . | |
| Did not reduce | Reduced coincidentally (energy policy) | Did not rely on LRTAP for knowledge of domestic damage | Creating knowledge of domestic damage | Linking to other issues |
| --- | --- | --- | --- | --- |
| Albania | Belgium | West Germany | Austria | Denmark (Nordic Council) |
| Czechoslovakia | France | Norway | Finland | U.K. (EC) |
| Bulgaria | Hungary | Sweden | Netherlands | USSR (détente) |
| Greece | Italy | | Switzerland | |
| Iceland | Luxembourg | | | |
| East Germany | | | | |
| Ireland | | | | |
| Poland | | | | |
| Portugal | | | | |
| Romania | | | | |
| Spain | | | | |
| Turkey | | | | |
| Yugoslavia | | | | |

The first column of countries simply did not reduce emissions. These are all poorer Western countries and East bloc countries.

In the second column, countries reduced emissions, but not because of environmental politics. These countries were switching fuels used to generate electricity, and that process coincidentally reduced their sulfur emissions. France undertook a massive nuclear program (with no environmental motivation) which generated enormous sulfur reductions. Italy switched to lower-sulfur petroleum, partly for reasons of improving urban air quality, but not because of any international pressure or commitments. A review of Italian air pollution policy published in 1988 makes no reference to either the sulfur protocol or to any policy aimed at achieving 30 percent reductions; there were measures aimed at reducing urban concentrations of sulfur dioxide for health reasons.[51] As table 3.5 shows, Italy has been unable to provide LRTAP with a forecast of its 1993 emissions, an indication that there is no policy.[52] Hungary's reductions are attributable to a switch from oil to gas in electricity plants, a nuclear program, and a recession. Neither the fuel switching nor nuclear programs had environmental motivations.[53] None of the countries in this column are large exporters of sulfur, and there was therefore much less external pressure on them than on other exporters such as Czechoslovakia, Poland, Germany, and Britain.

In the third column are countries that reduced emissions for environmental reasons, but reasons which cannot be causally traced through the international institutions. Sweden's and Norway's cuts are products of their prior concern with acidification, dating to the late 1960s. Germany's reductions are the consequence of the forest death which turned into a public crisis in 1982 and 1983.[54] Swedish, Norwegian, and German reductions would have occurred in the absence of a multilateral protocol.

In the two right-hand columns of table 3.9, emission reductions had strong causal connections to the sulfur protocol. Countries in the fourth column—Austria, Finland, Switzerland, and the Netherlands—were influenced primarily by LRTAP's knowledge-creation activities. All have ecosystems of economic importance that are sensitive to acidification, of which governments were unaware in 1980. As part of their participation in LRTAP these governments participated in collaborative research programs designed to ascertain the effects of acid rain. These programs

51. Laura Mottola Cutrera, "The Italian Republic," in Barbara Rhode, ed., *Air Pollution in Europe, Volume 1: Western Europe*, Occasional Paper No. 4, (Vienna: European Coordination Centre for Research and Documentation in the Social Sciences, 1988), 129–44.
52. Italy is one of the very few countries that fail to comply with their commitments to the EMEP protocol, and is frequently deficient in meeting its reporting requirements.
53. Interview with Hungarian environment official, Geneva, January 1991. See also Hungary's report to the September 1990 UN Meeting on Industrial Cooperation for Air Pollution Control Technology, ECE/UNDP/AP/15/R.5 (29 August 1990), which reports that sulfur emissions fell "due partly to the structural changes of the used energy sources and partly to economic recession" (p. 5).
54. The evolution of German sulfur emissions policy is covered thoroughly in Boehmer-Christiansen and Skea, *Acid Politics*, 185–204.

involved government research labs in measurements of acidification of lakes and forests, comparative assessments of forest damage, and measurement of damage to buildings and monuments. All of the governments were active participants in these collaborative programs, even though their official positions, initially, were that acidification was not a problem. Once these governments became aware of the extent of damage their countries suffered, they adopted positions favoring reductions in emissions.[55]

The conclusion that the sulfur protocol was responsible for such reductions requires proof that these countries would not have undertaken reductions in the absence of a protocol, and that the role of the protocol was in creating knowledge rather than promoting linkage. The first claim is more difficult to substantiate, because it lies in the realm of counterfactuals. The strongest evidence comes from the fact that acid rain was neither a subject of political debate nor the focus of government-sponsored research prior to the negotiation of the sulfur protocol. Rather, the negotiation of the protocol prompted these countries to debate the issue and to engage in serious acidification research (much of it under the auspices of LRTAP's working groups). The policy-making pattern during this crucial juncture was clearly externally driven, in sharp contrast to the internally driven policies of Norway, Sweden, and Germany.[56]

For the countries in the fourth column of the table, LRTAP transformed a situation of deadlock into one of harmony. Once these countries became aware of their own acidification damage, it was no longer a case of Sweden and Norway's seeking adjustments that would benefit only Sweden and Norway, but a case of all parties' engaging in self-interested reductions that happened to be mutually beneficial.

55. For another analysis that attributes LRTAP's "qualified success" in part to its knowledge-creation activities, see Jørgen Wettestad and Steinar Andresen, "The Effectiveness of International Resource Cooperation: Some Preliminary Findings," R:007-1991 (Oslo: Fridtjog Nansen Institute), 74–93.
56. For Austria, see John McCormick, *Acid Earth: The Global Threat of Acid Pollution*, revised edition (London: Earthscan, 1989), 138; Steve Elsworth, *Acid Rain* (London: Pluto Press, 1984), 98; Rhode, *Air Pollution in Europe*, vol. 1, 27–46. For Finland, see McCormick, *Acid Earth*, 137–38. For Netherlands, see McCormick, *Acid Earth*, 127–28; Elsworth, *Acid Rain*, 35, 98; Rhode, *Air Pollution in Europe*, vol. 1, 145–64. For Switzerland, see McCormick, *Acid Earth*, 139; Elsworth, *Acid Rain*, 97.

The argument that LRTAP induced these countries to reduce emissions by creating knowledge of domestic damage presumes that they would not have recognized such damage in the absence of LRTAP. Such a counterfactual argument is, of course, subject to debate. It is not implausible, for example, to presume that the discovery of forest damage in Germany in 1982, absent multilateral negotiations and research, would have prompted domestic research in similarly situated countries such as Austria and Switzerland. While this counterfactual conjecture cannot be decisively refuted, the experience of aquatic acidification is instructive. Sweden and Norway discovered severe aquatic acidification in the late 1960s, which had as strong an impact on domestic pollution policies there as the discovery of forest death had in Germany in the early 1980s. But the Scandinavian discoveries occurred in the absence of an international scientific and diplomatic framework, and generated virtually no political or scientific reorientations abroad. Even though other countries suffered similar aquatic damage (including the Netherlands), they did not realize it until the 1980s, when LRTAP prompted them to look for it. I argue that the Scandinavian experience of the late 1960s suggests that if LRTAP had not been present, the German forest death would not have had the international reverbations that we observe.

The last column in table 3.9 represents countries that were influenced by LRTAP through its effect on linkage politics. In the case of Denmark, local geological conditions simply meant that there was little damage to discover. But Denmark reduced emissions anyway because, as a member of the Nordic Council, it is required to consider transborder harm in other Council members according to the same standards governing such harm domestically. LRTAP served to signal precisely what Denmark's responsibilities were as a responsible Nordic Council member. One might argue that Denmark would have reduced even without LRTAP, because Sweden and Norway would have pressed it to do so as part of its Nordic Council commitments. But the fact is that Sweden and Norway had been pressing since the late 1960s, but it was only in 1982, after the LRTAP sulfur protocol was under negotiation, that Denmark committed itself to reductions.[57]

57. McCormick, *Acid Earth*, 121; Elsworth, *Acid Rain*, 98; Per Gunderson, "The Kingdom of Denmark," in Rhode, ed., *Air Pollution in Europe*, vol. 1, 47–61.

In the Soviet Union there was plenty of domestic damage to discover, but this was politically irrelevant. Emissions were reduced because LRTAP had come to be perceived as an issue of high politics. Transborder emissions had to be reduced to further the goals of détente. That the Soviets did not come to value sulfur reductions independently is evident from the fact that they just met their international commitments under the sulfur protocol, whereas other compliers were greatly exceeding their commitments.

Because the Soviets always planned to take an active role in LRTAP but did not care about acid rain, they had a strategic plan for doing so at the least possible cost. They argued strenuously for clauses in regulatory protocols that required them to reduce not total emissions, as everyone else did, but only transborder flows. Because the Soviet Union has such a huge land mass, and prevailing winds blow east, only about 3 to 4 percent of its sulfur emissions cross national borders. The Soviet Union could comply with the sulfur protocol by shifting a small part of its energy production eastward. There are indications that geographical shifting was a major component of Soviet policy. In 1980 the Soviet Union reported that its total emissions were scheduled to increase, but that large coal-fired plants would remain in the east "while it is planned to locate nuclear power stations in the European part of the country."[58] In 1983 the USSR report to LRTAP that it had established a special interagency commission on the implementation of the convention, reiterated that replacing coal plants with nuclear plants in the west was an important aspect of the policy, and stressed that it intended to target transborder fluxes as opposed to total emissions.[59] Only the "European part" of the Soviet Union, west of the Urals, is included within the EMEP monitoring system. Emissions in this area, which cover less than a quarter of the country, have fallen by over 30 percent.

The United Kingdom too was probably influenced by linkage politics promoted by the sulfur protocol, even though it never signed the protocol. Because of its refusal to sign, Britain was branded with the image of "dirty man of Europe," and the government was buffeted by political

58. ENV/IEB/R.2 (1 September 1980), 11.
59. Statement by V. G. Sokolovsky to Executive Body (8 June 1983), "On Strategies and Policies of the USSR for the Abatement of Air Pollution Caused by Sulphur Compounds."

pressure from a wide variety of sources. The United Kingdom is the largest west European emitter of sulfur, and the fourth-largest in all of Europe. It is highly unlikely that the sulfur reduction measures adopted by the British government would have been adopted in the absence of the sulfur protocol. The most significant of these measures include the installation of desulfurization equipment on a number of large coal-burning power stations. While this is a difficult argument to prove, I believe the evidence supports it. First, it is clear that the British desulfurization policies have been treated almost solely as a foreign policy concern, rather than a domestic issue.[60] Britain exports about 65 percent of its sulfur emissions, and suffers relatively little acid damage within its own territory as compared to what occurs in the countries where much of British sulfur falls. Norway, especially, suffers from British sulfur—some 16 percent of its nationwide deposition is traceable to British emissions, and the figure approaches 40 percent in southern Norway, where many very sensitive ecosystems are located. There is British acid rain damage in Scottish and Welsh aquatic systems, and British forest surveys reveal extensive damage that may be in part attributable to acidification, but the local effects have not generated nearly the political uproar of the transborder effects.[61]

The sulfur dioxide protocol figured prominently in all the political pressure placed on the British government. Beginning in 1984 (when the "30 percent club" was announced), a wide range of domestic actors referred to the LRTAP negotiations in an effort to embarrass the government. From that date on, the political opposition consistently promised to join the 30 percent club if elected, elements of the ruling Conservative party also urged the government to sign the protocol, and a prominent House of Commons Environment Committee report in 1984 urged the government to join other Europeans and sign the protocol.[62]

60. This observation is confirmed in interviews with British environment officials.
61. Interviews with British officials in Department of the Environment, July–August 1991, London. See Boehmer-Christiansen and Skea, *Acid Politics*, especially 205–29. For an opposing view which attributes much greater impact to local effects in the United Kingdom, see McCormick, *Acid Earth*, 91–113. My research finds little evidence for McCormick's view.
62. For more details on the domestic politics of the acid rain issue, see Marc A. Levy, "The Greening of the United Kingdom: Assessing Competing Explana-

The protocol served as a landmark that exerted a profound influence on the domestic debate: it is virtually impossible to find a supporter of acid rain controls in the United Kingdom who did not also favor signing the sulfur protocol.

The evidence for the protocol's influence on the British is murky because in the end the British government adopted a policy of sulfur reductions that fall just short of the protocol's requirements. It is therefore the largest Western European sulfur emitter outside of the protocol, and the second-largest European emitter. In 1986 the government announced plans to install desulfurization equipment on three large power plants. The decision followed a joint British-Scandinavian research project funded by Britain's national utility industry, the Central Electricity Generating Board, that provided conclusive proof that acid deposition was killing fish in southern Norway. The precise extent of promised British desulfurization has fluctuated since 1986, but it has never been enough to satisfy the requirements of the 1985 protocol.

To argue that the sulfur protocol did not play a role in Britain's limited desulfurization policies, one would have to argue that the Norwegian and Swedish pressure alone would have been sufficient to bring about the same policy changes. This is plausible, but the Scandinavians would have had a much harder time without the protocol. LRTAP meetings (regularly attended by British NGOs) provided a chance for domestic and international opponents to embarrass the British government, and regularly forced the issue onto the agendas of the government, political parties, and environmental activists. Today, the United Kingdom is bound by a 1988 European Community directive governing emissions from large power plants, which forced stricter standards than those adopted during the wrangling with the Scandinavians in 1984 through 1987. And only recently, the British government has committed itself in principle to adopting even stricter emission reduction standards, toward the goal of achieving "critical loads"—deposition levels that in theory will leave sensitive ecosystems unharmed.[63] The tightening of

---

tions," paper presented to Annual Meeting of the American Political Science Association, Washington, D.C., 1991.
63. *This Common Inheritance: Britain's Environmental Strategy*, Cm 1200 (London: HMSO, September 1990), 149.

British acid rain standards that began in 1988, unlike the reductions announced in 1986, are less directly connected to LRTAP. They have more to do with German pressure within the EC, and with a general reorientation of British environmental policy-making that has resulted in an across-the-board effort to take environmental threats more seriously. LRTAP had a contributory role alongside these factors, but more at the level of the framing of policy alternatives than at the level of mobilizing concern.

In conclusion, then, the sulfur protocol probably had significant effects on the emission reductions in seven countries, including the largest and fourth-largest emitters in Europe (USSR and United Kingdom). A protocol that affects only these seven probably counts as a success.

What is the impact of these sulfur reductions on the environment? The sulfur protocol, even with all the reductions that would have occurred anyway, has not produced a dramatic improvement in environmental quality. Forest surveys reveal damage just as extensive as before, and aquatic systems have not yet recovered. Much of this is explainable by the increase in nitrogen emissions over the 1980s. Nitrogen oxides are also acidifying, yet they have not been regulated to the same extent as sulfur dioxide. The sulfur reductions have kept acidification from growing worse than it would have otherwise.

Finally, it is highly possible that the sulfur protocol will exert a strong influence on the new regimes of central Europe. In both Poland and Czechoslovakia, the largest sulfur polluters in central Europe, there is a strong desire to acquire reputations as good citizens by striving for 30 percent reductions in sulfur dioxide emissions. Hungary hopes to achieve 30 percent reductions by 1993, and Poland by 2000; Czechoslovakia has not yet fixed a target. All three governments make frequent references to the sulfur protocol in their policy pronouncements.[64] For

64. Interviews with Hungarian, Polish, and Czech officials in Geneva (January–February 1991) and in Warsaw and Prague, June–July 1991. See also Hungary's report to the September 1990 UN Meeting on Industrial Cooperation for Air Pollution Control Technology, ECE/UNDP/AP/15/R.5 (29 August 1990), 1; Polish Ministry of Environmental Protection, Natural Resources and Forestry, *National Environmental Policy* (Warsaw, November 1990), 12–15, 19–20; and Bedrich Moldan et al., *Environmental Recovery Program for the Czech Republic* (Prague: Academia, 1991), 37–39 and 89–93. The effects of the changes

all of post–Cold War Eastern Europe, international legal instruments such as the sulfur protocol derive their power from an intense and widespread desire to show that they are worthy partners for political and economic integration.

## Conclusion

The first institutional responses to European acid rain took place when there was very little consensus regarding the severity of the problem. Thirty parties joined together to address a problem only two of them worried about. In this light, any success that LRTAP has achieved must be considered a great accomplishment.

Some countries escaped LRTAP's effects almost entirely. Tote-board diplomacy had no effect on the the emissions policies of the poorer countries of Western Europe and on all of Eastern Europe. None of the poorer western countries were considered politically important, because their exports to sensitive countries were minimal. Therefore LRTAP does not present a good test for how effective normative and scientific persuasion can be on lower-income countries. Eastern European emissions *did* damage sensitive ecosystems and were the focus of political strategies; these countries were both poor and autocratic, however, and it is not clear from this case which factor mattered more.

A significant number of other countries did succumb to LRTAP's influence, though, including the United Kingdom (Western Europe's largest sulfur emitter). LRTAP influenced these other states not because it solved a collective action problem for them, nor because it enmeshed them in an ironclad enforcement mechanism, but because it induced them to reevaluate their interests. Three institutional features helped LRTAP achieve this. First, LRTAP was organized in a way that was initially unthreatening to laggards. The secretariat was small and underfunded, all decisions were made by unanimous vote, and the membership was chock full of opponents to regulation. These un-

---

in Eastern Europe on LRTAP are discussed at greater length in Marc A. Levy "East-West Environmental Politics after 1989," in Stanley Hoffmann, Robert O. Keohane, and Joseph P. Nye, Jr., *After the Cold War: State Strategies and International Institutions in Europe* (Cambridge: Harvard University Press, forthcoming).

**Appendix table 3.1** Status of the convention on long-range transboundary air pollution and its related protocols (as of 15 march 1991)

| | Convention (a) | | EMEP protocol (b) | |
|---|---|---|---|---|
| | Signature | Ratification* | Signature | Ratification |
| Austria | 13.11.1979 | 16.12.1982 (R) | 25. 2.1985 | 4. 6.1987 (Ac) |
| Belgium | 13.11.1979 | 15. 7.1982 (R) | 4. 4.1985 | 5. 8.1987 (R) |
| Bulgaria | 14.11.1979 | 9. 6.1981 (R) | | 26. 9.1986 (Ap) |
| Byelorussian | | | 28. 9.1984 | |
| SSR | 14.11.1979 | 13. 6.1980 (R) | 3.10.1984 | 4.10.1985 (At) |
| Canada | 13.11.1979 | 15.12.1981 (R) | | 4.12.1985 (R) |
| Czech and Slovak | | | | |
| Federal Republic | 13.11.1979 | 23.12.1983 (R) | 28. 9.1984 | 26.11.1986 (Ac) |
| Denmark | 14.11.1979 | 18. 6.1982 (R) | 7.12.1984 | 29. 4.1986 (R) |
| Finland | 13.11.1979 | 15. 4.1981 (R) | 22. 2.1985 | 24. 6.1986 (R) |
| France | 13.11.1979 | 3.11.1981 (Ap) | 26. 2.1985 | 30.10.1987 (R) |
| Germany (5) | 13.11.1979 | 15. 7.1982 (R) (2) | | 7.10.1986 (R) (2) |
| Greece | 14.11.1979 | 30. 8.1983 (R) | | 24. 6.1988 (Ac) |
| Holy See | 14.11.1979 | | 27. 3.1985 | |
| Hungary | 13.11.1979 | 22. 9.1980 (R) | | 8. 5.1985 (Ap) |
| Iceland | 13.11.1979 | 5. 5.1983 (R) | 4. 4.1985 | |
| Ireland | 13.11.1979 | 15. 7.1982 (R) | 28. 9.1984 | 26. 6.1987 (R) |
| Italy | 14.11.1979 | 15. 7.1982 (R) | | 12. 1.1989 (R) |
| Liechtenstein | 14.11.1979 | 22.11.1983 (R) | 21.11.1984 | 1. 5.1985 (Ac) |
| Luxembourg | 13.11.1979 | 15. 7.1982 (R) | 28. 9.1984 | 24. 8.1987 (R) |
| Netherlands | 13.11.1979 | 15. 7.1982 (At) (3) | 28. 9.1984 | 22.10.1985 (At) (3) |
| Norway | 13.11.1979 | 13. 2.1981 (R) | | 12. 3.1985 (At) |
| Poland | 13.11.1979 | 19. 7.1985 (R) (2) | | 14. 9.1988 (Ac) |
| Portugal | 14.11.1979 | 29. 9.1980 (R) | | 10. 1.1989 (Ac) |
| Romania | 14.11.1979 (1) | 27. 2.1991 (R) | | |
| San Marino | 14.11.1979 | | | |
| Spain | 14.11.1979 | 15. 6.1982 (R) | 28. 9.1984 | 11. 8.1987 (Ac) |
| Sweden | 13.11.1979 | 12. 2.1981 (R) | 3.10.1984 | 12. 8.1985 (R) |
| Switzerland | 13.11.1979 | 6. 5.1983 (R) | 3.10.1984 | 26. 7.1985 (R) |
| Turkey | 13.11.1979 | 18. 4.1983 (R) | 28. 9.1984 | 20.12.1985 (R) |
| Ukrainian SSR | 14.11.1979 | 5. 6.1980 (R) | 28. 9.1984 | 30. 8.1985 (At) |
| USSR | 13.11.1979 | 22. 5.1980 (R) | 20.11.1984 | 21. 8.1985 (At) |
| United Kingdom | 13.11.1979 | 15. 7.1982 (R) (4) | 28. 9.1984 | 12. 8.1985 (R) |
| United States | 13.11.1979 | 30.11.1981 (At) | | 29.10.1984 (At) |
| Yugoslavia | 13.11.1979 | 18. 3.1987 (R) | | 28.10.1987 (Ac) |
| European | | | 28. 9.1984 | |
| Community | 14.11.1979 | 15. 7.1982 (Ap) | 21 | 17. 7.1986 (Ap) |
| Total: | 34 | 32 | | 30 |

* R = Ratification, Ac = Accession, Ap = Approval, At = Acceptance

(1) With a declaration upon signature
(2) With a declaration upon ratification
(3) For the Kingdom in Europe
(4) Including the Bailiwick of Jersey, the Bailiwick of Guernsey, the Isle of Man, Gibraltar, the United Kingdom Sovereign Base Areas of Akrotiri and Dhekhelia in the Island of Cyprus
(5) The former German Democratic Republic signed the Convention on 13 November 1979 and ratified it on 7 June 1982; acceded to the EMEP Protocol on 17 December 1986 with a declaration upon accession; signed the SO$_2$ Protocol on 9 July 1985 and the NOx Protocol on 1 November 1988.

| | SO$_2$ protocol (c) | | NOx protocol (d) | |
|---|---|---|---|---|
| | Signature | Ratification | Signature | Ratification |
| Austria | 9.7.1985 | 4. 6.1987 (R) | 1.11.1988 | 15. 1.1990 (R) |
| Belgium | 9.7.1985 | 9. 6.1989 (R) | 1.11.1988 | |
| Bulgaria | 9.7.1985 | 26. 9.1986 (Ap) | 1.11.1988 | 30. 3.1989 (R) |
| Byelorussian | | | | |
| SSR | 9.7.1985 | 10. 9.1986 (At) | 1.11.1988 | 8. 6.1989 (At) |
| Canada | 9.7.1985 | 4.12.1985 (R) | 1.11.1988 | 25. 1.1991 (R) |
| Czech and Slovak | | | | |
| Federal Republic | 9.7.1985 | 26.11.1986 (Ap) | 1.11.1988 | 17. 8.1990 (Ap) |
| Denmark | 9.7.1985 | 29. 4.1986 (R) | 1.11.1988 | |
| Finland | 9.7.1985 | 24. 6.1986 (R) | 1.11.1988 | 1. 2.1990 (R) |
| France | 9.7.1985 | 13. 3.1986 (Ap) | 1.11.1988 | 20. 7.1989 (Ap) |
| Germany (5) | 9.7.1985 | 3. 3.1987 (R) (2) | 1.11.1988 | 16.11.1990 (R) |
| Greece | | | 1.11.1988 | |
| Holy See | | | | |
| Hungary | 9.7.1985 | 11. 9.1986 (R) | 3. 5.1989 | |
| Iceland | | | | |
| Ireland | | | 1. 5.1989 | |
| Italy | 9.7.1985 | 5. 2.1990 (R) | 1.11.1988 | |
| Liechtenstein | 9.7.1985 | 13. 2.1986 (R) | 1.11.1988 | |
| Luxembourg | 9.7.1985 | 24. 8.1987 (R) | 1.11.1988 | 4.10.1990 (R) |
| Netherlands | 9.7.1985 | 30. 4.1986 (At) (3) | 1.11.1988 | 11.10.1989 (At) (3) |
| Norway | 9.7.1985 | 4.11.1986 (R) | 1.11.1988 | 11.10.1989 (R) |
| Poland | | | 1.11.1988 | |
| Portugal | | | | |
| Romania | | | | |
| San Marino | | | | |
| Spain | | | 1.11.1988 | 4.12.1990 (R) |
| Sweden | 9.7.1985 | 31. 3.1986 (R) | 1.11.1988 | 27. 7.1990 (R) |
| Switzerland | 9.7.1985 | 21. 9.1987 (R) | 1.11.1988 | 18. 9.1990 (R) |
| Turkey | | | | |
| Ukrainian SSR | 9.7.1985 | 2.10.1986 (At) | 1.11.1988 | 24. 7.1989 (At) |
| USSR | 9.7.1985 | 10. 9.1986 (At) | 1.11.1988 | 21. 6.1989 (At) |
| United Kingdom | | | 1.11.1988 | 15.10.1990 (R) (4) |
| United States | | | 1.11.1988 (1) | 13. 7.1989 (At) |
| Yugoslavia | | | | |
| European | | | | |
| Community | | | | |
| Total: | 20 | 20 | 26 | 18 |

(a) = Convention of Long-range Transboundary Air Pollution, adopted 13.11.1979, entry into force 16.3.1983

(b) = Protocol to the 1979 Convention on Long-range Transboundary Air Pollution on Long-term Financing of the Cooperative Program for monitoring and Evaluation of the Long-range Transmission of Air Pollutants in Europe (EMEP), adopted 28.9.1984, entry into force 28.1.1988

(c) = Protocol to the 1979 Convention on Long-range Transboundary Air pollution on the Reduction of Sulphur Emissions or their Transboundary Fluxes by at least 30 percent, adopted 8.7.1985, entry into force 2.9.1987

(d) = Protocol to the 1979 Convention on Long-range Transboundary Air Pollution concerning the Control of Emissions of Nitrogen Oxides or their Transboundary Fluxes, adopted 31.10.1988, entry into force 14.2.1991

| | EMEP (a) | | ICP forests (b) | |
|---|---|---|---|---|
| | Steering body | Stations | Task force | 1988 survey |
| Austria | x | 3 | x | N |
| Belgium | x | 1 | x | R |
| Bulgaria | x | | x | N |
| Byelerussian SSR | x | * | x | |
| Canada | x | | x | |
| Czechoslovakia | x | 2 | PCC-East | N |
| Denmark | x | 3 | x | N |
| Finland | x | 3 | x | N |
| France | x | 2 | x | N |
| East Germany | x | 2 | x | N |
| West Germany | x | 15 | PCC-West | N |
| Greece | x | 1 | x | N |
| Holy See | | 1 | | |
| Hungary | x | 1 | x | N |
| Iceland | x | 1 | | |
| Ireland | x | 1 | x | N |
| Italy | x | 4 | x | R |
| Liechtenstein | x | | x | N |
| Luxembourg | x | | x | N |
| Netherlands | x | 2 | x | N |
| Norway | CCC,MSC-West | 8 | x | N |
| Poland | x | 2 | x | N |
| Portugal | x | 2 | x | N |
| Romania | | 6 | | |
| San Marino | | | | |
| Spain | x | 4 | x | N |
| Sweden | x | 6 | x | N |
| Switzerland | x | 2 | x | N |
| Turkey | x | | x | |
| Ukrainian SSR | x | * | x | |
| USSR | MSC-East | 11 | x | R |
| United Kingdom | x | 5 | x | N |
| United States | x | | x | |
| Yugoslavia | x | 6 | x | R |
| European Economic Community | x | 1(in Italy) | x | |
| Total: 35 | 32 | 95 | 31 | 25 |

Source:  ECE/EB.AIR/22
CCC = Chemical Coordinating Center           SC = Subcenter
MSC = Meteorological Synthesizing Center      N  = National Forest Damage Survey
 *   = Listed under USSR                       R  = Regional Forest Damage Survey
PCC = Program Coordinating Center

| ICP freshwaters (c) | | ICP materials (d) | | ICP crops (e) | |
|---|---|---|---|---|---|
| Task force | Laboratories | Task force | Sites | Task force | Laboratories |
| x | | | | x | |
| x | 1 | | | x | 1 |
| x | | | | | |
| | | | | | |
| x | 1 | x | 1 | | |
| | | SC | 3 | x | 1 |
| x | 1 | | | x | 1 |
| x | 1 | x | 3 | x | 1 |
| | | | | x | 1 |
| | | | | | |
| x | 1 | SC | 6 | x | 2 |
| | | | | x | 1 |
| | | x | | | |
| | | | | | |
| | | | | | |
| x | 1 | | | x | 1 |
| x | 1 | x | 4 | x | 1 |
| | | | | | |
| | | | | | |
| x | | x | 4 | x | 1 |
| PCC | 1 | SC | 3 | x | |
| | | | | x | 1 |
| | | x | 1 | | |
| | | | | | |
| | | | | | |
| | | x | 3 | x | 1 |
| x | 1 | PCC | 3 | x | 1 |
| | | | | x | 1 |
| | | | | | |
| | | | | | |
| x | | x | 2 | | |
| x | 1 | SC | 4 | PCC | 2 |
| x | 1 | x | 2 | x | 2 |
| | | | | | |
| x | | x | | x | |
| 16 | 11 | 15 | 39 | 19 | 19 |

(a) = Cooperative Program for Monitoring and Evaluation of the Long-range Transmission of Air Pollutants, established in 1977

(b) = ICP for Assessment and Monitoring of Air Pollution Effects on Forests, established in 1985

(c) = ICP for Assessment and Monitoring of Acidification of Rivers and Lakes, established in 1986

(d) = ICP for Effects on Materials, including Historic and Cultural Monuments, established in 1986

(e) = ICP for Research on Evaluating Effects of Air Pollutants and Other Stresses on Agricultural Crops, established in 1987

threatening characteristics ensured that all the relevant countries were engaged in LRTAP's activities from the start. A more ambitious start would have scared many of them off.

Second, LRTAP focused its early energies on establishing an open-ended process of knowledge building. It built the most extensive monitoring program to accompany an environmental treaty, and established an expanding range of scientific working groups which harmonized data collection, evaluated competing explanations of damage, and assessed environmental threats. This process was crucial for keeping alive political momentum after political crises faded from view, and for enabling the institution to enter its current stage, in which the regulatory agenda is determined more by scientific consensus than political shocks.

Finally, LRTAP protocols were crafted as instruments of normative persuasion instead of as regulatory rules. If they had been designed as regulatory rules, they would have been crippled by problems of free-riding and bickering over distributive gains. Using instruments that have the appearance of rules, but serve the function of normative persuasion (a process here called "tote-board diplomacy"), was central to LRTAP's success.

LRTAP's influence was also facilitated by events external to the institution. Chief among these were the bilateral diplomatic efforts of Sweden, Norway, and Germany, which put pressure on Britain; the German decision to take the issue to the European Community, which influenced most of Western Europe; the 1982 shock engendered by the German forest death; and transnational links among acid rain researchers. But had LRTAP not been present, these exogenous factors would have generated less change than actually occurred. LRTAP held states publicly accountable to principles they accepted on paper but violated in practice, boosted the power of domestic proponents of action, and created a multilateral knowledge base supporting the need for action. The experience of LRTAP shows that institutions that enter life weak and symbolic can, under the right circumstances and with the right design, evolve into more powerful instruments with the ability to alter state policies.

# 4
# Protecting the Baltic and North Seas

Peter M. Haas

The North Sea and Baltic states have been seeking to control marine pollution of their seas since the early 1970s. Thirteen governments signed the Convention for the Prevention of Marine Pollution by Dumping from Ships and Aircraft (Oslo Convention) to protect the Northeast Atlantic in 1972. Twelve Northeast Atlantic governments signed the Convention for the Prevention of Marine Pollution from Land-Based Sources (Paris Convention) in 1974. The Oslo Commission (OSCOM) was established in 1974 to control marine dumping in the Northeast Atlantic, and the Paris Commission (PARCOM) was established in 1978 to control land-based sources of Northeast Atlantic pollution. Seven Baltic governments signed the Convention on the Protection of the Marine Environment of the Baltic Sea Area (Helsinki Convention) in 1974. The Helsinki Commission (HELCOM) was established in 1980 to control all sources of Baltic marine pollution.

Taken together, these commissions constitute a single international institution which is responsible for developing a single policy system and a set of legally binding rules for both the Baltic and North seas. The commissions stipulate emission standards for very hazardous sub-

Documentary access was provided by the Norwegian Department of the Environment in Oslo, and the Baltic Environment Protection Commission in Helsinki. Interviews were conducted with over forty officials from governments, international organizations, and NGOs. I am grateful to Antonia Chayes, Michael Hatch, Ton IJlstra, Robert O. Keohane, David Victor, and the participants in the International Environmental Institutions project for their comments on earlier drafts. Research assistance was provided by Joseph Amitrano, Denise Barton, Anilla Cherian, Bruce Martin, Jon Birger Skjaerseth, and Juila Wormser. Financial support came from the Rockefeller Brothers Fund and NSF grant SES-9010101.

stances, design licensing procedures for less hazardous substances, organize regional environmental monitoring, and identify least polluting technologies. While discrete organizations have been established to deal with the problems of each sea, they are intricately interlocked. Organizational interlocking is based on the ecological interdependence among the seas, and on overlapping memberships. Denmark, Germany, and Sweden are members of each commission. Since 1985, agenda setting, international policy formulation, and national policy action in the North Sea–Baltic region have become much more vigorous in setting emission values for regulated substances, with deadlines for their implementation; and there are signs of increasing institutional effectiveness.

This chapter seeks to explain that increasing activity and probable effectiveness. My argument is that international institutions helped to amplify domestic environmental concern. High-profile Ministerial Conferences made it difficult for environment ministers from laggard countries to oppose environment measures proposed by leader countries. Institutional change became self-reinforcing, as national bodies became better equipped to protect the environment and as public expectations of their accountability mounted.

Consistent with the framework of this volume, this chapter will consider, in turn, agenda setting, international policies, national policy responses, and institutional effectiveness. Since the Baltic and North Sea arrangements constitute a single international institutional network, they will be considered together. Before discussing processes of institutional and policy change, however, it is necessary to describe the major actors in Baltic–North Sea institutions and the formal institutional arrangements that had been established before the 1980s.

### The Actors: Leaders and Laggards

The most important actors have been national governments (states), which are responsible for formulating policies and adopting international agreements. International policy coordination occurs in a region with no great disparities in state capabilities, so no one government can compel others to do anything. A key source of national power relative to other governments in environmental issues is control over environmental information. All governments have access to indigenous science.

While there is variation in the number of national scientists and laboratories, such numbers do not imply relative influence among countries, the way that, say, differences in numbers of comparable weapons systems may. Ultimately any country is free to say no to decisions it does not regard as necessary or politically tolerable.

Coordination between states in the regions has been difficult because interests conflict regarding the economic costs of harmonizing environmental standards. By the time international discussions on marine pollution control for the North Sea and Baltic began, most European countries had already developed their own styles of protecting the marine environment, often applying different standards, regulating different substances, and using different policy instruments.[1] Thus, real costs were entailed for countries that had relatively weaker environmental standards.

Most governments formulated domestic environmental policies before foreign environmental policies, so the North and Baltic seas were effectively regulated through a composite of national water quality, pollution, waste control, and conservation measures. Some countries adopted single environmental laws (Sweden, 1969; West Germany, 1972) while others lacked comprehensive laws and have adopted ad hoc collections of measures for discrete activities (such as Belgium). Another problem that inhibited agreeing on strong measures was a difference in fundamental approaches to environmental standard setting. Until 1987 the United Kingdom and Portugal adhered to the principle of environmental quality objectives (EQO), which set ambient standards for the receiving water. Other countries applied uniform emission standards (UES), which set actual limits on substances released at the ends of pipes.

Countries typically had two motivations in seeking international environment policy. Firstly, they sought to minimize the possible relative costs from environmental protection to their industries in highly competitive markets. Countries with strong prior environmental standards sought to encourage other countries to adopt similar standards, to re-

1. Turner T. Smith and Renee R. Falzone, "Foreign Environmental Legal Systems—A Brief Review," *International Environment Reporter*, November 1988, 626.

duce any competitive disadvantages to their own industries. Much of the marine pollution of these regions comes from land-based activities. Eighty percent of the Baltic pollution comes from rivers and the coast. Significant industries in the North Sea region include agriculture, shipping, fishing, nuclear power generation, steel production, chemical manufacturing, ports, oil refineries, pulp and paper mills, metal finishing, and offshore oil and gas production.[2] The Baltic lacks offshore industry but has many of the same onshore sources of pollution. The pulp and paper industry, concentrated entirely in Sweden, Finland, and the USSR, is a major source of Baltic contamination.

These polluting industries are much stronger and better organized politically than groups concerned about reducing pollution, including fishermen. They are widely consulted by governments before intergovernmental meetings in order to formulate national positions. Their prevailing concerns have been to avoid additional production costs and to avoid losing relative competitive advantage to manufacturers in other countries that lack environmental standards. Through the mid-1980s, when public opinion and scientific understanding were weak, the industry position prevailed in most countries. Industry in Germany, however, has tended to be pro-environment in order to gain local approval for new development plans in such a densely populated country.

Secondly, governments, and particularly environment ministries, have been accountable to their domestic electorates. In countries with strong environmental movements there were strong pressures on governments to adopt stringent domestic environmental measures, as well as to stand up for stringent foreign environmental policies. Growing environmental concern in Western Europe has increased the demands on governments to appear "green." In Eastern Europe similar changes in popular concern have only emerged since 1989.

Nongovernmental organizations (NGOs) exercised little regional influence until the late 1980s. Other than Greenpeace International and

2. M. M. Sibthorp (ed.), *The North Sea Challenge and Opportunity* (London: Europe Publications, 1975), chap. 3; Steinar Andresen, "A Comprehensive North Sea Convention," *Reasons for Concern Proceedings of the 2nd North Sea Seminar '86* (Amsterdam: Werkgroep Noordzee, 1986); Steinar Andresen, "The Environmental North Sea Regime: A Successful Regional Approach," in Elisabeth Mann-Borgese et al. (eds.), *Ocean Yearbook 8* (Chicago: University of Chicago Press, 1989), 378–401.

**Table 4.1**  Lead ministries

| Country | North Sea | Baltic |
| --- | --- | --- |
| Denmark | Environment | Environment |
| Finland | | Agriculture (pre 1983) Environment (post 1983) |
| W. Germany | Transport until 1986 for PARCOM, 1989 for OSCOM, Environment thereafter | Transport (until 1987) Environment (post 1987) |
| Norway | Environment | |
| Sweden | Environment | Environment |
| Netherlands | Transport, Water Management and Public Works | |
| United Kingdom | Environment | |

Friends of the Earth, few regional NGOs existed, and there was little transnational logistic support for coordinating efforts by national groups. Most national environmental groups were not involved with marine issues, focusing instead on energy and nature conservation.[3]

Differences of opinion exist within governments as well. While environment ministries often serve as the lead agency in formulating foreign environmental policy, they are often pitted against other, more powerful ministries with larger staffs, bigger budgets, and more influential constituencies. As relative newcomers, environment ministries lack clout, particularly with regard to such other functional agencies as agriculture (Denmark, Norway), trade and commerce (United Kingdom), and transportation (Germany). Table 4.1 indicates this organizational division of labor. Environment ministries tend to express greater concern for environmental quality than other ministries, which focus on their own sectoral responsibilities. For instance, countries whose North

3. Interviews at Aktionsconferenz Nordsee (Bremen), World Wildlife Fund (Stockholm), Greenpeace International (Copenhagen, Amsterdam).

Sea policies were dominated by marine authorities had the greatest trouble in identifying alternative disposal options for pollutants. Conversely, countries where waste regulators were responsible for North Sea policy generated more flexible policies.[4] The German transportation ministry opposed incineration at sea, while the environment ministry opposed incineration anywhere.

Environment ministries thus strive to enhance their own bureaucratic power relative to other ministerial bodies, as well as to expand their domain of regulatory influence. International standards help legitimate domestic efforts that would otherwise be blocked at home by more powerful domestic interests, such as the control of agricultural pesticide use. In Germany the federal environment ministry also sought to gain leverage over the Lander, which have much greater legal authority for policy making.

Collective pollution control efforts for the Baltic and the North Sea have developed through a "leader-laggard" dynamic. Leader governments are pressed by both industry and public opinion to draw other governments up to their levels of environmental protection. "Leaders" are countries with stringent sectoral environmental measures, which promote their sectoral standards for universal adoption. Thus, talks focus on controlling specific substances and emissions from economic sectors, such as metal plating, rather than on overall protection of the marine environment. "Laggards" are countries with relatively weak measures, which are reluctant to accept more stringent measures. Without any way of offsetting the laggards' reluctance, regional policy coordination yielded a least-common-denominator outcome, as the leaders lacked institutional mechanisms to compel compromise. I argue below that the major institutional role in the region has been to help states transcend the least-common-denominator pattern of agenda setting and international policy making by increasing laggard governments' political costs from recalcitrance. The paths of influence are depicted in the figure 4.1.

The strongest environmental advocates in both regions have been Sweden, Germany, and Denmark. Sweden and Germany had developed

4. Daryl Ditz, "The Phase Out of North Sea Incineration," *International Environmental Affairs* 1, 3 (Summer 1989): 196.

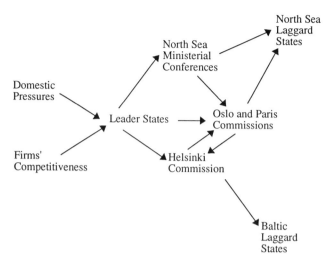

**Figure 4.1**
North Sea and Baltic paths of influence

fairly sweeping environmental protection programs by the early 1970s, and also had active, mobilized, and politically influential domestic environmental constituencies; thus they were leaders for collective controls on most economic sectors. With less industry, Denmark tended to lead only in sectors for which it had developed strong domestic controls, such as reducing nutrient deposition and pollution from agriculture. All three countries pressed for common measures for both regions, in order to avoid having to apply different standards to plants on different coasts. Sweden and Germany still disagree about the flexibility with which measures should be applied and have differing styles of international policy making. Germany relies on universal compliance, while Sweden, which relies on licenses concluded between licensing authorities and individual firms or industrial groups, is willing to tolerate more variation in actual implementation of limit values. Sweden tended to be ideologically green, promoting across-the-board cuts of substances, while Germany was more pragmatic, merely ensuring that its own Federal Code was universally respected. Many other states (the United Kingdom, France, West Germany) were suspicious of Sweden, whom they suspected of pursuing any environmental measures that would play well at home (such as controlling mothproofing agents), regardless of the feasibility and importance of such measures. Belgium, France, and Norway were North Sea laggards.

The Wadden Sea states (Germany, Netherlands, Denmark), facing more pollution, have also been strong advocates in the North Sea region for stringent pollution controls. Netherlands was often an entrepreneurial leader in negotiations, offering constructive suggestions and seeking compromise solutions, particularly in the areas of nutrients, pesticides and some heavy metals.

In the Baltic, Finland and the Eastern Europeans were laggards. Finns say "what is good in Sweden is good after ten years in Finland." Most industries in the USSR and Eastern Europe were antiquated, with little investment or change in process engineering since the 1940s, and would have been severely hit by virtually any environmental standards. Thus, they were concerned less with the substance of arrangements than were countries in the west because they realized that complying with any new standards would entail eliminating entire plants and possibly even industrial sectors. Recently, East European countries have supported standards in hope of attracting financial support to reach the standards as well as modernize their industries. The USSR was responsive to others' proposals through the 1980s, but did not lead. After 1989 the USSR transferred the responsibility for controlling Baltic coastal pollution to the Baltic republics.

The EC has exercised a major restraint on agenda setting and international decision making. As a party to the Oslo and Paris Commissions, an EC representative even chaired the PARCOM Commission. More importantly, the EC Commission asserts its competence to speak for the European Community when prior EC directives exist, or when similar EC discussions are under way. Under such circumstances the EC delegate gets to vote for all the EC members at the meeting, guaranteeing it the Community a majority in North Sea decisions. Since EC decisions were reached by least-common-denominator formulas before the qualified majority voting was introduced in 1987, the EC's assertion of competence has had the effect of yielding less stringent measures than some of the more environmentally activist countries desire on cadmium, mercury, and hexachlorocyclohexane.[5] EC competence has also yielded

5. Eckard Rehbinder and Richard Stewart, *Environmental Protection Policy*

non-decisions, as when the North Sea states postponed discussions on PCBs for five years and abandoned talks on environmental impact assessment when they found it impossible to reach agreement on a text more stringent than extant EC directives.[6]

Suspicions that leaders' actions are merely efforts to garner comparative advantages for their industries can be easily dismissed in this case. Through NGO and media publicity, leaders' actions are fairly transparent, and observers can calculate the likely costs and benefits of action to all the parties.

## Formal Institutions

All legally binding international decisions have been taken through the Oslo and Paris Commissions for the Northeast Atlantic and North Sea, and the Helsinki Commission (HELCOM) for the Baltic Sea.

The Convention for the Prevention of Marine pollution by Dumping from Ships and Aircraft (Oslo Convention) was signed on 15 February 1972 and entered into force in April 1974. It covers parts of the Northeast Atlantic which include coastal areas of Belgium, Denmark, France, Germany, Iceland, Ireland, Netherlands, Norway, Portugal, Spain, Sweden, and the United Kingdom. Finland also signed the Oslo Convention because it transported material to the North Sea for incineration in the 1970s. While the Oslo Convention was designed only to regulate dumping and offshore incineration, its designers intended to turn their attention to other land-based sources of marine pollution in the future, and the Convention's preamble suggests land-based sources as a future topic.

---

(Berlin: Walter de Gruyter & Co., 1985), 213; Ton IJlstra, "Regional Co-Operation in the North Sea: An Inquiry," *International Journal of Estuarine and Coastal Law* 3, 3 (1988): 201–3; Ton IJlstra, "L'action Communautaire dans les Commissions de Paris et d'Oslo," in J. Lebullenger and D. Demorvan (eds.), *La Communaute Europeene et la Mer* (Editions Economica, 1990).
6. Environmental impact assessment procedures were proposed by West Germany in 1986, with support from Denmark, Sweden, and Norway, but were blocked by the EC because they would exceed measures anticipated in a draft EC decision. Paris Commission, Eighth Meeting of the Paris Commission, 1986; Greenpeace International, "The Oslo and Paris Commissions: Review of Past Performance, Part 2," mimeo (1991) submitted to the Thirteenth Joint Meeting of the Oslo and Paris Commissions, Den Haag, 13–15 June 1991, 9.

The Oslo Convention parties adopted the Convention for the Prevention of Marine Pollution from Land-Based Sources (Paris Convention) on 4 July 1974; it entered into force in May 1978. The EC is a signatory party to the Paris Convention but not the Oslo Convention. A 1986 protocol extended the Paris Convention's coverage to include airborne transmission of pollutants reaching the North Sea; it entered into force in September 1989.

While the Oslo and Paris Conventions cover the Northeast Atlantic region, since 1983 regional attention has focused more extensively on the North Sea through the medium of the North Sea Ministerial Conferences (described in the international policies section below). Portugal and Spain attend the North Sea meetings as observers, and many of the North Sea decisions are subsequently applied to the broader North Atlantic region.

The Oslo Convention controls marine pollution from dumping, while the Paris Convention controls pollution from land-based sources, including offshore oil platforms. Both apply black and gray lists. Annex 1 to the conventions lists particularly hazardous substances—black lists—whose dumping or emission is prohibited. Annex 2 lists less hazardous substances—gray lists—whose dumping or emission require special care and for which permits must be issued by signatory governments.[7] To be included on the lists, substances must be toxic, persistent, and must bioaccumulate in the sea.

While the decisions regarding substances to be included on the black and gray lists is not known or remembered by the current generation of policymakers, the substances appear to reflect general consensual knowledge available at the time in marine chemistry textbooks. Few governments were aware of their major emissions, and many lacked data on emissions of many of the substances included on the list.[8] The lists reflect concern about pollutants unique to the regions, as they differ from other similar efforts which were under way at the same time.

7. Peter Hayward, "Environmental Protection: Regional Approaches," *Marine Policy*, April 1984, 106–119; and Peter Hayward, "The Oslo and Paris Commissions," *International Journal of Estuarine and Coastal Law* 5, 1–3 (1990): 91–100.
8. Sonya Boehmer-Christiansen, "Marine Pollution Control in Europe—Regional Approaches, 1972–80," *Marine Policy* 8, 1 (1984): 49.

While applying the same criteria as the EC, which was in the process of identifying substances for control under its First Environmental Action Program, the Paris Convention's list is much shorter than the eventual list of 127 substances which the EC developed. The Oslo Convention also covers incineration of PCBs, although these were left off the list developed by the International Maritime Organization (IMO) during its concurrent talks for the 1973 London Dumping Convention.

The Convention on the Protection of the Marine Environment of the Baltic Sea Area (the Helsinki Convention) was signed on 22 March 1974 by Denmark, Finland, East and West Germany, Poland, Sweden, and the USSR. The Convention finally entered into force on 3 May 1980. Between 1974 and 1980 decisions were taken through an Interim Commission. Sweden and the USSR have blocked the EC's becoming a member.[9]

The Helsinki Convention is a unique piece of international law, covering a comprehensive list of pollution sources. Unlike the North Sea conventions and the UN Environment Program's Regional Seas treaties, the Helsinki Convention covers sources of pollution rather than pollutants. It commits parties to control airborne and waterborne sources of hazardous substances in the Baltic, in particular PCBs, PCTs (poly chlorinated triphenols), and DDT. It also governs land-based sources of pollution and land-based emissions transmitted through the atmosphere, with corresponding lists of sixteen substances whose release should be eliminated or reduced. It also has detailed provisions against pollution by tankers and other ships carrying oil in quantities over 400 metric tons. Coverage is limited to the open waters of the Baltic. Coastal waters were not covered to accommodate the Soviet Union's concern for coastal security.

The Oslo and Paris Conventions are supported by annual meetings of the Oslo Commission and Paris Commission. The commissions share a small joint secretariat in London (OSPARCOM) with four professional staff and three clerks. Meetings are staggered to fall on sequential days. Joint meetings are held as well. Some national officials service both commissions. Chairmanships rotate annually.

9. Interviews and United Kingdom House of Lords Select Committee on the European Communities, *Dumping of Waste at Sea*, Session 1985–86, 17th Report (London: Her Majesty's Stationery Office, 1986), 6.

While much of the real work in OSCOM and PARCOM is conducted in working groups, conflicts are passed up to the commissions for resolution. Many technical disagreements are ultimately only resolved at the top level. PARCOM issues decisions and recommendations. Decisions are reached by unanimous consent and are legally binding within two hundred days. Recommendations are adopted by a three-fourths majority vote, and are only binding on the approving parties. This decision rule gives great influence to "the least enthusiastic party which cannot be accepted as a free rider."[10] Thus, contentious decisions may take several years to be adopted and then are likely to reflect a least-common-denominator compromise.

All decisions and reports in working groups are made according to the lead country principle. A country with an interest in the substance or industrial process under consideration conducts a study of national practices and monitors practices at home. It then provides background material for proposed measures and drafts the measures for discussion. Lead countries typically have the most experience with a specific substance or sector. They commonly propose more stringent standards or procedures than are widely applied. Table 3.2 indicates the frequency with which countries have volunteered to lead in several working groups in the North Sea and the Baltic. The Helsinki Commission for the Baltic operates according to the same principle. A sample of lead countries is presented in table 4.2.

In practice, the use of the lead country principle eliminates the possibility that countries that lack a given sector will insist on regulating it to the discomfort of those countries with the sector. For instance, regulating the offshore oil and gas industry is only subject to initiatives from Denmark, the Netherlands, Norway, and the United Kingdom.

Environmental protection efforts for the Baltic Sea have been conducted through organizational channels similar to those of the North Sea region. A tiny permanent secretariat of only five professions is located in Helsinki. The Helsinki Commission (HELCOM) meets annually to administer the Helsinki Convention. Each contracting party has one vote, and decisions are taken by consensus at all stages. Thus,

10. Sunneva Saetevik, *Environmental Cooperation Between the North Sea States* (London: Belhaven Press, 1988), 20.

Table 4.2  Lead countries in selected working groups

| | PARCOM industrial sectors working group | PARCOM diffuse sources working group | HELCOM point sources working group | HELCOM diffuse sources working group | HELCOM industrial discharges working group |
|---|---|---|---|---|---|
| Norway | 1 | 1 | | | |
| Netherlands | 3 | 2 | | | |
| United Kingdom | 0 | 1 | | | |
| Belgium | 1 | 0 | | | |
| France | 1 | 0 | | | |
| Spain | 2 | 0 | | | |
| Sweden | 3 | 3 | 7 | 1 | 3 |
| West Germany/ Germany | 2 | 0 | 0 | 2 | 4 |
| Denmark | 0 | 0 | 0 | 1 | 0 |
| Finland | | | 1 | 1 | 2 |
| USSR | | | 2 | 2 | 1 |
| Poland | | | 0 | 1 | 1 |

HELCOM meetings are fairly amicable as disagreements in working groups never progress up to the Commission. All decisions are taken by the lead country procedure. Yet, some effort is expended to use lead countries that have less experience, such as the USSR, in order to encourage learning by doing.

Since 1979 HELCOM has coordinated the Baltic Monitoring Program for the region, which yielded, among other studies, a 1987 compilation on the load of pollution entering the marine environment from land-based sources. A monitoring program for airborne pollution was started in 1986, and a monitoring program for radioactive substances began in 1987. OSPARCOM and HELCOM refer pollution problems that are not covered by their conventions to other functional international organizations. Most navigational issues, vessel-based oil pollution, and operational pollutants are explicitly left to IMO (see Chapter 5). The control and monitoring of airborne pollutants entering the North Sea and Baltic is left to LRTAP (see Chapter 2). Problems related to the conservation of nature and species preservation are left to regional fisheries commissions and international law.

The North Sea and Baltic secretariats were intended by governments to be ineffective. They have small staffs and meager budgets. Autonomous initiatives are discouraged by governments, and the secretariat exists solely to coordinate joint activities and support annual meetings. No one government is able to dominate either the secretariat or decision making in the commissions because budgetary commitments are allocated on a proportional scale based on gross national product (roughly similar to the standard scheme used by the United Nations).

Other subregional treaties cover elements of regional pollution, but are not widely referred to. The Nordic Council offers a small forum for Nordic states to coordinate their policies before going to the other bodies.[11] The 1971 Copenhagen Agreement concluded between Denmark, Finland, Norway, and Sweden coordinates measures against oil pollution. North Sea states adopted agreements in 1969 and 1983 for cooperation in dealing with oil spills. Bilateral agreements have also been concluded between Denmark and East Germany and between Denmark and West Germany to combat oil in the western Baltic and pollution in the Flensborg Fjord; between Denmark and Sweden for sewage treatment in the Oresund; and between Finland and Sweden for the Gulf of Bothnia. Additional multilateral arrangements exist for the rivers Rhine and Elbe.

### Agenda Setting

Two phases of agenda setting have occurred in the regions. First was the identification of regional pollution as a problem and the specification of specific substances requiring regulation. Agendas for each region were largely embodied in the original conventions. Subsequently, additional substances were identified for priority action and choices were made to accelerate attention to the already specified agenda.

Agenda setting has largely been the consequence of public concern. Environmental shocks were initially responsible for agenda setting. Most agenda setting was a response to publicized local problems which prompted individual governments to raise their concerns at internation-

11. Nordic Council of Ministers, *Nordic Action Plan on Pollution of the Seas* (Copenhagen: Nordic Council, 1990), 90–94.

al meetings. Both the identification of substances for control and the timing of major meetings have been responses to domestic public pressure and media attention. Subsequent agendas have been catalyzed by publicized environmental disasters and by occasional scientific reports. With renewed public concern in the mid-1980s, the institutional agendas were recharged as well.

The 1967 *Torrey Canyon* accident led to universal concern over ship-based pollution. In 1969 the North Sea governments adopted the Bonn Agreement for Cooperation in Dealing with Pollution of the North Sea by Oil. In July 1971 another maritime shock (but not a disaster) focused public attention on the issue of marine dumping: Five North Sea governments refused to allow the Dutch coastal freighter *Stella Maris* to dump its load of chlorinated hydrocarbons in their waters.[12] The media offered daily reports of the ship's location.

Norway pressed the North Sea states to adopt a treaty to control offshore dumping, and in October 1971, Norway convened a drafting conference. It was easy for Norway to promote dumping controls, as most of Norway's wastes were disposed of on land. Norway was also responding to domestic pressures from fishermen who were alarmed that their yields were threatened by dumping of aluminum-industry wastes in fjords. Still, drafting occurred in the general climate of preparations for the United Nations Conference on the Human Environment (UNCHE), and many Norwegian and Finnish officials were enamored of the holistic ecological views then being applied to public policy for the first time. Norway's leadership led to the 1972 Oslo Convention.

In 1972 France convened a conference to draft a convention on land-based sources of North Sea pollution. Countries participated to "obtain more information and a better knowledge concerning the connection between emissions and environmental damage," because they wished to control industrial emissions, and because there were no strong reasons against cooperating.[13] The Paris Convention was adopted in 1974.

The Baltic lacked a potent attention-getting incident. While experts feared for the health of the sea, such concerns were not shared outside

12. Stuart W. Lehman, "Controlling Sediment Contamination by Toxics in the North Sea," a report to the German Marshall Fund of the United States (January 1986), 23.

the immediate community of scientists and international organization officials.[14] Scientists had in the 1950s detected signs of environmental contamination that was linked to large-scale industrialization and chemical-intensive agriculture.[15] By the late 1960s it was clear that an agreement was necessary to protect Baltic fisheries. In 1969 the International Council for the Exploration of the Seas (ICES) Working Group on Pollution of the Baltic released an influential report which identified sewage and heavy metals as major pollutants. Low-level government meetings in 1969 and 1970 yielded agreement on a treaty to control oil pollution, but inter-Germany recognition problems delayed an immediate signing. In 1973 the Convention on Fishing and Conservation of the Living Resources in the Baltic Sea and the Belts was signed.

Finland proceeded to draft an unusually comprehensive treaty to control multiple sources of pollution reaching the Baltic. Officials in the newly created Environment Ministry hoped to use the treaty as an expedient way to create a diplomatic opening to the USSR and East Germany, as well as to convert their holistic ecological views into practice. Many of these officials lacked clear training or understanding of Baltic conditions but were infused with the holistic vision that permeated the climate of UNCHE preparations. They were also influenced by Rachel Carson's book *Silent Spring*, which identified DDT as a substance meriting control and justified controls of a host of substances which might be transported through the air. European environmental policy making was still nascent, so few parties were committed to adhering to national or international precedents that stressed control of substances over sources. Officials in the region who participated in later phases of the regime believe that the Eastern Europeans' unfamiliarity with environmental protection led them to prefer to regulate sources of pollution rather than unfamiliar contaminants.

Subsequent agenda setting has been generally shaped by public opinion in the leader states. Concern started earliest in West Germany,

13. Sunneva Saetevik, *Environmental Cooperation Between the North Sea States*, 33.
14. J. E. Carroz, "The Management of Living Resources in the Baltic Sea and the Belts," *Ocean Development and International Law* 4, 3 (1977): 213.
15. Stockholm Environment Institute, "Forward to 1950," *AMBIO* Special Report No. 7 (September 1990), 22.

largely in response to the widely publicized 1982 forest dieback. Elsewhere such concerns did not become salient until the later 1980s, to some extent in response to the 1986 Chernobyl disaster. Extensive media reports in 1988 of unrelated instances of "algae invasions" and mysterious seal deaths in the North Sea led to the treatment of those concerns at the Third North Sea Ministerial Conference in 1990. Scientists suggested that the seal deaths may have been due to a virus, but environmentalists argued that seals' immune systems were inhibited by pollution. The Swedish government convened Baltic Ministerial Conferences in 1988 and 1990 to demonstrate its "greenness" before upcoming elections. To a large extent such intermittent public concern has not proved troublesome for protecting the environment because the initial lists of substances in the black and gray lists were sufficiently accurate to offer real opportunities for environmental protection.

New scientific information has seldom been responsible for agenda setting. Scientists were highly uncertain about the sources and degree of contamination of the North Sea and the Baltic. Regional scientists were unable to specify causal ties between emissions of pollutants into the sea and their concentrations in water or in fish. Until recently, scientists have not paid much attention to any of the more exotic chemical pollutants.

Scientific reports and monitoring kept the marine contamination issue alive in both regions by providing material for the media and NGOS to demonstrate a need for environmental action, but reporting and monitoring have not themselves catalyzed agenda setting. The first well-regarded systematic summary of North Sea environmental conditions was not released until 1987, and the first thorough study for the Baltic appeared in 1990.[16] Tributyltin in marine anti-fouling paint was controlled in the North Sea in response to findings of high levels of tributyltin (TBT) in mariculture waters, but the monitoring had initially been undertaken in response to French mussel growers' complaints of con-

16. Second International Conference on the Protection of the North Sea, *Quality Status of the North Sea*, September 1987; Helsinki Commission Report, Baltic Sea Environment Proceedings No. 35A, Summary, and 35B, "Second Periodic Assessment of the State of the Marine Environment of the Baltic Sea." See also National Swedish Environmental Protection Board, *Monitor 1988: Sweden's Marine Environment—Ecosystems Under Pressure* (Solna, June 1988), 85–145.

taminated water. At times scientists have borrowed from scientific literature on problems outside the region to suggest potential substances for HELCOM control. The 1984 to 1988 quality assessment of the Baltic proposed further action to reduce pollution from nitrogen and phosphorus (a policy focus borrowed from North Sea action), tributyltin in marine paints (borrowed from North Sea action), and polychlorinated camphenes (borrowed from the literature). Governments have shown little interest in pursuing such suggestions.

While scientific advice has been provide by the International Council for the Exploration of the Seas (ICES), which does much of the nongovernmental research and monitoring, that advice has had little impact on agenda setting in the regions. ICES is itself a political body: delegates to ICES are chosen by governments, and ICES projects reflect a least common denominator of parameters and environmental media chosen by government representatives. The advice of its Advisory Committee on Marine Pollution is disregarded by delegations, and its "management principles" are often harshly criticized. Efforts by ICES to identify new problems or substances for control are discouraged by government delegates who fear that they may lose control of the agenda.

**International Policies**

OSPARCOM and HELCOM have developed measures for most of the major pollutants identified in the conventions and devised limit values for many of them, as well as stipulating industrial processes by which the values may be reached.

Fifty-eight decisions, recommendations and agreements have been adopted for the North Sea since 1978, and 112 recommendations have been adopted for the Baltic. Until 1987 these measures were developed and applied on a substance-by-substance basis, which led to a disorganized and incoherent set of policy efforts. Some substances were regulated according to common emission standards, and others by common ambient standards. While reflecting scientific consensus about environmental capacity, such an approach was slow and unwieldy. Moreover, removed from public scrutiny and subject to industrial capture, many decisions were delayed or were subject to standards that merely satisfied a least-common-denominator approach, using the measure acceptable to the most recalcitrant government.

Institutional change contributed to more forceful environmental protection. Following the establishment of Ministerial Conferences and the spread of mass environmental concern in the region, international efforts became much more vibrant and requirements became more stringent. Across-the-board cuts of 50 percent were established for thirty-seven significant pollutants, and 70 percent cuts in dioxins, mercury, cadmium, and lead are required by 1995. Many countries have accelerated or broadened national programs for pollution control. Since 1987 most of the Commissions' activities have been directed at implementing decisions reached at Ministerial Conferences.

Several decisions have flowed between the North Sea and Baltic, brokered by Denmark, Germany, and Sweden as lead countries. With only minor phrasing changes, arrangements for offshore installations, mercury and cadmium emissions, and dumping practices for dredging spoils were initially adopted in the North Sea and subsequently adopted in HELCOM. A standard for oil emissions from refineries was first adopted by HELCOM and then transferred to PARCOM. A small number of policies were also informed by prior EC decisions. PARCOM regulations for mercury, cadmium, and hexachlorocyclohexane (HCH) were lifted from prior EC decisions, and subsequently adopted in HELCOM.

### North Sea

OSCOM developed a series of measures to control the dumping of industrial wastes, sewage sludge, and dredging spoils as well as offshore waste incineration. In 1977 OSCOM adopted a Code of Practice governing incineration at sea. In 1988 OSCOM banned all offshore incineration in the North Sea and Northeast Atlantic by 1994, following the refusal the previous year by the United Kingdom, Ireland, and Spain to accept a Scandinavian termination date of 1991.[17] OSCOM established a system of national licensing through which each country reports its dumping and incineration operations to the Commissions, which pub-

17. Daryl Ditz, "The Phase Out of North Sea Incineration," 177.

lish the data in annual reports. In 1987 OSCOM banned industrial waste dumping at sea from the end of 1989 in the North Sea, and in the broader North Atlantic OSPARCOM waters by the end of 1995.

PARCOM has adopted a total of 58 decisions, recommendations, and agreements since 1978. Mercury and oil have received more attention than any other substances. Fifteen recommendations and decisions were taken on mercury between 1978 and 1990, and of the twenty programs and measures adopted by PARCOM at its first five meetings (1978–1983), ten involved mercury and seven concerned oil.[18] PARCOM has grown more active since 1985, moving from an average of 3.8 decisions per year through 1985 to 5.7 decisions per year since 1986.

Only a small number of PARCOM's actions may be said to significantly influence existing practices. PARCOM's most important decisions apply limit values for the emission of major sources of pollution with deadlines for their application. PARCOM prohibited the use of PCBs and PCTs in new equipment after 1985, established chlorine emission limits from pulp and paper mills, set standards for the production and disposal of mercury and cadmium, regulated the use of TBTs, established oil discharge limits from refineries, reduced nutrient emissions from agricultural runoff, and established a variety of regulations on offshore oil platforms. Guidelines were developed for the use of oil-based muds and for the disposal of oil-contaminated cuttings, limits were set for oil and chemical emissions from offshore platforms, and monitoring arrangements were developed for various platform emissions. Detailed requirements also exist for municipal sewage treatment facilities, although no deadline has been established by which they must be implemented. A recommendation to phase out the use of "the drins" (aldrin, dieldrin and endrin) was adopted in 1978 and upgraded to a decision in 1985, but no timetable has yet been developed.

While PARCOM has adopted many decisions, most of the most effective ones were concluded in the late 1980s. During its first decade PARCOM was only able to conclude relatively toothless agreements which lacked limit values or timetables.[19] Observers generally regard

18. Greenpeace International, "The Oslo and Paris Commissions: Review of Past Peformance," 8.
19. Sunneva Saetevik *Environmental Cooperation Between the North Sea States*, 20.

the development of North Sea Ministerial Conferences as the turning point for active international decisions for the region.[20]

In 1984 Germany convened a conference of North Sea environment ministers in Bremen. These conferences became institutionalized, with subsequent ones held in 1987 and 1990. Participation is limited to the environment ministers of the eight North Sea states and the EC, although OSPARCOM members frequently attend as observers. East Germany, Czechoslovakia, and Switzerland also attended the 1990 North Sea Ministerial Conference as observers. Ministerial declarations are not legally binding, and their implementation is generally left up to OSPARCOM. Ministerial conferences do not use the lead country principle. Thus, countries without polluting sectors can propose strong environmental measures for those sectors with no repercussions on their economies, generating a broader agenda than OSPARCOM. The host country is responsible for preparations, and others expect the host country to provide a fruitful conference so they can show their "green" colors.

A 1980 German report had identified a variety of North Sea pollution sources and suggested that precautionary action was a "requirement for a successful environmental policy for the North Sea ecosystem ... (and) required in international, supranational and national law."[21] The new German interior minister, whose responsibility included the environment, found this proposal to be a convenient way for a weak and low-profile ministry to appeal to growing domestic environmental concern, while also promoting his own political career. He called for a North Sea Ministerial Conference. Germany's formal objectives were to adopt the precautionary principle, which had already been encoded into domestic environmental practice; to ban industrial waste dumping; and

20. Jorgen Wettestad, "Uncertain Science and Matching Policies," in Steinar Andresen and Willy Ostreng (eds.), *International Resource Management: The Role of Science and Politics* (London: Belhaven Press, 1989); Greenpeace International, "The Oslo and Paris Commissions: Review of Past Performance, interviews in the United Kingdom and Sweden.
21. Peter Ehlers, "The History of the International North Sea Conferences," *International Journal of Estuarine and Coastal Law* 5, 1–3 (1990); Lothar Gundling, "The Status in International Law of the Principle of Precautionary Action," *International Journal of Estuarine and Coastal Law* 5, 1–3 (1990): 24; interview in Frankfurt, 12 July 1991.

to declare the North Sea a special area for the 1973 International Convention for the Prevention of Pollution from Ships (MARPOL), thus prohibiting the dumping of chemicals and of all dangerous waste. Germany hoped to attract the United Kingdom to an international meeting where it might be pressured or embarrassed into adopting more stringent environmental protection measures.

The conference yielded moderate results, as few countries were yet as ambitious as Germany in pursuing environmental protection. The parties agreed to strengthen existing surveillance measures on ships and their discharges, to reduce sewage discharge from rivers, to attempt to reduce dumping of radioactive waste, and to intensify research on the impact of air pollution on the sea. Germany failed to achieve endorsement of its proposal to declare the North Sea a "special area" under MARPOL or to adopt the precautionary principle. The conference did prompt the creation of a new German NGO, the Aktionsconferenz Nordsee, which has since then publicized the problems of North Sea degradation, used the media to press the government to adopt more stringent measures, and coordinated activities with Dutch (and other) North Sea interested groups through the broader Dutch umbrella organization, Seas at Risk.

The Second North Sea Ministerial Conference was held in London in 1987, with far more dramatic results.[22] Environment ministers were more familiar with the issues, and pressures from domestic environmentalists were much more acute throughout Europe, as evidenced by recent strong showings by "green" parties in local and EC parliamentary elections. Sweden, with a strong green showing in recent elections, pushed for stringent measures across the board. The countries with the weakest domestic showing by green parties, such as France, continued to be the least aggressive at the meeting.

Success at the meeting was guaranteed when Britain abandoned much of its prior resistance. The United Kingdom withdrew its opposition to the use of uniform emission standards, and accepted controls on marine dumping. Prior British reluctance was overcome by a combination of growing domestic environmental concern, the pressure incumbent on a

22. Second International Conference on the Protection of the North Sea, *Ministerial Declaration*, London, 24–25 November 1987.

host country to have a productive conference, and Britain's desire to ameliorate its reputation as the "dirty man of Europe" so that concerns high on its own agenda would receive a hearing in the future. Prince Charles also publicly called for such a policy reversal.

The Conference Declaration called for "a substantial cut (on the order of 50 percent)" of toxic, persistent and bioaccumulative substances reaching the North Sea via rivers and estuaries between 1985 and 1995. Nitrogen and phosphorus inputs to sensitive areas were to be cut by 50 percent between 1985 and 1995. The conference encouraged controls of refineries and the elimination of pollution by oil-contaminated cuttings, both of which had been deadlocked at PARCOM.

Strong decisions were reached on marine dumping, which overcame many stalled efforts in OSCOM. The Conference Declaration stated that "no material should be dumped after 1 January 1989 unless there are no practical alternatives on land and it can be shown to the competent international organizations that the materials pose no risk to the marine environment."[23] The parties decided to phase out hazardous waste incineration by 31 December 1994, with a 65 percent reduction in marine incineration by 1 January 1991. Industrial waste dumping was to be banned by 31 December 1989. Sewage sludge dumping was to be kept below 1987 levels. States would increase their efforts to limit dumping of dredging wastes. The Second Ministerial Conference also established a North Sea Task Force (NSTF) to draw up a synoptic environmental quality report by 1993. Begun in 1988, the NSTF is high profile and politicized. It is made up of scientists and senior administrators from the North Sea states who are designated by their governments. Consequently, domestic administrative forces prevail over transnational scientific ones in establishing priority concerns and identifying future problems.

The Conference also endorsed the use of "best available technology" (BAT) as a regulatory ideology for reducing pollution at the source. BAT means that policies should stress the least polluting technology rather than specifying specific emission values. Since 1987, countries have attempted to apply BAT to control point source pollution, and "best environmental practices" for non-point sources. Yet countries dis-

23. *Ministerial Declaration*, 12.

agree about what factors should be considered when choosing the BAT. The United Kingdom applies the principle of "best practicable environmental option" (BPEO) and "best available technology not entailing excessive cost" (BATNEEC). When determining emission licensing, inspectors consider all disposal options, and go for the cheapest. Finland also chooses the "best available economically feasible technology."[24] Other countries have much less pragmatic styles of environmental policy setting which conflict with the British insistence on considering economic considerations of the possible measures. Denmark, Sweden, and Germany are considering principles of "clean technology," which entail the adoption of any measures that will reduce the generation of wastes at any point in the production process—not merely at the end of the pipe as the British method involves—virtually regardless of cost. A few research plants are under way that utilize entirely closed systems for their production processes, assuring that no wastes escape the plant. Eastern Europe imitates whatever is popular in the West. Environmental NGOs continue to chastise their governments for not adopting more measures to reduce waste generation rather than its management.

Real policy differences follow from these approaches. The United Kingdom approach stresses technologies that will be most cost-effective for protecting the overall environment. Other countries have stressed without regard to cost only those measures that will reduce the amount of wastes going into the marine environment. In principle, a combination of the two would be most effective for the environment as a whole.

The Second Ministerial Conference also adopted the precautionary principle as a general planning notion:

[The ministers] accept the principle of safeguarding the marine ecosystem of the North Sea by reducing pollution emissions of substances that are persistent, toxic and liable to bioaccumulate at source by the use of the best available technology and other appropriate measures. This applies especially when there is reason to assume that certain damage or harmful effects on the living resources of the sea are likely to be caused by such substances, even where there is no scientific evidence to prove a causal link between emissions and effects ("the principle of precautionary action").[25]

24. Finland, Ministry of the Environment, *National Plan for Reduction of the Load of Pollution on the Baltic Sea*, (no date), 31. *Ministerial Declaration* London, 21–25 November 1987, Finnish National Report, 31.
25. Second International Conference on the Protection of the North Sea, 9. See

The precautionary principle constitutes a fundamental shift in the burden of proof regarding pollution. Firms and countries are expected to apply the best available technologies even in the absence of compelling evidence of environmental degradation from a given substance. Applying the precautionary principle, and the associated technique of BAT, means that future policy is based on technology assessment rather than the determination of tolerable environmental limits. A corresponding effect is a shift from relying on scientists to identify pollutants and determine appropriate environmental limits to relying on engineers to identify least polluting technologies and processes.

The adoption of across-the-board emission cuts and the precautionary principle reflected public impatience at the slow pace with which OSPARCOM had been dealing with discrete pollutants. The 50 percent cut was a triumph of politics over economics or ecology. Such cuts are inefficient and introduce inequitable distribution of costs between countries. It is not clear that all substances in the region require such extensive cuts, and the declaration does not take into account to any differential efforts already taken by governments. Thus, states that had not yet undertaken domestic measures would find it easier and cheaper to cut emissions by 50 percent than states that had already started to cut their emissions.

The policy decisions reflected some compromises between the participating countries. The hazardous waste incineration timetable is a compromise between the Nordic countries and Germany, which desired a ban by the end of 1991, and Belgium, which wanted to delay it until 1995. Germany, which generates 55 percent of the wastes burned at sea, will have to make major policy alterations. Curiously, the countries with the heaviest reliance on marine incineration for the disposal of wastes were some of the most active promoters of controls, while those little affected by offshore incineration were the most adamantly opposed.[26] Britain is the only country significantly affected by the industrial waste dumping decision, as Belgium and West Germany were the only other countries to engage in dumping titanium dioxide wastes

also Lothar Gundling, "The Status in International Law of the Principle of Precautionary Action."
26. Daryl Ditz, "The Phase Out of North Sea Incineration."

and had already banned them by 1989. The United Kingdom was also the only country still actively dumping sewage sludge, which the Germans hoped to control.[27] The United Kingdom opposed a decision on riverine inputs to the North Sea, although it was adopted in 1990.

The 1987 Ministerial Conference had rapid effects on PARCOM. In 1989 PARCOM adopted the principle of precautionary action and the principle of the use of best available technology (BAT) as bases for current and future activities. The adoption of the precautionary action principle and BAT "is an important shift in the philosophy behind the Commissions' work and means that the piecemeal substance-by-substance, sector-by-sector approach will have to be supplemented, and in some cases replaced, by a more holistic view," and implies a move from "preventing an increase" in pollution to "preventing pollution."[28] PARCOM had endorsed a "waste stream approach" in 1984, but had done little to develop it. In 1989 PARCOM established the Industrial Sectors Working Group to review BAT in ten industrial branches with a view to proposing process-based discharge standards.

The Third International Conference on the Protection of the North Sea met in The Hague in 1990.[29] Ministers felt that they had to do better than the previous ministerial conference to prove their green credentials. At the Third Ministerial Conference, environment ministers expressed their desire to "achieve a significant reduction (of 50 percent or more) of inputs via rivers and estuaries between 1985 and 1995, and atmospheric emissions by 1995, or by 1999 at the latest, so long as the application of BAT makes it possible." They designated thirty-seven significant pollutants to qualify for the 50 percent cuts which had already been established and applied 70 percent cuts from 1985 to 1995 for dioxins, mercury, cadmium, and lead. Leaders agreed that sewage discharges should receive secondary treatment, rather than being emitted through long outflows, and that the efforts to eliminate offshore incin-

27. "U.K. Policy Shifts on Dumping, Discharges Pave Way for Successful North Sea Meeting" *ENDS Report* 154 (November 1987): 3–4.
28. Oslo and Paris Commissions, *Progress Report on the Activities of the Oslo and Paris Commissions November 1987–March 1990* (London: Oslo and Paris Commissions, 1990), 1, 8.
29. Third International Conference on the Protection of the North Sea, *Ministerial Declaration of the Third International Conference on the Protection of the North Sea*, The Hague, 8 March 1990.

eration should be accelerated. PCB use is to be phased out by 1999 and existing stores are to be destroyed. Ministers also adopted a Memorandum of Understanding to protect small cetaceans in the North Sea; this eventually led the parties in 1991 to adopt a weak agreement to protect dolphins and porpoises in the North Sea and Baltic. The memorandum was weakened through Norway's efforts to protect its fishery interests in the regions.[30]

Decisions at the Ministerial Conference were reached by compromise. The thirty-seven substances were chosen during six or seven prior meetings of technocrats. Countries preferred substances which reflected existing national priorities, policies, and established practices. Compromise entailed concessions by all to accept additional substances to those previously covered at home.[31] The 70 percent target was a compromise figure worked out between the countries who wanted cuts up to 90 percent, such as Norway, Sweden, and the Netherlands, and those who were reluctant to go beyond the original 50 percent figure. The dates for PCB elimination reflected a compromise between Scandinavian preferences for 1995, West German desire for 1999, Netherlands, Belgium, and the United Kingdom's wish for 2005, and France's preference for 2010.[32] The United Kingdom blocked agreement on nuclear waste dumping.

Popular concern and close monitoring of the conferences swamped subtle diplomatic deals made at the conferences. For instance, phrasing

---

30. John Zarocostas, "Ecologists Criticize New Baltic, North Sea Pact," *Journal of Commerce*, 16 September 1991, 5A.
31. Swedish Environmental Protection Agency, *Marine Pollution '90–Action Programme* (Solna: Swedish Environmental Protection Agency, 1990), 50; Denmark Progress Report on Measures to Reduce Inputs of Nutrients, 144. Germany, Federal Ministry for the Environment, Nature Conservation and Nuclear Safety, *Environmental Report 1990 by the Federal Minister of for the Environment, Nature Conservation and Nuclear Safety* (Bonn: Federal Ministry for the Environment, Nature Conservation and Nuclear Safety, May, 1990); Norway, The Norwegian State Pollution Control Authority (SFT), *Micropollutants in Norway* SFT Report No. 80 (Oslo: The Norwegian State Pollution Control Authority, 1987); *ENDS Report* 162 (July 1988), pp. 15–17, *ENDS Report* 171 (April 1989), pp. 24–26; United Kingdom Department of the Environment News Release 194 (10 April 1989); R. J. Otter, "The Red-List and Prescribed Processes," paper presented to the IBC Conference on Integrated Pollution Management (7–8 February 1991).
32. Roger Milne, "Britain in Row with Neighbours Over North Sea Dumping," *New Scientist* 125 (27 January 1990): 28.

loopholes created to allow the United Kingdom to sign proved meaning-less in subsequent public debate. The Second North Sea Ministerial Conference determined that dumping practices would be banned unless "the materials pose no risk to the marine environment." The United Kingdom contended that offshore disposal of sewage and sludge were not harmful. However, public opinion took the language to mean the elimination of all dumping and the United Kingdom was pressed by domestic environmental groups to rescind most of its dumping licenses for sewage and sludge. The Third North Sea Ministerial Conference set nutrient cuts only for vulnerable areas "where these inputs are likely, directly or indirectly, to cause pollution," thus offering a possible out for the United Kingdom. Yet the Declaration was widely interpreted without such subtle differentiation.

The Fourth North Sea Ministerial Conference is scheduled for 1995 in Denmark. The period between conferences was expanded to enable environment ministers to announce more decisions, as national policy changes in the interim would make them possible.

## Baltic Sea

HELCOM has adopted 112 recommendations, most of which deal with navigation, oil spill management, operational discharges, and reception facilities. The most important decisions are the 38 recommendations aimed at reducing emissions from land-based sources, including DDT, PCBs, PCTs, oil, mercury, cadmium, treatment of municipal sewage and industrial waste water, discharges from agriculture, pulp and paper in-dustry, iron and steel industry, and chemical industry. The Commission has also adopted 42 recommendations relating to maritime issues and 17 recommendations for oil combating.[33]

Since 1987, HELCOM has pursued a more active approach to the control of marine pollution. Twenty-one recommendations were adopted from 1980 to 1987, while 14 were adopted from 1988 to 1991, for a shift from 2.5 per year to 3.5 per year. Three of HELCOM's four most stringent recommendations were reached after 1987. HELCOM, like PARCOM, has moved from controlling emissions of individual

33. J. T. Kohonen, "Protection of the Marine Environment of the Baltic Sea," *Marine Pollution Bulletin* 23 (1991): 543.

substances to identifying best available technologies for industrial branches or sectors.

HELCOM's most meaningful recommendations cover emissions from pulp and paper mills, offshore platforms, airborne and marine emissions from iron and steel mills, oil refineries and municipal waste treatment, and controls on organotin compounds used in marine anti-fouling paint. HELCOM also conducts seminars on providing information for environmental decision making. HELCOM has collected, published and offered on-line bibliographic information drawn from the scientific and technological studies made by the contracting parties.

Borrowing a lesson from the North Sea Ministerial Conferences, Sweden convened a meeting of Baltic environment ministers in March 1988. The ministers agreed to target levels of 50 percent reduction of discharges of nutrients, heavy metals, and organic toxins into the Baltic Sea by 1995. As with the North Sea, the 50 percent cuts are to be applied by each country.

In September 1990 in Ronneby, Sweden, the Baltic Sea Declaration on Environment was adopted by heads of government and high political representatives. In addition to the seven Baltic states, Norway, Czechoslovakia, and the EC attended. The ministers called for "ensuring the possibility of self-restoration of the marine environment and preservation of its ecological balance." They endorsed the principles of BAT, precautionary action, and "cleaner technologies, including low-waste and non-waste processes and environmentally non-hazardous products" to safeguard the marine ecosystems of the Baltic Sea. HELCOM adopted the principle of BAT in 1991, and the reconstituted Technological Committee has undertaken to identify BATs for major industrial sectors.

The ministers also created a Baltic Task Force composed of HELCOM members plus Czechoslovakia, Norway, the EC, European Bank for Reconstruction and Development (EBRD), European Investment Bank (EIB), Nordic Investment Bank, and the World Bank. The task force is to identify and analyze investment projects for pollution control in the Baltic Sea, estimated to cost between 5 and 6.5 billion dollars, to control industrial and municipal wastes.[34] Preliminary reports have

34. *European Chemical News*, 26 March 1990, 14.

largely documented national environmental problems, rather than identifying fruitful investment opportunities.

The international financial institutions approached by the Baltic Task Force may begin to provide the necessary capital to enable laggard states to take action as well, although many observers suspect that the largest short-term reduction in marine pollution will come from dismantling the uncompetitive plants as they are purchased by western firms. With the reunification of Germany, pollution control in the former East German regions improved. Germany aspires to build sewage treatment plants for most of the towns in Mecklenberg and Saxony, which had emitted untreated wastes into the Baltic.

Since 1990, NGOs have become directly involved in OSPARCOM and HELCOM. In response to growing public concern, environmental NGOs were invited to participate in HELCOM and PARCOM. In 1990, two environmental NGOs and two industry groups were awarded formal observer status at regional Commission meetings.[35] Greenpeace International has been the most aggressive NGO at international meetings, pressing for zero discharges into the North Sea by the year 2000.[36] With such expanded public scrutiny, government officials are concerned that it will be harder to veto unpopular decisions or to fashion political deals.

The roles of OSPARCOM and PARCOM are being reconsidered. Both PARCOM and HELCOM are presently revising their conventions. Many decisions have been supplemented or superseded by subsequent actions. OSCOM has been made obsolete by the regulation of dumping, and PARCOM is looking for a new organizational mission now that it has been eclipsed by the Ministerial Conferences. Parties are considering an umbrella framework convention to integrate the Oslo and Paris conventions supplemented by protocols on offshore activities and land-based sources. A Ministerial Conference is planned for 1992 in France to adopt the revised treaty. HELCOM is seeking to add the precaution-

35. At the 1991 Commission meetings, OSCOM received Friends of the Earth, Seas at Risk, E&P Forum, and the International Association of Ports and Habors. PARCOM received Greenpeace, World Wildlife Fund, CONCAWE, and the Conseil Europeen des Federations de l'Industrie Chimique (CEFIC). HELCOM also received NGOs.
36. *European Chemical News*, 5 March 1990, 21.

ary principle and best available technology to its recommendations, as well as extending its coverage to internal waters in the convention area and authorizing pollution verification inspections. No effort is being made to coordinate HELCOM and PARCOM. While observers wonder about the future of OSPARCOM in an expanded EC (if all the OSPAR-COM members are EC members, what organizational justification is there for OSPARCOM?), OSPARCOM may serve as a smaller vanguard body in which leader countries can mobilize support for more stringent EC measures.

Domestic environmental concern has been an important factor in making international policy decisions and for subsequent national policy actions. Germany, Denmark, and Sweden are the countries where domestic green sentiment has been strongest for the longest period of time. Thus, these countries were some of the first to adopt strong domestic environmental policies and to press others to harmonize their policies with their more stringent ones. The upsurge in North Sea and Baltic activity after 1985 followed increases in public environmental concern throughout Europe. Green parties fared increasingly well in national and European Parliament elections. While such parties received relatively small shares of the total vote, in countries with coalition governments 5 to 7 percent of the vote can be extremely significant. Traditional parties responded to growing environmental concern as well by adding environmental planks to their platforms. Public opinion seemed to be associated with broad environmental issues such as Chernobyl or with very localized issues of industrial siting, rather than with issues of North Sea or Baltic water quality. Still, an expedient way for environment ministers and their governments to gain public approval was to undertake measures to control marine pollution—measures which remained relatively inexpensive compared to other, purely domestic environmental issues. Countries in which green parties fared most poorly in the mid-1980s, such as France and the United Kingdom, were the most recalcitrant at North Sea ministerial meetings.

It has been easier to take international and national policy decisions for substances for which states anticipate the cost of controls to be low, or for which technologies already exist. States' willingness to adopt OSCOM's dumping controls was facilitated by transferring to land-based options, which were already required in lead countries such as

Germany, and which were available in England at a relatively low cost. In Germany, industries have been instructed since 1977 to first search for land-based disposal options. The move to land-based incineration options greatly eased the elimination of offshore incineration because Germany accounted for a high percentage of hazardous wastes incinerated offshore. In the United Kingdom, one of the major dumpers, a total shift to onshore incineration would involve a maximum capital expenditure of 200 million pounds, with operating costs rising by about 50 million pounds annually.[37] Some of the most effective policy choices were adopted in areas for which technological options were already available at a fairly low cost. For instance, PARCOM's decisions banning the use of oil-based muds in drilling new oil and gas wells were greatly facilitated by the alternative of water-based muds.

While technological availability is important for getting some countries to support international decisions and to apply them at home, such decisions still have unanticipated effects on other laggard states who are encouraged over time to adopt more stringent measures than they may initially have intended. Moreover, while for each sector or substance many laggard countries may be relatively unaffected by the decisions, other laggard countries, including the United Kingdom and the countries of Eastern Europe, have subscribed to measures for which real adjustment costs will be required.

**National Policy Actions**

All countries have ratified the relevant treaties. Indeed, most have gone ahead and developed more stringent environmental measures for the substances regulated by OSPARCOM and HELCOM.

States have made extensive changes in their marine dumping practices. Virtually all offshore dumping and incineration has ceased or has been scheduled for termination. Germany eliminated offshore dumping of industrial wastes and offshore incineration. In the mid-1980s three vessels were used to incinerate wastes offshore in the North Sea; now only one operates. The Belgian *Vulcanus 2* stopped operations in

37. "The Ever-Widening Agenda for the North Sea Environment," *ENDS Report* 181 (February 1990): 14.

the late 1980s. Germany stopped issuing incineration permits in 1989 for the incineration vessel *Vesta*, and in February 1991 its license was canceled and the ship was converted into a chemical tanker, leaving only one vessel operational. The third vessel, the Belgian registered *Vulcanus 1* is scheduled for decommission by 1994, at which time virtually all European wastes will have to be disposed of on land, and Belgium continues to import wastes for incineration aboard the *Vulcanus 1*.[38]

Land-based regulations have also changed. Both leaders and laggards have changed national policies. A closer study of two of the more demanding policy outcomes revealingly demonstrates how international decisions led to changes in national practices through the interplay of international institutions and domestic demands for environmental protection.

Denmark was a leader in seeking to control nutrient pollution of the North Sea and the Baltic. Danish foreign environmental policy in this regard was driven by domestic and bureaucratic pressures, as unilateral Danish efforts would have had little impact on the quality of the seas. Denmark is responsible for only 10 percent of yearly nitrogen inputs into the Baltic (fifth ranked of the Baltic states), and 18 percent of phosphorus into the Baltic (ranked second).[39]

The Danish Environment Ministry staff had wanted an opportunity to regulate agricultural emissions since 1981, when fish kills were prominently covered by the media. The Environmental Protection Agency conducted a number of studies of the problem, suggesting strict enforcement of agricultural emissions of nitrogen and phosphorus. The Environment Ministry pushed Parliament to adopt a National Action Plan in 1987, calling for 50 percent cuts in nitrogen discharges and 80 percent cuts in phosphorus discharges by 1993, as well as developing a sophisticated comprehensive national monitoring system and demands for periodic reporting to determine if further governmental action was necessary. While Denmark was ruled by the conservative party which strongly supported agriculture, the government was a minority coalition

38. Third International Conference on the Protection of the North Sea, *The Implementation of the Ministerial Declaration of the Second International Conference on the Protection of the North Sea* (February 1990).
39. Swedish Environmental Protection Agency, *Marine Pollution '90–Action Programme*.

that required broader support, and had decided that it would not risk a confidence vote on environmental issues. The costs of such unilateral measures are estimated at 12 billion crowns from 1987 to 1995, as well as increased annual operating costs of 480 million crowns for municipal waste water treatment and industrial waste water treatment plants, an increase of 70 percent over the 1977 through 1985 average.[40]

Having adopted stringent domestic controls for nutrients, the Danish government moved to encourage international nutrient controls, in part to protect Danish agriculture and in part because much of the Danish eutrophication was believed to come through the Elbe River from Germany, and Germany appeared indifferent to controlling nutrients. While the Environmental Protection Agency had successfully introduced the National Action Plan, the international efforts bolstered the legitimacy of its efforts with regard to the Agricultural Ministry (which naturally opposed increased costs for farmers) as well as modifying the distributional consequences for Danish farmers. Denmark approached PARCOM and got it to approve a new Working Group on Nutrients, for which Denmark served as lead country. However, Spain and Portugal argued at PARCOM in 1987 that the problem was limited to the North Sea, and did not pertain to the broader North Atlantic region governed by PARCOM.[41] Denmark presented the issue to the Second North Sea Ministerial Conference, where it was approved and referred back to PARCOM for action. PARCOM reached decisions regulating nutrient emissions in 1988 and 1989. Denmark also submitted nutrients proposals to HELCOM, where Danish leverage over Germany was stronger because Germany could not ally with the EC states. In 1988 HELCOM adopted a decision to limit nutrient emissions.

Other countries have now adopted measures to control nutrient emissions as well. Belgium has increased the enforcement powers of local authorities for dealing with environmental issues, and has accelerated construction plans for sewage treatement facilities. Most actions involve

---

40. Ministry of the Environment, Denmark, *Environmental Impacts of Nutrient Emissions in Denmark* (Copenhagen: National Agency of Environmental Protection, 1991), 179–180. The 1987 Action Plan is also described in this document.
41. Paris Commission: Ninth Meeting of the Paris Commission, paragraph 5.58.

educating farmers, encouraging efficient manuring practices, better manure storage, attention to herd sizes, and the use of cover crops in winter.[42]

A second instance of change in land-based regulation at the national level is Sweden's efforts to control bleach from pulp and paper mills. In 1988 Sweden and Finland struck a bilateral arrangement for pulp and paper mill emissions in the Gulf of Bothnia.[43] Sweden then went on to promote standards for the North Sea and the Baltic.

Swedish efforts in PARCOM's Industrial Sectors Working Group were originally blocked. Sweden, as lead country, proposed chlorine emission standards for sulfate kraft mills of 2, 1, 1 according to AOX (Adsorbable Organic Halogen) measures: 2 kg/ton for sulfate softwood pulp, 1 kg/ton for sulfate hardwood pulp, and 1 kg/ton of sulfite hardwood and softwood pulp based on estimates of actual Swedish emissions.[44] Sweden, however, had already introduced domestic measures to reduce chlorine emissions to 1, 0.5, 0.5 by 1995 and 0.5, 0.3, 0.3 by the year 2000, at a total cost of about three billion crowns to the industry.

The Third North Sea Ministerial Conference in March 1990 adopted standards of 2, 1, 1, and the proposal was reintroduced to PARCOM for legal adoption. PARCOM in June 1990 actually adopted a lower figure of 1, 1, 1, as delegates got caught up in the heat of the exercise. France, Norway, and Portugal filed reservations because they wouldn't go below the 2, 1, 1 figure approved at the Third North Sea Ministerial Conference.[45]

---

42. Third International Conference on the Protection of the North Sea, *The Implementation of the Ministerial Declaration of the Second International Conference on the Protection of the North Sea* (February 1990). Greenpeace International, "Present Difficulties with 50% Reductions," Greenpeace Paper 29, Third North Sea Conference (1989). Greenpeace International released studies of policies taken by different governments, as well as efforts to regulate individual substances.
43. Ulla-Britta Fallenius, "Water Pollution Problems in the Finnish and Swedish Pulp and Paper Industry," Report 3443 (Solna, Sweden: Environmental Protection Board, September 1988).
44. Swedish Environmental Protection Agency, *Marine Pollution '90–Action Programme*, 27–28.
45. Convention for the Prevention of Marine Pollution from Land-Based Sources, "Twelfth Meeting of the Paris Commission," Rejkjavik, 1–14 June 1990, PARCOM 12/13/1-E p 5, Annex 5.

HELCOM also adopted a Swedish-led pulp and paper decision in 1990. The actual discharge values reflected a compromise between Sweden and Finland: Sweden wanted shorter time frames and lower limits than Finland. The final discharge limits were 2, 1, 1.4 kg/ton to reflect the capability of Finnish mills. While critics like Greenpeace contend that the best approach would be to ban the use of chlorine for pulp bleaching, the figures are still a significant cut below existing levels, with significant benefits for the environment.[46] While Sweden and Finland will be able to reach the new targets with existing technology, both countries still have to increase expenditures and accelerate investment programs in the pulp and paper industry. The laggard USSR was the big loser, and will probably have to entirely close down a number of older mills.

Other evidence exists for national support of international policy decisions. Sweden has adopted HELCOM's more stringent recommendations on oil content of refinery cooling water. Three of Sweden's four refineries introduced biological treatment of their waste water. Sweden has undertaken aggressive measures to reduce mercury pollution, including banning the sale of alkaline batteries with a mercury content greater than 0.025 percent. Mercuric acid batteries are to be banned by the year 2000. The Swedish chloralkali industry intends to replace mercury methods with mercury-free methods by 2010, with all plants examined by 1995 to enable the drawing up of conversion plans.[47] Denmark immediately applied HELCOM's 1985 standards for oil discharges from refineries.

National policy change is most evident in laggards, who of course had not yet adopted many of the institutional decisions. Finland is changing its forestry policy to encourage growing trees whose pulp requires less bleaching. The Belgian ministers of the environment and agriculture adopted the precautionary principle in May 1989.[48]

The United Kingdom was forced by the OSCOM procedures to can-

46. Baltic Marine Environment Protection Commission, "Activities of the Commission 1989," 35–37.
47. Swedish Environmental Protection Agency, *Marine Pollution '90–Action Programme*, 109, 123.
48. Folkert de Jong, "The Second International Conference on the Protection of the North Sea: National Implementation," *International Journal of Estuarine and Coastal Law* 5,1–3 (1990): 32–33.

cel many industrial dumping permits. In 1987 the British Ministry of Agriculture, Fisheries and Food (MAFF) awarded twenty full and ten standby licenses for liquid industrial waste. In late 1989 MAFF awarded four license renewals following the OSCOM-mandated prior justification procedure. Four of the North Sea states promptly lodged objections, and Greenpeace aired them in front of the media. One of the firms awarded a license withdrew its application, having located a land-based disposal option.[49] In February 1990, MAFF announced that all but two licenses for 207,000 metric tons of industrial wastes per year would be canceled by the end of 1992. ICI and Sterling Organics, the firms responsible for generating the wastes, are now building a 30-million-pound recycling facility and treatment plant.

Profound policy reappraisals were instigated by the emission cuts called for at the Ministerial Conferences. Many governments are now reappraising domestic measures in order to identify which sectors can easily reach the cuts and which will require assistance, or exclusions. Denmark, Sweden, Germany, the Netherlands, Norway, and Finland are all conducting such reappraisals, though few can yet demonstrate success at achieving widespread cuts in emissions of the targeted substances.

Eastern Europe and the USSR have adopted fewer policy changes than the Western European states. They lack the financial means to make the technological modifications to the antiquated state of much of their capital stock that will be necessary to bring their industry into compliance with international standards.

Monitoring others' actions has not been an important factor influencing states' actions. Few effective measures exist to verify states' adoption of international decisions. Direct studies of environmental quality, such as by OSPARCOM's Joint Monitoring Program and the North Sea Task Force, are not yet well established. Dumping activities are subject to national monitoring. Although individual countries conduct surveillance with airplanes, most coastal countries have only one or two planes allocated for such activities.[50]

49. "The Ever-Widening Agenda for the North Sea Environment" *ENDS Report* 181 February 1990, p. 13; *The Economist*, 3 March 1990, 55.
50. Ton IJlstra, "Enforcement of International Environmental Instruments in the North Sea: The Missing Link," in G. Peet (ed.), *The Status of the North Sea*

Reports on national policy measures and actual industrial practices are also scarce. Governments periodically submit standardized reports to PARCOM, OSCOM, and HELCOM about many of their activities subject to the commission's supervision. Such reporting is voluntary, though. Governments report to OSCOM the number of permits issued for dumping and incinerating wastes. In PARCOM, the United Kingdom, France, and Spain have been remiss in responding to questionnaires about industrial practices.[51] Baltic reports are very detailed, down to specifying emissions from individual factories.

Reporting is ultimately a voluntary system, but the incentives and pressures on individual technocrats to provide information to their colleagues in other countries are complex. Because many of the PARCOM delegates are middle-level technocrats, and because the PARCOM meetings have a certain clubby atmosphere, delegates exert a form of peer pressure on one another, which encourages them to press their own staffs at home to collect sufficient information for the reporting schemes.

**Institutional Effectiveness at Improving Environmental Quality**

North Sea and Baltic agendas grew from elaborating schedules and limit values for substances identified on the black and gray lists to identifying technological means for across-the-board cuts of those and more emissions from a variety of industrial sectors. Virtually all the issues that were on the original agendas of the black and gray lists were subsequently treated by OSCOM, PARCOM, and HELCOM. The lists of substances identified for 50 percent cuts at North Sea and Baltic Ministerial Conferences are more extensive than the original black and gray lists.

Both regions have progressed toward more aggressive control mechanisms, from setting weak limit values to forcing technological change. Many more decisions are in the works, as the approach is still fairly new. All marine dumping and offshore incineration has been eliminated. Many national efforts mirror international policies.

While studies of overall environmental quality in the North Sea and Baltic are not yet able to demonstrate overall trends, localized measures are available. National reports from the United Kingdom, Denmark, and Sweden indicate reduced concentrations of PCBs, PCTs, and DDT in fish—substances which were regulated under PARCOM. In the Baltic, DDT levels are sharply reduced and PCBs have fallen moderately. Some reductions in the formerly high levels of phosphorus and nitrogen concentrations have been observed. However, in the North Bothnian Bay, concentrations in fish of cadmium, zinc, and copper are still rising. Overall assessments have indicated that the Baltic as a whole is not endangered, and countries are now focusing on the causes of two hundred "hot spots" of localized pollution.[52]

Emissions of a number of specific substances into the regions have been reduced. Reported quantities of oil discharged into the Baltic from refineries fell by 62 percent from 1980 to 1990.[53] The volume of industrial wastes dumped in the North Sea fell from 7.2 million tons in 1976 to 5.8 million metric tons in 1986. By 1990 the United Kingdom remained the sole country engaged in marine dumping of industrial wastes: in 1988, 2.3 million tons of fly ash, liquid industrial wastes, and colliery wastes were dumped.[54] Titanium dioxide dumping in the North Sea fell by 42 percent from 1979 to 1989. Changes in national releases are presented in table 4.3 below. As one of OSPARCOM's few presentations of aggregated data, it reveals the general gaps in such data and indicates the general form in which it is made available.

Total discharges of oil from offshore installations fell by 24 percent from 1986 to 1989, due to a decrease in discharges from accidental spills and flaring operations in the United Kingdom, and dramatic de-

52. "Current Status of the Baltic Sea," *AMBIO* Special Report No. 7 (September 1990); Helsinki Commission Report, Baltic Sea Environment Proceedings No. 35A, Summary, and 35B, "Second Periodic Assessment of the State of the Marine Environment of the Baltic Sea."
53. Baltic Marine Environment Protection Commission, "Draft Progress Report on HELCOM Recommendation 6/2 Concerning Restriction of Discharge from Oil Refineries," TC Point 1/8/1.
54. Jon Birger Skjaerseth, "Towards the End of Dumping in the North Sea; An Example of Effective International Problem Solving?" mimeo, Oslo, 1991, 13 fn 32.

**Table 4.3**    Changes in North Sea titanium dioxide emissions, 1979–1989

| Country | Dumping | Land-based discharges |
| --- | --- | --- |
| Belgium | −60% | i. |
| Denmark | n.p. | n.p. |
| France | i | +20% |
| Germany | −14% | i |
| Netherlands | i | +2% |
| Norway | i | −80% |
| Portugal | n.p. | n.p. |
| Spain | +58% | n.i. |
| Sweden | n.p. | n.p. |
| United Kingdom | i. | −20% |

i–insignificant dumping
n.i.–no information
n.p.–no titanium dioxide produced

Source: Convention for the Prevention of Marine Pollution from Land-Based Sources, "Thirteenth Meeting of the Paris Commission The Hague 17–20 June 1991," PARCOM 13/6/1-3, Annexes 1 and 2.

creases in discharges of oil-contaminated cuttings from offshore oil plat-forms in the Netherlands (off by 87 percent) and Norway (off by 53 percent).[55]

Relatively nonpartisan observers concur that the North Sea efforts have led to moderate successes at containing marine pollution.[56] Finland concluded that "the state of the Baltic Sea today is definitively better than it would have been without the many efforts and concrete . . . measures by the Baltic Sea States."[57]

While the North Sea and Baltic institutions had little to do with the static phases of regional environmental protection at particular points in time, the institutions had much more to do with the improved effec-

55. Triennial Report of Discharges from Offshore Exploration and Exploitation Installations in 1989, PARCOM 13/4/7-3, 2.
56. Jorgen Wettestad and Steinar Andresen, "The 'Effectiveness' of International Resource Cooperation: Some Preliminary Findings," Fridtjof Nansen Instit Report R:007-1991 (Oslo, 1991).
57. "Protection of the Marine Environment of the Baltic Sea," submitted by the Delegation of Finland to the CSCE meeting on Environmental Protection in the Mediterranean, Palma de Mallorca, October 1990, 5.

tiveness of regional efforts over time. The dramatic increase in regional activity since 1985 is a consequence of institutional change.

Before 1985 decisions were reached by a least-common-denominator process, because domestic pressures were not widespread and laggard countries could simply say no to anything they were not willing to apply at home. After the introduction of the Ministerial Conferences, and following changes in domestic environmental sentiments, it became much more difficult for laggards to say no, and a new dynamic institutional process of progressive improvements emerged. Leader countries were encouraged for reasons of economic competitiveness to promote their own standards for others. Laggards, given increased domestic environmental concern, found it increasingly difficult to say no, because ministers were encountering new accountability expectations at home. Moreover, environment ministers in laggard countries could benefit entrepreneurially by making stringent statements at international meetings which would not be possible domestically, where they would be squelched by their domestically stronger colleagues in other ministries.

Ministerial Conferences have made the delegates directly responsible to their populaces. The Ministerial Conferences became high-profile events, widely covered by the media, with great public expectations for significant decisions. Issues relegated to the back burner at OSPARCOM have moved to the front burner at the Ministerial Conferences. Institutional changes amplified domestic political influences on governments, compelling governments to adopt more ambitious agendas as well as to adopt and enforce more stringent control measures internationally and domestically.

The Ministerial Conferences received much wider public attention than OSPARCOM. In the face of growing environmental consciousness in Europe, the Ministerial Conferences provided a convenient forum for ministers to play to the home audience, and to bring home international decisions to compel their own governments to become more environmentally inclined. A 1990 ENDS report noted: "Environment Ministers [are] under pressure to provide a public demonstration of their green credentials. The greenest Minister will, by definition, be he or she who demands the earliest phase-out dates of the largest percentage reductions applicable to the longest possible list of chemicals or waste disposal practices. It is this political competition which has become a driving force for North Sea policy which was never in evidence when the matter was left to the Oslo and Paris Commissions.[58] Conversely, OSPARCOM was characterized by its clubby atmosphere, based on frequent interactions, often of the same individuals, who were insulated from public scrutiny. Information presented at the meetings was not circulated outside. Trust and familiarity bred inertia.

The consequence of this insitutional reform was the establishment of a moving standard for new factories over time. The institutions generate a common set of industrial practices with which new factories are expected to comply. As the standards are increasingly upgraded, new plants will be constructed according to the new technological possibilities. Indeed, thirty-one of the HELCOM decisions supersede prior decisions. Also, as institutions progressively foreclose discrete waste disposal options, companies are forced to search for alternative production procedures that will generate fewer wastes and contaminants.

Institutions had direct and indirect effects on changes in agenda setting, international policy decisions, and national actions. Institutions affected international policy decisions and national policy actions through the identification of new pollution control technologies and techniques by lead country reports. The discussions with industry engendered by international talks often alert governments to new possibilities. For instance, during the process of negotiating a HELCOM recommendation restricting discharges from the kraft pulp industry, Finland discovered that a reduced emission level of 1.4 kg of chlorine per metric ton of air-dry bleached kraft pulp was technically and economically feasible.

Institutions helped fashion additional side-payments for laggards without extensive domestic environmental concern. Promises of financial rewards attracted Eastern European states to support stronger international policy decisions.

The political costs of supporting international policy decisions in the North Sea for other laggards without strong domestic environmental concern were relatively slight. Countries like France could still offer reservations to international decisions it did not like, and neglect to sub-

58. "The Ever Widening Agenda for the North Sea Environment," *ENDS Report* 181/February 1990, 13.

mit reports about its national actions. Even so, with the broader growth of domestic concern among the laggards, it would have been politically unwise for France to appear as a blocking figure in environmental negotiations while hoping for cooperation from other countries on other issues. In short, as the number of laggards declined, the incentives for the remaining laggards to publicly oppose international decisions diminished as well.

National policy action has been indirectly affected by the information generated by the institutions about national policies and sources of pollution. Environmentalist groups in Denmark, Sweden, Germany, and the United Kingdom have used information made available to the institutions by national authorities to compel their own governments to comply more fully with international measures. For instance, Greenpeace used OSCOM data to embarrass the British government over dumping. Greenpeace prevented a ship belonging to U.K. National Power from dumping 500 metric tons of coal ash into the North Sea on 16 January 1990.[59] Since 1988, information has become much more widely available and less politically dangerous to circulate in Eastern Europe as well. Submitting information to the international institutions has also led laggard countries such as Poland to institute new domestic information-gathering measures, and to begin building the necessary new bureaucratic units.[60]

Institutional decisions also helped domestic groups to press their governments to enforce prior standards or accelerate the introduction of new measures. For instance, in the aftermath of the Second North Sea Ministerial Conference, West Germany moved up from 1992 to 1989 its compliance with new measures regulating nitrogen and phosphorus emissions from sewage treatment plants.[61]

The institutions often provided incentives for increased enforcement of existing measures or for the application of more stringent standards by licensing authorities over time. Many countries had already

59. *Keesing's Record of World Events* vol. 36, no. 2, 37293.
60. Piotr Kryzanowski, "Rules of Protection of Gulf Sea Waters in Poland in the Light of International Co-Operation within HELCOM," *Marine Pollution Bulletin* 23 (1991): 545–549.
61. "Germany to Cut Nutrient Pollution of North Sea," *New Scientist* 118 (30 June 1988), 39.

embarked on pollution reduction programs, in the form of granting emission permits from water boards or licensing boards, before the various institutional decisions and most environmental decisions were taken. Such decisions are generally taken at the municipal level, where authorities enjoy a high degree of autonomy from national authorities. Consequently, tracing compliance links to international standard-setting is difficult.

Still, as the local authorities periodically reissue licenses and permits subject to changing conditions and new information about tolerable emission levels or environmental concentrations, the internationally developed standards are applied at this stage.[62] Local decisions are also subject to local pressure, using the information obtained from the regional institutions. Because many staffs are relatively small (the U.S. Environmental Protection Agency is enormous in this regard) there is extensive reliance on standards applied elsewhere for choices for domestic standards.

Even so, such authorities often find it extremely difficult to compel industries to change their practices, or to effectively monitor or verify actual industrial and municipal practices. Offending firms are not faced with weighty fines, and appeal processes may last years. Effective leverage exsits more for the construction of new plants. For new projects the investment climate is often paramount, leading managers to agree much more readily to costly new environmental demands in order to get a new factory operational while the market is still favorable. Domestic environmental groups use the international commitments sustained at the Ministerial Conferences and through PARCOM and HELCOM to exercise such leverage.

Institutional overlap has also contributed to the progressive formulation and adoption of stronger measures to protect the environment. Lead countries have used the institutional overlap between OSPARCOM, HELCOM, and the Ministerial Conferences to break the EC's stranglehold on environmental agenda setting and international policy decisions in the regions. Lead countries deliberately use the linkages between PARCOM and HELCOM to promote their own preferences, as well as to circumvent the EC's conservative impact on outcomes. North

62. Interviews in Norway, Finland, Sweden (June, July 1991).

Sea countries that are members of the EC and desire stringent environmental measures first go to the North Sea institutions to drive a wedge into the EC decision-making process. North Sea and Baltic states (Sweden, Germany, Denmark) go to the insitution in which they think have a better chance before approaching the EC. Baltic Sea states go first to HELCOM, then to PARCOM, then to the EC. Ministerial Conferences helped to override objections in the Commissions. Having secured agreement in PARCOM it is easier to go to the EC, with a 75 percent majority already established. For example, although the EC delayed talks in PARCOM regarding three substances, over time lead countries have invoked this mechanism to upgrade the EC standards. The Third North Sea Ministerial Conference adopted Sweden's targets of .025 percent mercury content in alkaline batteries, which PARCOM promptly adopted in excess of the EC standards of 0.1 percent.

## Conclusion

Institutional changes in the Baltic and North seas led to altered incentives for states to set agendas, adopt international decisions, and take national action. With expanded public demands for action and increased visibility of government actions, leaders and laggards were faced with stronger inducements for effective environmental protection.

Institutional effectiveness in protecting the North Sea and Baltic from pollution built on the "three Cs" analyzed in this volume (see Introduction and Chapter 8) OSPARCOM, HELCOM, and the Ministerial Conferences increased governmental concern by making information available to environmentally active NGOs through their publications and by inviting NGOs as observers to recent meetings. The public nature of the Ministerial Conferences created opportunities to magnify domestic public pressures. The institutions enhanced the contractual environment by providing a forum where states could seek to make their disparate policies more commensurate. More important, though, the overlapping jurisdictions of the different organizations overwhelmed the conservative tendencies present in any individual body. The environmental and policy-monitoring data released by the organizations was useful to domestic groups which hold their own governments accountable for environmental protection by enabling such groups to assess their governments' performance in living up to public commitments. The institutions also helped increase national capacity in Eastern Europe.

For institutions to generate more effective environmental behavior, though, additional factors were necessary. The institutional analysis offered here is a contingent one. Increasing governmental concern by amplifying public pressure required relatively open societies in which information could be safely deployed against governments. Societies' abilities to exercise governmental pressure based on relatively technical information, and governments' abilities to respond to such pressures, also required a base level of national capacity to assess and publicize technical studies of the environment. The North Sea and Baltic institutions only encouraged greater environmental protection because of a concurrent change in domestic climates of opinion. The institution would not have been increasingly effective if there was no domestic constituency to whom the ministers could play. Still, changed domestic opinion alone is insufficient to explain the observed change in institutional effectiveness because, in the absence of the institutions, government leaders would have no way in which to respond to such pressures while assuring domestic industrial sectors that they would not be losing comparative advantage.

Claims about the institutional role in promoting environmental protection in the regions can be supported by a counterfactual consideration. Collective efforts proved more effective with the institutional mechanism than they would have in a reasonable counterfactual scenario in which decisions were confined to OSPARCOM or HELCOM without the accountability conferred by the Ministerial Conferences. Even with increasing domestic pressures on governments, without the high profile of the ministerial meetings, talks would have persisted out of the limelight in PARCOM, where entrepreneurial environment ministers from laggard countries would have lacked the opportunity for grandstanding and playing green. Without the high-profile ministerial meetings to focus the domestic pressures on governments, environmental ministries would have been unable to compel more powerful agricultural and industrial ministries to introduce environmental control measures, and few countries would have been willing to undertake measures without guarantees of reciprocity from others. Institutions also provided side-payments for laggards for whom the cost of domestic embarrassment was not high or compelling. There would still have been fewer and weaker coordinated efforts without even the minimum of OSPARCOM or HELCOM.

These efforts remain open to criticism. The Organization for Economic Development and Cooperation criticized HELCOM for its focusing excessively on pollution control instead of heeding contending needs and uses of the Baltic Sea by taking an integrated approach to resource management.[63] PARCOM delegates now express similar concerns about the North Sea, where a concern with preserving the quality of the marine environment has increased pressures for land disposal of hazardous wastes (which may be more hazardous to public health), and focused in an ad hoc manner on individual threats to the sea, without formulating an alternative, comprehensive approach to guide industries in the choice of appropriate technologies. It remains unclear whether the across-the-board cuts introduced in 1987 are efficient ways to improve environmental quality, or even if such cuts are necessary for many of the substances for which they are demanded.

It is hard to imagine that the institutions could have done any better. Other arrays of forces which would have been likely to contribute to effective environmental cooperation were not present. No other environmental constituencies had access to governments; consequently, decisions were always driven by politicians' calculations of domestic political gain. Delegates commented that one "may win an argument, but won't change minds" and that "decisions are made by mustering votes, not by scientific argument." A 1984 Dutch study indicating that British pollutants were transported to other parts of the North Sea was denied by the United Kingdom. More comprehensive policies were not widely considered by governments because no constituencies promoted them.

Transnational networks of scientists, epistemic communities, and consensus scientific opinion, which have served as bases for comprehen-

63. OECD Environment Directorate, "Review of the Effectiveness of the Helsinki Convention as a Tool for Integrated Coastal Resources Management," February 1990.

sive policy making in other settings, were all absent.[64] Scientists play only a minor role in these regions. Virtually no informal policy networks exist, and those that exist lack access to national administrations. Most applied marine science is conducted in government laboratories. When governments assign experts to international working groups, the scientists are generally chosen from these government bodies and are accountable to the relevant ministries.

Few nonpartisan sources of scientific information existed. The scientific community does not actively engage in policy work, nor is its work widely circulated, although it does make it into the media. Regional scientific culture further proscribed most scientists' involvement. Career advancement resulted from brief research projects on specific substances rather than the sustained monitoring programs supported by the institutions. "Data isn't science," scoffed the director of a prominent marine research institute; and the Baltic Marine Biologists, composed of marine biologists from all seven Baltic states, limits most of its attention to harmonizing laboratory and monitoring techniques. No tradition of policy-oriented scientists exists as in the United States. Science policy activism has been limited to a few isolated scientists publicizing their findings, largely on fish diseases.

Scientifically derived agendas would have been unlikely. Research agendas were controlled by governments. Most monitoring and research is conducted by national laboratories. Initial monitoring was limited to familiar substances, and subsequent international monitoring projects have generally been a reflection of national monitoring measures. Parameters and techniques and substances are limited to those with which national laboratories were familiar, or for which they were already obligated to monitor by national environmental law.

Research and monitoring activities also reflected a disciplinary orientation toward fishery interests. Fisheries scientists were initially consulted for advice by ICES and by most governments. Consequently,

64. See Peter M. Haas, *Saving the Mediterranean: The Politics of International Environmental Cooperation* (New York: Columbia University Press, 1990); Peter M. Haas, "Save the Seas," in Elizabeth Mann Borgese et al. (eds.), *Ocean Yearbook 9* (Chicago: University of Chicago Press, 1991); Ernst B. Haas, *When Knowledge is Power* (Berkeley: University of California Press, 1990).

research and policy efforts have focused on contaminants associated with fishery yields, rather than on protection of ecosystems. Univariate models rather than ecosystemic models were applied, and potential contaminants, such as nutrients, tended to be neglected along with more exotic metals for which no studies on fish diseases existed.

The North Sea and Baltic arrangements for controlling regional pollution are likely to persist. Feedback from institutionalized environmental monitoring programs provide the input for NGOs and environmental movements to supervise their governments' activities. Continuing high-level international meetings provide a forum for domestic groups to assess their governments' activities. Institutional monitoring provides a source of data for identifying new pollution control technologies and circulating information about them. Absent a dramatic decline in public environmental concern, the North Sea and Baltic institutions are well designed to amplify domestic environmental concern at an international level and to guide governments to adopt effective measures for regional pollution control.

# 5

# Intentional Oil Pollution of the Oceans

Ronald Mitchell

Mention oil pollution and most people conjure up images of accidents like the *Exxon Valdez*.[1] Yet the intentional discharge of oil during tanker operations has consistently overshadowed accidents as the major source of the ship-related oil pollution that soils beaches and oils seabirds (see table 5.1).[2] Indeed, for more than six decades, nations have sought international regulations to address this problem. Yet only in the last decade and a half has oil entering the ocean from tanker operations begun to decrease. This raises two questions. First, can we attribute recent progress in reducing oil pollution to these international efforts? Second, if so, what components of these efforts account for their success?

This chapter answers these questions by arguing that international regulations to control intentional discharges of oil at sea have had re-

I am grateful for research funding to the Center for International Affairs, the Harvard MacArthur Scholarships in International Security, and the Eisenhower World Affairs Institute. I am also grateful for travel funding provided through the Center for International Affairs by the Delegation of the Commission of the European Communities, and by the Rockefeller Brothers Fund. Personnel at the International Maritime Organization and the U.S. Coast Guard provided me with invaluable assistance. I would like to thank Antonia Chayes, Gail Osherenko, Oran Young, Mark Zacher, and the authors and editors of this volume for helpful comments on previous drafts of this paper. The work was conducted at the Center for International Affairs, Harvard University.

1. The *Exxon Valdez* spilled 35,000 tons of oil into Prince William Sound, Alaska on 24 March 1989.
2. See National Academy of Sciences, *Petroleum in the Marine Environment* (Washington, D.C.: National Academy of Sciences, 1975); National Academy of Sciences and National Research Council, *Oil in the Sea: Inputs, Fates and Effects* (Washington, D.C.: National Academy Press, 1985); and MEPC 30/INF.13 (19 September, 1990) (All subsequent document citations refer to IMCO documents.)

cent, if limited, success. Success has depended on strong concern and pressure from the United States supported by increased concern among other countries. By providing an ongoing diplomatic forum, however, the Inter-Governmental Maritime Consultative Organization (IMCO) and its successor the International Maritime Organization (IMO) have, since the 1970s, facilitated the transformation of this concern into global agreements and has established effective equipment standards that have removed practical and legal barriers that impeded enforcement of earlier agreements. Expert assessments suggest that oil discharges have decreased even after accounting for a simultaneous reduction in seaborne oil trade, and, while oil price increases have caused some of the reduced discharge levels, the price increases do not explain the techniques adopted by industry (see figures 5.1 through 5.3).[3] To fully explain recent progress, we must acknowledge the role of international conventions in 1973 and 1978 which supplemented essentially un-

3. Sources for figure 5.1: David W. Abecassis, *The Law and Practice Relating to Oil Pollution from Ships* (London: Butterworth and Co., 1978); G. Boos, "Revision of the International Convention on Oil Pollution," in *International Conference on Oil Pollution of the Sea*, (Rome, 1968); GESAMP (IMCO/FAO/UNESCO/WMO/WHO/IAEA/UN Joint Group of Experts on the Scientific Aspects of Marine Pollution), *Impact of Oil on the Marine Environment* (Rome: Food and Agriculture Organization, 1977); International Conference on Pollution of the Sea by Oil, "General Committee: Minutes of 5th Meeting Held on 5 May 1954" (1954); J. H. Kirby, "The Clean Seas Code: A Practical Cure of Operational Pollution," in *International Conference on Oil Pollution of the* · *Sea* (Rome, 1968); MEPC 30/INF.13; Arthur McKenzie, "Letter to the Honorable John L. Burton," in House Committee on Government Operations, *Oil Tanker Pollution—Hearings*, 95th Congress, 2nd session, House 401-8 (Washington, D.C.: GPO, 1978); James E. Moss, "Character and Control of Sea Pollution by Oil" (Washington, D.C.: American Petroleum Institute, 1963); National Academy of Sciences, *Petroleum in the Marine Environment* (Washington, D.C.: National Academy of Sciences, 1975); National Academy of Sciences, and National Research Council, *Oil in the Sea*; J. D. Porricelli, V. F. Keith, and R. L. Storch, *Tankers and the Ecology* (New York, N.Y.: Society of Naval Architects and Marine Engineers, 1971); Sonia Zaide Pritchard, "Load on Top: From the Sublime to the Absurd," *Journal of Maritime Law and Commerce* 9 (1978); Y. Sasamura, *Petroleum in the Marine Environment: Inputs of Petroleum Hydrocarbon Into the Ocean Due to Marine Transportation Activities* (London: IMCO, 1981); Study of Critical Environmental Problems, *Man's Impact on the Global Environment: Assessment and Recommendations for Action* (Cambridge, Mass.: The MIT Press, 1970); J. Wardley-Smith, ed., *The Control of Oil Pollution*, rev. ed. (London: Graham and Trotman Publishers, 1983). Source for figure 5.2: Gilbert Jenkins, *Oil Economists' Handbook* (New York, N.Y.: Applied Science Publishers, 1990).

enforceable performance standards—limiting where and how tankers could discharge oil—with easy-to-verify equipment standards that required installation of equipment that eliminated the need for such discharges. Compliance with these rules, rather than economic factors, explain why so many tanker owners have so quickly adopted certain expensive, in some cases non-cost-effective, oil retention technologies. Unfortunately, while international rules have changed industry behavior, they have had little influence on government behavior. In addition, the extended phase-in period for equipment requirements, continued illegal discharges by some tankers, and the lack of successful control of land-based sources of oil most likely account for the continuing environmental damage by oil to birds and beaches.

Even this limited success is not strictly due to the institution, how-

**Table 5.1**  Input of oil into the sea

|  | Year of estimate: | | |
|---|---|---|---|
|  | 1971 | 1980 | 1989 |
|  | (million metric tonnes per year) | | |
| Transportation |  |  |  |
| Tanker operations | 1.080 | 0.700 | 0.159 |
| Dry-docking | 0.250 | 0.030 | 0.004 |
| Terminal operations | 0.003 | 0.020 | 0.030 |
| Bilge and fuel oils | 0.500 | 0.300 | 0.253 |
| Accidents | 0.300 | 0.420 | 0.121 |
| Scrappings | No est. | No est. | 0.003 |
| Combination carriers |  |  |  |
| Subtotal | 2.133 | 1.470 | 0.569 |
| Offshore production | 0.080 | 0.050 | No est. |
| Municipal and industrial wastes and runoff | 2.700 | 1.180 | No est. |
| Natural sources | 0.600 | 0.250 | No est. |
| Atmosphere-emissions fallout | 0.600 | 0.300 | No est. |
| Total | 6.113 | 3.250 | 0.569 |
| Discharges from tanker operations | 1.080 | 0.700 | 0.159 |
| Crude traded (mta) | 1100.0 | 1319.3 | 1097.0 |
| Discharges as percent of crude trade | 0.0982% | 0.0531% | 0.0145% |

Sources: National Academy of Sciences, 1975, 1985, 1990.

ever. These rule changes depended on deeper changes in the interests of the governments negotiating the agreements. Efforts to control discharges failed for decades because concern over the problem was neither sufficiently strong nor widespread. While they might have, international efforts have not played a major role in increasing understanding or concern over the oil pollution problem. Support for strong rules required changes in three factors. First, growing environmentalism led the U.S. government to champion more stringent measures than had previously been considered, backing their proposals with threats of unilateral action. Second, European states increased their support for strong measures in the face of similar public concern evoked by several major tanker accidents. Third, the many developing countries who joined IMO in the early 1970s supported these measures, either out of environmental concern or to increase jurisdictional power in the linked Law of the Sea negotiations. Only this combination of factors allowed concerned governments to overcome the resistance of the oil and shipping interests, and the maritime governments which supported them, to get agreement on the expensive but effective equipment requirements necessary to reduce intentional discharges.

This chapter examines the various efforts to achieve international regulation of operational, or intentional, oil pollution.[4] While many analysts essentially ignore the "unsuccessful" efforts before 1973,[5] this author reviews the various attempts at regulation beginning with those made in the 1920s and extending through the most recent amendments, in order to better demonstrate the conditions that explain why oil pollution control has succeeded or failed. The chapter begins by describing the intentional oil pollution problem. It delineates the actors involved in the bargaining over international oil pollution control and describes how changes to their interests and power have altered the nature of the

---

4. I will use the terms intentional discharges and operational discharges interchangeably. The point is to distinguish them from accidental oil spills.
5. For example, see Jeff B. Curtis, "Vessel-source Oil Pollution and MARPOL 73/78: An International Success Story?" *Environmental Law* 15 (Summer 1985); and Alan B. Sielen and Robert J. McManus, "IMCO and the Politics of Ship Pollution," in David A. Kay and Harold K. Jacobson, eds., *Environmental Protection: The International Dimension*, (Totowa, N. J.: Allanheld, Osmun & Co., 1983).

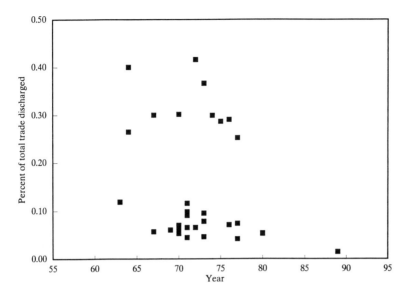

**Figure 5.1**
Discharge as percent of crude trade
Sources: various (see note 3).

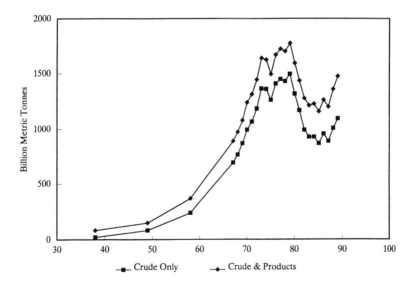

**Figure 5.2**
World seaborne trade
Source: BP Statistical Review.

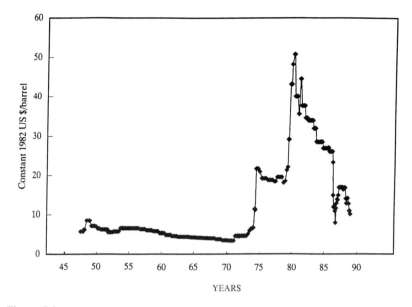

**Figure 5.3**
World crude oil prices
Source: *Oil Economists' Handbook*, 1990.

international bargain over time. I then describe the history of international oil pollution control by breaking it into three periods: the 1920s until 1954, during which efforts failed to produce signed agreements; 1954 through 1967, during which signed agreements failed to change industry behavior; and 1967 through the present, during which intentional discharges have begun to decrease. This history develops the evidence for the subsequent analysis of agenda setting for, international policies on, and industrial and national policy responses to, intentional oil pollution regulation. This section is followed by conclusions regarding the overall effectiveness of international oil pollution control and some lessons for other international environmental institutions.

Intentional oil pollution arises from deliberate discharge into the ocean of oil-water mixtures produced during three processes of oil transport. First, tankers have historically filled cargo tanks with sea water ballast to remain seaworthy when returning from a delivery. Second, tankers often used water to clean their tanks before receiving more oil. Third, oil and lubricants leak into all ships' bilges and mix with seawater. Captains have traditionally discharged the oil-water mixtures from all three processes at sea prior to arrival in port. These discharges are not essential to the oil transportation process, but arise because the cost of recovering the oil exceeds the value of the oil recovered.

Historically, these procedures have put close to a million tons of oil into the world's oceans each year. They represent 60 to 70 percent of all ship-generated oil pollution, with accidents and non-tankers making up the rest. But ship-generated oil represents only a third of all oil entering the oceans, with the rest due to land-based sources, natural seeps, and offshore production. Thus, operational discharges are responsible for only some 20 percent of all ocean oil pollution. These discharges, while they do not persist indefinitely, as believed by the United States and Britain in the 1920s, can remain afloat over long distances. Indeed, the maximum distance that oil can travel before evaporating or being broken down by bacteria depends on numerous factors, and has never been conclusively determined. The inherently international nature of the oil transportation market and the fact that a single tanker can discharge oil that pollutes the resorts and kills the seabirds of numerous countries, has produced frequent calls for international regulation.

Three solutions to the problem have been considered: banning oil-water discharges in zones close to shore, banning oil-water discharges oceanwide, and requiring equipment which reduced the oil-water mixtures created. Zones of 50 to 100 miles inside of which discharges were prohibited by early agreements have reflected low levels of concern rather than scientific assessments of the distance beyond which discharges would not cause coastal pollution. Leader states, like the United Kingdom, saw zones as an ineffective but acceptable initial compromise to demonstrate international commitment to action and to start a process, while states unconcerned about pollution accepted zones to avert activist states from unilaterally creating a patchwork of rules impairing their ships' involvement in oil transportation markets. The subsequent adoption of oceanwide bans and equipment requirements reflected the recognition that, at least in some circumstances, discharges made outside 50- to 100-mile zones could still harm the coastal environment.

## Domestic Concern and International Bargains

An international environmental problem consists not only of an environmental harm, but also of the political barriers to its mitigation. Thus, before examining the history of international efforts to regulate oil pollution, it will help to examine the factors influencing the interests of parties to the international bargain and the obstacles that impeded the growth of international concern. Effectively, international negotiations have involved an ongoing three-way bargain between national governments, their domestic publics and environmental nongovernmental organizations (NGOs), and the international oil and shipping industries. It has been a negotiation between people concerned about the effects on birds and resorts of coastal oil pollution, the maritime and oil interests for whom discharging oil at sea was cheaper than alternatives, and the governments mediating between these two groups.

What obstacles, prior to the 1970s, prevented the international bargain necessary to successfully eliminate coastal oil pollution? The largest impediment has been an absence of sufficient concern, indeed an absence of a perception that a bargain needed to be struck. It has not been insufficient knowledge of oil's impacts or uncertainty regarding the sources of the oil. The primary impacts of oil that drive public concern—dead seabirds and oiled beaches—have always been highly visible and scientists have found no evidence that oil spills "have unalterably changed the world's oceans or marine resources," which, if found, might have provided the impetus for quick and dramatic international action.[6] There has also been little contention over the major con-

---

6. National Academy of Sciences, and National Research Council, *Oil in the Sea*, 489. Even major accidental pollution from oil spills seems to have only limited, nonpermanent environmental effects. As a 1990 study noted, oil "continues to be a matter of concern locally after accidents have released large amounts of oil that accumulate in sheltered areas, affecting amenity and living resources, especially bird life. While the damage is not irreversible, recovery can be slow"; GESAMP (IMO/FAO/UNESCO/WMO/WHO/IAEA/UN/ UNEP Joint Group of Experts on the Scientific Aspects of Marine Pollution), *The State of the Marine Environment* (New York, N.Y.: United Nations, 1990), 2. For other examples, see Second International Conference on the Protection of the North Sea, *Quality Status of the North Sea* (London: Her Majesty's Stationery Office, 1987), 72–73; United Kingdom, Royal Commission On Environmental Pollution, *Eighth Report: Oil Pollution of the Sea* (London: Her Majesty's Stationery

tribution of intentional discharges to coastal oil pollution. Nations have neither lacked the capacity to adopt, nor been ignorant of, techniques and technologies which could immediately and effectively have eliminated the problem. States have also not found it difficult to make agreements; indeed, states have regularly drafted agreements to control oil pollution since the 1920s. Rather, the major obstacle until the 1970s to the strong international action needed to eliminate coastal oil pollution has been a lack of adequate concern—a lack of widespread concern in the majority of states and a lack of sufficiently deep concern in powerful states—to lead to their proposing strong action and pressuring reluctant states to support them.

At least three obstacles have hindered development of the international concern necessary for strong international action.[7] The first has been lack of concern among domestic publics. In the United Kingdom from the 1920s to the 1960s, bird protection societies pressed the government for regulations to halt coastal pollution. In the United States, environmentalist groups in both the 1920s and the 1970s conducted letter-writing and lobbying campaigns to raise the salience of the issue. After the 1967 *Torrey Canyon* disaster, growing tanker traffic due to increased imports, widespread media coverage of oil tanker accidents, and increased environmentalism also helped strengthen public concern and calls for international action in Europe and the United States. In contrast, states with little oil pollution, like Germany and the Netherlands during the 1920s, and developing states more recently, have shown little interest in international action except if it protected the access of domestic shipping interests to the U.S. market. Essentially, until the 1970s, most governments did not feel an oil pollution problem existed that needed an international solution.

A second obstacle has been that, even when domestic calls for action

---

Office, 1981), 38, 46–49, 266; and J. M. Baker, *Impact of Oil Pollution on Living Resources* (Gland, Switzerland: International Union for Conservation of Nature and Natural Resources, 1983), 40.
7. The following discussions draw extensively on Sonia Zaide Pritchard, *Oil Pollution Control* (London: Croom Helm, 1987); United Kingdom Ministry of Transport, *Report of the Committee on the Prevention of Pollution of the Sea by Oil* (London: Her Majesty's Stationery Office, 1953); and R. Michael M'Gonigle and Mark W. Zacher, *Pollution, Politics, and International Law: Tankers at Sea* (Berkeley: University of California Press, 1979).

have been loud, a government's international support for strong measures depended on the level of opposition from domestic oil and shipping concerns.[8] Oil companies have initially resisted any regulation, but have supported international negotiation to avert the competitive disadvantage inherent in unilateral regulation while simultaneously weakening the stringency of regulation. In the 1950s and 1960s, cross-cutting pressures meant that an international conference allowed Britain to placate environmental critics while using the resistance of other states to achieve less stringent internationally agreed rules that would be more palatable to domestic industry than unilateral laws.[9] Likewise, the French and Danish had reported serious coastal pollution as early as the 1950s but opposed the 1973 SBT requirements out of deference to their shipping industries' concern at the expense involved and their shipbuilding industries' concern that tanker buyers would defer new orders.[10] However, by the 1950s, enough states had domestic pollution concerns that they felt the necessity to take some initial international steps and that they could convince oil and shipping interests, and the states representing them, to accept some no-cost pollution controls to avoid patchwork unilateral legislation. However, when efforts to impose real costs on industry began to emerge in 1962, the industry quickly showed its power both to ignore existing regulations and to demand less costly rules.

The third obstacle to effective international regulation has been the difficulty of developing a coalition of states willing to support strong international action. Increased concern in the 1970s in part reflected a much larger problem: even if each tanker discharged a smaller fraction of cargo than previously, the problem would have increased as seaborne

8. Oil is shipped by sea in tankers owned by oil companies and in tankers owned by independent shipping companies from which oil companies charter. The interests of the shipping and oil industries frequently converge with respect to oil pollution regulations. However, the larger size and higher visibility of oil companies makes them more susceptible to public political pressure than small (sometimes single-ship) independent companies.
9. Pritchard, *Oil Pollution Control*, 75. See also U.K. Ministry of Transport, *Report of the Committee*, 37.
10. See United Nations Secretariat, *Pollution of the Sea by Oil* (New York, N.Y.: United Nations, 1956); and IMCO, *Pollution of the Sea by Oil* (London: IMCO, 1964) for state positions regarding oil pollution during the 1950s and 1960s. See also M'Gonigle and Zacher, *Pollution, Politics, and International Law*, 86, 90, 114.

oil trade went from 84 million tons per year in 1938, to 264 in 1954, to 1695 in 1973. Through a combination of policy compromise and diplomatic pressures, the United Kingdom in 1954 and 1962, and the United States in 1973 and 1978, succeeded in building coalitions willing to support international controls. Only in 1973 and 1978, however, was concern deep enough in the activist state, and sufficiently widespread in other countries, that nations agreed to effective international rules. Under environmentalist pressures at home, the United States threatened strong unilateral action if other states did not agree to international regulation. While it made compromises to its initial stringent proposals, these nonetheless pushed many states well beyond what they would have legislated on their own. The ranks of IMCO willing to support effective oil pollution control had also swelled to include new developing countries, many of whom had little domestic experience of, or concern over, oil pollution, but supported strong controls because they expected few direct costs from such regulation and hoped that pollution control would help establish jurisdictional precedents favorable to their interests in the Law of the Sea negotiations. Developed states lacking strong oil and shipping interests, like Canada, Australia, and New Zealand, also took environmentalist positions and supported the U.S. proposals. By 1973, these changes provided the votes needed to counter the power of maritime states and industry and pass international regulations that began to require real national and industrial policy responses.[11] While the shift took more than overnight, the political bargain was no longer weighted exclusively in favor of shipping interests. If, prior to the 1970s, industry had always dictated oil pollution policy, they now had to negotiate it.

## The History of International Regulation

### Unsigned Agreements: 1920–1954[12]
**The 1926 Draft Convention**   Oil pollution first became a problem in the 1920s, as ships began to use oil and gas, rather than coal, as fuels.

11. See M'Gonigle and Zacher, *Pollution, Politics, and International Law*, especially chapters 4 and 5, for an extended discussion of the changes in political bargaining at IMCO between 1954 and 1978.
12. This section draws heavily on Pritchard's detailed account of the early years of oil pollution regulation in her book *Oil Pollution Control*.

During the 1920s and 1930s most oil pollution came from the discharge of oil from the bilge and fuel tanks of such ships.[13] In the 1920s, the Royal Society for the Protection of Birds in the United Kingdom and the National Coast Anti-Pollution League in the United States lobbied legislators to regulate the increasing discharges evidenced in the growing numbers of oiled birds and soiled beaches.[14] Politicians also heard complaints from resorts and tourists, local authorities responsible for beach and harbor cleanup, and fire underwriters paying for fires in ports.[15] While oil pollution was not provoking widespread public concern, NGOs were vocal enough in the United States and United Kingdom to get the attention of governmental and industrial interests.[16]

Lobbied by such groups, many nations unilaterally restricted ship discharges near their ports. The United Kingdom passed the Oil in Navigable Waters Act in 1922, the United States passed the Oil Pollution Act of 1924, and other countries passed similar legislation.[17] The U.S. and British laws banned oil discharges within their three-mile territorial waters. It was these two main shipping countries that drove most international action on oil pollution. The U.S. governmental committee formed to investigate the oil pollution problem worked closely with the British government to develop practical, economical solutions before calling an international conference on oil pollution.[18]

The United States convened the conference in 1926 with the goal of eliminating intentional discharges of oil. Delegates from thirteen countries attended. While most nations faced no significant oil pollution problems at home, agreement would avert diverse unilateral rules, especially growing claims of extended territorial seas with their implications far beyond the issue of oil pollution.[19] As discussed above, positions reflected the interplay of shipping and environmental concerns as well

13. As noted later, as oil moved by sea increased, so did the discharges from cargo tank cleaning and ballasting.
14. Pritchard, *Oil Pollution Control*, 12–13.
15. U.K. Ministry of Transport, *Report of the Committee*, 1. See also United Nations Secretariat, *Pollution of the Sea by Oil*.
16. Pritchard, *Oil Pollution Control*, 11.
17. Pritchard, *Oil Pollution Control*, 25–30, U.K. Ministry of Transport, *Report of the Committee*, 3.
18. Pritchard, *Oil Pollution Control*, 10.
19. Spain and Portugal banned discharges within six miles. Pritchard, *Oil Pollution Control*, 27–28.

as scientific perceptions of the problem. "The U.K., the U.S., Germany and the Netherlands were big shipping nations, but whereas Germany and the Netherlands had relatively short coasts, both the U.K. and the U.S. had long coasts which were exposed to oil pollution."[20] International action also held the promise of averting more stringent regulations which would harm shipping (especially British shipping) while quieting domestic environmental pressures.[21]

During the conference, a significant scientific debate arose over how long oil persisted in the ocean. The Dutch and Germans contended that biological processes eliminated oil quickly. The United States, United Kingdom, and Canada believed that crude, fuel and diesel oils persisted indefinitely. Thus, the United States sought to require that all oil-water mixtures be kept on board using expensive separators and then discharged into reception facilities in port. Given the resistance of other states to such measures, the conference debate turned to interim measures involving zones within which discharges would be restricted. While the United States proposed 500-mile zones, the final draft convention established 50-mile coastal zones within which discharges over 500 parts of oil per million parts of water (ppm) would be prohibited. A chart of the discharge provisions adopted is provided in table 5.2. Ships were to retain oil on board within these zones and discharge oil "slops" outside the zones or into reception facilities in ports. Neither the equipment for retaining slops on board nor reception facilities were required, however.[22]

In addition to their unilateral legislation, the United States threatened to ban from its ports those ships that violated the unsigned 1926 agreement. Within months of the convention, the British government responded with a request to its shipping industry to voluntarily comply. The latter in turn convinced the members from seven other countries in the major shipowners' trade organization, the International Chamber of Shipping, to adhere voluntarily to the zones established in the agree-

20. Jesper Grolin, "Environmental Hegemony, Maritime Community, and the Problem of Oil Tanker Pollution," in *North-South Perspectives on Marine Policy*, Michael A. Morris, ed., (Boulder, Colo.: Westview Press, 1988), 22.
21. Pritchard, *Oil Pollution Control*, 15.
22. The rules did require removal of economic disincentives to providing the on-board equipment, however. Such clauses have never been reinstated in subsequent agreements.

**Table 5.2**    Intentional oil pollution discharge standards, 1926 through present

| Convention date | Dates in force | Age of ship | Discharge limit within zones* | Discharge limit outside zones* | Maximum total discharge |
|---|---|---|---|---|---|
| 1926 | Never | All | < 500 ppm | None | None |
| 1935 | Never | All | < 500 ppm | None | None |
| 1954 | 1958–1967 | All | < 100 ppm | None | None |
| 1962 | 1967–1978 | Old | < 100 ppm | None | None |
| | | New | | < 100 ppm | None |
| | 1978–1983 | All | Clean ballast | < 100 ppm −60 1/m | < 1/15,000 tc |
| 1973/1978 | 1983–present | Old | < 15 ppm | < 60 1/m | < 1/15,000 tc |
| | | New | < 15 ppm | < 60 1/m | <1/15,000 tc |

\* = Zones of 50 miles plus special areas.
ppm = Parts per million.
1/m = Liters per mile.
tc = Total cargo capacity.

ment.[23] Pressures from countries advocating adoption of the convention faded as ships apparently complied with this voluntary agreement and with the unilateral U.S. and British legislation.[24] The United States also had new scientific tests which convinced it that oil did not persist indefinitely. In light of these factors and the continued strong resistance of some countries, especially Germany, the agreement was never adopted.

**The 1935 Draft Convention**    By the 1930s, most experts believed that "the problem was less severe than a decade ago."[25] However, continued pressure by British environmentalists, who saw the zone system as inadequate, led the British to reinitiate international efforts at oil pollution regulation. Caught between a strong environmental lobby and a

23. Pritchard, *Oil Pollution Control*, 202–3.
24. Pritchard, *Oil Pollution Control*, 39. Indeed, the major U.S. anti–oil pollution group disbanded shortly after the U.S. Oil Pollution Act of 1924 was passed. Pritchard, *Oil Pollution Control*, 12.
25. Pritchard, *Oil Pollution Control*, 51.

strong shipping industry, the British asked a League of Nations' Committee of Experts in 1934 to draft a new version of the 1926 accord.[26] A survey by the committee showed that most countries still had little direct experience of serious oil pollution. There also remained considerable scientific uncertainty about how persistent oil was and how far it would float from the point of discharge. But the panel concluded that international action was nonetheless desirable.[27]

The League's redrafting built on the 1926 negotiation. The discharge limit of 500 ppm was retained, although the zones could be expanded from 50 to 150 miles. Extensive discussions took place over requiring ships to install the oily-water separators which the United States had initially proposed in 1926. While retrofitting existing ships received little support, eighteen of twenty-eight countries supported requiring separators on new ships. However, that eighteen countries did not include the United States and United Kingdom, without whose support any agreement would fail. For the Americans, an apparent reduction in coastal pollution due to shipowners' voluntary compliance with the 1926 agreement supported the view that zones were proving effective and equipment requirements were unnecessary.[28] The contradiction between British support for international agreement but lack of support for equipment requirements illustrated their conscious use of the international negotiations to quell domestic environmental concerns without imposing significant costs on their own shipping industry.[29] A requirement that ports provide reception facilities for oil (essential to effective use of retention on board) was discussed but replaced with a recommendation because of the resistance of the United States and other countries and the acknowledged unlikeliness of compliance: only seven of thirty-four countries had port reception facilities at the time.[30]

26. Pritchard, *Oil Pollution Control*, 48. One British politician commented at the time, "We would welcome international action . . . to still the protests of the bird societies and to safeguard our mercantile marine from the risk of suddenly being subjected to arbitrary and possibly ill-advised or unworkable rules which . . . other countr[ies] might seek to impose upon foreign shipping" (Geoffrey Thompson in Pritchard, *Oil Pollution Control*, 44).
27. Pritchard, *Oil Pollution Control*, 52.
28. Pritchard, *Oil Pollution Control*, 200.
29. Pritchard, *Oil Pollution Control*, 48.
30. Pritchard, *Oil Pollution Control*, 53, 60–61.

Three attempts to improve enforcement were also made. The French proposed that coastal states rather than flag states (the state of a ship's registry) be given exclusive jurisdiction to prosecute treaty violations. While this proposal failed, two other efforts succeeded. States were required to impose fines severe enough to discourage violations. And, "ship masters would be required to enter into the ship's log all incidents involving the discharge of oil".[31] Each of these discussions foreshadowed debates that would recur in subsequent negotiations.

The League Committee of Experts completed the draft treaty in 1935 and received "overwhelmingly favorable" responses.[32] Most countries were ready to attend a planned signing conference. Indeed, U.S. interest in oil pollution control, which had abated during the late 1920s and early 1930s, revived after a spate of accidental spills. As they had in 1924, the Americans took unilateral action. Congress passed the 1936 Tank Vessel Act with "stricter construction and operational standards for American tankers."[33] The U.S. State Department also succeeded in getting American and British shipowners to expand their voluntary adherence to the 1926 agreement to 100 miles around U.S. coasts.[34] While the British were the major maritime state pushing the League draft agreement, their ambivalent stance—seeking to placate domestic environmentalists without hindering their shipping industry—led them to balk at convening a conference that looked doomed to failure given German, Italian, and Japanese resistance.[35] Oil pollution got pushed off the international agenda as German expansion and World War II loomed on the horizon. The planned conference was never held and the draft treaty was never signed.

Despite their failure to achieve agreement, these international efforts induced some response by industry. Seven nations' shipping interests did, under governmental pressure, "volunteer" to discharge outside 50-mile zones. Of course, since the treaties never entered into force, enforcement was impossible, and no data on compliance is available.

31. Pritchard, *Oil Pollution Control*, 57. Why negotiators expected shipmasters to log self-incriminating information is unclear, however.
32. Pritchard, *Oil Pollution Control*, 60.
33. Pritchard, *Oil Pollution Control*, 62.
34. U.K. Ministry of Transport, *Report of the Committee*, 4.
35. Pritchard, *Oil Pollution Control*, 70.

However, oil pollution along the U.S. coast decreased enough to defuse U.S. pressures for international action. In part, this was due to ship-building improvements that had the environmental side benefit of reducing leakage and oil clingage.[36] The combination of reduced U.S. pressure and continued British pressure suggests that tankers complied with the voluntary agreement when it was cheap and easy and violated it when it was not. Thus, en route to the United States, discharging wastes in the mid-Atlantic outside U.S. zones involved few costs. In contrast, en route to European states, tankers would have needed to swing far outside normal routes to comply. They proved unwilling to incur the corresponding costs of delays and extra fuel, and the United Kingdom's pollution problem remained unabated.[37]

**Signed but Ineffective Agreements: 1954–1967**[38]
**The 1954 International Convention for the Prevention of Pollution of the Sea by Oil**   While efforts prior to World War II failed to achieve any signed agreements, the draft agreements shaped the negotiations that arose after the war. The oil pollution problem had changed since before the war. Before the war, oil discharges were mainly from the bilges and deballasting of the fuel tanks of non-tankers. After the war, growing demand for crude oil, shipped from the Middle East but refined in Western countries, meant that more tankers were discharging the more persistent crude (verse refined) oils after tank cleaning and ballast operations.[39] Complaints of spoiled beach resorts and of large numbers of dead sea birds grew rapidly in the United Kingdom and elsewhere in Europe.[40] The United Kingdom continued to lead the call for international regulation. Particular interest groups rather than the public at large continued to be the major source of pressure for action by the United Kingdom. Nongovernmental organizations including bird

36. Pritchard, Oil Pollution Control, 64.
37. Of course, the stronger sustained concern of British environmental NGOs, discussed below, suggests that activism in the United Kingdom may well have continued even had the level of pollution decreased.
38. All of the following sections build extensively on the excellent analyses in M'Gonigle and Zacher, *Pollution, Politics, and International Law*; and Pritchard, *Oil Pollution Control.*
39. Kirby, "The Clean Seas Code," 203.
40. U.K. Ministry of Transport, *Report of the Committee,* 1.

protection societies, hotel and tourist organizations, and local governments banded together to form the U.K. Advisory Committee on the
Prevention of Pollution of the Sea by Oil (ACOPS).

In response to such pressures, the United Kingdom established the
Committee on the Prevention of Pollution of the Sea by Oil, the Faulkner Committee.[41] Its 1953 report concluded that the persistence of
crude oils made the prewar zone system merely a "palliative." It recommended an international ban on discharges above 100 ppm by all ships
(tankers and non-tankers) throughout the ocean. In the interim, U.K.–
registered ships should be banned from discharges over 100 ppm "within a wide zone around the United Kingdom.[42] In contrast, the United
States, feeling it had solved its pollution problems through unilateral
measures and voluntary compliance by industry with the zone system,
had lost interest in international regulation.[43] As the U.S. delegate
phrased it, "The pollution problem in the United States today is less critical than it was a quarter century ago, notwithstanding we are consuming three times as much petroleum and products today as we did in
1926."[44]

The British belief that zones were inadequate, and the desire to avoid
encumbering their domestic shipping and oil interests, led them to press
for international action. They were also under pressure to do so from
ACOPS, which held a conference in 1953, inviting environmental
groups, national governments, and oil and shipping interests.[45] At the
conference, the British government announced they would host the
intergovernmental conference recommended in the Faulkner report.[46]

Thirty-two countries attended the intergovernmental conference of
1954 in London. While many European nations considered oil pollution
a problem, most developing and Soviet bloc nations still did not.[47]

41. U.K. Ministry of Transport, *Report of the Committee.*
42. U.K. Ministry of Transport, *Report of the Committee*, 33.
43. Pritchard, *Oil Pollution Control*, 84.
44. International Conference on Pollution of the Sea by Oil, "General Committee: Minutes of 3rd Meeting Held on 30th April 1954," 4.
45. M'Gonigle and Zacher, *Pollution, Politics, and International Law*, 84.
46. While the Intergovernmental Maritime Consultative Organization
(IMCO)—established under the United Nations in 1948—was the obvious
forum to hold such negotiations, it did not start operation until 1958.
47. For a discussion of particular states' views of the seriousness of oil pollution during the 1954 Conference, see Pritchard, *Oil Pollution Control*, Figure 2,

Both the size and biological effects of the oil pollution problem were debated.[48] The United Kingdom proposed to limit discharges throughout the ocean, a dramatic change from the prewar zonal approach that would have required tankers to stop discharging waste oil at sea, rather than merely discharging far from shore.[49] Tankers could largely eliminate oil pollution if they "refrained from cleaning their cargo tanks and mixed oily ballast residues with new cargo oil".[50] Ships could also pump oil-water mixtures from ballasting and tank-cleaning operations to a slop tank where the oil would separate and the water could be decanted from the bottom. Such requirements prompted resistance from two quarters. Industry resisted because discharging slops at sea could be done while underway, whereas complete oil retention required lengthy port delays to discharge slops. Governments resisted the complementary requirement to provide expensive reception facilities to receive these slops. Most countries felt such costs were unwarranted given that they themselves were not experiencing severe costs from oil pollution. The United Kingdom attempted to increase concern, even flying delegates to its beaches to demonstrate the problem, but "if domestic experience had little effect on states' policies, this predictably had even less."[51] Rather than trying to establish an international scientific review process to increase concern over the long term, they opted to develop the most stringent regulations possible given the current level of concern, in hopes of establishing a regulatory base from which more stringent measures could be adopted once concern increased.

------

98–99); and responses to the U.N. survey conducted in 1956 United Nations Secretariat, *Pollution of the Sea by Oil*.
48. For example, the Faulkner report itself concluded that there was no evidence that fish or shellfish beds were harmed by oil pollution (U.K. Ministry of Transport, *Report of the Committee*, 2–3). The French argued at the 1954 conference that their research had "produced no proof that its effects upon marine life were harmful" (International Conference on Pollution of the Sea by Oil, "General Committee: Minutes of 5th Meeting Held on 5 May 1954," 5). By this time, crude oil tankers clearly had become the major source of oil pollution.
49. M'Gonigle and Zacher, *Pollution, Politics, and International Law*, 90. While the final agreement addressed both tankers and non-tankers, the subsequent discussion will focus exclusively on regulations relating to tankers, as they had become by far the major source of the problem.
50. Pritchard, *Oil Pollution Control*, 95.
51. M'Gonigle and Zacher, *Pollution, Politics, and International Law*, 87.

The failure to limit discharges throughout the ocean left a final agreement in 1954 which looked very much like the prewar agreements. The International Convention for the Prevention of Pollution of the Sea by Oil (OILPOL) reflected "the fact that most governments were still not willing to accept any important control costs themselves or even to impose such costs on their industries."[52] It prohibited discharges above 100 ppm within 50-mile zones.[53] This was some progress from the 500 ppm limit of the prewar draft agreements. Outside the zones, discharges remained unrestricted. The 1954 convention, like the prewar agreements, required no reduction in the amount of oil discharged, only its redistribution outside the zones, from where it nonetheless might reach shore. The final agreement also refrained from requiring the reception facilities without which tankers were forced to discharge at sea.[54] Regarding enforcement, the countries modified the 1935 draft language and required ship masters to record all tanker ballasting, cleaning and discharge operations in a newly developed Oil Record Book instead of in the ship's log.[55] Port states could inspect these books but not delay the ship, and were limited to providing evidence to flag states for prosecution of violations.[56] In 1958, the convention received the requisite ten ratifications, with five from major shipping states,[57] and the first international rules regulating oil discharges entered into force.

Given the design of the 1954 regulations, enforcement capabilities were quite limited and compliance was unlikely. The difficulty of enforcement under zonal arrangements had been noted at the 1926 conference, when one delegate stated: "We know the difficulties of getting evidence within our own three-mile limit. A fortiori what are the difficulties going to be in enforcing it when it comes to a matter of 50 to 150 miles?"[58] As with the prewar period, data on

---

52. M'Gonigle and Zacher, *Pollution, Politics, and International Law*, 89.
53. Some wider zones were established near Australia, the North Sea states, and in the Atlantic off the European and British coasts.
54. Pritchard, *Oil Pollution Control*, 108.
55. This had been recommended in the Faulkner report as an amendment to the Oil Pollution Act of 1922 as well (Ministry of Transport, *Report of the Committee*, 32).
56. Pritchard, *Oil Pollution Control*, 112.
57. Defined as states having aggregate shipping tonnage of over 500,000 tons.
58. Pritchard, *Oil Pollution Control*, 23.

enforcement and compliance with discharge regulations is virtually nonexistent.[59] A 1962 survey of twelve countries showed essentially only two countries detecting and prosecuting violations of the 1954 regulations. Enforcement by flag states and beyond states' territorial waters of three miles was nonexistent despite the treaty's 50-mile zones.[60]

**The 1962 Amendments** The years following the 1954 OILPOL agreement saw a rapid increase in the amount of oil transported by (and discharged at) sea. More states became concerned about pollution, especially in the Mediterranean. Without wasting time and fuel to go beyond prohibition zones off Europe's Atlantic coast, tankers could deballast and clean their tanks in the still-legal discharge area in the central Mediterranean.[61] This assumed they observed OILPOL's requirements at all. Dissatisfied with the results of OILPOL, ACOPS sponsored a conference of eleven countries in 1959 which recommended extending the 1954 zones and globally banning operational discharges.[62]

In 1958, the Inter-Governmental Maritime Consultative Organization (IMCO) had come into existence. Its mandate encompassed the full range of international shipping regulation. Among other responsibilities, it assumed secretariat responsibilities for the 1954 OILPOL agreement from the British government and helped prepare the amending conference that parties to the 1954 Conference had urged take place after a few years of experience with the rules. IMCO sponsored the conference in 1962. Thirty-eight states attended. Negotiators maintained 50 miles as the minimum coastal zone, but extended the zones to cover 100 miles from many coastlines and the whole of the North and Baltic seas.[63] Discharges below 100 ppm remained legal within these zones.

59. As Congressman John Burton remarked, IMO "has seldom monitored compliance with [its] rules. It has certainly never enforced the rules" (House Committee on Government Operations, *Oil Tanker Pollution—Hearings*, 95th Congress, 2nd session, House 401-8 [Washington, D.C.: GPO, 1978] 4).
60. Pritchard, *Oil Pollution Control*, 112. See also M'Gonigle and Zacher, *Pollution, Politics, and International Law*, 220–221.
61. Kirby, "The Clean Seas Code," 203.
62. Pritchard, *Oil Pollution Control*, 119.
63. An intriguing French proposal to increase the speed of signatures by *decreasing* the size of prohibition zones off non-party states failed (Pritchard, *Oil*

Industry raised little objection to these extensions. Whatever the nominal zone width, whether 50 or 100 miles, experience since 1954 had shown that enforcement never extended beyond a country's three-mile limit.

Making their 1954 proposal more palatable, the British proposed that *new* tankers over 20,000 tons be banned from discharging anywhere in the ocean. However, they did not complement this performance standard with the obvious equipment requirements that these ships install oily-water separators and that ports provide reception facilities to receive the wastes generated. Indeed, they explicitly rejected requiring governments to provide the latter and exempted even new ships from the discharge ban when going to ports without facilities. While these qualifications did not remove opposition from states with large shipping interests, such as the United States and Japan, the proposed restriction on new tankers was adopted. As with the zone extensions, "the industry was strangely silent."[64]

Other policy changes in 1962 included resurrection of the 1935 clause that penalties be severe enough to discourage violations. Provision was also made to allow future amendments to occur within the IMCO structure rather than requiring a conference.[65] The 1962 Amendments entered into force in 1967, but seemed to produce little improvement in compliance. While data was still hard to obtain, pollution remained a problem. The performance standards still meant that "the harmful consequences of an illegal discharge from ships at sea is often evident but tracing the offender and prosecuting him is sometimes almost impossible."[66] As late as 1975, a British oil pollution expert did not think "there was a tanker over 20,000 [tons] in the world complying with the 1962 Amendments."[67] No significant increase in re-

---

*Pollution Control*, 133). Unfortunately, such an effort at reciprocity has received little serious consideration.
64. M'Gonigle and Zacher, *Pollution, Politics, and International Law*, 95–96.
65. Recommendations from IMCO's Maritime Safety Committee approved by the IMCO Assembly would become effective upon receipt of a qualified majority of ratifications (Pritchard, *Oil Pollution Control*, 122).
66. G. Boos, "Revision of the International Convention on Oil Pollution."
67. M'Gonigle and Zacher, *Pollution, Politics, and International Law*, 99.

ception facilities occurred. However, the rules did induce increased research into alternative means to reduce discharges: the United States developed segregated ballast tanks, the Soviet Union developed chemical washing techniques, and British oil companies developed the load on top (LOT) technique.[68]

Although the 1962 Amendments had not required them, oil companies recognized that expensive equipment requirements were needed for new ships to comply with the general prohibition. The 1962 conference had also left environmentalists still unsatisfied and so, under British pressure, Shell developed the load on top technique, in which, during the return voyage, oil-water mixtures from ballast and tank cleaning would be transferred to a single cargo tank where the water would settle out and be discharged at sea. Then the next load of cargo would be loaded directly on top of the remaining oil residues. Oil companies had previously required tankers to clean their tanks between each load of cargo to preserve crude oil quality. Only the threat of expensive international equipment rules led them to "discover" that "most crude oil cargoes are compatible," thus removing their major objection to mixing residues from one delivery with subsequent cargoes.[69]

Oil companies preferred LOT to equipping new tankers with the equipment needed to meet the 1962 general prohibition. Since discharging residues occurred as part of delivery of the subsequent cargo, LOT also eliminated the need to spend additional time in port discharging residues. Governments liked LOT because it also removed the need to build reception facilities. And, when used properly, LOT significantly reduced total oil discharged from ships. However, since oil companies designed LOT to avoid equipment costs, it required tanker operators to determine by sight when to stop discharging water from beneath oil slops. Oil companies admitted that, in practice, this would frequently produce discharges exceeding 100 ppm by large amounts, violating the

---

68. Pritchard, *Oil Pollution Control*, 145. As James Kirby noted, "It was only our close study of the solution recommended by the [1962] conference of discharging oil ashore into slop facilities that really drove us towards the Load-on-top method." "Background to Progress," *The Shell Magazine* 45 (January 1965): 26.
69. Kirby, "The Clean Seas Code," 206.

1954 and 1962 discharge limits.[70] Nonetheless, by 1964, Shell had allegedly gotten LOT adopted by some 60 percent of tankers, including most American and European ships.[71]

### Progress Toward Effective Control: 1967–1991

**The 1969 Amendments**    Since the 1920s, pressure to reduce oil pollution rested on the belief that "once the stuff is in the sea, it is there for ever."[72] By the late 1960s, however, the evidence was "overwhelming" that natural processes made oil "unobjectionable" over time.[73] Nonetheless, by then, the history of international regulation had made it "axiomatic that the less oil discharge into the sea, the better."[74] In this context, the grounding of the *Torrey Canyon* in 1967 provided a major new impetus to oil pollution control. The accident raised public concern in many European countries, and major international agreements to address tanker accidents were quickly signed. Growing environmentalism was also raising broader concerns over all ocean pollution.

ACOPS once again hosted a conference which helped push operational discharges onto the international agenda. Their Rome conference of 1968 occasioned a major proposal by Shell to scrap the existing zonal system and the implicit equipment requirements of the 1962 amendments in favor of LOT, or what Shell called the Clean Seas Code.[75] The issue of modifying international regulations to legitimize LOT and eliminating equipment requirements had already been raised in IMCO's newly established Subcommittee on Oil Pollution (SCOP) in 1965.[76] The British, who had been the major force for reduced oil pollution up

70. Indeed, accurate oil content meters had not yet been developed.
71. Kirby, "The Clean Seas Code," and M'Gonigle and Zacher, *Pollution, Politics, and International Law*, 97.
72. Sir Gilmou Jenkins in Kirby, "Background to Progress," 26. See also the U.S. Bureau of Mines study to the 1926 Conference and the Report on the Second Session of the League of Nations Committee of Experts (par. 21) of Oct. 26, 1935 (both cited in U.K. Ministry of Transport, *Report of the Committee*, 6–9) as well as the Ministry of Transport conclusions themselves.
73. C. T. Sutton, "The Problem of Preventing Pollution of the Sea by Oil," *BP Magazine* 14 (Winter 1964): 9.
74. Kirby, "The Clean Seas Code," 210.
75. Kirby, "The Clean Seas Code."
76. M'Gonigle and Zacher, *Pollution, Politics, and International Law*, 99.

until the 1962 conference, now began working much more closely with their oil companies. In 1968, they proposed to the IMCO subcommittee that all governments promote LOT. At the same time, growing domestic environmentalism was leading the United States to seek stronger international controls.[77]

The conflicting efforts to modify the convention came to a head in the Subcommittee on Oil Pollution during 1968. Oil and shipping companies, with British and French support, wanted to avoid expensive equipment requirements aboard ships and the need to build reception facilities. Environmental states, led by the United States, wanted to strengthen the regulations. The oil companies succeeded in getting the 100 ppm rule for tankers replaced with a rule prohibiting discharges at rates over 60 liters per mile.[78] They eliminated the 1962 rules regarding new tankers.[79] They also blocked new requirements for construction of reception facilities.

However, their efforts to scrap the zones failed. The 50-mile zones were retained with the discharge limit of 60 liters per mile applying *outside* them. Within the zones, only discharge of "clean ballast" which did not leave a visible sheen was allowed. Therefore "any sighting of a discharge from a tanker . . . would be much more likely to be evidence of a contravention."[80] The United States also seized on the oil industry's contention that LOT would make the convention "automatically enforced world wide." A U.S. proposal was accepted to require total discharges be limited to 1/15,000 of a tanker's cargo capacity. Without requiring precise measurements, these rules allowed port authorities to assume that any tanker with clean tanks had blatantly violated the agreement.[81] However, international law barred port states from such

77. M'Gonigle and Zacher, *Pollution, Politics, and International Law,* 100.
78. By limiting the rate of discharge rather than the oil content, this rule removed the requirement for oil content monitors and separators, which were expensive and had technical problems. The 60 l/m rate posed few problems for tankers since it was "a figure within which any responsibly run ship, no matter how big, could operate" (J. H. Kirby, "The Clean Seas Code," 208).
79. IMO, *International Convention for the Prevention of Pollution of the Sea by Oil,* 1954 (as Amended in 1962 and 1969) (London: IMO, 1983), Article 3(b)(ii).
80. Resn. A.391(X) (1977), Annex, par. 5.
81. Kirby, "The Clean Seas Code," 200, 209; and William T. Burke, Richard Legatski, and William W. Woodhead, *National and International Law Enforce-*

intrusive inspections of vessels, a legal barrier that was not removed until the 1973 convention.

The IMCO Assembly adopted these amendments in October 1969, dramatically changing the underlying principle of oil pollution regulation. The 1926, 1935, 1954, and 1962 rules had all permitted discharges except in prohibited zones. In contrast, the new rules prohibited discharges except under certain conditions.[82] And, for the first time, international rules required that oil entering the ocean be reduced rather than merely redistributed.

Progress on paper did not mean progress on the ground, however. Ratifications were so slow that the 1969 Amendments only entered into force in 1978. Since then, discharges have been essentially limited to "clean ballast" of 15 ppm within 50 miles from land, rates of 60 l/m outside these zones, and a maximum of 1/15,000 of total cargo capacity. Since changes to these standards in 1973 and 1978 have left them essentially unchanged,[83] compliance and enforcement with these standards will be discussed after the sections on the 1973 and 1978 conferences.

**The 1973 International Convention for the Prevention of Pollution from Ships**    The growing environmental interest of the late 1960s became manifest in the early 1970s with the UN Conference on the Human Environment and the London Dumping Convention. The oil pollution problem also continued to grow as oil transported by sea con-

---

*ment in the Ocean* (Seattle: University of Washington Press, 1975), 129. Imagine a new tanker that loads 150,000 tons of oil in Kuwait. It delivers 149,400 tons in Rotterdam, leaving 600 tons remaining as "clingage" of oil to the tanks' sides. On its return voyage to Kuwait, it ballasts several tanks with seawater and cleans others with seawater. It allows the oil to separate from the resulting oil-water mixtures and discharges the water overboard. If it arrives in Kuwait with less than 590 tons of oil residues ("slops"), it would clearly have discharged more than 1/15,000 of its 150,000 tons. The more likely scenario would involve arrival in Kuwait with completely clean tanks or negligible slops.
82. Samir Mankabady, *The International Maritime Organization*, vol. 1, *International Shipping Rules* (London: Croom Helm, 1986), 318.
83. The 1973 Amendments superseded and essentially incorporated the 1969 standards, the only changes being a total discharge standard of 1/30,000 for new tankers and a redefinition of "clean" ballast as 15 ppm. As discussed below, the major innovation was to complement discharge limits with equipment requirements.

tinued to increase (see figure 5.2). Countries such as Greece and Italy that had previously opposed strict regulations adopted more environmentalist stances as they experienced more operational pollution and greater calls for environmentalism at home.[84]

These forces had their strongest impact in the United States, which pushed for regulations stricter than the 1969 Amendments. While the LOT system had only been legally legitimized in 1969, oil companies allegedly had been using it since 1964. And the United States believed this experience proved LOT was far less effective than the oil companies claimed.[85] Therefore, in the early 1970s, the United States proposed supplementing the existing performance standards with equipment standards. These included requirements for existing tankers and ports to install the equipment necessary to comply with the 1969 performance standards, such as oil discharge monitors, oily-water separators, dedicated slop tanks and reception facilities. They also sought measures beyond those needed to implement the 1969 amendments. They sought to widen the prohibition zones to 100 miles while restricting allowable discharges within them to 10 ppm, and to reduce rate limits outside the zones from 60 to 30 l/m. To reduce oil-water mixtures from ballast operations, new tankers over 70,000 tons were to have piping that completely segregated ballast tanks from cargo tanks, a design known as SBT. In addition, to reduce spills during accidents they proposed that new ships have double bottoms. The last two proposals were especially expensive.

The domestic pressures behind the United States' international efforts also found expression in congressional passage in 1972 of the Ports and Waterways Safety Act. It required the Coast Guard unilaterally to adopt strict equipment standards by 1976 unless other countries agreed to rules similar to those the United States was proposing. The Coast Guard was also to deny entry to any ships violating such rules.[86]

At the same time, Canada began an "aggressive diplomatic campaign" to lobby for protection of coastal state environmental rights.[87]

---

84. M'Gonigle and Zacher, *Pollution, Politics, and International Law*, 118.
85. M'Gonigle and Zacher, *Pollution, Politics, and International Law*, 108.
86. U.S. Public Law 92-340, Ports and Waterways Safety Act of 1972, 10 July 1972, Sec. 201(13).
87. Grolin, "Environmental Hegemony," 27.

Motivated by both environmental and territorial concerns, Canada worked with other developed coastal states like Australia and New Zealand to persuade developing states to attend the 1973 International Conference on Marine Pollution. That conference and the International Convention for the Prevention of Pollution from Ships (known as MARPOL) which emerged from it were far broader in scope than previous agreements. They applied to oil platforms as well as ships, included refined as well as crude oil, and used five annexes (including Annex 1 for oil) to address liquid chemicals, harmful packaged substances, sewage, and garbage discharged by ships. This broader perspective on pollution had been foreshadowed in IMCO's renaming of the Subcommittee on Oil Pollution as the Subcommittee on Marine Pollution in 1969, and in the creation of the Marine Environment Protection Committee in 1973 as a full committee answering directly to the IMCO Assembly.

The U.S. proposals provided the basis for most of the conference's discussion on oil tankers, however. Despite U.S. pressure, the final agreement maintained essentially the same performance standards. The zones remained at 50 miles, though special areas were designated in the Mediterranean, Baltic, Black, and Red seas and in the Persian Gulf, but not the North Sea.[88] Outside the zones, discharges below 60 l/m remained legal (see table 5.2). Inside the zones, the negotiators defined the "clean ballast" limitation of the 1969 Amendments as 15 ppm, although the United States was seeking a 10 ppm definition. Total allowable discharges were kept at 1/15,000 of cargo capacity for existing tankers, although new tankers were limited to 1/30,000.[89]

The far more controversial aspects of the proposals involved the equipment standards. The final outcomes required equipment for compliance with the discharge standards—oily-water separators and monitoring devices—on all new tankers delivered after 1979[90] and on

---

88. The special areas in the Red Sea and Persian Gulf were designated as part of the 1973 Convention. However, only the 50-mile zones applied until a sufficient number of states had provided reception facilities at all oil-loading terminals (International Conference on Marine Pollution, *International Convention for the Prevention of Pollution from Ships*, 1973. (London: IMO, 1973), Annex 1, reg. 10 (hereafter cited as MARPOL Convention).
89. MARPOL Convention, Annex 1, reg. 9.
90. "New" tankers were defined as tankers with building contracts placed after

existing tankers from three years after the treaty entered into force. The segregated ballast tank requirement for new tankers initially evoked strong opposition from states with large shipping interests and from oil companies. Two factors reduced resistance to the SBT requirement. First, it promised to dissuade the United States from unilaterally adopting the even more expensive double bottoms. Second, the recent construction boom meant that the cost of building new tankers with SBT would not be felt until far into the future.

Large increases in the quantity of oil transported by sea, and a corresponding increase in discharges, prompted new concern in many coastal states. Developed states with long coastlines and small shipping industries—like Australia, Canada, and New Zealand—supported the United States' SBT proposal. Italy, traditionally opposed to stringent requirements, joined the environmental ranks as it experienced increased coastal pollution. Developing states—such as Egypt, Argentina, and India—lent their support since they faced growing pollution from developed countries' ships and saw few direct costs to their own small-sized tanker fleets. They also supported SBT as a means to reduce oil wastes generated and thereby deflect growing pressures to require them to build expensive reception facilities. In an era of détente, Soviet bloc countries saw support as having low economic costs and both political and environmental benefits. This diverse coalition was large enough to pass the requirement. However, "it was opposed to the end by states with large independent shipowning interests, and by the two states anticipating the construction of" new tankers, France and Japan. Finally, while states were required to "ensure provision" of reception facilities in all tanker ports, this left ambiguous whether states or industry would be responsible for constructing them.[91] Table 5.3 details the final equipment requirements.

The 1973 conference also sought to improve implementation, enforcement and compliance. Continuing ratification delays were addressed through a tacit acceptance procedure which permitted entry

---

31 December 1975, or whose keel was laid after 30 June 1976, or whose delivery occurred after 31 December 1979 (MARPOL Convention, Annex I, reg. 1, par. 6).
91. M'Gonigle and Zacher, *Pollution, Politics, and International Law*, 114–120.

**Table 5.3**    MARPOL 1973/1978 SBT and COW requirements for crude oil carriers

| Tanker size | Existing ship | New ship under MARPOL 73 but existing ship under 78 Protocol | New ship under 78 Protocol |
|---|---|---|---|
| 70K< = DWT | SBT or COW | SBT* | SBT* and COW |
| 40K< = DWT<70K | SBT or COW | SBT or COW | SBT and COW |
| 20K< = DWT<40K | No requirement | No requirement | SBT and COW |
| DWT<20K | No requirement | No requirement | No requirement |

* SBT required under MARPOL 1973, all other requirements under Protocol of 1978.

DEFINITION OF NEW SHIP:
MARPOL 73: Building contract after 31 December 1975 or keel laid after 30 June 1976 or delivery after 31 December 1979.
Protocol 78: Building contract after 1 June 1979 or keel laid after 2 February 1980 or delivery after 1 June 1982.

Source: Sasamura, 1990.

into force of certain amendments unless more than one-third of the signatories explicitly objected. The conferees also applied construction standards to ships built after set dates, regardless of the number of ratifications.[92] Compliance with the equipment standards was to be established by initial surveys by national governments and ship classification societies documented in an International Oil Pollution Prevention (IOPP) Certificate. States were given expanded rights to inspect the IOPP certificates of ships entering their ports and to determine whether they met the equipment requirements. If found in violation, governments were obligated to "take such steps as will ensure that the ship shall not sail until it can proceed to sea without presenting an unreasonable threat of harm to the marine environment".[93] Negotiators hoped that providing more environmentalist port states with such enforcement powers would improve compliance. The conference also established a technical cooperation program to train developing countries' merchant

92. This built on the approach of amendments adopted in 1971, limiting tank size to address the size of accidental spills (Pritchard, *Oil Pollution Control*, 159).
93. MARPOL Convention, art. 5(2).

marines to mitigate marine pollution and to help fund reception facilities.[94]

While the MARPOL agreement did not enter into force until 1983, it began to have an impact as soon as January 1976, after which time large contracts for new tankers had to include SBT. All evidence suggests that ship buyers began complying with this regulation on schedule. "No company ordering a new ship could afford to ignore draft regulations which they knew would be adopted and enter into force whilst the ship was still comparatively new."[95] An extended discussion of compliance with these equipment requirements, the 1978 Protocol additions to them, and amendments during the 1980s, follows the discussion of the 1980s period.

**The 1978 Protocol to the 1973 Convention**[96]   The 1973 MARPOL Convention failed to gain quick ratification, both because of the strong resistance that the new equipment and reception facility requirements generated and because adoption of Annex 1 addressing oil pollution was legally linked to adoption of Annex 2 on chemical pollution, which imposed even higher costs on states. Then, just as the *Torrey Canyon* incident had motivated the 1969 Amendments and the 1973 conference, a series of accidents in December 1976 and January 1977, including the *Argo Merchant* grounding off Nantucket, Massachusetts, combined with activist pressures, including lawsuits by the Center for Law and Social Policy and other environmentalist groups,[97] to produce unilateral U.S. action and put oil pollution back on the international agenda.

94. Michelle Sieff, "An Analysis of the IMO's Technical Cooperation Program" (unpublished paper, Dartmouth College, 1991), 3.
95. G. Victory in James Cowley, "The International Maritime Organisation and National Administrations," *Transactions of the Institute of Marine Engineers* 101 (1989): 129.
96. The following discussion relies extensively on M'Gonigle and Zacher, *Pollution, Politics, and International Law*, and Sielen and McManus, "IMCO and the Politics of Ship Pollution."
97. Attorneys from the Center for Law and Social Policy, representing fifteen environmental groups, were among the U.S. delegates to the 1973 and 1978 conferences. Clifton E. Curtis, "Statement" in Senate Committee on Foreign Relations, *Hearings on Protocol of 1978 Relating to the International Convention for the Prevention of Pollution from Ships, with Annexes and Protocols*, 96th Congress, 2nd session, Exec. Rept. No. 96–36 (Washington, D.C.: GPO, 1980), 9.

In response to the accidents and congressional pressure, the Carter Initiatives were proposed. These included double bottoms and other systems to prevent accidental spills, but also addressed operational pollution by requiring that the Coast Guard unilaterally require SBT on all tankers above 20,000 tons and annual tanker inspections, unless international negotiations produced stronger standards. Under direct threats that "if IMCO tailors its moves to suit and protect the U.S., we will accept; if not, we reserve the right to impose our own rules," IMCO called the Tanker Safety and Pollution Prevention Conference in 1978.[98] This conference produced a protocol that became integral to the 1973 MARPOL agreement, together known as MARPOL 73/78.

At the 1978 conference, the United States proposed to expand the application of the 1973 SBT rule from *new* tankers over 70,000 tons to new *and existing* tankers over 20,000 tons, but found little support. Various alternatives were proposed. The most important of these, pressed by the oil industry and the United Kingdom, involved requiring existing tankers over 70,000 tons to install a tank-cleaning system that used crude oil to wash tanks. As had occurred with LOT in the 1960s, the oil industry had reevaluated its technological options in light of the growing political imperative to reduce oil pollution that had become evident in MARPOL 73's SBT requirements. The crude oil washing technique (COW), which had been available since the late 1960s, became more attractive as U.S. pressures to require SBT on all existing tankers increased. While rising oil prices also played a role, the political pressures undoubtedly helped promote industry support for a COW requirement. COW significantly reduced oil residues without requiring additional time in port, since the process occurred during cargo delivery. While proposed as an alternative to SBT, in fact COW addressed the oil-water mixtures from tank cleaning, not ballasting operations. The placement of segregated ballast tanks in protective locations was proposed as an adequate alternative to the U.S. double bottom proposal.

The support that met the United States' 1973 proposal for SBT on large new ships evaporated with the 1978 proposal to expand it to all ships. The high costs of retrofitting revealed just how much countries

---

98. Brock Adams in M'Gonigle and Zacher, *Pollution, Politics, and International Law*, 130.

were willing to pay for environmental protection. A few states with very heavy pollution supported the SBT retrofit proposal, as did states with laid-up tanker fleets, which would have benefited by reducing the current over-capacity of the world tanker fleet.[99] But most states, including Soviet bloc and developing ones, saw SBT as too costly, preferring the cheaper COW. The oil and shipping industries, and countries representing them such as the United Kingdom, also preferred COW.[100] Given the "power and determination" of the United States, supporters of the British alternative recognized the need for compromise.[101] In contrast to the debates of the late 1960s, even the latter no longer believed in exclusive reliance on performance standards. The final protocol required new crude tankers over 20,000 tons to install SBT and COW, while requiring existing tankers over 40,000 tons to install either SBT or COW.[102] Existing tankers were sure to choose the cheaper COW option.

While the 1978 Protocol left performance standards unchanged, it added language requiring regular unscheduled inspections to verify compliance. The IOPP certificate and Oil Record Book were modified. In addition, to speed entry into force, the negotiators de-linked ratification of Annex 1 on oil pollution from ratification of Annex 2 on chemicals. As with the 1973 rules, applying the equipment requirements to ships delivered after June 1982 (regardless of the entry into force date) removed incentives for countries to delay ratification to slow the rule's impact. Ratifications from the requisite fifteen states, with not less than

99. Since installing SBT on a tanker removed some 15 percent of its cargo capacity, retrofitting requirements provided a means to bring the numerous laid-up tankers of Norway, Sweden, and Greece back onto the world market. M'Gonigle and Zacher, *Pollution, Politics, and International Law*, 135.
100. As discussed below, COW actually produced net savings for oil companies.
101. M'Gonigle and Zacher, *Pollution, Politics, and International Law*, 138.
102. "New" tankers under the Protocol were defined as tankers with building contracts placed after 1 June 1979, or whose keel was laid after 1 January 1980, or whose delivery occurred after 1 June 1982 (International Conference on Tanker Safety and Pollution Prevention, 1978, *Protocol of 1978 Relating to the International Convention for the Prevention of Pollution from Ships, 1973* (London: IMO, 1978), Annex I, reg. 1, par. 26). Existing tankers, instead of retrofitting SBT or COW, could dedicate certain tanks to ballast for an interim period—until 1985 for tankers over 70,000 tons and until 1987 for tankers over 40,000 tons. For a chart of the application of the various regulations, see Y. Sasamura, "Oil in the Marine Environment," in *IMAS 90: Marine Technology and the Environment* (London: Institute of Marine Engineers, 1990), 3–4.

half the world's merchant tonnage, led to entry into force of the combined MARPOL 73/78 in 1983.

**The 1980s**  Having finally achieved stringent regulations on paper, many nations and the International Maritime Organization, or IMO (IMCO was renamed but left otherwise unchanged in 1981), sought to redirect its focus to compliance. By 1981, the frequent changes in and proliferation of oil pollution regulations and the problem of adopting new regulations before entry into force of old ones were inhibiting compliance. This led the IMO Assembly to resolve that the Marine Environment Protection Committee (MEPC) should consider amendments only "on the basis of clear and well-documented compelling need."[103] While this has not prevented amendments, they have been largely technical in nature. All have been adopted through the MEPC and have entered into force via the tacit acceptance procedure of the 1973 Convention.

The long delay in ratification of MARPOL 73/78 meant that several amendments to the agreement were proposed before it even entered into force. These amendments were agreed to during regular meetings of the Marine Environment Protection Committee in 1981, 1982, and 1983 and adopted in September 1984.[104] The changes sought to improve the existing equipment requirements or, at the request of shipping interests, to remedy implementation problems that had become evident with initial experience with MARPOL 73/78. They improved specifications for the MARPOL oil monitoring, separating, and filtering equipment whose details had plagued IMO for years, waived equipment requirements under strict conditions, and again modified the oil record book. Since 1984, IMO has adopted three other amendments to MARPOL. First, in 1987, the Gulf of Aden was designated a special area. Second, in 1990, guidelines for surveys under MARPOL were harmonized with surveys required under other IMO conventions. Third, in 1990, Antarctica was designated a special area.[105]

103. Resn. A.500(XII) 1981.
104. "First Amendments to MARPOL 73/78 Adopted," *IMO News*, no. 4 (1984): 8.
105. IMO, *Status of Multilateral Conventions and Instruments in Respect of Which the International Maritime Organization or Its Secretary-General Performs Depositary or Other Functions, as at 31 December 1990* (London: IMO, 1991).

Since 1978, concern over enforcement also grew in Europe. The *Amoco Cadiz* spilled 223,000 tons of oil off France on 16 March 1978, prompting the Commission of the European Communities to start working on directives on oil pollution enforcement and France to call a 1980 conference which led to fourteen European states adopting a Memorandum of Understanding (MOU) on Port State Control.[106] The MOU promulgates no new rules but has had some success at increasing enforcement of MARPOL's equipment requirements.[107] It requires each participating state to inspect 25 percent of ships entering its ports and to report deficiencies in certificates or equipment to a central computer processing facility. This facility gives inspectors in each country access to recent data on violations by any ship arriving in its ports.[108] The United States, Japan, and Canada have taken similar steps unilaterally.

As late as 1975, enforcement of the 100 ppm standard set in 1954 and 1962 was still considered "dismal, with very few cases being prosecuted, and even fewer penalties being assessed for violations."[109] The 1969 changes appear to have helped very little. Despite hopes at the time, the "clean ballast" provision has not led to aerial photographs becoming widely accepted as clear legal evidence of a violation.[110] And the improved enforcement that the 1/15,000 rule was hoped to provide seems not to have materialized.[111] In 1983, IMO noted that flag state

---

106. Member states include Belgium, Denmark, Finland, France, West Germany, Greece, Ireland, Italy, Netherlands, Norway, Portugal, Spain, Sweden, and the United Kingdom. The 1982 MOU replaced a similar MOU signed in The Hague by eight North Sea states in 1978 (Secretariat of the Memorandum of Understanding on Port State Control, *The Memorandum of Understanding on Port State Control* (The Hague: The Netherlands Government Printing Office, 1989), and George Kasoulides, "Paris Memorandum of Understanding: Six Years of Regional Enforcement," *Marine Pollution Bulletin* 20 (June 1989): 255–61).
107. "Control on compliance with operational [discharge] requirements did not strictly fit in the present framework of the MOU" (Secretariat of the Memorandum of Understanding, 1989, 16).
108. See Kasoulides, "Paris Memorandum of Understanding"; and Kasoulides, "Paris Memorandum of Understanding: A Regional Regime of Enforcement," *International Journal of Estuarine and Coastal Law* 5 (February 1990): 180–92 for extensive discussions of the Memorandum of Understanding on Port State Control.
109. Burke, Legatski, and Woodhead, *National and International Law Enforcement*, 48.
110. M'Gonigle and Zacher, *Pollution, Politics, and International Law*, 328.
111. Interviews at IMO in summer 1991 confirmed that the loading port in-

prosecution of violations was "often inadequate."[112] While it is often assumed that increased port state control and national aerial surveillance programs undertaken in the 1980s have helped deter violations, there is no hard evidence to confirm such an assumption.[113] Dutch studies conducted in 1988 and 1989 suggest that prosecution and penalty situations remain dismal.[114] Fines have traditionally averaged only $5,000 to $10,000 per violation.[115]

This enforcement record gives little reason to expect high compliance with the discharge standards. Given that oil companies had proposed LOT as an alternative to the standards existing during the 1960s, it seems unlikely that many ships were complying with the 1954/1962 standards. Those ships that adopted LOT before 1978, the year the 1969 Amendments entered into force, would frequently and admittedly violate the 100 ppm standards, since they lacked the meters needed to measure oil content. And, while oil representatives claimed that 80 percent of the fleet were using LOT in 1968,[116] oil company data for 1972

---

spections for clean tanks—which would indicate discharges exceeding the 1/15,000 limit—have never been systematically conducted and that no prosecutions have depended on this rule. "Since 1972, the industry has offered to provide the information discovered to the oil-exporting states for referral to the flag states for prosecution under the 1969 Amendments. No interest has been shown by these states despite the entry-into-force of the amendments" (M'Gonigle and Zacher, *Pollution, Politics, and International Law*, 333).

112. Resn A.542(13), 1983, Annex, Appendix 2.

113. Cowley, "The International Maritime Organisation," 138–139; Secretariat of the Memorandum of Understanding on Port State Control, *Annual Report 1989* (The Hague: The Netherlands Government Printing Office, 1989), and Secretariat of the Memorandum of Understanding on Port State Control, *Annual Report 1988* (The Hague: The Netherlands Government Printing Office, 1988).

114. In only 17 percent of cases reported to IMO did flag states follow up on violations reported to them by coastal or port states. Only 6 percent actually were fined and "in these cases it is clear that the fines imposed on the vessel were too small to have a significant effect upon the vessel's crew or master" (MEPC 29/10/3 (15 January 1990)), 5; also see the data in N. Smit-Kroes, *Harmonisatie Noordzeebeleid: Brief Van de Minister Van Verkeer en Waterstaat, Tweede Kamer der Staten-Generaal* 17–408, 23 September 1988 (The Hague: The Netherlands Government Printing Office), 5.

115. Paul Stephen Dempsey, "Compliance and Enforcement in International Law—Oil Pollution of the Marine Environment by Ocean Vessels," *Northwestern Journal of International Law and Business* 6 (1984): 488.

116. Kirby, "The Clean Seas Code."

through 1977 show that two-thirds of the world fleet essentially ignored the not-yet-in-force 1969 standards, and the other third failed to operate LOT efficiently enough to meet these standards.[117] In 1985, the National Academy of Sciences estimated that only 50 percent of all crude oil tankers were meeting the 1969 discharge standard.[118] Their 1990 estimates assume that, of tankers not facing equipment standards, 15 to 20 percent violate the total discharge standard.[119] Critics argue that even these compliance rates are "grossly exaggerated; indeed most estimates quote a figure of 80% upwards, when actual performance rates seem suspect."[120] Recent Dutch and Belgian studies confirm that even in ports with reception facilities to receive waste oil, most oil wastes generated by tankers still get discharged at sea.[121] Indeed, as recently as 1989, tanker owners admitted that they do not always fully comply with MARPOL's discharge requirements, although they blame it on the failure of governments to provide reception facilities.[122]

In contrast to the discharge standards alone, all available evidence suggests that equipment and construction standards have achieved essentially perfect compliance. Initial surveys of compliance with equip-

117. For the one-third figure see Pritchard, "Load on Top," 214; and M'Gonigle and Zacher, *Pollution, Politics, and International Law*, 228. Data on the effectiveness of the load on top technique between 1972 and 1977 was presented to Congress in 1978. Since the 1969 rules only took legal effect in 1978, the oil companies were quick to point out that this data was not evidence of treaty violations. Indeed, the oil companies claimed the visible decreases in intentional discharges before 1978 were "a tangible measure of the voluntary progress . . . of the industry in advance of any formal regulation requiring such performance." William Gray, "Testimony" in House Committee on Government Operations, *Oil Tanker Pollution—Hearings*, 95th Congress, 2nd session, House 401-8 (Washington, D.C.: GPO, 1978), 92.
118. National Academy of Sciences, and National Research Council, *Oil in the Sea*, 59.
119. The 1990 National Academy of Sciences (MEPC 30/INF.13, 12) study uses the MARPOL 73/78 distinction between the 1/15,000 standard for existing ships and the 1/30,000 standard for all new ships. Existing tankers using load on top are estimated to discharge 1/25,000 of total cargo capacity.
120. Pritchard, "Load on Top," 218.
121. See P. Vanhaecke, *Verontreiniging Door Schepen* (Antwerp, Belgium: ECOLAS, 1990); and Marja den Boer et al., *'Loos'-alarm: Afvalolie Van de Scheepvaart in de Waddenzee* (Groningen, The Netherlands: Werkgroep Eemsmond Van de Landelijke Vereniging Tot Behoud Van de Waddenzee, 1987) which estimate that less than 15 percent and 35 percent, respectively, of tankers' waste oils are actually received in port reception facilities.
122. MEPC 27/5 (17 January 1989).

ment and construction standards are required before issuance of the required International Oil Pollution Prevention certificate required by
MARPOL 73/78 will be issued. Some governments conduct these surveys, while others rely on private classification societies. Since tankers
are only built on order, ordering a boat without SBT would require a
buyer to elicit cooperation in an admittedly illegal act from at least
three other actors—a builder, a classification society, and an insurance
company. Classification society representatives in shipyards reserve
their highest classifications for ships built to all international requirements. While insurance companies do not link premiums to compliance
with international rules, they do link them to classification, providing
strong incentives for tanker buyers to conform with international rules.
In essence, a tanker owner wants the highest classification and lowest
premiums possible, and one element of securing them requires building
to internationally required standards.[123] Since MARPOL 73/78, most
governments also have broadened traditional safety inspections of
tankers arriving in port to include pollution-related equipment and
construction criteria. Some states have made use of the new MARPOL
73/78 enforcement language to detain, or bar the unloading of, ships
found violating the equipment and construction standards—although
such incidents appear to be quite rare.[124]

No study has examined actual compliance with the equipment and
construction standards established by the 1973 Convention. However,
two 1990 studies assume that 100 percent of tankers built after the requisite dates do have COW and SBT.[125] Ships that meet the SBT and

123. M'Gonigle and Zacher, *Pollution, Politics, and International Law*, 330–
331.
124. For example, in November 1990, the U.S. Coast Guard in Boston detained a Chinese tanker and ordered a Norwegian tanker to leave U.S. waters
because the tankers violated MARPOL 73/78 requirements for existing tankers
(William P. Coughlin, "2 Ships Barred from Unloading Oil in Boston," *Boston
Globe*, 1 November 1990).
125. Coast Guard inputs to the 1990 National Academy of Sciences study presumably support this assumption. MEPC 30/INF.13, 8. A study conducted for
IMO makes a similar assumption. P. G. Sadler and J. King, "Study on Mechanisms for the Financing of Facilities in Ports for the Reception of Wastes from
Ships" (Cardiff, Wales, 1990). Oil companies and classification societies do
maintain databases which probably contain such data. However, neither IMO,
national governments, nor private academics have made use of this data. Inter-

COW requirements are estimated to be significantly more likely to comply with the discharge standards. In contrast to the 50 to 85 percent figures the National Academy of Sciences has used for existing tankers, which barely meet the 1/15,000 requirement, the NAS estimates that 85 to 99 percent of new tankers with COW and SBT do better than required, achieving discharges averaging 1/50,000 and 1/100,000 respectively.[126] While ships with SBT and COW could still violate MARPOL's zonal and discharge proscriptions, retention of oil slops proves economically advantageous once the equipment has been installed.

Having examined the response of industry to international regulations, we must also examine government responses. The requirement for reception facilities seems to have induced little change in compliance. While developed countries generally have such facilities, oil-loading states—where discharging of the tank-cleaning and deballasting slops of a return voyage is most needed—have few. Violation of the requirement that governments "ensure provision" of reception facilities is evident from frequent complaints at IMO.[127] Indeed, the Red Sea and Persian Gulf, both designated as special areas in 1973, and the Gulf of Aden, designated in 1987, have yet to be "implemented" because of the continuing lack of adequate reception facilities.[128] The IMO's technical cooperation program has sought to encourage developed member states to provide developing states with the financial assistance necessary to build such facilities, but to date has made little progress.[129]

---

views during summer 1991 at IMO suggest that most experts are comfortable assuming that all new tankers meet the SBT and COW rules.

126. While the National Academy of Science estimates in 1973, 1985, and 1990 are widely cited, they provide little support for those elements of their oil pollution estimates which involve compliance (National Academy of Sciences, *Petroleum in the Marine Environment*; National Academy of Sciences and National Research Council, *Oil in the Sea*; and MEPC 30/INF.13).

127. See, for example, Resn A.585(14) (1985); "Cleaner Oceans: The Role of IMO in the 1990s," *IMO News*, no. 3 (1990): 10; "Concern Over Lack of Reception Facilities," *IMO News*, no. 1 (1984): 10; and MEPC 30/INF.30.

128. L. Andren and D. Liu, "Environmentally Sensitive Areas and Special Areas Under MARPOL 73/78," in *IMAS 90: Marine Technology and the Environment* (London: Institute of Marine Engineers, 1990).

129. Sadler and King, "Study on Mechanisms."

## Analysis

The preceding history allows us to identify and explain the agenda setting for, international policies on, and national and industry policy responses to, international control of oil pollution. The following section examines the role and effectiveness of the international environmental institution in influencing each of these elements. The section concludes by examining how effective the institution has been at solving the fundamental problem of oil pollution.

### Agenda Setting

Unilateral action has been the most frequent impetus placing international oil pollution onto the international agenda.[130] The threat or taking of unilateral action by countries controlling significant fractions of the oil or shipping markets has consistently preceded major international conferences. The following list summarizes the various examples which have been detailed above:

| Conference | Preceding unilateral legislation |
|---|---|
| 1926 Conference | U.K.: Oil in Navigable Waters Act, 1922 |
|  | U.S.: Oil Pollution Act, 1924 |
| 1954 Conference | U.K.: Faulkner Report recommendations, 1953 |
| 1973 Conference | U.S.: Ports and Waterways Safety Act, 1972 |
| 1978 Conference | U.S.: Carter Initiatives, 1977 |

While in the 1920s the United States controlled some 60 percent of the world's oil exports, more recently the United States or United Kingdom has controlled a significant fraction (usually between 10 percent and 20 percent) of the oil import trade or the tankers that carry oil. The United States and British governments, under pressure from NGOs and their domestic publics to take some action, pushed other states to discuss international oil pollution control either as a means to pacify domestic critics or in a more sincere effort to achieve an effective solution to an international problem. The United States or United Kingdom "would take the strongest possible position at the conference, mainly in order to please a domestic audience, but anticipating resistance from other major

130. Sielen and McManus, "IMCO and the Politics of Ship Pollution," 155.

maritime powers, it would prepare a number of fallback positions more acceptable to its own domestic commercial interests."[131] Given industry and maritime states' strong aversion to multiple regulations with respect to shipping, the threat of unilateral action would readily prompt a willingness by other states at least to discuss international regulation.

Unilateralism did not arise from any deep-seated governmental commitment to environmental protection, however. "Only domestic pressure from within the state has motivated governments—and maritime governments in particular—to advocate costly environmental initiatives. . . . All environmental initiatives at IMCO have been a direct result of democratic governments seeking international solutions to problems being loudly mooted at home."[132]

These domestic pressures in turn have been driven by two different processes. Until the *Torrey Canyon* grounded in 1967, it was not widespread public concern but pressures from small but loud domestic NGOs such as British bird protection societies, that induced governments to take unilateral action at home and seek international agreement abroad. Only one international environmental NGO, ACOPS, through its conferences in 1953, 1959, and 1968, played any significant role in heightening concern over the issue or initiating proposals for discussion at the subsequent international conferences. Since the 1970s, Friends of the Earth International has played a less visible role as the main environmental observer at MEPC meetings. While environmental NGOs have played little role in setting agendas, the International Chamber of Shipping played an important role in keeping oil pollution off the agenda by coordinating the voluntary agreement with the 1926 draft agreement. During the mid-1960s, oil companies themselves pushed oil pollution regulation onto the agenda, though they sought to have rules loosened, not strengthened.

131. Pritchard, *Oil Pollution Control*, 75. Congress and environmental groups have criticized the U.S. Coast Guard for not adopting stricter standards than those acceptable to the international community at IMCO and IMO. See, for example, Burton in House Committee on Government Operations, *Oil Tanker Pollution—Hearings*, 95th Congress, 2nd session, House 401–8 (Washington, D.C.: GPO, 1978), 4; and M'Gonigle and Zacher, *Pollution, Politics, and International Law*, 119, 127.
132. M'Gonigle and Zacher, *Pollution, Politics, and International Law*, 273, 285.

Since the late 1960s, however, it has been crises that have placed oil pollution on the agenda. While pollution from accidents has quite different causes and solutions than does intentional pollution, governments and IMCO/IMO have responded to general public pressures induced by accidents to also address operational pollution. A consistent pattern flows through the 1967 *Torrey Canyon* disaster leading to the 1969 Amendments and the 1973 conference, the spate of accidents in the winter of 1976–77 leading to the 1978 conference, and the 1978 *Amoco Cadiz* accident leading to France's 1980 hosting of the conference that produced the MOU on Port State Control. In contrast to the crises that have motivated the ozone debate (see Chapter 1), scientific assessments of "pollution in the marine environment have had little discernible influence on the timing or substance of decisions taken by IMCO."[133]

Getting oil pollution on the international agenda thus seems to depend considerably on factors exogenous to any actions by IMO. Yet, once on the agenda, the contractual environment has been enhanced by having an international organization to facilitate the transformation of international concern into international policy. In most cases, major new international policies have been agreed to at diplomatic conferences that might well have occurred even absent IMCO. Even in those

133. Sielen and McManus, "IMCO and the Politics of Ship Pollution," 154. A British House of Lords report on the dumping of waste at sea noted the divergence between scientific and political perceptions of environmental problems: "The Committee have been struck by the lack of scientific evidence to support the proposal [an EC Council Directive (8805/85) on dumping of waste at sea]. . . . There is of course, no dispute that the dumping of certain wastes in large enough quantities causes pollution. . . . But there seems to be little scientific evidence of pollution attributable to present dumping practices. Alternatively pollution may be assessed 'politically', that is to say judgments may be taken that the risk of abuse of the disposal system is unacceptably high or, in accordance with the precautionary principle, that the risk of pollution is unacceptable because pollution, once identified, could be irrevocable. . . . The public have a natural and reasonable concern about the long-term consequences of waste disposal practices. In this area where scientific proof is difficult—it is easier to prove the positive, that damage has occurred, than the negative, that damage will not occur—public acceptance of waste disposal methods is vital." U.K. House of Lords, and Select Committee on the European Communities, *Dumping of Waste at Sea: With Evidence*, Session 1985–86, 17th Report. (London, England: Her Majesty's Stationery Office, 1986), 21.

cases, however, IMCO supported the conferences, making them less dependent on the goodwill of an individual national government. Just as importantly, regular technical discussions within IMO committees have provided the foundations for successful conferences. Nations negotiated the 1969 amendments within the Subcommittee on Oil Pollution during the mid-1960s, and the 1984, 1987, and 1990 Amendments in the Marine Environment Protection Committee. The latter's regular meetings also "provided an amiable forum for regular consultations and negotiations," which facilitated agreement at the 1978 conference and have helped resolve numerous implementation issues.[134]

Nations and regional groups have universally deferred to IMO's exclusive cognizance over intentional oil pollution regulation, thus helping to achieve the preference of states and industry for uniform international regulations. Individual and regional groups of states have refrained from promulgating independent control measures for operational oil pollution.[135] The Paris and Oslo Conventions and the U.N. Environment Program regional seas agreements leave operational oil pollution control to IMO. The North Sea states have, to date, refrained from reducing discharge limits from 60 l/m to 30 l/m within the regional Bonn Agreement forum, preferring to propose such changes to the MEPC, where agreement would lead to their adoption globally rather than just regionally.[136] IMO's dominance in intentional oil pollution control encourages states to seek global rules before proceeding unilaterally or regionally.

In summary, global agreements have probably been easier to reach because of IMO and its ongoing pollution committee meetings than they would have been had negotiations only taken place within intermittent, ad hoc, regional conferences. If the exigencies of debating regulation at the global rather than regional level have made agreements weaker than they might otherwise have been, they have also made them more broadly applicable.

134. Sielen and McManus, "IMCO and the Politics of Ship Pollution," 152–153.
135. Only the United States has imposed rules stricter than those set internationally (Cowley, "The International Maritime Organisation," 134).
136. MEPC 31/5/1 (4 April 1991).

**International Policies**

Once an issue is on the agenda, we need to look at the effectiveness of an international environmental institution in producing international policies. First, we can ask, how effective have international efforts been at achieving negotiated agreements? These efforts have been quite successful. Since 1926, delegates have achieved five major agreements (1926, 1935, 1954, 1973, 1978) and as many amendments (1962, 1969, 1984, 1987, 1990). But signatures proved elusive until 1954. Even after signature, necessary ratifications have been consistently slow throughout IMO's history. All conventions and amendments have required ratification by a majority of the world's shipping fleets before entry into force. While this delays entry into force, it ensures that once in force, an agreement has at least the nominal support of the major players. The pattern in oil pollution suggests that the delegates to an international conference tend to be more environmentalist then their governments (hence the draft 1926 and 1935 agreements) and that negotiation and signature of conventions confer more domestic political benefits than does the administrative chore of ratification (hence the long ratification delays).

Since the tacit acceptance procedure adopted in the 1973 Convention became operational in 1983, it has improved this process considerably. IMCO/IMO has regularly passed resolutions, and its secretary-general has at times made concerted efforts, calling upon states to speed up ratification of existing conventions.[137] However, these have had little apparent impact on the domestic political factors, often including low levels of concern and long bureaucratic processes, that impede ratification. Eliminating the need for two-thirds of signatory states to ratify, the tacit acceptance procedure incorporated into most IMO conventions involves a technical amendment's entry into force within sixteen months of its adoption so long as no more than one-third of these states, representing more than fifty percent of world shipping tonnage, submit objections. This allows entry into force procedures to take advantage of, rather than fall victim to, bureaucratic and political inertia. Certainly, part of the improvement since 1983 (see chart below) reflects the less substantively controversial nature of the amendments adopted in the

137. See, for example, Resn. A.119(V) (1967) and Resn. A.347(IX) (1975).

1980s. However, it seems unlikely that even these amendments would have entered into force so quickly absent the tacit acceptance provision.

| Agreement | Period until entry into force |
|---|---|
| 1926 Agreement | Never signed or ratified |
| 1935 Agreement | Never signed or ratified |
| 1954 Convention | 4 years |
| 1962 Amendments | 5 years |
| 1969 Amendments | 9 years |
| 1973 Convention | 10 years |
| 1978 Convention | 5 years |
| 1984 Amendments | 16 months |
| 1987 Amendments | 16 months |
| 1990 Amendments | 16 months |

A signed and ratified convention is not necessarily equivalent to an effective one, however. We must ask, would the treaty rules solve the problem? During the first two stages of oil pollution control, the answer is definitely no. Even though many negotiators thought oil persisted indefinitely, they could only agree to the palliative adoption of a zonal approach. Indeed, the zonal approach initiated in 1926 was changed little until 1969, suggesting that initial solutions wield strong influence over the approach underlying subsequent agreements. Early agreements reflected the dominance of shipping and oil interests. Once IMCO was formed, it immediately fell victim to "regulatory capture," and it became commonplace to think of the IMCO as a "shipowner's club."[138] International policies either reflected the lowest common denominator positions of major maritime nations with little concern over oil pollution, as in 1954, or reflected the strong interests of shipping and oil companies in averting stringent measures while ensuring that all policies adopted were universal in character, as in the voluntary agreement of the 1920s and 1930s and the legitimation of LOT in the 1969 Amendments. Negotiators depended on industry for information regarding the costs and feasibility of all the solutions to the oil pollution problem. However, the lowest-cost options that industry proposed eventually proved ineffective.

It took the increased strength and breadth of environmentalism in the late 1960s and early 1970s to alter the bargaining structure of the prob-

138. Sielen and McManus, "IMCO and the Politics of Ship Pollution," 141.

lem. International agreements now reflected the product of negotiations
between a coalition of developed states facing domestic pressures and
developing states, seeking to extend "their general rights of regulation,"[139] and an opposing coalition of governments representing shipping and oil interests and those industries themselves, seeking the
lowest-cost, most politically viable, international alternative. The
former coalition had gained strength by the early 1970s due to three
factors. First, oil pollution had grown with the dramatic growth in oil
transported by sea. Second, the United States, due to domestic environmentalist pressures, assumed a leadership role in pressing for international action on the environment. Third, desiring to create precedents
for extended jurisdictional claims in pollution control that would influence the Law of the Sea negotiations, new developing state members
of IMCO supported regulations that, while having few direct benefits,
also imposed no direct costs. The conflict of interests between environmentalists and shipping concerns was as strong as ever, but the former
had gained in numbers and power. These conditions were essential to
breaking the shipping interests' control of IMCO in 1973. However, by
1978, the first coalitions' weak commitment to environmental protection was highlighted by the unwillingness to support the expensive U.S.
proposal to retrofit SBT on all ships.

Notwithstanding the above, IMO and its member states have learned
from their mistakes. The equipment approach adopted in MARPOL 73/
78 was a response to the perceived failure of the existing performance
standards and the load on top technique. Consider what policies the environmentalist pressures of the 1970s would have produced absent the
poor compliance of the 1950s and 1960s. Conferences would have been
held and agreements reached, surely. International policies might even
have involved strict performance standards. However, it seems unlikely
that countries would have switched immediately from no international
regulation to expensive equipment standards.

Effectiveness can also be evaluated by the scope of the policies
adopted. This involves both the number of countries involved and the
definition of the problem. International efforts to address oil pollution
have broadened dramatically over the years. What began as a thirteen-

139. Grolin, "Environmental Hegemony," 33.

country negotiation in 1926 has become an ongoing negotiation of over seventy countries. The breadth of agreement has also increased in terms of the sources of marine pollution addressed. While only operational oil discharges from tankers have been discussed in this article, international regulation has broadened to encompass other pollution sources. While initial regulatory efforts involved only operational discharges from tankers and non-tankers, after the *Torrey Canyon* disaster, IMCO and the oil industry began addressing accidental pollution under several government and industry agreements.[140] The 1973 Convention exploded the scope of regulations—they now applied to oil-drilling platforms at sea and also addressed other pollution from ships, including chemicals, hazardous packaged substances, garbage, and sewage. Problems that have remained outside IMO's purview, due to its focus on shipping, are the oil and other pollutants generated from land-based sources. IMO has not attempted to address these issues. The number of countries attending relevant conferences is shown below.

| Year of conference | Number of countries attending |
| --- | --- |
| 1926 | 13 |
| 1954 | 32 |
| 1962 | 38 |
| 1973 | 71 |
| 1978 | 58 |

## National and Industrial Policy Responses

In trying to assess how international oil pollution control has affected the behavior of international actors, we can look at both enforcement

---

140. These include private industry conventions—the Tanker Owners Voluntary Agreement Concerning Liability for Oil Pollution (TOVALOP, 1969), and the Contract Regarding an Interim Supplement to Tanker Liability for Oil Pollution (CRISTAL, 1971)—and intergovernmental conventions—the Intervention Convention on Civil Liability for Oil Pollution Damage (1969), the International Convention Relating to Intervention on the High Seas in Cases of Oil Pollution Casualties (1969), and the International Convention on the Establishment of an International Fund for Compensation for Oil Pollution Damage (1971). M'Gonigle and Zacher, *Pollution, Politics, and International Law*, (chapter 5) provide an excellent analysis of the negotiation of these conventions. It is worth noting that the deference shown by regional groups of states to IMO on operational oil pollution has not carried over into accidental oil regulation. Various regional agreements have been arrived at to address the local impacts and cleanup arrangements needed for major oil spills.

**Table 5.4**  Number of ships detained or barred from entry, countries reporting during 1988–1990

| Country | 1988 | 1989 | 1990 |
|---|---|---|---|
| Australia | 0 | 0 | 0 |
| Bulgaria | 0 | 0 | 1 |
| Canada | 0 | 0 | NA |
| China | 0 | 0 | 0 |
| Egypt | 0 | 0 | NA |
| Germany (East plus West) | 0 | 0 | 11 |
| Greece | 0 | 0 | 0 |
| Hong Kong | 0 | 0 | 0 |
| Japan | 0 | 0 | 0 |
| Norway | 1 | 0 | 1 |
| United Kingdom | 47 | 2 | 3 |
| United States | 339 | 10 | 14 |
| Total | 387 | 12 | 30 |

Sources: MEPC 29/10 (1989), MEPC 29/10 Add.1 (1990), MEPC 30/17, (1990), MEPC 30/17 Add. 1 (1990), MEPC 30/17 Add. 2 (1990), MEPC 30/17 Add. 3 (1990), MEPC 31/16 (1991), MEPC 32/14 (1991), and MEPC 32/14/Add.1 (1991).

and compliance. In the latter, four different patterns emerge in this case: (1) no change, (2) spurious change, (3) preemptive change, and (4) rule-induced compliance.

The resources governments dedicate to enforcing oil pollution rules appear to be little affected by international requirements to enforce. While required to detain ships threatening the marine environment under MARPOL, the table above shows that most states rarely do so, seeing the provision as a right, not an obligation.

Table 5.4[141] also supports other analyses suggesting that most states ignore IMO's annual reporting requirements on enforcement activity, with only five to fifteen of some sixty signatory states providing reports

141. Sources: MEPC 29/10 (6 November 1989), MEPC 29/10/Add.1 (9 February 1990), MEPC 30/17 (20 July 1990), MEPC 30/17/Add.1 (16 August 1990), MEPC 30/17/Add.2 (4 October 1990), MEPC 30/17/Add.3 (11 October 1990), MEPC 31/16 (18 April 1991), MEPC 32/14 (13 November 1991), and MEPC 32/14/Add. 1 (6 December 1991).

in a given year.[142] IMO also fails to use the reports it does receive, merely copying and distributing them, with little analysis or effort to make the data comparable. Only in 1985 did IMO establish a standard format to facilitate comparison of enforcement data between different countries over time.[143] Discussion of enforcement and compliance is often postponed and states rarely "call each other on the carpet" for lax compliance or lax enforcement.[144] While governments do not attempt to shame other governments, industry often harangues governments for failing to supply adequate reception facilities, and environmental NGOs often criticize lax government enforcement.[145] The fact that most states conduct little if any enforcement, while the United States, Japan, and Germany have quite strong enforcement suggests that domestic political factors, rather than IMO requirements, determine enforcement. The Memorandum of Understanding on Port State Control provides an exception, where international cooperation has increased the attention and resources states dedicate to enforcement.[146] European states facing similar domestic pressures for environmental improvement to the United States and Canada required the cooperation reflected in the MOU to reassure themselves and each other that all countries would increase their levels of enforcement together. This allowed states to increase their enforcement without fear of free-riding by others. While states have failed to achieve the 25 percent inspection targets established in the MOU, all members have increased their enforcement efforts.[147] However, continuing problems within the MOU highlight the

142. Paul Stephen Dempsey, "Compliance and Enforcement," 487.
143. MEPC/Circ.138 (15 May 1985).
144. Information on how IMO uses its enforcement data was collected through interviews at IMO during summer 1991.
145. MEPC 30/INF.30, MEPC 29/10/3, and C. J. Camphuysen, *Beached Bird Surveys in the Netherlands, 1915–1988: Seabird Mortality in the Southern North Sea Since the Early Days of Oil Pollution* (Amsterdam: Werkgroep Noordzee, 1989).
146. Kasoulides, "Paris Memorandum of Understanding," *Marine Pollution Bulletin* 20 (June 1989): 255–61.
147. Secretariat of the Memorandum of Understanding on Port State Control, *Annual Report 1990* (The Hague: The Netherlands Government Printing Office, 1990). Indeed, like pollution compliance itself, enforcement presented these nations with a classic public goods problem which the MOU helped resolve. See Kenneth Waltz, *Theory of International Politics* (Reading, Mass.: Addison-Wesley, 1979), 196, and Henk E. Huibers, "Statement to the Seminar on Port

costs and evidentiary problems involved in policing performance standards. Even with visible evidence of a violation, linking that evidence with a particular ship remains difficult.[148]

MARPOL 73/78 did improve enforcement in one major way, however. That improvement came from switching from performance standards to equipment standards. While this switch did not increase any state's interest in enforcing oil pollution regulations, it did make effective enforcement easier and cheaper for those states interested in enforcing. With equipment rules, violations are easy to detect during regular port inspections. Just as important, under the legal changes in 1973, port states can bar ships suspected of violations from their ports and detain ships that threaten the marine environment. This authority provides those developed port states having domestic political incentives to enforce with the potent sanctions needed to induce compliance.

In the area of compliance, "no change" best describes the response of governments to reception facility requirements. Since 1954, the obligation to provide facilities has been neither strong nor clear. MARPOL only requires that governments "ensure provision" of facilities; governments prefer to impose this expense on industry while industry argues that they must spend large sums complying with MARPOL equipment requirements and should not also have to finance reception facilities. Very little of the Technical Cooperation Program funding has been used to build reception facilities. While the number of reception facilities worldwide has increased over the years, many ports still have inadequate facilities to receive oil wastes, thus providing rationales, if not reasons, for tanker captains to continue discharging at sea. "No change" also describes industry responses prior to the early 1960s. While no hard evidence exists, the voluntary agreements prior to 1954 and the zones under the 1954 agreement seem unlikely to have substantially changed shipping behavior. National legislation, especially in the United States, and improvements in tanker design and construction techniques adopted for other reasons during the 1930s and 1940s, easily account for reduced U.S. concern about oil pollution at the 1954

---

State Control" in *Report on the Joint IMIF/MOU Seminar on Port State Control* (London: International Maritime Industries Forum, 1991).
148. Smit-Kroes, *Harmonisatie Noordzeebeleid*.

Conference.[149] Continued British concern suggests that discharges remained the standard procedure for most of the industry.

Spurious change is change that correlates with rule changes but is caused by other factors. Oil has traditionally been discharged at sea because the costs of retrieval have usually exceeded the economic value of doing so. As oil prices increased, shipping and oil company interests in retrieval followed. Can this increase explain the change in the type of tankers purchased? In the case of crude oil washing, the answer is yes. By cleaning tanks with crude oil during unloading, COW reduced the amount of oil lost between initial loading and final delivery. While installing a COW system would have cost a company $5,500 per voyage at the 1972 price of oil, it would have *saved* the company $9,000 per voyage at the 1976 price of oil.[150] This certainly explains why some tanker owners installed COW equipment even prior to the dates required by MARPOL.[151] COW was adopted after it became technically available but before it was internationally required, suggesting that the pre-MARPOL adoption was due to the oil price rise. However, COW installation did involve front-end capital costs of about $400,000.[152] While most owners would eventually have installed COW, many owners would have deferred such an investment absent international regulations.[153] While no detailed data exists on when ships retrofitted with COW, logic suggests that MARPOL probably led industry to install COW more widely and quickly than it would have done otherwise. Similarly, load on top, which oil companies had been promoting since

149. Pritchard, *Oil Pollution Control*, 64.
150. Based on a recalculation of the data in table 7-4 of William G. Waters, Trevor D. Heaver, and T. Verrier, *Oil Pollution from Tanker Operations—Causes, Costs, Controls* (Vancouver, B.C.: Center for Transportation Studies, 1980), 124, with 1972 oil prices of $21 per ton (1976 dollars) substituted for the figure of $80 per ton (1976 dollars) used in their calculations. These savings would have grown as the price of oil continued to rise in the late 1970s.
151. M. G. Osborne and J. M. Ferguson, "Technology, MARPOL and Tankers—Successes and Failures," in *IMAS 90: Marine Technology and the Environment* (London: Institute of Marine Engineers, 1990), 6-2, M'Gonigle and Zacher, *Pollution, Politics, and International Law*, 131.
152. Waters, Heaver, and Verrier, *Oil Pollution from Tanker Operations*, 99.
153. More accurate annual data on COW installations would allow us to discriminate between those tanker owners who installed COW for economic reasons prior to MARPOL requirements and those who did so only on the schedule laid out in MARPOL 73/78.

the early 1960s, was practiced far more efficiently after the OPEC oil price increase of 1973 than it was before. In these cases, economics rather than international law explains behavior change.

Preemptive change by industry has also occurred. The development and adoption of LOT during the 1960s involved a major change in tanker operations, though by no means a technological break-through,[154] and was a direct response to the 1962 conference.[155] Given their stability from the 1940s through the 1960s, oil prices can not explain oil companies' discovery in 1963 that tankers could reduce waste by combining new cargoes with the oil residues from a previous ballast voyage. Rather, it was these interests' desire to derail growing pressure for equipment requirements, and international pressures to reduce oil pollution, that explain development and promotion of LOT as a better alternative which eliminated the need for expensive oily-water separating equipment and the long delays needed to discharge slops in reception facilities. While LOT did reduce discharges and was a response to international action, LOT remained, at least until the 1969 Amendments entered into force in 1978, an admitted violation of the 1962 discharge prohibitions for new tankers.

Finally, segregated ballast tank adoption in the late 1970s provides an example of rule-induced compliance. Very few tankers built prior to the MARPOL dates have SBT; almost no tankers built since those dates are without it.[156] Economics argued against complying with the SBT standards. A new SBT tanker costs 5 to 10 percent more than an equivalent non-SBT tanker. It also reduces the tanker's carrying capacity, further increasing transportation costs. Overall, SBT increases ship costs by almost $1,600 per voyage at 1976 oil prices.[157] In short, SBT required that money "be invested with an anti-economic result" and placed the owner at a competitive disadvantage.[158] Tanker owner be-

154. Indeed, the 1953 Faulkner report elaborated all the major elements of the procedure except for the combining of slops with subsequent loads of cargo.
155. Kirby, "Background to Progress."
156. Clarkson Research Studies, *The Tanker Register* (London: Clarkson Research Studies, Ltd., 1990).
157. Waters, Heaver, and Verrier, *Oil Pollution from Tanker Operations*, 92–94, 124; and Sadler and King, "Study on Mechanisms," 6.
158. Studies at the time concluded that even after accounting for social be-

havior confirms this analysis: MARPOL required existing tankers to retrofit either COW or SBT and the vast majority have opted for COW
rather than SBT. Taken together, this evidence suggests that the international requirement for SBT has been largely responsible for the technology's adoption.

SBT proved far more effective at changing behavior than did discharge regulations, for three reasons. First, unlike discharge regulations,
violations of equipment requirements could be readily detected. Second,
the treaty provided port states with the legal authority to detain in their
ports any ships violating these regulations. While few states have
proven willing to take such actions, at the time of construction, an owner could not be sure how few states that would be, or what share of the
market they would represent. Therefore, in buying a ship without SBT,
an owner was taking a large risk of being forced to retrofit or losing the
tanker altogether. Third, the ease of detecting and prosecuting equipment violations also eliminated each tanker owner's fear that complying
would place him at a competitive disadvantage. In contrast to discharge
standards, each owner could be confident that no other owner could get
away with an equipment violation. While SBT was expensive, this fact
removed the strong and continuing incentives to violate that even a conscientious tanker owner faced with respect to discharge standards.
Indeed, "mitigation of competitive disadvantage is so central to the shipping industry's perception of IMCO that it is this factor, probably more
than any other, that has brought the maritime community to embrace
costly requirements it would not have otherwise been willing to
accept."[159] Having said this, however, most tankers had no reason to
support SBT requirements absent international pressures for environmental protection. And, as already noted, once SBT or COW is installed, compliance with the performance standards can, relatively
safely, be assumed.

nefits, SBT adoption was unjustified. See, for example, Waters, Heaver, and
Verrier, *Oil Pollution from Tanker Operations*, 136; MEPC VI/Inf.7 (6 September 1976), and MEPC V/Inf.4 (8 March 1976), A18–A19. See also Osborne
and Ferguson, "Technology, MARPOL and Tankers", 6-2.
159. Sielen and McManus, "IMCO and the Politics of Ship Pollution," 154.

## Institutional Effectiveness

We now need to ask, how effective has this international environmental institution—its rules and procedures—been in solving the problem? The answer involves addressing at least three subsidiary questions. First, what definition of "the problem" should be used as the metric for effectiveness? Second, given a certain definition, has that problem been mitigated? Third, to what extent and by what means did the institution contribute to that mitigation?

How was the problem defined and against what standard should the institution's effectiveness be measured? While others could be used, I believe the most appropriate basis for evaluation is success in reducing intentional oil pollution from tankers—a standard that has been one of the nominal goals of the institution since the 1920s. From then until the late 1960s, international action sought to address coastal oil pollution due to intentional discharges from ships. The international environmental institution has gone on to expand the definition of the problem in some directions but not in others. After the *Torrey Canyon* accident of 1967, IMCO and the nations that had negotiated the 1954 Convention and 1962 Amendments began to address accidental oil pollution. The 1973 MARPOL Convention expanded in scope to include chemical, garbage, and sewage pollution from tankers and to apply relevant tanker regulations to oil platforms. Current discussions are under way to regulate air pollutants generated by ships.[160] International attempts were not made within this framework to address land-based sources of oil pollution, a problem that has been left to other, regional institutions. The institution could be judged on its success or failure at addressing any one of these other important environmental problems. However, a fair evaluation of any of these efforts would require an equally lengthy analysis of the institutional history involved. Therefore, the following analysis answers the first question by evaluating the effectiveness of the international institution at reducing intentional discharges. While it is no longer the only problem, it has remained a major problem addressed in the institutional framework.

This raises the second question, is there any evidence that intentional

160. Y. Sasamura, "Prevention and Control of Marine Pollution from Ships." (Paper prepared for the 25th Annual Conference of the Law of the Sea Institute, Malmo, Sweden, 1991).

discharges have decreased? Unfortunately, consistent efforts have not been made to collect high-quality data on oil pollution, whether by measuring oil found on beaches, oil content in ocean water, or even the number of operational oil spills. Indeed, perhaps the first criticism we can make of institutional effectiveness is that the institution has not established a research program to better understand the size and nature of the oil pollution problem and its change over time. Table 5.5 shows British and Dutch data that shed some light on the problem. The British data suggests a significant decrease in discharge incidents in port between 1961 and 1974 when normalized to tanker traffic (tonnage and number of ships), but provides no data on coastal and high seas spills or on observation efforts. The Dutch figures on observed North Sea spills show no significant decline between 1969 and 1988 when normalized to observation time, but do not account for tanker traffic.[161] Neither data set successfully excludes double counting of the same spill by different observers or clearly separates accidental from intentional spills. In 1989, a comprehensive Dutch study found that "the density of oiled sea birds found dead on the Dutch coast has fluctuated during the last forty years, and it has not decreased significantly".[162] In short, direct data has not been collected in a way sufficiently rigorous and systematic to clearly show whether coastal oil pollution or water quality has been decreasing or not.[163]

Rather than trying to observe oil pollution once it is introduced into the ocean, most analysts have attempted to estimate the amount of oil that tankers could be expected to discharge each year. The best estimates were based on oil company surveys conducted in the mid-1970s. Data collected by oil companies on oil retained aboard tankers showed that most tankers were not using LOT efficiently and that an average of 0.1 to 0.3 percent of a tanker's cargo, and hence of total seaborne trade, was discharged at sea. This produced estimates of operational discharges totaling 3.5 to 5 million tons per year.[164] Most analysts,

161. Smit-Kroes, *Harmonisatie Noordzeebeleid.*
162. Camphuysen, *Beached Bird Surveys,* 13.
163. Satu Nurmi, "Issues and Problems in the Protection of the Marine Environment," in *International Environmental Diplomacy: The Management and Resolution of Transfrontier Environmental Problems,* John E. Carroll, ed., (Cambridge: Cambridge University Press, 1988), 208.
164. Arthur McKenzie, "Letter to the Honorable John L. Burton," in House

Table 5.5   A.  Milford Haven oil spill statistics

| | 1961 | 1962 | 1963 | 1964 | 1965 | 1966 | 1967 | 1968 | 1969 | 1970 | 1971 | 1972 | 1973 | 1974 |
|---|---|---|---|---|---|---|---|---|---|---|---|---|---|---|
| Spills detected | 45 | 33 | 28 | 34 | 83 | 72 | 50 | 52 | 58 | 55 | 49 | 56 | 48 | 43 |
| No. of ships in port | 1066 | 1192 | 1236 | 1392 | 1985 | 2378 | 2680 | 2669 | 3266 | 3359 | 3490 | 3465 | 3886 | 4200 |
| Spills per 100 ships | 4.2 | 2.8 | 2.3 | 2.4 | 4.2 | 3.0 | 1.90 | 1.9 | 1.8 | 1.6 | 1.4 | 1.6 | 1.2 | 1.0 |
| Million tons of oil | 9.9 | 11.5 | 13.0 | 17.7 | 24.9 | 28.9 | 28.2 | 30 | 39.9 | 41.2 | 43.2 | 45.7 | 53.1 | 59.2 |
| Spills per million tons | 4.5 | 2.9 | 2.1 | 1.9 | 3.3 | 2.5 | 1.8 | 1.7 | 1.4 | 1.3 | 1.1 | 1.5 | 0.9 | 0.7 |

Source:  Dudley, 1976, 29.

B. Dutch sector of the North Sea oil spill statistics

| | 1969 | 1970 | 1971 | 1972 | 1973 | 1974 | 1975 | 1976 | 1977 | 1978 | 1979 | 1980 | 1981 | 1982 | 1983 | 1984 | 1985 | 1986 | 1987 | 1988 |
|---|---|---|---|---|---|---|---|---|---|---|---|---|---|---|---|---|---|---|---|---|
| Oil spills | 24 | 96 | 145 | 105 | 151 | 128 | 154 | 187 | 692 | 488 | 500 | 376 | 660 | 466 | 1024 | 649 | 571 | 378 | 535 | 429 |
| No linked to ships | | | | | | | | 100 | 127 | 82 | 47 | 74 | 77 | 107 | 92 | 72 | 62 | 70 | | |
| Detection rate | | | | | | | | 14% | 26% | 16% | 13% | 11% | 17% | 10% | 13% | 13% | 16% | 13% | | |
| Total slicks per hour of observation | | | | | | | | | | | | | | | 2.4 | 1.3 | 1.2 | 0.9 | 1.2 | 0.8 |
| Vessel slicks per hour of observation | | | | | | | | | | | | | | | 0.12 | 0.06 | 0.06 | 0.08 | 0.13 | 0.13 |
| Platform slicks per hour of observation | | | | | | | | | | | | | | | 0.13 | 0.06 | 0.07 | 0.03 | 0.04 | 0.02 |

Source: Camphuysen, 1989, 41 and 248.

largely due to lack of empirical data, have assumed LOT was both more widely and more efficiently used, and have estimated annual discharges in a range below 2 million metric tons. Although the accuracy of any of these estimates is subject to doubt, in the absence of better data, the range of expert estimates graphed in figure 5.1 suggests a decline in intentional oil pollution from ships, with the most notable decrease occurring after the mid-1970s. Perhaps more convincingly, the three National Academy of Sciences estimates also show a steady decline in intentional discharges.

Many analysts estimate reductions and attribute them directly to the international efforts to control oil discharges. In 1965, oil companies claimed that LOT had eliminated 60 percent of the estimated one million metric tons (Mt) of oil discharged annually.[165] A 1990 study concluded that "if there were no international pollution control, the annual amount of oil discharged from tankers could be as high as 6 Mt; if MARPOL 73/78 were strictly adhered to, this figure could be as low as 0.1 Mt. The actual figures could lie between 6 and 0.1 Mt, but the author optimistically assumes that it would be much nearer to the latter figure at present and could be further reduced in the future."[166] Similarly, a 1990 study by GESAMP concluded that MARPOL "regulations have resulted in a major reduction of operational pollution, not only from tankers but also from all other types of vessels."[167]

Without putting much faith in such assertions, the above analysis of industrial responses supports the accuracy of their direction if not their magnitude and the attribution of the adoption of SBT, and some adoption of LOT and COW, to international regulations. Since proper use of each technology does reduce oil discharges, and there is evidence that compliance has been quite high with SBT and COW, their adoption should have produced corresponding decreases in total oil inputs to the ocean. Indeed, their continuing phasing into the fleet over the past and

Committee on Government Operations, *Oil Tanker Pollution—Hearings*, 95th Congress, 2nd session, House 401-8. Washington, D.C.: GPO, 1978).
165. SCOP I/21, (1965), 6.
166. Y. Sasamura, "Oil in the Marine Environment," in *IMAS 90: Marine Technology and the Environment* (London: Institute of Marine Engineers, 1990), 3–6.
167. GESAMP 1990, 21.

next two decades will eventually account for major reductions in the intentional oil pollution that initially prompted international action. Without quantifying these reductions or the share for which the international institution is responsible, we can have some confidence that the world's oceans receive less oil from ships today than they would have absent these efforts. The lack of data demonstrating unambiguous reductions in oil slicks or sea bird deaths may be due to poor data, an inability to distinguish intentional discharges from other sources, and the fact that ships required to have SBT under MARPOL 73/78 still represent only 20 percent of the current world fleet.[168] Major observable environmental improvement from MARPOL 73/78 may await the total replacement of the fleet in the early twenty-first century, and enhanced control of other oil sources.

How did the institution overcome the obstacles that initially prevented effective action? What does this experience suggest about the value of increasing concern over, enhancing the contractual environment of, or improving national capacities to address, international environmental problems?

**Increasing Concern**   Most intergovernmental action has reacted to, rather than stimulated, concern over intentional oil pollution. Domestic nongovernmental organizations in both the United States and the United Kingdom have consistently played a significant role in raising the salience of oil pollution, widening public support, and pressuring lawmakers. Indeed, international concern has almost always been evinced by unilateral action by the United States or the United Kingdom, which in turn has been driven by domestic pressures. During the 1950s and 1960s, a single international NGO, ACOPS, also played a role in increasing attention to the issue by holding independent conferences.

Early on, most states, especially those with shipping and oil interests, viewed oil pollution as not enough of a problem to warrant strong international action. During the 1950s and early 1960s, British concern, due mainly to NGO activism, was high enough to prompt calls for action,

168. Lloyd's Register of Shipping, *Statistical Tables* (London: Lloyd's Register of Shipping, 1990), and Sadler and King, "Study on Mechanisms," 19.

but not widespread enough for the government to take strong measures. International action provided a means to weaken rather than widen the application of stringent pollution control. Even if compliance with 50-mile zones had been adequate to eliminate coastal oil pollution, enforcement measures would have failed to ensure compliance. It took increased concern, ignited by major oil spills in the late 1960s and 1970s and fanned by NGOs, their expression in threats of tough unilateral U.S. action, and wider support for such measures as the oil problem and other countries' concern over it grew, to shift the bargain from industry control over international policies to negotiation between industry and environmental concerns. Equally strong concern in less powerful states would have been unlikely to overcome the resistance or indifference of most states; indeed, major maritime states failed to support many U.S. proposals, though they eventually signed and ratified agreements containing those that passed. At the same time, if high concern in the United States had not found support in other states, the weak policies that had been the outcome of the British efforts in the 1950s and 1960s would have continued. While U.S. concern and unilateralism was crucial to adoption of stringent control measures, U.S. action alone would likely have failed to achieve the same results absent international agreement. Industry would probably have responded to exclusively unilateral U.S. requirements for SBT by equipping enough ships with SBT to service the U.S. market, rather than equipping all ships with SBT. The United States also could have attempted to achieve more stringent rules among fewer countries through bilateral agreements, but this would have involved far higher transaction costs than did the use of IMO meetings and associated conferences. It required the combination of strong concern in a major power coupled with a background level of concern in other states to overcome the resistance of shipping and oil interests that had preempted stringent international control prior to 1973.

The British and Americans, during their various phases as leaders of international action, consistently chose to compromise and achieve near-term regulatory rules within the constraints of current levels of concern, rather than to opt for a framework agreement reflecting general norms. They did not press for an ongoing research program to overcome low concern in hopes of developing support for stronger measures in the long term. Research into the impacts of oil pollution have neither been promoted by, nor had much influence on, the international institution. Indeed, scientists have found little conclusive evidence that oil pollution has major environmental impacts beyond the readily visible ones of oiled resort beaches and dead sea birds. Therefore, an extensive research program would likely have done little to speed up the process of increasing concern that eventually led to adoption of strong international rules. Research into technologies to reduce discharges might have proved helpful, however, in reducing international dependence on industry development of, and reluctance to release information regarding, options like LOT and COW which promised environmental benefits.

Thus, stringent controls depended on strong concern in a major developed state, its expression in a willingness to take unilateral action and to bring diplomatic pressure to bear, and a willingness among many other states to support such measures for many reasons— including, but by no means limited to, concern over coastal pollution. While strong concern has been a precondition for effective rules, the institution has done little to promote the growth of such concern.

**Enhancing the Contractual Environment**    International efforts to control oil pollution have achieved greater success by enhancing the contractual environment for international agreement. By holding regular committee and subcommittee meetings and sponsoring diplomatic conferences, IMCO has provided a forum where nations could raise their views and concern regarding oil pollution and current or proposed solutions. These forums have facilitated global rather than regional or unilateral regulation, an outcome also preferred by oil and shipping interests. While this approach produces less stringent measures at a slower pace than "leaders" and many environmentalists might prefer, it has produced more stringent rules than most states would have promulgated absent international agreement. For example, while the double bottoms promoted by the United States in 1973 were never required internationally, tankers from most states would still be unlikely to have SBT absent the MARPOL 73/78 accord. The Subcommittee on Oil Pollution facilitated discussions of LOT in the 1960s, and the Marine Environment Protection Committee conducted extended discussions on retrofitting SBT in the 1970s and on amendments since

1978, thus helping to work out the technical details essential to implementing the oil pollution agreements effectively.

The institution also learned from past experience to make it easier for agreements to enter into force and for nations to enforce agreements. After decades of excruciatingly slow ratification processes, adoption of the tacit acceptance procedure dramatically reduced the time between amendment adoption and entry into force. MARPOL adopted not merely a more stringent, but a fundamentally different, equipment-based, approach to oil pollution control because of the dismal record of discharge standards, which had proved ineffective not because they were too lenient—MARPOL left them largely unchanged—but because violations were hard to detect or sanction effectively. MARPOL established equipment standards that increased the effectiveness of enforcement resources and removed the international legal impediments to effective enforcement. Requirements for SBT and COW also helped reassure otherwise conscientious tanker owners that their compliance would not be matched by clandestine violations by others, leaving them at a competitive disadvantage. The institution dramatically increased the transparency of oil pollution control through adoption of these measures.

IMO has been relatively unsuccessful, however, at enhancing transparency regarding, and thereby increasing, governmental enforcement. Most states regularly ignore IMO's reporting requirements. Outside of the Memorandum of Understanding, little concerted effort has been made to improve enforcement of IMO conventions. Enforcement continues to depend on the domestic political incentives states have to expend resources on monitoring and sanctioning violations.

**Increasing Capacity**  Finally, the institution has a mixed record at increasing the capacity of states to address oil pollution. IMO and developed states concerned about the problem have done little to increase the capacity of developing states to address intentional oil pollution. The failure of many governments to comply with the requirement to ensure provision of adequate reception facilities has provided tanker operators with an excuse for discharging oil at sea. Yet, the voluntary financial assistance measures under IMO's Technical Cooperation

Program have rarely been used to fund installation of reception facilities, or to pay for enhanced enforcement, in developing countries.[169]

More than from increasing capacity, IMO has achieved progress by reducing barriers to the effective use of states' existing capacities. Initial reliance on flag state enforcement inhibited successful prosecution of discharge violations. While the MARPOL 73/78 provisions allowing port states the right to fully inspect ships and to detain those posing a threat to the marine environment did not create new incentives for enforcement, they did remove barriers restraining port states that had existing incentives to enforce. Full inspections have become commonplace, and some states have detained ships for equipment violations— procedures which were unheard of prior to removal of the jurisdictional barriers that were still reflected in the 1969 Amendments. MARPOL's shift from discharge standards to equipment standards enhanced enforcement capacity by ensuring that the relatively few states willing to enforce treaty provisions had the legal authority and practical ability to do so.

### Conclusions and Lessons

International efforts to control intentional oil pollution from ships had essentially no impact on improving the marine environment until the rules promulgated in the 1973 and 1978 agreements came into force. The institution succeeded by improving the contractual environment to facilitate global agreements, and by removing the barriers to states' ability to exercise their capacity to enforce those agreements. The institution's success awaited, rather than created, concern over oil pollution. Stringent measures were agreed to only after strong public concern in a powerful country like the United States met with willing support from

169. This continuing problem produced a call within the Preparatory Committee for the United Nations Conference on Environment and Development to raise $80 million per year for oil reception facilities in developing countries (UN Document A/Conf.151/PC/100/Add.21 United Nations, and Preparatory Committee for the United Nations Conference on Environment and Development, *Protection of Oceans, All Kinds of Seas Including Enclosed and Semienclosed Seas, Coastal Areas and the Protection, Rational Use and Development of Their Living Resources* (New York, N.Y.: United Nations, 1991).

states concerned over the problem or little affected by the proposed solution. Having regular international meetings delayed and diluted, but also broadened, the impact of these proposals. Adoption of tacit acceptance procedures helped bring these measures into force more quickly than previously. Adoption of equipment standards removed practical and legal barriers to effective detection and enforcement, and violations have been almost nonexistent. The institution's success in the past decade depended on taking advantage of exogenous increases in concern to enhance the contractual environment and remove constraints on capacity that had previously impeded effective mitigation of the intentional oil pollution problem.

What lessons for environmental institutions can we draw from this examination of the lengthy history of oil pollution control efforts? I see the lessons as twofold. The first lesson is not especially encouraging. The story laid out here suggests that significant progress in environmental improvement depends on development of strong public concern that in many cases may be outside the control of international policymakers, negotiators, and others concerned about the health of the global environment. Early on, so few governments considered oil pollution a problem that international agreements went unsigned. While some states sought international action, others simply saw no benefits from such action. After 1954, enough governments saw oil pollution as a problem that international action became desirable, but only as long as it involved no significant costs. It took until the 1970s before governments began to impose the high costs—on industry, notably, not on themselves—necessary to reduce intentional oil discharges. Major progress to reduce intentional oil discharges has required environmental crises or shocks sufficient to prompt widespread public concern. NGO action without such broad concern within and across countries proved insufficient to produce effective regulations. Even once support for action developed, it took a combination of three factors—unilateral action by powerful states, a lowering of political resistance among many (though not all) developed states, and a willingness on the part of developing states to support such action—to bring the issue to the international agenda in a way which produced effective regulations.

The second lesson seems more hopeful, however. Once sufficient concern has developed, the right international rules can improve the environment. Their effectiveness will certainly be constrained by the breadth of support and commitment to achieving real environmental progress. However, the oil pollution story suggests that sometimes even quite strict and expensive rules can induce levels of compliance that promise, over time, to significantly reduce environmental degradation. The very nature of oil pollution has meant that reductions in oil wastes will often be due to self-interested behavior on the part of oil transportation interests. However, oil and shipping interests have adopted technologies to decrease intentional discharges into the ocean even when facing large and direct economic costs. While the lack of progress against oil pollution before the late 1970s must have frustrated many people concerned with the environment, the experience with ineffective rules over that period helped point the way to the rules that were needed to get tankers to stop discharging their oil at sea. Policymakers seeking to mitigate environmental pollution could benefit by developing rules that remove the barriers to states with the capacity and incentives to enforce international agreements, so that during periods when support for action develops, they can use those opportunities to put effective environmental regulations into place.

# 6

## International Fisheries Management

M. J. Peterson

National and international efforts to regulate ocean fisheries, including the taking of marine mammals, have addressed three issues. Before the twentieth century, the greatest issue was allocation of rights to fish in particular areas or for particular species. Even before any overfishing occurred, certain rich fishing grounds became crowded and fishers sought explicit agreements defining rights of access. As fishing technology improved in the twentieth century, the problems of overfishing and overinvestment in equipment became more prominent. Actual or feared overfishing led governments to devise ways to limit fishers' catches through restricting gear, establishing closed seasons, areas, or both, specifying minimum sizes to prevent taking immature fish, and determining catch quotas. Effective policy has long been defined as keeping catches steady over the long term, permitting neither short bursts of high catch nor periods of low or no catch. Overinvestment has never received as much attention as overfishing, but is important in its own right. Resource economists identified overinvestment as a problem not only because it results in a socially suboptimal allocation of resources among different economic endeavors, but also because they believed that preventing overinvestment would reduce both crowding on the grounds and pressures to permit overfishing.[1] The early optimism that it would

The author thanks the Rockefeller Brothers Fund for financial support, James Smith for research assistance, and Gary D. Brewer and the other members of the project team, particularly Peter M. Haas, Robert O. Keohane, Marc Levy, and Ron Mitchell, for comments on earlier drafts.
1. E.g., H. S. Gordon, "The Economic Theory of a Common Property Resource: The Fishery," *Journal of Political Economy* 62 (1954): 124–42; Milner B. Schaefer, "Biological and Economic Aspects of the Management of Marine Fisheries," *Transactions of the American Fisheries Society* 88 (1959): 100–104;

be easy to attain sustainable catches and economically efficient levels of investment simultaneously was challenged later,[2] but few would deny the broad proposition that overinvestment greatly increases the pressures to permit unsustainably high catches.

Of these three concerns—access, overfishing, and overinvestment—only the second directly poses an "environmental" issue to which the expertise of natural science is relevant. The strong link between overinvestment and overfishing means that failure to attack that problem makes failure to prevent overfishing more likely. At minimum, then, effective regulation of fishing requires a combination of biological and economic expertise coupled with administrative effectiveness.

Ocean fishing has been an international problem since access problems were first recognized. The international aspect stemmed from the legal doctrines treating the high seas as a common area open to all. On the high seas, no single government had the right to regulate all fishing. Each government could regulate its own fishers, but regulation of all fishers depended on cooperation among all their governments. Local overfishing problems were first recognized in the 1880s and began inspiring international action after the turn of the century. As overfishing became more widespread and the problems of overinvestment were recognized, international efforts proliferated.

The history of twentieth-century international fisheries management must be divided into two eras: before and after widespread adoption of the 200-nautical-mile exclusive economic zone in 1976–77. This change in the wider normative framework within which international fisheries commissions operated transformed the contractual environment, and with it nearly every aspect of international fisheries management. Though this change was partly a reaction to perceived failures to prevent overfishing, it occurred through a separate negotiating process that is not the subject of this chapter.[3] Thus multilateral responses to over-

---

Francis T. Christy, Jr., and Anthony Scott, *The Common Wealth in Ocean Fisheries* (Baltimore: Johns Hopkins University Press, 1965), 14.
2. E.g., Colin Clark, "The Economics of Overexploitation," *Science* 181 (17 August 1973): 630–34; Geoffrey Waugh, *Fisheries Management: Theoretical Developments and Contemporary Applications* (Boulder, Colo.: Westview, 1984).
3. On that negotiating process, see e.g., Ann Hollick, *U.S. Policy and the Law*

fishing can be divided into two broad types: international commissions charged with making joint decisions about managing a common pool resource, and regional commissions invigorated after 1977 to help coastal states cope with managing their EEZs.

This study focuses first on eleven international fisheries commissions established before 1977. Four concerned a single species while seven concerned all commercially valuable species in a particular ocean area. Their main features are summarized in table 6.1.

Most of these commissions remained in existence after 1977, though their terms of reference were shifted to accommodate national jurisdiction in the EEZ. Reorganization was most thorough in the Northwest Atlantic, where the older commission was replaced by a new Northwest Atlantic Fisheries Organization. A new multispecies body, the Commission for the Conservation of Antarctic Marine Living Resources, was established in 1982 to deal with the Southern Ocean. While the Inter-American Tropical Tuna Commission lost most of its functions in the late 1970s, and the North Pacific Fur Seal Commission was terminated in 1984, the other single-species commissions remained in existence. A new one, covering North Atlantic salmon, was established in 1982. The main features of these commissions are summarized in table 6.2.

Eight regional commissions (including the one for the East Central Atlantic noted in table 6.2) covering developing areas extended their activity to include discussion of management issues. Basic features of the nine are given in table 6.3. While distant fishing states remain members of most of the commissions sponsored by the UN Food and Agriculture Organization (FAO), their management committees, like the three independent commissions, include only coastal states.

Effective fisheries management is the end point of a process that involves getting the matter on the political agenda, choosing measures from among those being urged as solutions to the problems of overfishing and overinvestment, and assuring action consistent with the de-

*of the Sea* (Princeton: Princeton University Press, 1982); D. P. O'Connell, *The International Law of the Sea* (2 vols. Oxford: Oxford University Press, 1982–83); Guilio Pontecorvo, ed., *The New Order of the Oceans: Advent of a Managed Environment* (New York: Columbia University Press, 1986); Clyde Sanger, *Ordering the Oceans: The Law of the Sea in Practice* (Toronto: University of Toronto Press, 1986).

**Table 6.1**  International commissions established before 1977

| Commission | Focus | Active | Members |
|---|---|---|---|
| North Pacific Fur Seal Commission | Fur seals of Pribilof, Robbin, & Commander Islands | 1911–40; 1957–84 | America: Canada, U.S.; Asia: Japan; Europe: USSR |
| International Whaling Commission (IWC) | Great whales in all oceans, main emphasis on Southern Ocean | 1949– | Africa: South Africa; America: Brazil, Canada, Mexico, Panama, U.S.; Asia: Japan; Europe: Iceland, Sweden, U.K., USSR; Oceania: Australia, New Zealand. (membership increased to 40 in early 1980s) |
| Interamerican Tropical Tuna Commission (IATTC) | Tuna and tuna-like species of S.E. Pacific | 1950–79 | America: Mexico, U.S., Nicaragua, Panama; Asia: Japan; Europe: France |
| International Commission for the Conservation of Atlantic Tunas (ICCAT) | Tuna and tuna-like species of Atlantic | 1969– | Africa: Angloa, Benin, Cape Verde, Cote d'Ivoire, Eq. Guinea, Gabon, Ghana, Morocco Sao Tome e Principe, Senegal, South Africa; America: Brazil, Canada, Cuba, U.S., Uruguay, Venezuela; Asia: Japan, S. Korea; Europe: France, Spain Portugal, USSR |
| North Sea Commission | Major commercial species of North Sea and Belts | 1954–59 | Europe: Belgium, Denmark, France, W. Germany, Iceland, Ireland, Netherlands Norway, Poland, Portugal, Spain, Sweden, U.K., USSR |
| North Pacific Fisheries Commission | Major commercial species of NE Pacific | 1952– | America: Canada, U.S.; Asia: Japan |

**Table 6.1**  (*continued*)

| Commission | Focus | Active | Members |
|---|---|---|---|
| International Commission for Northwest Atlantic Fisheries | Major commercial species off U.S., Canada, Greenland eastern Iceland | 1950–79 | America: Canada, U.S.; Europe: Denmark, France W. Germany, Iceland, Italy, Norway, Portugal, Spain, U.K., USSR |
| North East Atlantic Fisheries Commission (NEAFC) | Major commercial species in North Sea, Irish Sea, Atlantic off Scandinavia and Iceland | 1959–78 | Europe: Belgium, Denmark, France, W. Germany, Iceland, Ireland, Netherlands Norway, Poland, Portugal, Spain, Sweden, U.K., USSR |
| International Commission for Southeast Atlantic Fisheries (ICSEAF) | Major commercial species off west coast of South Africa, off Namibia and Angola | 1971– | Africa: Angola, S. Africa; Amerian: Cuba; Asia: Iraq, Israel, Japan, S. Korea; Europe: Bulgaria, France, E. Germany, W. Germany, Italy, Poland, Portugal, Romania, Spain, USSR, Belgium (to 1981) |
| Baltic Fisheries Commission | Major commercial species of Baltic | 1974– | Europe: Denmark Finland, E. Germany, W. Germany, Poland Sweden, USSR |
| Committee for the East Central Atlantic Fisheries (CECAF) | Stocks off northern Atlantic coast of Africa and Gulf of Guinea | 1969– | Africa: Benin, Cameroon, Cape Verde, Cote d'Ivoire, Eq. Guinea, Gabon, Gambia, Congo, Ghana, Guinea, Guinea-Bissau, Liberia, Mauritania, Morocco, Nigeria, Sao Tome e Principe, Senegal, Sierra Leone, Togo, Zaire; America: Cuba, U.S. Asia: Japan, S. Korea; Europe: France, Greece, Italy, Norway, Poland, Romania, Spain |

**Table 6.2**    International commission established after 1977

| Commission | Focus | Active | Members |
|---|---|---|---|
| Revised NEAFC | stocks beyond 200-mile limit in same area as NEAFC | 1980– | America: Cuba; Europe: Belgium, Bulgaria, Denmark, France, Germany, Greece, Greenland, Faroes, Iceland, Ireland, Italy, Luxembourg, Netherlands, Norway, Poland, Portugal, Spain, Sweden, USSR, U.K., European Community |
| North Atlantic Fisheries Organization (NAFO) | stocks straddling 200-mile limit off Canada | 1980– | America: Canada; Europe: Denmark, France, Iceland, USSR, European Community |
| North Atlantic Salmon Conservation Organization (NASCO) | North Atlantic salmon | 1982– | America: Canada, U.S.; Europe: Denmark, Finland, Iceland, Norway, USSR, Sweden, European Community |
| Commission for the Conservation of Antarctic Marine Living Resources (CCAMLR) | Krill, finfish in Southern Ocean | 1982– | Africa: S. Africa; America: Argentina, Brazil, Chile, U.S.; Asia: India, Japan, S. Korea; Europe: France, E. Germany, W. Germany, USSR; Oceania: Australia, New Zealand |

**Table 6.3**   Regional commissions

| Commission | Focus | Membership |
|---|---|---|
| General Fisheries Council for the Mediterranean (GFCM) | Stocks in Mediterranean and Aegean Seas | Africa: Algeria, Egypt, Libya, Morocco, Tunisia; Asia: Israel, Syria, Lebanon; Europe: Bulgaria, Cyprus, France, Greece, Italy, Malta, Monaco, Romania, Spain, Turkey, Yugoslavia |
| Committee for the East Central Atlantic Fisheries (CECAF) | Stocks off northern Atlantic coast of Africa and in Gulf of Guinea | Africa: Benin, Cameroon, Cape Verde, Congo, Cote d'Ivoire, Eq. Guinea, Gabon, Gambia, Ghana, Guinea, Guinea Bissau, Liberia, Mauretania, Morocco, Nigeria, Sao Tome e Principe, Senegal, Sierra Leone, Togo, Zaire; America: Cuba, U.S.; Asia: Japan, S. Korea; Europe: France, Greece, Italy, Norway, Poland, Romania, Spain |
| Western Central Atlantic Fishery Commission (WECAFC) | Stocks in Gulf of Mexico, Caribbean | Africa: Guinea, Zaire; America: Antigua and Barbuda, Bahamas, Barbados, Belize, Brazil, Colombia, Cuba, Grenada, Dominica, Guatemala, Guyana, Haiti, Honduras, Jamaica, Mexico, Nicaragua, Panama, St. Kitts-Nevis, St. Lucia, St. Vincent-Grenadines, Suriname, Trinidad-Tobago, U.S., Venezuela; Asia: Japan, S. Korea; Europe: France, Italy, Netherlands, Spain, U.K. |
| Regional Fisheries Advisory Commission for the Southwest Atlantic (CARPAS) | Stocks off coasts of member states | America: Argentina, Brazil, Uruguay |
| Indo-Pacific Fisheries Commission (IPFC) | Stocks off Southeast Asia and east coast of India | America: U.S.; Asia: Bangladesh, Burma, India, Japan, Cambodia, S. Korea, Malaysia, Nepal, Pakistan, Philippines, Sri Lanka, Thailand, Vietnam; Europe: France, U.K.; Oceania: Australia, New Zealand |

**Table 6.3** (*continued*)

| Commission | Focus | Membership |
|---|---|---|
| Indian Ocean Fisheries Commission (IOFC) | Stocks in Indian, Ocean, Bay of Bengal, Red Sea, Persian Gulf, and off east coast of Africa | Africa: Comoros, Ethiopia, Kenya, Madagascar, Mauritius, Mozambique, Seychelles, Somalia Tanzania; America: Cuba, U.S.; Asia: Bahrain, Bangladesh, India, Indonesia, Iran, Iraq, Israel, Jordan, Japan, S. Korea, Kuwait, Malaysia, Maldives, Oman, Pakistan, Qatar, Saudi Arabia, Sri Lanka, Thailand, United Arab Emirates, Vietnam; Europe: France, Greece, Netherlands, Norway, Portugal, Spain, Sweden, U.K.; Oceania: Australia |
| South Pacific Permanent Commission | Stocks off coasts of member states | America: Chile, Colombia, Ecuador, Peru |
| South Pacific Forum Fisheries Agency | Stocks in S. Pacific and off Oceania | Oceania: Australia, Cook Islands, Fiji, Kiribati, Marshall Islands, Micronesia, Nauru, New Zealand, Palau, Papua-New Guinea, Samoa, Solomon Islands, Tonga, Tuvalu, Vanuatu |

cisions. Conceptually, overinvestment is simple: it consists of putting more capital (generally in the form of ships and gear) into a fishery than is justified by the long-term return on investment. Overfishing has two components: growth overfishing and recruitment overfishing. Growth overfishing occurs when fishers take a smaller average size fish though the overall population size is not yet affected. In a typical fishery, the largest fish are taken first, since they yield the best price. As they are depleted, fishers concentrate their effort on smaller (and younger) ones. Growth overfishing can be avoided by regulations that discourage or prevent the taking of juveniles. Closing spawning areas, banning fishing during spawning season, and setting trawl net mesh size large enough that juveniles can escape all address this problem. The main difficulties with these measures occur in mixed fisheries where different species spawn at different times, or grow to such different sizes that a net permitting escape of juveniles of one species retains juveniles of another. In such fisheries, regulations involve trade-offs of over- and underfishing different species. Recruitment overfishing is more serious; it involves taking so many fish that those left to spawn produce a smaller number of young than before, reducing the total population size. Recruitment overfishing can be avoided only with more stringent measures limiting fishing effort by imposing catch quotas, limiting gear to less efficient forms, limiting the number of boats and fishers involved, or allocating exclusive rights to fish particular areas. While it is possible to have growth overfishing without passing on to recruitment overfishing, the great increase in fishing gear efficiency during the twentieth century has meant that in most cases growth overfishing was simply the prelude to recruitment overfishing.

Evaluation of any management effort must look at the policy process within its wider context. International management efforts occur within the decentralized the international system, in which autonomous units bargain their way to cooperation. The effectiveness or ineffectiveness of international management stems from both the constraints imposed by context and the features of the policy process.

**The Contractual Environment**

Before adoption of EEZs in 1977, ocean fisheries formed an open-access common pool resource. Prevailing international law restricted coastal state jurisdiction to a narrow band of water, usually three nautical miles wide, adjacent to its coasts. Within that area, a coastal state could regulate fishing as it wished; outside that area, all comers had an equal legal right to fish. The contractual environment involved mixed parallel and divergent interests, with the latter prevailing. All parties acknowledged enough common concern to accept the establishment of joint commissions and the creation of mechanisms for securing expert advice. Yet enough parties had sufficient interest in keeping the costs of adjustment as low as possible to delay agreement on serious restrictions of fishing. Some parties also tolerated their fishers' cheating on the limits. At any particular moment enough parties suspected cheating (usually with good reason) to make stable cooperation in the maintenance of restrictions impossible. Though all would benefit from restraining current catching activity to ensure decent catches in the future, most governments heavily discounted the future. Restricting the time horizon to the immediate term meant that the gain from free-riding (cheating on the regulations while others follow them) was viewed as sufficiently greater than the gain from mutual cooperation to encourage cheating. This forced even those considering longer time horizons to acknowledge that their cooperation was likely to go unreciprocated, which reduced their own commitment to restraint. Altering the contractual environment sufficiently to evoke stable cooperation would have required both changing the time horizons so that the value of free-riding over mutual cooperation was reduced and finding effective ways to prevent cheating so that all parties would have assurance of reciprocal restraint.

Provision of common scientific advice did not lead to any lengthening of time horizons for several reasons. Through the 1950s and much of the 1960s, world fish catches were actually increasing as fishers located unexploited stocks in other parts of the world. Thus depletion of stocks in a particular area was not taken as cause for alarm, but as a signal to start shifting effort somewhere else. Though world fish catches leveled off in the 1970s and the collapse of the Peruvian anchoveta fishery from a catch of 10.25 million metric tons in 1971 to one of 1.75 million metric tons in 1973 was taken as a warning by some governments and in scientific circles,[4] it was still possible to locate unexploited stocks. This helped distract the governments whose fleets exploited such stocks from the need to accept regulations on already heavily exploited ones. Governments' support for expansion of national fishing fleets, whether working in areas near home or in distant waters, was strong. Even as understanding of the limits of the world's fisheries increased during the 1970s, many governments still expected to shift adjustment costs onto others. Governments of distant-water fleets sought to maintain opportunities; governments of coastal fleets looked more and more to modifying the bargaining situation through a redefinition of the resource by national enclosure. In addition, as will be noted below, the policy process offered little assistance in upgrading the common interest.

4. FAO *Yearbook of Fisheries Statistics*, vol. 1: *Catches and Landings* 1973, 106.

Most particular bargaining situations were affected by significant asymmetries. This was not true in the North Pacific, where well-equipped fleets from several states participated in the fishery, and each government had the administrative capacity to bring relevant scientific and economic expertise to bear and to implement programs. In other areas, some fleets were larger and better equipped than others, and thus were able to catch faster and further from home. This gave them ability to outrace others and to shift to other grounds if currently fished areas became less productive. In many of these situations interstate asymmetries occurred as well; more powerful fishing states were able to resist the initiatives of less powerful coastal or conservationist states. Unevenness of fleet capacity marked all North Atlantic fisheries; imbalances in overall state capability were particularly pronounced in the fisheries off Iceland, the Scandinavian Peninsula, and Canada. Other bargaining situations were even more asymmetrical because a weak coastal state with little or no fishing fleet and little administrative capacity ended up watching while others took the riches. This situation appeared in the Eastern Pacific tuna fisheries in the 1940s, and spread to others off the west coast of Latin America soon after. Fisheries off the west coast of Africa, particularly off Angola and Namibia, were similarly dominated by distant-water fleets by 1970. With sometimes the Soviets and sometimes the Japanese in the lead, distant-water fleets were pushing into new areas of the Pacific, the Indian Ocean, and the South Atlantic by the mid-1970s. A few developing countries, most notably Peru and Thailand, increased their capacity to fish in nearby waters. In all these areas, weak developing coastal states and their local fleets faced stiff challenge from the well-equipped distant-water fleets of industrial countries. While industrial coastal states supported EEZ proposals out of frustration with the international commissions, many developing coastal states supported such proposals even before the commissions' failure became apparent so they could control the resources rather than be forced to let others rake them off.

The distributional conflicts among states that impeded collaboration were fairly strong. Each of four domestic patterns resulted in severe reluctance to adjust. The first involved privately owned distant-water fleets importuning their own government to help them retain or expand fishing opportunities. Such demands had the greatest impact on government policy in Japan, but the British, South Korean, Norwegian, Spanish, Taiwanese, and U.S. governments responded similarly when their important distant-water fleets were involved. A second pattern, in which government fostered and protected state-owned distant-water fleets, occurred most clearly in the USSR, but also in Bulgaria, East Germany, Poland, and Romania. The third, where governments owned or encouraged private coastal fleets, occurred in developing countries anxious to build a new industry to acquire additional food supplies or products for export. The west coast Latin American states, particularly Peru, had adopted such policies in the 1950s; by 1975 they had been joined by other developing states. The fourth pattern, another variant of industry importuning government, occurred in states where coastal fleets sought assistance against distant-water competitors. This had the greatest effect on policy in Iceland, but also affected Canada, European countries without distant-water fleets, and the United States. Some governments were beset by strong tensions between coastal and distant-water fishers in the same country. The U.S. policy in particular suffered from contradictions between what was advocated for fisheries where United States coastal fleets were most important, and what was advocated when U.S.–flagged distant-water fleets were the most important. The major distant-water fleet states and the developing countries were far less divided domestically. The overlapping of these four patterns of fisher-government relations guaranteed that in virtually every fisheries commission, the common realization that overfishing should be avoided was subordinated to the struggle over who should adjust, and how much.

How severely these asymmetries and domestic pressures for continued fishing were felt in each commission depended on the precise mix of environmental leaders, followers, and laggards among the members. Greater fleet mobility encouraged distant-water states to be laggards by reducing incentives to take a long view of the particular stock. If the fishing became poor, their fleets could just move on to another area and fish another stock. The Soviets, Japanese, and Eastern Europeans all had deserved reputations for energetic and abusive fishing, but other distant-water fleets displayed the same tendencies. In general, the British, Canadian, Scandinavian, and U.S. governments tended to be leaders. The West German government became a leader in the mid-1970s, even to the point of reducing the size and capacity of its distant-water fleets.[5] Most governments can be classified as followers—concerned about conservation in waters near their own shores when others point out problems, but less concerned about more distant areas.

Those who wanted cooperation had to overcome the obstacles imposed by the highly conflictual nature of the contractual environment. Success would have involved transforming that environment sufficiently that adjustment would be accepted by all participants, not just leaders. Issue-linkage, the securing of concessions in one area by providing rewards in another, is often an efficacious method of transforming situations. Such linkage was seldom attempted in international fisheries management. Fisheries commissions were restricted to managing fishing of particular species or in a particular ocean area. This tight compartmentalization made issue-linkage, apart from trading off greater or fewer restrictions on different parts of the fishery, impossible. This limited the opportunities for inducing cooperation through side-payments.

Only the North Pacific Fur Seal Commission, spurred by severe stock depletion, was based on arranging a trade. That arrangement was reached only after a long bilateral wrangle between the United States and Britain (then sovereign over Canada) over protection of the stocks. In 1882, an arbitral tribunal rejected U.S. claims of a unilateral right to stop pelagic sealing on the high seas, but recommended the basic settlement adopted among Britain, Japan, Russia, and the United States in the 1911 North Pacific Fur Seal Convention. Canada, Japan, and Russia traded their nationals' right to hunt fur seals on the high seas for a percentage of the skins "in number and value" taken by licensed American, Japanese, and Russian sealers working the island breeding grounds.[6] The managing states also had the right to patrol the seas where their seal stocks lived and arrest any ship engaged in pelagic sealing. Though prosecution remained a matter for the flag state, this gave the managing states effective control over activity at sea. This solution was encouraged by the particular features of the fishery. The seals bred on islands that were within the sovereignty of individual states, and were best

5. Compare figures in 1970 and 1980 volumes of Lloyd's of London, *Lloyd's Registry of Shipping: Statistical Tables* (London: Lloyd's, annually).
6. *North Pacific Fur Seal Convention*, 1911, Article 1.

hunted when on the islands because adults could be distinguished from juveniles, females from males, and females with calves from females without. Yet they also spent a considerable portion of their lives at sea, where they could be taken by any comer. Considerations of efficiency favored confining the hunt to the breeding grounds; high seas rights meant that ocean hunting could not simply be banned. The potential gain from restoring the stocks gave Japan, Russia, and the United States incentive to offer rewards, and Canada, Japan, and Russia incentive to accept them. Even this trade-off broke down temporarily when the Japanese used claims that stocks were restored to justify a return to ocean taking.[7]

A number of coastal states did attempt a trade of sorts in the early 1970s, using threats to assert broader fisheries jurisdiction as a way to restrain others. The United States was able to do this with some effect vis-à-vis both the USSR and Japan. Iceland waged a long legal and ocean battle with the United Kingdom. Yet these efforts were stopgaps; once EEZs were accepted, this sort of trade was no longer possible— but it was also unnecessary unless stocks ranged beyond the 200-mile line.

In some cases where depletion had not gone as far, the desire of some states to avoid adjusting was strong enough to change the situation from conflict to deadlock. The Whaling, Northwest Atlantic, Northeast Atlantic, and Southeast Atlantic commissions all faced such a situation. The Soviet fleets active in the first, and the Soviet and Eastern European fishing fleets active in the latter three, always had different economic calculations than others. They were concerned not with selling on a market guided by price, but with supplying a planned economy where the cost of fishing was compared not to the return from sales but to the cost of producing an equivalent amount of animal protein in an inefficient (hence, high-cost) agricultural sector.[8] Japanese whaling fleets had markedly different economic incentives than their Western counter-

7. William C. Herrington and John L. Kask, "International Conservation Problems, and Solutions in Existing Conventions," in *Papers Presented at the International Technical Conference on the Conservation of the Living Resources of the Sea*, Rome, 1955 (United Nations Documen A/CONF.10/7), 152–53.
8. S. V. Mikhailov, "On the Comparative Efficiency of Production of Some Products of Land and Sea," *Okeanologiia* 2: 385–92; discussed in Christy and Scott, *Common Wealth*, 122.

parts because they had a market for whale meat as well as whale oil. In 1955, a whale worth about $3,500 to a British or Norwegian whaling company was worth over $11,000 to a Japanese one because of this second, and more lucrative, product.[9] Even Japanese fishing fleets had better markets because of the high demand for fish at home. This made restraint relatively more expensive for Japan, the Soviet Union, and Eastern European countries. Though stock depletion would be as bad for them as for others, it would not be as bad as quickly, which allowed their fleets to try outlasting others'. Their behavior gives credence to the theory that a sufficiently high discount rate makes it economically rational to deplete stocks to exhaustion, if not to actual extinction.[10]

The change in international law, legitimizing coastal state jurisdiction over all fishing within 200 nautical miles of its coasts, transformed the game. Most ocean fisheries were no longer open-access common pools. Rather, property rights were attributed to states, with governments acting as their agents. In many areas, then, the contractual environment acquired a new asymmetry because the holder of property rights was able to extract cooperation from others by threatening to deprive them of all access. In other areas, where coastal states lacked sufficient administrative capability to manage their EEZs, the actual situation remained asymmetrical in favor of the better-equipped fishers—usually the distant-water fleets of industrial states—though this could change as the coastal states developed management capacities.

Attributing property rights through the EEZ concept did not, however, eliminate the need for international cooperation. Fish continue to swim and migrate without regard to human boundaries. While about 90 percent of edible species range within 200 nautical miles of some coast, a much smaller proportion remain neatly within the confines of one state's EEZ. Some stocks range across the 200-mile line, meaning that fishers outside as well as inside the EEZ need to observe a common overall catch limit. Yet those outside are not under the jurisdiction of the coastal state; they remain under the jurisdiction of their own. Unless the flag states of these fleets cooperate with the coastal state, the latter's

9. George Small, *The Blue Whale* (New York: Columbia University Press, 1971), 39–42.
10. R. Michael 'M'Gonigle, "The 'Economizing' of Ecology: Why Big, Rare Whales Still Die," *Ecology Law Quarterly* 9 (1980): 119–237.

property rights mean little because there is a "hole in the fence" through which resources can be taken. Other stocks of fish stay within 200 nautical miles of shore, but are either constantly spread across, or migrate between, the EEZs of two or more neighboring states. Here, effective management requires cooperation among all coastal states sharing part of the stock. A third reason for international cooperation arose from developing states' realization that they lacked the capability to administer their EEZs. They saw in regional organization—whether established locally or fostered by the UN's Food and Agriculture Organization—a way to acquire greater capacity and redress the asymmetries of dealing with industrial state fleets by presenting a group position.

In the areas still subject to international management, the old conflict situation continued. Though there was greater mutual awareness that overfishing needed to be avoided, this did not provide a common focus sufficient to override or abate the concern about costs of adjustment. The strength of these dynamics was also manifest at the domestic level in those states with administrative capacity to pursue fisheries management within their own EEZs. In most such states, fishing industry reluctance to adjust, sometimes coupled with new local entrants as reduction of foreigners' access seemed to create new opportunities, prevented effective management. Overinvestment was not avoided in systems that ran the national fishery as an open-access resource, and this increased the pressures to allow overfishing.

There were some differences in the new contractual environments. Management of stocks staying within 200 nautical miles of shore but traversing the EEZs of different states became an issue for those coastal states. Nothing assured, however, that they would be any more successful at focusing on common interests than the larger groups of states involved in the pre-1977 bargaining. While they jointly could control all local and distant-water fishing, the segmentation of jurisdiction meant that any one could erode the work of the others by adopting less restrictive regulations or by enforcing less energetically. Where each of a group of neighboring countries was seeking to build local fisheries through a variety of joint ventures with foreign fishers, there was potential for competitive bidding for foreign interest that could undermine stock management.

Management of stocks that spilled over the 200-nautical-mile limit led to two sorts of situations. The less complicated occurred when, as in the Grand Bank off Canada, the stock straddled the 200-mile limit of only one state. There, a coastal state with jurisdiction over most of the stock faced fishing states with fleets actually or potentially exploiting that portion lying beyond the line. The more complicated situation occurred when the same stock not only straddled the 200-mile limit, but also ranged across the EEZs of several states. Then, several coastal states had to coordinate with each other as well as with the distant-water fleets' states. In the first situation, the single coastal state could try to offer incentives by conditioning access to fish within the EEZ on cooperative behavior beyond the zone. As the Canadians discovered in the 1980s, this works only when domestic pressures to reduce foreign fishing in the EEZ are low, and the foreign fleets involved desire EEZ access.[11] If local fishers succeeded in securing explusion of the foreigners, or the foreigners decided that they were content to stay outside the EEZ, such a trade could not occur. Serious conflict, or even deadlock, would ensue.

**The Policy Process in the Commissions**

Despite the unpromising contractual environment, the fisheries commissions attempted to deal with the issues placed before them. The policy process was a relatively closed one, with government delegates (generally regulators from national fisheries agencies) weighing possible courses of action. The fishing industry of each country kept an eye on the process, but usually confined its activity to lobbying its own government and ensuring that industry people as well as scientists served as advisers to the national delegation. Only occasionally did other social groups become interested in the commissions' activity.

**Agenda Setting**

In all the fisheries commissions, the agenda remained confined to the species or ocean areas defined in their founding treaties. The commis-

11. Karl M. Sullivan, "Conflict in the Management of a Northwest Atlantic Transboundary Cod Stock, *Marine Policy* 13 (1989): 119–36.

sions dealing with ocean areas could be more flexible, adding species or stocks as the situation warranted. The single-species commissions remained concerned solely with the species they were established to help manage. Adoption of EEZs transformed the agendas of most commissions. Stocks lying within 200 miles of shore were removed from the purview of multispecies commissions. Even single-species commissions were affected if a significant portion of the membership believed that the species should be managed by coastal states, as happened with tuna. On the other hand, the agendas of the FAO-sponsored and other regional commissions expanded as developing coastal members adapted to their new rights and responsibilities as coastal states.

Certain aspects of agenda setting were reactions to "crises"—newly perceived difficulties serious enough to merit immediate attention. Clear stock depletion led to creation of the North Pacific Fur Seal Commission, while widely perceived overfishing spurred creation of the North Sea, Northeast Atlantic, Northwest Atlantic and Southeast Atlantic commissions. The Whaling Commission was created in hopes of preventing a repeat of past depletion while the North Pacific Commission was an effort to protect work that had restored herring, halibut, and salmon stocks from depleted condition. Of the pre-1977 bodies, only the Inter-American and Atlantic Tuna commissions were established before overfishing. Once established, the commissions' attention was most often drawn to additional stocks by complaints about actual overfishing, though warnings were sometimes enough to trigger leader concern. The record becomes little better after 1977. The Antarctic Commission came into existence before heavy fishing of krill, but not until after overfishing of some finned stocks; the North Atlantic Salmon Commission was a continuation of an earlier bilateral effort.

Perception of crisis does not explain the pattern of alternative specification within the commissions. In all of the commissions, a wider set of possible measures for dealing with overfishing was considered in the late 1960s and early 1970s than in the 1950s. While the pressure to widen alternatives can be traced to concern about observed stock depletion, the content of most of the alternatives discussed reflected the changing consensus among members of the broad bioeconomic discipline of fisheries management. This consensus reached the commissions directly through their scientific advisory committees or research staffs, and indirectly via the national members who were generally aware of the current theoretical work.

Governments have long been receptive to the idea that scientific advice is needed for the framing of effective fisheries management plans. The International Council for the Exploration of the Sea (ICES), a collaborative body drawing scientists from the states fronting the North Sea, began coordinating studies of fisheries in 1902. Though it and other advocates of cooperation failed to secure creation of an international commission before World War II, the most active fishing states did agree on certain mesh size rules in 1937.[12] The highly successful bilateral Canada—United States halibut and salmon commissions had their own research staffs, which contributed much to the management process and to the development of fisheries science generally. The original North Pacific Fur Seal Commission lacked any research staff or scientific advisory committee, but all the other commissions had some provision for direct input of scientific advice. The Inter-American Tropical Tuna Commission had its own research staff; the North Sea, Northeast Atlantic and Baltic commissions secured advice from ICES; other international commissions had advisory committees made up of scientists named by their governments; and the post-1977 regional commissions secured assistance from FAO's Fisheries Department.

These research staffs and advisory committees provided the intergovernmental tip of a broader transnational fisheries science community engaged in an active process of research, mutual discussion, refinement of theoretical models applicable to the study of fish population dynamics, and elaboration of alternate methods of regulation. In large part, the process of refining the alternatives laid before fisheries commissions was the result of changes in the consensus views of this transnational expert community.

By 1950, the experts agreed that imposition of minimum mesh size and minimum size requirements for keeping fish was necessary to preventing overfishing. Mesh size requirements had been proposed in the 1930s, but met with skepticism from those who still believed nets would simply be pulled tighter and effectively close up when filled with fish. Though experiments conducted in 1932 showed this was not true,

---

12. Christy and Scott, *Common Wealth*, 200.

the skeptics were won over only after wide dissemination in the early 1950s of underwater films showing that nets stayed open.[13] The international commissions then in existence moved to adopting such regulations, sometimes adding closed seasons or closed areas to further protect spawning.

Neither governments, fishers, nor experts then realized that while such measures were effective against growth overfishing, they were not effective against recruitment overfishing. Even while taking only large fish, it was possible to take too many adults for the long-term stability of the population. This only became clear in the late 1950s with development of better models of fish population dynamics. It was also in this period that the implications of overinvestment, at least in the form of too many boats, were recognized as well. The improved models of population dynamics rested on the contributions of many scientists.[14] This work established two related traditions of management advice, one (more prevalent in North America) focusing on estimating maximum sustainable yield from the whole population, and the other (more prevalent in Europe) basing estimates of safe fishing levels on cohort analysis combining the size of additions to the stock in earlier years and yield-per-recruit equations to work out annual quotas.

The first policy response to this revised version of the problem was imposition of quotas before depletion. Though quotas had been used in the Whaling Commission since 1949 and in bilateral Canada—United States management of North Pacific fur seal, halibut, and salmon since at least the 1930s, they were inspired and explained to fishers by the obvious need to rebuild stocks. The newer models of fish population dynamics permitted, at least in principle, anticipating overfishing and setting quotas before depletion. Most of the fisheries commissions be-

13. Cyril E. Lucas, "Regulation of North Sea Fisheries under the Convention of 1946," in *Papers presented at the International Technical Conference on the Conservation of the Living Resources of the Sea*, Rome 1955 (UN Document A/CONF.10/7), 167–81.
14. Including H. R. Hulme, R. J. H. Beverton, and S. J. Holt, "Population Studies in Fisheries Biology," *Nature* 159 (1947): 714–15; Gordon, "Economic Theory of a Common Property Resource"; W. E. Ricker, "Stock and Recruitment," *Journal of the Fisheries Research Board of Canada* 11 (1954): 559–623; R. J. H. Beverton and S. J. Holt, "The Theory of Fishing," in M. Graham, ed., *Sea Fisheries: Their Investigation in the United Kingdom* (London: Arnold, 1956), 372–441; and Schaefer, "Biological and Economic Aspects."

gan to discuss quotas as soon as the state of the stocks they were han-dling suggested a need.

Yet even before many of the commissions moved to quotas an addi-tional problem was identified. Most dramatically in whaling, but also in the Pacific halibut fishery, it became apparent that an overall quota, coupled only with a rule closing the season when the quota was reached, spurred overinvestment. This happened because each compet-ing company or boat acquired additional and more sophisticated gear to improve its chances of landing a good catch before the season was halted. The race went to the swift, and all were equally anxious to be swift because the penalty for slowness was little or no catch. Though a few specialists noted the problem early,[15] only in the mid-1960s was it generally acknowledged. The first response was subdivision of quotas into national allocations; per-boat allocations and limits on the number of boats were also suggested but not adopted.

Alternative specification shifted again in the 1970s and 1980s to reflect new ideas on two points, the efficacy of the models underlying management decisions, and the efficacy of suballocated quotas as a brake on overinvestment. Both debates began within the expert com-munity, but quickly came to the attention of governments and the fisheries commissions.

The models used for determining quotas came under four attacks. In the late 1960s and early 1970s, criticism focused fairly narrowly on use of maximum sustainable yield (MSY) as the criterion for setting quotas. A growing number of experts demonstrated that using MSY encouraged a level of effort that promoted, if not assured, overinvestment. They be-gan advocating greater integration of economic factors to produce a hybrid model that would limit fishing to an optimal yield (OY) calcu-lated by taking into account the marginal cost of fishing each additional unit of catch.

The second line of attack became more prominent in the mid-1970s. Though fisheries biologists were aware that species in the same area often affected each other, either through predator-prey relations or competition for the same food, the standard models assumed that these

15. E.g., H. A. Dunlop and F. A. Bell, "New Problems in the Regulation of Pacific Halibut Stocks," *ICES Journal* 18 (1952): 167; Lucas, "Regulation of North Sea Fisheries," 175–76.

effects were minor and could be ignored in determining safe levels of catch. The more holistic views encouraged by rise of the environmentalist movement soon bred a challenge based on arguments that interspecies effects were significant and needed to be taken into account. The leading experts were advocating multispecies management in 1975.[16] Fisheries experts then proposed several possible models.[17] However, managers could not adopt them because neither the data nor the computational tools for applying them existed. The computational tools became available by 1981 with improvements in computer technology;[18] the data requirements are still not yet met. Certain data is not yet available, and there is also considerable uncertainty about what additional data is really needed.[19] The result has been a retreat into rule-of-thumb modifications of single-species models that yield lower recommended quotas to accommodate interspecies relations and other sources of fluctuation in recruitment.

A third line of criticism peaked in the late 1970s then receded in the early 1980s. A number of experts, some from industrial and some from developing states, argued that tropical population dynamics were so distinct that separate models had to be devised. By the mid-1980s, however, scientific consensus had settled on a belief that the differences were relatively minor and could be accommodated within the framework of the basic models.[20]

The fourth line of attack is potentially the most serious. It takes perceptions of variations in recruitment much further than the older

16. Airlie House Workshops of 1975, discussed in James E. Scarff, "International Management of Whales, Dolphins, and Porpoises," *Ecology Law Quarterly* 6 (1977): 395–97.
17. See Taivo Laevastu and Herbert A. Larkins, *Marine Fisheries Ecosystem: Its Quantitative Evaluation and Management* (Farnham, Surrey, Eng.: Fishing News Books, 1981); Keith M. Brander and David M. Bennett, "Norway Lobsters in the Irish Sea: Modelling on One Component of a Multispecies Resource," in John F. Caddy, ed., *Marine Invertebrate Fisheries: Their Assessment and Management* (New York: Wiley, 1989), 183–204.
18. Laevastu and Larkins, *Marine Fisheries Ecosystem*, xi.
19. Marinelle Basson and John R. Beddington, "CCAMLR: The Practical Implications of an Eco-System Approach," in Arnfinn Jørgensen-Dahl and Willy Østreng, eds., *The Antarctic Treaty System in World Politics* (London: Macmilland, 1991), 54–69.
20. Daniel Pauly, "Problems of Tropical Inshore Fisheries: Fishery Research on Tropical Soft-Bottom Communities and the Evolution of its Conceptual Base," *Ocean Yearbook* 6 (1986): 29–37.

realization that birth rates and rates of survival to maturity depend on water temperature during spawning season, circulation of currents, disease, and changes in predator populations as much as on human taking. However, this remained a general awareness not always accommodated in the standard models. In 1983, John Caddy proposed distinguishing among four types of stock, only the first of which could be analyzed well by the standard MSY or cohort models. He argued for distinctive "steady-state stocks" experiencing little fluctuation in total population, "cyclical fisheries," which experience relatively predictable levels of abundance and scarcity independent of human fishing, "irregular stocks," which vary from year to year in no apparent cycle, and "spasmodic stocks," which have periods of abundance alternating with periods of such scarcity that any fishing effort in those years is uneconomic.[21]

Of the four attacks, this last has the greatest potential for changing fisheries management. All the others could be accommodated within the two prevailing traditions of changing quotas, the reliance on recalculating MSY favored by North Americans and the reliance on changes in catch per unit of effort favored by Western Europeans. The MSY users found the relevance of their analysis restricted; the catch per unit effort users were forced to realize, partly through that analysis and partly through separate research on stock behavior,[22] that schooling species could be overfished even before declines in catch per unit effort were noticed because the reduced populations would tend to huddle together and seem as abundant to fishers as before. Though these developments are only beginning to affect fisheries managers' alternative specification, they have contributed to current perceptions that the goal of maintaining steady levels of prudent fishing was always overambitious.

By the end of the 1970s, there was also considerable agreement that quota systems with national suballocations could not fully protect stocks because they failed to curb overinvestment. Some experts advo-

21. John F. Caddy, "An Alternative to Equilibrium Theory for the Management of Fisheries," paper presented to the FAO Expert Consultation on the Regulation of Fishing Effort (Fishing Mortality), 17–23 January 1983 (Rome: FAO), summary in J. F. Caddy and J. A. Gulland, "Historical Patterns of Fish Stocks," *Marine Policy* 7 (1983): 267–78.
22. Trond Bjørndal and Jon M. Conrad, "Capital Dynamics in the North Sea Herring Fishery," *Marine Resource Economics* 4 (1987): 63–74.

cated addressing overinvestment more directly by limiting entry, that is, restricting the number of boats licensed for particular fishery. As limited entry proved difficult to implement, particularly in well-established fisheries where the number of active boats had to be reduced, opinion shifted again. By the late 1980s, there was considerable interest in moving away from managing a common pool resource to division by imposing per-boat quotas or granting exclusive rights to fish in particular areas to individual fishers or small groups of fishers.[23] In essence, these proposals advocated doing nationally what had been done internationally with EEZs: moving from a common pool situation to the vesting of property rights.

The extent of expert influence on agenda setting depended on the particular aspect of the issue involved. Fishers and governments were most often the source of concern about the condition of particular stocks; most frequently the start of directed research was triggered by perceptions that catches had deteriorated. The experts influenced the range of broad alternatives considered as their work suggested the possibility and usefulness of various types of measures. Even here, however, governments' complaints about other fleets' fishing practices led them to propose particular regulations.[24] Agenda setting in the international commissions was heavily influenced by experts. At the same time, only governments could do the political persuading that might induce followers and laggards to take up an issue seriously. Governments could also slow the whole policy process by bringing in considerations that were not on the formal agenda but which colored their attitudes.

**Policy Choices**

Most of the international fisheries commissions concentrated on formulating management choices, not joint scientific research or building of national capacity. The Inter-American Tropical Tuna Commission,

23. Specific proposals discussed in Philip A. Neher and Ragnar Arnason, Introduction to special issue on "Rights-Based Fishing," *Marine Resource Economics* 5 (1988): 285–87; more general treatment in Elinor Ostrom, *Governing the Commons* (Cambridge: Cambridge University Press, 1990).
24. E.g., Norwegian proposals based on complaints that Polish-design chafers on the underside of bottom trawl nets effectively shrunk the mesh size below the Northeast Atlantic Commission minimum, noted in Arild Underdal, *The Politics of International Fisheries Management: The Case of the North Atlantic* (Oslo: Universitetsforlaget, 1980), 51.

though its own research staff, and the Northeast Atlantic and Baltic commissions, through reliance on ICES, did promote joint science. The other commissions relied on scientific advisory committees, which had the effect of encouraging member governments to promote domestic science, but governments responded unevenly. Increasing of both local catching and regulatory capacity is a major focus of the regional fisheries commissions in the Third World. The effort to recommend management procedures helps guide decisions about the sort of expert and administrative capacity needed by member states; FAO and other aid donors organize aid programs along regional and subregional lines that mirror commission areas. FAO and the regional commissions also help foster the transnational ties that link the new developing country experts with their industrial state counterparts. This effort is important not only for broadening discussion and fostering speedier transfer of knowledge and ideas, but also because developing countries are often reluctant to take the word of foreign (particularly industrial country) experts. In 1950, Wilbert Chapman urged the American Tunaboat Association to support giving the Inter-American Tropical Tuna Commission a multinational scientific staff "to gain the facts in conjunction with the Latinos so they will believe them. . . ."[25] This advice is no less pertinent today.

All the commissions attempt to formulate specific management policies. Here they face the problem that agreeing on a type of measure is far easier than agreeing on its specific character. It is one thing to accept the need to regulate mesh size; quite another to pick a particular size as the legal minimum, because that will impose different costs on different fleets depending on the mesh they currently use. Agreeing to the idea of quotas is fairly easy; agreeing on a particular quota raises all the questions of adjustment that make fisheries a conflict situation. If disagreements are great enough, laggards may well hold off agreeing in principle lest that start them on a slippery slope toward limitations they do not wish to accept.

The ability of fisheries commissions to frame particular measures, especially to get members to accept specific quotas, was weakened by

25. Letter of 25 August 1950, quoted in Harry N. Scheiber, "Pacific Ocean Resources, Science, and the Law of the Sea: Wilbert M. Chapman and the Pacific Fisheries," *Ecology Law Quarterly* 13 (1986): 465.

the imperfect state of fisheries science in the 1950s and early 1960s. While the models were reasonably good, there was not full scientific consensus supporting their use. In addition, their application depended on having more data than was available. This provided plenty of leeway for governments interested in arguing that there was no immediate need for serious restrictions. Uncertainty was used as an excuse for delay, as was typical in environmental affairs at the time. Laggards were never slow to exploit this. Even though the data has improved, it still falls short of providing the sort of certainty many fishers and regulators desire. In the 1960s and early 1970s, there was still enough uncertainty that the scientists themselves shied away from recommending particular regulations. Only later did they overcome this reticence.

Initially, government regulators tended to expect a single recommendation. Quotas might be expressed in a range, but the range was usually not terribly broad. A few governments, notably Canada in the Northwest Atlantic Organization, some members of the Northeast Atlantic Commission after 1980[26] and the non-fishing members of the Antarctic Commission starting in 1987,[27] have pressed for expert advice about the likely impact of alternative management policies. Yet the old habit of expecting a specific single answer and policy recommendation from the experts dies hard. Most experts would probably agree with John Gulland that "the relations between the fisheries administrator or manager and his scientific advisors would be different if there were better recognition that the predictions of the scientist have the reliability typical of the weather forecaster, or the economist predicting next year's rate of inflation. At present there is too often the feeling that in a properly run fishery the scientific advice should have the reliability of the predictions of the time of sun rise or of eclipses."[28] Reducing the pressure on scientists to acquire "perfect" data would remove a major source of delay—the old argument that uncertainty

26. John Farnell and Manes Elles, *In Search of a Common Fisheries Policy* (Aldershot, England: Gower, 1984), 115.
27. Francisco Orrego Vicuna, "The Effectiveness of the Decision-Making Machinery of CCAMLR," in Jørgensen-Dahl and Østreng, eds., *The Antarctic Treaty System*, 32.
28. John A. Gulland, "Managing Fisheries in an Imperfect World," in Brian J. Rothschild, ed., *Global Fisheries: Prospects for the 1980s* (New York: Springer Verlag, 1983), 120.

means that action should be deferred. It would also focus responsibility back on the fisheries regulators. This would increase the potential for politicization, but whether that harmed or helped the stocks would depend on whether it served to perpetuate the distributional conflicts or became a channel for pressures to pay more attention to the common purpose.

The fisheries regulators also provide an independent source of inertia favoring standard MSY or cohort analysis models over others. Both provide an apparently objective biological standard less subject to political manipulation than others. Optimum yields vary from fleet to fleet depending on each one's particular costs of and revenues from fishing, while explicit inclusion of social considerations, like preserving the ways of life of coastal groups, add further nonquantifiable complications. The models are also useful to governments, which find quantifiable biological criteria particularly helpful when attempting to persuade their nationals of the need for restraint.[29]

The speed with which individual commissions moved to quotas and then to national allocations was marginally affected by whether the commission had been given, or could be presumed to have, legal authority to set them. The Whaling Commission had authority to set a total quota, but not national allocations. Since changing the convention required unanimity, the members with Antarctic fleets solved the problem by negotiating allocations among themselves starting in 1960. The North Sea Commission lacked authority to set quotas, much less allocations.[30] It was superseded by the Northeast Atlantic Commission in 1963, which was given such authority, but which established no general quota scheme until 1974 (though it set some indirectly through exceptions to fishing bans).[31] The Northwest Atlantic Commission had a broad enough mandate to set quotas and allocations, but did not start doing so until 1970 after an intense five-year debate on the issue.[32] The

29. Rognualdor Hannesson, "Inefficiency through Government Regulations: The Case of Norway's Fishery Policy," *Marine Policy* 12 (1985): 31–39, 131.
30. Douglas M. Johnston, *The International Law of Fisheries* (New Haven, Conn.: Yale University Press, 1965), 361.
31. Underdal, *Politics*, 166.
32. W. G. Doubleday, A. T. Pinhorn, R. G. Halliday, R. D. S. MacDonald, and R. Stein, "The Impact of Extended Fisheries Jurisdiction in the Northwest Atlantic," in Edward L. Miles, ed., *Management of World Fisheries* (Seattle: University of Washington Press, 1989), 35–36.

Southeast Atlantic Commission had authority to set total quotas, which it began using in 1976, its fifth year of activity. It did not have authority to make allocations; this was left to direct agreement among member states whose fleets fished a particular stock put under quota.[33] The Inter-American Tuna Commission imposed a quota on yellowfin in 1966, and began setting allocations in 1969. The Atlantic Tuna Commission set its first quotas in 1982, and the Antarctic Commission in 1987.

Far more important was the mix of leaders, followers, and laggards in a particular commission and their relative shares of the catch. The voting rules usually gave important advantages to the participants most resistant to restrictions. Both the consensus rule used in a few commissions, and the simple or qualified majority plus opt-out clause used in others, pushed decisions toward the least common denominator. In a consensus system any party can veto; in a majority plus opt-out system, any party taking a significant amount of the catch can effectively veto. These rules have not been changed; in no case have governments been prepared to transfer authority to make immediately binding decisions to an international fisheries commission. At most, procedures have been streamlined so that the interval for opting out has been exhausted by the beginning of a new fishing season. The Southeast Atlantic and Antarctic Commission experiences suggest that even when having authority to set quotas and faced with an overfished stock, a new fisheries commission with strong and stubborn laggards among the members needs five years to adopt its first quotas. The situation in the post-1977 regional commissions is not much different; they produce recommendations that members either adopt or ignore, and laggards are likely to ignore.

The exact mix of leaders, followers, and laggards did vary some among the commissions. The North Pacific was fairly neatly divided into American-Canadian zones on one side and Japanese-Russian zones on the other. This separated the leaders and laggards into matched pairs, each wrangling over one side of the ocean. Thes wrangles were generally worked out in bilateral agreements. In the North Atlantic,

33. Gunnar Saetersdal, "Fisheries Management in the Northeast Atlantic and in Namibia: A Comparative Description," in Miles, ed., *Management of World Fisheries*, 26.

leaders and laggards were mixed together in the commissions regulating both sides of the ocean. On both commissions, laggard influence, mainly from the USSR and those Warsaw Pact allies engaged in distant-water fishing, but also from Western European distant-water fleets, was very strong. The same was true in the Southeast Atlantic Commission, where laggards were not balanced by conservation-minded coastal states. Leaders and laggards have been roughly balanced in the Antarctic Commission. Laggards held an advantage in the Whaling Commission until the early 1980s, when a transnational environmentalist campaign led to accession by numerous states with no whaling industry and great readiness to adopt highly conservationist goals. By the time it had to make regulations, the Atlantic Tuna Commission had a heavy proportion of leaders; the Inter-American Tropical Tuna Commission was composed this way from the start.

The North Atlantic Commissions not only had stubborn laggards, but suffered from broader disagreements as well. Two streams of conflict were involved. The first, starting in the early 1970s, stemmed from all governments' reluctance to make any agreements that might prejudice their positions at the Third U.N. Conference on the Law of the Sea (UNCLOS III). This exacerbated conflicts about quotas and allocations. The second conflict was triggered in the mid-1970s when the members of the European Community decided to manage their 200-mile zones in common. They were fully aware that the USSR would oppose any such move, partly out of a general reluctance to give intergovernmental organizations more status, and partly because it would make older games of divide-the-opposition more difficult to pursue. Fearing that the USSR would use the Northeast Atlantic Commission to block an EC common fisheries policy, EC members moved to forestall the Soviets in November 1976 by announcing their withdrawal from the commission.[34] A revised agreement geared to the realities of coastal state management in EEZs and the EC's common fishery zone was worked out in 1980. On the other side of the North Atlantic, Canada precipitated the demise of the Northwest Atlantic Commission because it wanted more leeway in managing its own 200-mile zone. EC members supported the Canadian move because it would also permit them

34. Farnell and Elles, *In Search*, 72–73.

to write the EC into a revised agreement. Again, the Soviets were un-happy about both developments, but could do little about them. The Northwest Atlantic Commission was replaced by the Northwest Atlantic Fisheries Organization (NAFO) in 1979. In both cases broader considerations injected an additional level of conflict into the distributional wrangles.

The domestic and transnational processes creating pressures for decisions giving greater weight to the common interest that have arisen in other cases have seldom developed in the fisheries commissions. Overfishing has not become an issue of widespread public concern like ozone depletion, acid rain, or toxic wastes. The only cases of extended non-governmental attention involve the Whaling Commission, where the issue was framed in the simple terms of "stop whaling," the Antarctic Commission, where the pressures are a part of the wider effort to preserve Antarctica's wilderness character, and the recent campaign against the use of large, untended driftnets. In the 1970s and early 1980s, coastal fishers in many countries put pressure on their governments to restrict foreign fishing, but only so locals could increase their catches. These were economically, not ecologically, inspired campaigns. Though cases of overfishing are known and receive occasional attention in the media, the issue has not attracted wide attention. As long as this remains true, all the domestic pressures on governments work in the direction of laxity. The restricted salience of the issue also means that top political leaders are unlikely to take up the issue, and even less likely to use it in contests to prove who is "greener" than whom. While such contests occur in intergovernmental forums, they, too, rest ultimately on the presence of mobilized voters and interest groups at home that value "greenness" and use it as a standard of policy evaluation on the issue at hand. Thus, leaders have not been able to compensate for their lack of ability to offer material incentives for restraint by getting laggard governments into a policy vise consisting of intergovernmental pressure in the commission and domestic popular pressure outside.

## National Action

Implementation of fisheries management decisions requires eliciting compliant behavior. Monitoring ocean fisheries has always been hard; the fishers spread out over fairly large areas of the sea and follow irregular work schedules. As in other areas, implementation is eased if compliance can be elicited voluntarily; similarly, monitoring of activity and penalizing of violators is needed to assure the compliant that they are not being "suckered" by others.

Efforts to elicit compliant behavior pose real dilemmas for managers. The fishing industry, which consists of vessel owners, skippers, crews, fish processors, and investors, generally resists restraint in the short term. To recognize this, however, is not to argue that industry influence should be eliminated. First, in any democratic state the fishing industry is a social group with the same rights to press its case and seek government attention as any other. It does not have the right to monopolize government attention, but it does have the right to have its needs taken into account. Second, eliciting voluntary compliance reduces enforcement costs considerably. Voluntary compliance is more likely when fishers have a chance to participate in the framing of management measures. Fisheries regulators are aware that they must steer a course between contrasting dangers: They cannot ignore industry views, but even without explicit reference to the public policy literature on "regulatory capture," they know that it is easy to let industry have too much influence.[35]

The traditional rules of ocean fisheries, and most national systems of fisheries management under the EEZ regime, made implementation of management decisions more difficult by replicating among fishers the same open-access common pool situation that existed among governments. Individual fishers, too, were reluctant to adjust their effort downward. In principle, governments can change the contractual environment by imposing a new payoff structure or even a new situation. Most have opted for retaining the open-access common pool, and so have concentrated on altering payoff structures. Framing incentive-compatible regulations whenever possible, educating fishers about the overall effect of their simultaneous individual behavior, and providing serious, effective punishments of infractions could transform the outcome by modifying fishers' incentives.

35. E.g., Marver Bernstein, *Regulation by Independent Commission* (Princeton: Princeton University Press, 1955); George J. Stigler, "The Theory of Economic Regulation," *Bell Journal of Economics and Management Science* 2 (1971): 3–21.

Few of the measures for regulating ocean fisheries have been incentive-compatible. One of the few exceptions is minimum mesh size requirements in reasonably unmixed fisheries. Nova Scotia fishers adopted the newer $4\frac{1}{2}$-inch mesh nets introduced in the New England haddock fishery after they saw that it gave better yields, by hauling up only larger fish, than their old $2\frac{7}{8}$-inch mesh.[36] Efforts of the North Sea Commission to compare the effects of different size mesh were complicated by fishers' eager adoption of the larger mesh sizes as they saw the boats using them coming in with more profitable hauls.[37] While helpful, the effect of mesh size regulations was limited. First, they worked only in those fisheries where species of similar size were being taken and the main target species were larger than the associated ones. Second, their effect was often temporary: once recruitment overfishing became severe, fishers responded by taking smaller individuals again to maintain their incomes. The open-access common pool nature of the resource meant that most regulations were not incentive-compatible because they could not of themselves modify the danger that individual self-restraint would not be reciprocated by others. Such assurance would have to be provided by the fisheries regulators. This meant that the nature of monitoring and the effectiveness of punishing violators became crucial to success at protecting stocks.

Few of the pre-1977 fisheries commissions created situations in which governments were encouraged to apply effective implementation schemes. Themselves caught in a contractual environment marked by strongly divergent interests, governments had little incentive to help their fishers escape the dilemmas raised by the scramble for fish. Imposing restraints on individual fishers would not help them in the long term unless other governments imposed equal restrictions on theirs. Only the North Pacific Fur Seal Commission escaped this problem, by eliminating the open-access character of the common pool. Not only were the parties given incentive to respect others' management efforts by sharing

36. Erik N. Poulsen, "Conservation Problems in the Northwestern Atlantic," in *Papers Presented at the International Technical Conference on the Conservation of the Living Resources of the Sea*, Rome, 1955 (UN Document A/CONF.10/7), 190.
37. Lucas, "Regulation of North Sea Fisheries," 174.

in the proceeds, but the managing states could arrest pelagic sealers and turn them over to their home states for prosecution. The North Pacific Commission also faced a situation in which ocean areas could be effectively parceled out among the active fleets. The unilateral or smaller-group management schemes involved were protected by the "abstention principle," under which parties kept their nationals from fishing fully exploited stocks protected by others' management programs.[38]

The other pre-1977 commissions saw their efforts to encourage diligent enforcement vastly complicated by the traditional international legal rule that only the flag state may exercise jurisdiction over a vessel on the high seas. Since most fishing occurred on the high seas, each government had an exclusive right to monitor its own fishers and deal with violations. Even when rules were agreed in a joint commission, their effect could be weakened by lax enforcement on the part of any state. Thus, the first element of the implementation problem was getting all governments to take enforcement of the incentive-incompatible rules equally seriously.

Members of all the international commissions were aware of the problem, but there was considerable disagreement about how to proceed. All the commissions had a mandate to discuss implementation and propose improvements. They could thus raise the issue of lax enforcement. However, there was little they could accomplish under a flag state–only enforcement scheme. Members from other states could voice opinions about relative diligence in enforcement, but no one had definite information on how particular governments were responding, because all information about actual and suspected infractions came from the individual flag states.

Three solutions to this problem were proposed at various times. The least intrusive was the joint monitoring scheme, in which fisheries inspectors from any commission member could board, inspect, and note

38. William C. Herrington, "Comments on the Principle of Abstention," in *Papers Presented at the International Technical Conference on the Conservation of the Living Resources of the Sea*, Rome, 1955 (UN Document A/CONF.10/7), 344–49; and Harry N. Scheiber, "Origins of the Abstention Doctrine in Ocean Law: Japanese–U.S. Relations and the Pacific Fisheries, 1937–1958," *Ecology Law Quarterly* 16 (1989): 23–99.

any violations found. The foreign fisheries inspector could not assess a penalty; rather, the matter was referred to the flag state for action. More intrusive were schemes for exchange of observers between fleets, with observers from one member country assigned to vessels of another. Even though violations would still have to be handled by the flag state, this modified the situation by letting at least some foreigners have access to direct information about fishing routines. Most intrusive was the idea of sending out commission-appointed inspectors or observers who would report violations back to the commission directly, with the commission then holding the flag state responsible for taking action.

The first procedure could be applied in any situation. The second was financially feasible only in certain situations. Observers, who are generally berthed and fed at the carrying ship's expense, could be stationed with integrated catching and processing fleets. This was true in pelagic whaling, where catch was brought to factory ships for processing at sea, and in certain Japanese and Soviet bloc distant-water operations where a fleet of trawlers, processing ships, and associated transport ships worked together as an integrated whole. Observers could also be stationed with individual catching vessels if those vessels were large enough to carry an observer and the catch was valuable enough for the fishers to accept the extra cost as a reasonable price of fishing. The third solution is also applicable to any situation, since the commission appointees can operate either as observers aboard fishing vessels or as inspectors patrolling fishing areas and visiting individual fishing vessels as needed.

Before 1977, there was no case of commission-appointed inspectors or observers. The Whaling Commission sponsored an exchange observer scheme that began operation in 1970, but this was limited to the two fleets—Soviet and Japanese—still active in the Antarctic. All the other international commissions managing an open-access common pool fishery got no further than sponsoring a joint monitoring scheme. Most of these came after significant delays. The Northwest and Northeast Atlantic commissions, founded in 1950 and 1959 respectively, were supplemented by an Atlantic-wide agreement on mutual monitoring in 1967 and by more specific arrangements among their own members in 1969 and 1970 respectively. In the mid-1960s there were mutual arrangements covering the North Pacific, but most were contained in bilateral agreements.[39] The Southeast Atlantic Commission never began any mutual monitoring scheme, though provision for one had been made in the constituent treaty.

Assuring compliance was also complicated by the weakness of data reporting. Individual fishers had incentive to underreport when they could, and most governments had little incentive to cross-check the data. Even those that wanted to cross-check found it hard because of the large number of vessels involved and the large number of ports where catch could be landed. Unlike the situation with air pollution, contemporaneous monitoring of fish stocks cannot identify who is fishing how much, or even distinguish fishing-induced decline from that caused by other factors. It can only estimate the total population size and give information about whether that size appears to be increasing or decreasing. As populations decrease in an open-access fishery, and quotas become more restrictive, individual fishers and their governments have even more incentive to underreport. Nor did the shift to national suballocations within overall quotas change the situation very much. Governments and fishers still had enough interest in keeping their own quotas high, which required keeping the total high, that they persisted in underreporting. The net result in most commissions was considerable suspicion. Most of the commissions were also limited by the fact that catch data all came from national sources. Though fishers submitted data on common forms, they sent their reports to their own governments, which forwarded the information to the relevant commission.

Only the Inter-American Tuna Commission escaped this problem. It managed a fairly concentrated fishery operating out of a relatively small number of ports. By assuring individual skippers of confidentiality, its staff collected catch reports directly from the boats when they returned from fishing. In this case, separating reporting from enforcement (and particularly from the severe controversies about reallocating quotas to newcomers) permitted the commission to acquire better-quality catch

39. J. E. Carroz and A. G. Roche, "International Policing of High Seas Fisheries," *Canadian Yearbook of International Law* 6 (1968): 61–90.

data than most of its counterparts. This was particularly important since the wide migratory range of tuna makes population surveys difficult.

Implementation was transformed with adoption of the EEZ regime. The right to enforce fisheries regulations on all non–highly migratory species within 200 miles of shore was vested in the coastal state. In most areas, then, the intergovernmental open-access situation was ended. A coastal state willing and able to impose restrictions on all comers could do so. The situation was more complicated in the tuna fishery, with stocks that straddle the 200-mile limit, and in the Southern Ocean. With tuna, the situation was affected by the long dispute about their status under the EEZ regime. The United States, and to a lesser extent Japan, insisted that tuna were among the highly migratory species that should be managed jointly rather than by each coastal state. Developing countries with tuna off their shores, particularly the west coast Latin Americans and the South Pacific Islanders, insisted equally vehemently that tuna should be managed like any other species. The dispute made it impossible for the Inter-American Tuna Commission to function after 1979, and shifted effective tuna management from the Atlantic Tuna Commission to a series of bilateral agreements among the parties. Though Japanese and U.S. resistance has ended,[40] the dispute long colored efforts to manage tuna.[41]

The enforcement complications arising from other stocks that straddle the 200-mile line remain unabated. The coastal state is faced, in those situations, with the pre-1977 situation of needing cooperation from all the flag states if enforcement is to be effective. The international commissions faced with such situations have not been much more

40. Paul Addison, "Fishing for Praise," *Far Eastern Economic Review*, 18 May 1989, 25; Jim Fullilove, "Senate moves on Magnuson Act," *National Fisherman*, August 1990, 7.
41. See, e.g., James Joseph, "International Tuna Management revisited," in Rothschild, ed., *Global Fisheries*, 123–50; Alberto Szekeley, "Implementing the New Law of the Sea: The Mexican Experience," in Rothschild, ed., *Global Fisheries*, 51–72; Edward L. Miles and William T. Burke, "Pressures on the United Nations Convention on the Law of the Sea of 1982 Arising from New Fisheries Conflicts," *Ocean Development and International Law* 20: 343–57 (1989); Christopher M. Weld, "Critical Evaluation of Existing Mechanisms for Managing Highly Migratory Species in the Atlantic Ocean," *Ocean Development and International Law* 20 (1989): 285–95.

effective than their pre-1977 counterparts. Governments have been unwilling to go much beyond the pre-1977 institutions. One exception seems to be developing in the North Atlantic, where the North Atlantic Salmon Commission has been the venue for deals under which ocean fishers would stop their activity in return for payments by coastal states.[42] These deals are not universally popular, however; considerable opinion in the coastal states holds that the new EEZ regime vests management of anadromous species in the coastal state and effectively ends the right to fish them on the high seas.[43]

The Southern Ocean is a huge anomaly because the lack of generally recognized territorial sovereignty over any part of Antarctica means that there are, in effect, no coastal states to possess and control EEZs. There, enforcement remains the prerogative of the flag state except within 200 miles of those subantarctic islands within the Southern Ocean where a territorial sovereign is acknowledged. The Antarctic Commission, much like its pre-1977 counterparts, has moved slowly on enforcement issues. Only after seven years of existence did the members begin implementing the enforcement provisions.[44]

The regional commissions face a different situation. Most of the stocks they discuss straddle different countries' EEZs, but not the 200-mile line. The problem for them, then, is coordinating enforcement among those with an undoubted legal right to enforce. This is further complicated by the fact that many of the members lack the capacity to enforce, even when they have the will. The regional commissions serve as mechanisms for increasing local capacity and as forums for spreading ideas—some from within the region and some from outside—about effective enforcement. Thus, the Indo-Pacific Commission was advising member states that their management authority would be strengthened if they regulated foreign fleets by access treaties with their flag state

42. Nelson Bryant, "High Seas reprieve of Atlantic Salmon" *New York Times*, 27 April 1991, sec. 8, p. 7.
43. William T. Burke, "Anadromous Species and the New Law of the Sea," *Ocean Development and International Law* 22: (1991), 113.
44. Jean-Pierre Puissochet, "CCAMLR - A Critical Assessment," in Arnfinn Jørgensen-Dahl and Willy Østreng, eds., *The Antarctic Treaty System* 2, 75.
45. Report of the 4th Session of the Standing Committee on Resources Research and Development of the Indo-Pacific Fishery Commission, Jakarta, Indonesia, 23–29 August 1984, *FAO Fisheries Report* no. 318, appendix J.

rather than through the terms of contracts with the fishers themselves.[45] The commissions have also encouraged coastal state experiments with requiring flag states to assist in enforcement.[46] Other regions have also expressed interest in emulating the South Pacific Forum Fisheries Agency's regional register.[47] Foreign vessels must be on the register to secure a fishing license from any member, and can be removed from the list for failure to pay duly assessed fines. Ignoring any one member can lead to loss of fishing rights in a far wider area. In these various ways, the regional commissions are helping member countries meet the challenge of regulating the activities of nationals of larger and wealthier states.

**Assessing and Explaining the Outcomes**

Assessing the success or failure of the international and regional fisheries commissions requires an easily identifiable performance yardstick. Two are available. The stricter is avoiding or reversing serious depletions of steady fish stocks. Though too much fishing is not the only reason for collapse of a stock, it is generally an important factor. Fisheries regulators today are also more aware of the variety of possible causes and try to take all into account. Thus, measuring success in terms of what happens to steady stocks is a fair test of effectiveness. Fluctuations of other types of stocks cannot be blamed on the managers, but even with them, continuing high levels of fishing during periods of low abundance represents a management failure. Many fisheries experts, particularly those concerned about overinvestment, would regard this as too easy a test. They would prefer one that takes into account both the state of the stocks and the state of the industry. Acquiring the information needed to apply the latter is very difficult, however; and for present purposes the simpler test of stock stability does distinguish among management efforts. A second, less stringent,

46. S. K. B. Mfodwo, B. M. Tsamenyi, and S. K. N. Play, "The Exclusive Economic Zone: State Practice in the African Atlantic Region," *Ocean Development and International Law* 20 (1989): 445–99.
47. Described in David J. Doulman and Peter Terawasi, "The South Pacific Regional Register of Foreign Fishing Vessels," *Marine Policy* 14: (1990), 324–32.

test is whether a commission's activity contributes to a lower level of fishing than would otherwise have occurred. This test will seem fairer to those who regard some level of depletion as highly probable if not inevitable. It is unlikely to appeal to environmentalists and those concerned with maximizing the availability of fish protein in the long term.

Assessing of success or failure is the first step; it then needs to be explained. In particular, it is important to identify those aspects of success or failure that can be attributed to national decisions, and those that can be attributed to the international fisheries commissions. Only in that way can lessons for international cooperation on environmental issues be drawn.

**Relative Success at Protecting Stocks**
The pre-1977 international fisheries varied considerably in their ability to restore and maintain populations. The North Pacific Fur Seal Commission had considerable success in restoring stocks and preventing later overfishing. Stock depletion was arrested in 1912, populations doubled by 1916, and the largest breeding stock was close to pre-depletion levels by 1930. Recovery was so strong that it was hard for others to deny—though they rightly suspected its motives—Japan's 1940 claim that populations were now so large that the commission regulations were no longer needed.[48] The North Pacific Fisheries Commission and the Inter-American Tropical Tuna Commission also inspired some restraint, though their success at preventing overfishing was not as striking as that of the Fur Seal Commission. The North Pacific Commission oversaw a framework agreement that protected a set of bi- and trilateral agreements about particular species. The salmon dividing line provided a rough separation of North American and North Asian stocks that greatly reduced ocean catching of the former. This preserved the gains of joint Canadian–United States regulations that restricted the fishery to inland rivers and limited how many fish could be taken. The "abstention principle," under which each party agreed not to let its fishers exploit stocks already being fully exploited under a regulatory program managed by one or more other parties, protected Canadian–

48. Herrington and Kask, "International Conservation Problems," 153.

United States management of halibut and salmon in the eastern North Pacific as well.[49] The Inter-American Tropical Tuna Commission case is a little more difficult to assess because of the high reproductive rate of tuna. However, fishing effort increased even faster after the commission lost effectiveness in 1979, and at least one expert concluded that over-fishing was occurring in the early 1980s.[50]

Other commissions experienced failure. The Northwest Atlantic, Northeast Atlantic, Southeast Atlantic, and Whaling commissions failed to prevent overfishing of all or some major stocks within their purview. They helped bring about restrictions on effort, and in some cases this restraint did lead to some recovery of the depleted stocks. In the Northeast Atlantic, some cod and herring stocks collapsed in the 1960s and others in the 1970s.[51] Northwest Atlantic herring and mackerel stocks collapsed in the 1960s.[52] The Southeast Atlantic Commission was unable to reverse the decimation of pilchard and hake stocks off Namibia.[53] The Whaling Commission was unable to respond to decreasing catches because of fishing state arguments about the distribution of quotas, and fleet resistance to restrictions before investments in equipment had been recaptured. The situation got so bad that the Whaling Commission declared a moratorium on commercial whaling, effective in 1986.

The performance of Atlantic Tuna Commission, the Baltic Commission, and the East Central Atlantic Committee cannot be evaluated. Catches of Atlantic tuna did not reach levels causing concern about recruitment overfishing, though concern about possible growth overfishing led to adoption of minimum size requirements on some species in 1972 and 1974.[54] The Baltic Convention entered into force in 1974,

49. Herrington, "Comments on the Principle of Abstention;" Scheiber, "Origins of the Abstention Principle."
50. Joseph, "International Tuna Management," 141.
51. John R. Coull, "The North Sea Herring Fishery in the Twentieth Century," Ocean Yearbook 7 (1988): 115–31; Albert W. Koers, "What Trends and Implications: The Northeast Atlantic: EEC," in Miles, ed., Management of World Fisheries, 77–120; Saetersdal, "Fisheries Management."
52. Doubleday et al., "The Impact of Extended Jurisdiction."
53. Richard Moorsam, A Future for Namibia, vol. 5: Fishing (London: Catholic Institute for International Relations, 1984); Saetersdal, "Fisheries Management."
54. Joseph, "International Tuna Management," 131.

giving its commission too little time to start work before adoption of EEZs transformed the situation. The East Central Atlantic Committee began work in 1967 with too little information about stocks to frame management measures, and by the time it had some information, governments were well on their way to adopting the EEZs.[55]

The state of many fisheries in the 1970s amply justified coastal state arguments that the open-access common pool regime was not working. Before condemning the commissions as entirely useless, however, it is worth asking what would have happened without them. The answer is most obvious with North Pacific seals: the stocks would not have recovered or remained sizable. In the North Pacific fisheries, interfleet competition and international tension would have been higher without the commission. There had been severe conficts, particularly over salmon, in the 1930s, and they would have broken out again. At the same time, it is possible that Japanese effort would not have been shifted into the South Pacific and then into other oceans quite as quickly if there had been access to more North Pacific stocks, so an effort-diverting effect can be observed as well. In other areas, both the stock-protecting and effort-diverting effects are less strong. At most, one can say that adjustment to change came somewhat more quickly, but not always quickly enough to prevent stock collapse. This can best be discerned by the extent to which catches fell below quotas for more than a season. Since fishers tend to overfish when possible, underfishing the quota significantly in successive years suggests that the fish are simply not there for the catching; the stock is in the precipitous decline that marks the transition from overfished to depleted stocks. Many Northeast Atlantic catches were significantly below quota in 1975 and 1976.[56] The same was true of hake and sardine catches off Namibia in the late 1970s.[57] The Whaling Commission provided the starkest example: catches were significantly lower than quotas between 1960 and 1966.[58] Southeast Pacific tuna would have been overfished earlier if the competition be-

55. S. Garcia and F. Ponsard, "The Committee for the East Central Fisheries (CECAF) and the Management of West African Fisheries," in Miles, ed., *Management of World Fisheries*, 128.
56. Underdahl, *Politics*, tables on pp. 92 and 94.
57. Saetersdal, "Fisheries Management," 28–29.
58. M. J. Peterson, "Whalers, Cetologists, Environmentalists and the International Management of Whaling," *International Organization* 46(1992): 165.

tween U.S. and Latin American boats had been carried on without the limit of the Inter-American Commission quota. Overall, the effects of having the international fisheries commissions ranged from considerable to very marginal.

Though a number of the post-1977 commissions have been operating only a few years, it is possible to make preliminary judgments about their success. In many cases, there are few reasons for optimism. Both the new Northwest Atlantic Organization and the restructured Northeast Atlantic Commission inherited difficult positions and have not had outstanding success at dealing with the questions left over after states asserted EEZ jurisdiction. The better overall performance in the Northwest Atlantic reflects the larger proportion of stocks under unilateral management, rather than any feature of the commission. International nonrecognition of South African rule over Namibia, and hence of any South African right to regulate fisheries off the Namibian coast, left the Southeast Atlantic Commission largely undisturbed until 1991, and the situation continued to deteriorate despite commission quota reductions. The North Pacific Commission was the lever for one important setback in halibut management. The Japanese were able to use rules about allocating quotas to get a quota on Bering Sea halibut because Canadian and U.S. members could not prove their contention that the Bering Sea population was not a separate stock, but only an assembly of juveniles which later migrated to augment other previously identified and managed stocks. The initial quota was set too high and had to be lowered after what William Herrington characterized as "drastic overfishing."[59]

With others, it is still hard to determine the commission's impact. The North Atlantic Salmon Commission, created in 1982, was assisted by a shift to salmon hatching and farming, but it has not been able to prevent levels of ocean fishing that the coastal states regard as excessive. The Antarctic Commission also inherited some depleted finfish stocks, and got off to a slow start. It first adopted regulations in 1986, and the slow growth of Antarctic finfish means it is still too soon to tell whether they are having any effect. The Antarctic Commission is only beginning to deal with the main potential challenge, that of regulating the krill

59. William C. Herrington, "In the Realm of Diplomacy and Fish," *Ecology Law Quarterly* 16 (1989): 10–11.

fishery. Krill fishing has been limited by high expense and low consumer interest in the product; non-fishing states would like to add "precautionary quotas" to keep effort modest. The Atlantic Tuna Commission was able to survive intense disagreements among members about the extent of coastal state regulatory authority because of lower pressure on the stocks and members' use of bilateral access agreements to paper over the legal disputes.[60] The quotas mandated since 1982 may or may not have led to some restoration of giant bluefin populations, depending on how the commission's most recent study is interpreted.[61] The Inter-American Tropical Tuna Commission still exists, but it is not the effective manager of tuna off South America because of the major contentions among members about the respective rights of coastal and distant-water fishers. Several former members, led by Mexico, are championing a rival organization and managing tuna in their own EEZs through national measures, while other members, led by the United States, prefer retaining the commission.[62]

The regional fisheries commissions present a more complicated picture. Their management discussions produce recommendations for coastal states, which then choose whether or not to adopt them. FAO statistics and estimates suggest that the Northwest Pacific, the Mediterranean and Black seas, the Eastern Indian Ocean, and the Southeast Atlantic are overfished to varying degrees.[63] Thus the South Pacific Permanent Commission, the Indian Ocean Fisheries Commission, and the Mediterranean Council face the greatest challenges. Overexploitation of particular stocks occurs in nearly every ocean, posing regulatory challenges for coastal states. In trying to meet them, most coastal states limit effort to less than what would otherwise occur.[64]

60. Mfodwo, Tsamenyi and Blay, "The Exclusive Economic Zone," 463.
61. William K. Stevens, "Appetite for Sushi Threatens Giant Tuna," *New York Times*, 17 September 1991, C1.
62. Miles and Burke, "Pressures," 346–47.
63. World Resources Institute, *World Resources 1990–91* (New York: Oxford University Press, 1991), table 23.3.
64. See discussions in, e.g., Report of the Eleventh Session of the Fishery Committee for the East Central Atlantic, Doula, Cameroon, 7–9 December 1989, *FAO Fisheries Report* no. 420; Report of the Seventh Session of the Committee on Resources Management of the General Fisheries Council for the Mediterranean, Livorno, Italy, 22–25 February 1989, *FAO Fisheries Report* no. 426; Report of the Ninth Session of the Indian Ocean Fisheries Commission, Mahe, Seychelles, 2–6 October 1990, *FAO Fisheries Report* no. 436.

Except in the Whaling, Southern Ocean and (until 1991) Southeast
Atlantic commissions, the efforts of international fisheries commissions
since 1977 have been less important than the effects of national fisheries
management policies. Adoption of EEZs triggered a massive realloca-
tion of fishing effort as coastal states became more assertive about re-
serving their share of the resource to their own nationals and to those
foreigners forming joint ventures with local nationals. In the Southern
Ocean and the Southeast Atlantic the absence of coastal state jurisdiction meant that the commission was the only source of fisheries regulations. The Antarctic Commission, buttressed by the broader cooperative
norms of the Antarctic Treaty system of which it is a part, has had more
effect than the Southeast Atlantic Commission, yet even the latter managed to inspire real reduction of fishing effort in the early 1980s. Quotas
were reduced and at least the hake stocks started recovering.[65] Canadians have been frustrated at the limitations of the new North Atlantic
Commission, but the Commission did help reduce Canada's transaction
costs in dealing with states fishing just outside its EEZ by bringing those
states together in one forum. Yet even this advantage withered after
Canada restricted foreign fishing in its own EEZ so severely that it could
no longer condition access there upon participation in the commission.

The regional fisheries commissions are another matter. Without them,
the spread of management adivce and the growth of indigenous contributions to the general pool of fisheries knowledge would have been
even more modest. Their effects are felt not so much in management,
since this is mainly the task of coastal state governments, but in their
ability to frame measures and, particularly in the South Pacific, their
ability to present groups positions vis-à-vis wealthier distant-fishing
states.

**Paths to Change**
Before 1977, there were few examples of successful international management of fisheries. The early international commissions operated in a
highly unfavorable situation. The contractual environment, the numbers
of countries involved, the low concern of most, and the institutional

65. Seatersdal, "Fisheries Management, 28–29.

**Table 6.4**   Size of pre-1977 commissions

| Size | Successful | Helpful | Failure |
|---|---|---|---|
| Large | | | NW Atlantic (12) |
| | | | NE Atlantic (22) |
| | | | SE Atlantic (15) |
| | | | Whaling (12) |
| Small | North Pacific Fur Seal (4) | Inter-American Tuna (5–8) | |
| | | N Pacific (3) | |

limits imposed by the decision-making process, all made conservation an uphill struggle.

The difficulties of the contractual environment were only exacerbated by the relatively large size of the pre-1977 commissions, most of which had at least ten members. As table 6.4 demonstrates, their experience bore out the collective choice theory insight that collaboration among large numbers is more difficult.

The full implications of size can be seen in the contrast between the international commissions and the bilateral United States–Canada Pacific halibut, herring, and salmon commissions that provided the initial model for the international commissions. The international commissions could not duplicate their success because of differences in fisher attitudes. Both U.S. and Canadian Pacific coast fishers realized that restoring stocks and enjoying continual good fishing afterward would require cooperation with their counterparts in the other country because the stocks they exploited were so intermingled.[66] This awareness of mutual dependence among fishers eased the governments' regulatory tasks considerably. The bilateral commissions were not only small; they had no laggard members. The larger a commission, the less likely this situation of mutually high awareness among fishers.

The centrality of fishing patterns for creating mutual interest in restraint is borne out in the experiences of the pre-1977 commissions.

66. Herrington and Kask, "International Conservation Problems"; Johnston, International Law of Fisheries; Scheiber, "Pacific Ocean Resources."

Neither actual nor institutional devices for reducing the number of parties had any effect when resistant laggards were involved. Actual reduction of the number of significant parties occurred in three cases. Until the late 1960s, the United States took more than 80 percent of the catch regulated by Inter-Amercian Tuna Commission. The USSR regularly took more than 50 percent of the catch regulated by the Southeast Atlantic Commission, and four, later two, members took more than 80 percent of the catch regulated by the Whaling Commission. From Olson on, the collective choice literature has argued persuasively that small subgroups ("k groups") of members with sufficient resources can provide desired public goods for the whole.[67]

However, Olson and others have been analyzing a process in which the providers as well as the others benefit from presence of the goods. Even the members of a small group are likely to succumb to the pressures of a conflictual contractual environment when the issue is one of distributing adjustment costs. This is exactly what happened here. The Soviets had no interest in restraint in the Southeast Atlantic because their fleet expected to be able to fish elsewhere once the stocks there were depleted. The markedly different economic calculations of the Japanese and Soviet whalers led them to prefer driving others out of the industry to cooperating with them. The Inter-American Tuna case is more complicated. There, a number of coastal states desired to increase their share of the catch and used threats to extend jurisdiction as a means to force the United States to agree to reducing its share so they could have more. However, they did not simply go out and ignore the quotas, so they cannot be regarded as laggards in conservation. Recent studies suggest that small groups with members able to monitor each others' conduct continually can manage such adjustment, but that was not the situation of governments dealing with ocean fisheries.[68] In ocean fisheries, concentration of catch was helpful only if leaders were the largest takers.

Institutional efforts to reduce the number of parties actually involved in particular negotiations were no more successful. The Northwest

67. Mancur Olson, *The Logic of Collective Action* (Cambridge: Cambridge University Press, 1965).
68. E.g., Ostrom, *Governing the Commons*.

Atlantic, Northeast Atlantic, and Southeast Atlantic commissions were all subdivided into "panels" dealing with particular sub-areas of ocean or particular stocks. This meant that most regulations were framed by those governments whose fleets were most actively catching a particular type of fish or fishing in a particular area. Yet even when the panels were significantly smaller than the full commission (some were not), they were no more effective than the full commissions.

In many areas, the distant-water fleets' temptation to avoid adjustment was reinforced by their belief, better founded in the 1950s than in the early 1970s, that they could move on to yet-unexploited stocks elsewhere once the local ones were exhausted. Those ready to move on developed a "frontier mentality" focused almost exclusively on immediate gain; those less interested in moving were faced with trying to outrace the more mobile fleets, or finding some way to reduce the frontier mentality inspiring them.

Overall, the record of the pre-1977 international fisheries commissions was dismal. Most of them were unable to provide mechanisms for reconciling the strong divergence of interests that led many governments to avoid adjusting as long as possible. The bargaining dynamics of open-access common pool resources were too strong for the institutions in most cases. Only where open access was formally ended, as with North Pacific Fur Seals, or where local fishers aware of mutual dependence were isolated from newcomers less dependent on a particular stock, as in the North Pacific Commission, was stable success in fisheries management assured.

Yet the pre-1977 record would have been even worse if the international fisheries commissions had not existed. Without them, it would have been difficult for conservationist governments or the transnational community of fisheries scientists to focus the attention of laggard governments on the issue. Even if laggards were agreeing to encourage scientific work only for the purpose of getting arguments that would bolster their case for avoiding regulation, engaging in the discussion imposed some scientific discipline on their arguments. This should not be taken too far; even in the 1970s there was enough scientific disagreement that laggards could find good arguments. The scientists themselves realized that many supposedly scientific arguments were political, as captured in William Herrington's only partly humorous distinction among "facts" (statements based on weak scientific evidence), "true facts" (statements based on strong scientific evidence), and "real true facts" (statements based on strong scientific evidence that also support one's own policy preference).[69]

Though unable to transform perceptions of interest or become the forum for trading of side-payments for compliance, the international fisheries commissions did contribute to spreading awareness of issues and new perspectives on dealing with them. They kept fisheries regulators, scientists, and economists talking to each other, thus providing peer pressure and learning networks for both the experts and the governments involved. In a situation where industry influence was not subject to countervailing influence by any other domestic social group, and second- or third-party monitoring of national efforts to maintain restrictions was generally absent, it is fair to conclude that the commissions helped regulators "hold the line" against worse outcomes. If overfishing had already gone too far, this "holding the line" was not sufficient to prevent stock collapse. If it had not, the commission sometimes helped the leaders and the experts persuade the laggards to avoid letting the situation become worse.

Fisheries regulators have been somewhat more successful at avoiding overfishing and stock depletion since 1977. Collapses of particular fisheries occur, but regulatory measures come more quickly, and there is considerable experimentation with new forms of regulation in various parts of the world. Most of the credit for this change must go to the change in the broader law of the sea that transformed most fishing from open-access common pool to enclosed resource. This redefined the contractual environment regarding most stocks by replacing a bargaining situation with a hierarchical one in which one government could impose outcomes on others. It also limited the influence of any lingering frontier mentality by enclosing most known fish stocks.

The extent to which fisheries management improved depended heavily, on the preferences and capabilities of coastal states. Conservationist leaders with sufficient capability (which did not mean strong power status, but rather availability of resources for enforcing rules) no longer

69. Herrington, "Of Diplomacy and Fish," 109.

had their desires frustrated by the inertia created by laggards. Even governments which were somewhat laggard regarding domestic fishers often limited distant-water fishing, as local industry lobbied for removal of foreign competitors from "their" waters. In other areas, the prospect of being excluded forced distant-water fleets to be more attentive to coastal state preferences on catch, technology transfer, and joint venture arrangements. Occasional violations of 200-mile zones occurred, but the fact that most strong powers were coastal states with their own 200-mile zones created a balance of interests favoring respect. Yet many governments are still failing to provide effective management.[70]

After 1977, the most important factor in international management of stocks is the extent to which they straddle the 200-mile limit. Where they do, the coastal states have less clear title to regulate than if stocks remain within 200 miles of shore, even if they pass through the EEZs of several states. The greater prevalence of such stocks in the Northwest Atlantic; the habits of tuna; the existence of good fisheries in smallish areas of water that happen to be just beyond any country's EEZ (the Barents Sea and Bering Sea "donut holes"); and the lack of coastal state jurisdiction in the Southeast Atlantic (until Namibia became independent in 1991) and in the Antarctic make these the most challenging regulatory situations and explain why cooperative regulation is more difficult. The Whaling Commission's turnaround does not weaken this generalization because it stemmed from an unusual situation where a fishing issue gained enough salience to inspire considerable public pressure for action.

In this new situation, commission size becomes unimportant. As table 6.5 shows, this holds even if attention is focused on the number of coastal states (second number in the table entry) rather than the total of fishing and coastal state membership.

70. Lisa Busch, "Southeast Halibut Fleet Exceeds Quota," *National Fisherman*, September 1990, p. WCF4; Todd Campbell, "World Fisheries Management Gets Poor Marks" (interviews with Edward Miles), *National Fisherman Yearbook 1991*, 42–45; Lawrence J. Goodrich, "New England Fishing Drops Off," *Christian Science Monitor*, 22 February 1990, 7; Lawrence Ingressia, "Dead in the Water," Wall Street Journal, 16 July 1991; James R. McGodwin, *Crisis in the World's Fisheries: People, Problems, and Policies* (Stanford: Stanford University Press, 1990); and Jin Bee Oii, *Development Problems of an Open-Access Resource: The Fisheries of Peninsular Malaysia* (Singapore: Institute of Southeast Asian Studies, Occasional Paper no. 86, 1990).

**Table 6.5**   Size of post-1977 commissions

| Size | Helpful | Some challenge | Ineffective |
|---|---|---|---|
| Large | E Central Atlantic 31, 20 | Indian Ocean 41, 25 | |
| | W Central Atlantic 33, 24 | South Pacific 16, 16 | |
| | | Indo-Pacific 17 | |
| | | Mediterranean 19, 17 | |
| Small | Baltic 6, 7[1] | | SE Pacific 4, 4 |
| | | | SW Atlantic 3, 4[2] |

[1] EEC replaces Denmark and Germany as member in accordance with Common Fisheries Policy; Estonia, Latvia, Lithuania not counted.
[2] British administration of Falkland Islands.

The poorer performance of the southern cone commissions is particularly striking, and stems mainly from failure to bring fishing states into the discussions. Both commissions deal with stocks that straddle the 200-mile line and attract significant fleets from elsewhere. Part of the reluctance to draw the fishing states in has been political: The most active distant-water fleets have been Soviet, and for many years the governments involved in both commissions were reluctant to entertain broad relations with the Soviet government. On the Atlantic side, the situation is also complicated by the Argentine-British dispute over the Falklands/Malvinas, and by weak traditions of cooperation among the three coastal states.

Since coastal states manage most stocks, either individually or in small groups, it is easy to conclude that the international and regional fisheries commissions are largely superfluous. Except where stocks straddle the 200-mile limit, management could, in this view, be just as effective if carried out among smaller groups of coastal states. It is easy to imagine the commissions as temporary institutions useful for dealing with the rearrangement of world fishing activity as distant-water fleets are excluded and local ones replace them.

This last scenario presupposes a more rapid rearrangement of world fishing activity than is likely to occur. First established distant-water fleets will continue to seek out stocks beyond 200 miles that they can fish without coastal state hindrance. It is true that many countries are moving to exclude foreign fleets. Yet some governments are considering foreign fleets as long-term partners in joint ventures, and some resource economists are suggesting that governments managing fluctuating stocks consider using them as reserve capacity to be brought in during good years, so that they need not allow the domestic fleet to grow above the size efficient for catching average yields.[71]

That scenario also ignores the importance of the commissions as a forum for discussion and for transmission of new scientific insights. It is true that the FAO's intergovernmental Committee on Fisheries and staff in its Fisheries Division perform such functions. However, the Committee on Fisheries does not meet often enough or long enough for discussion of rapidly developing or very complex problems, and the staff is too small to be anything but a catalyst. Furthermore it can be a catalyst only if it has frequent contact with regulators and scientists in various countries. The international and regional commissions provide a structure for just such contact.

Industrial countries might get along without the international commissions; they have strong research and regulatory capabilities. For developing countries, the regional commissions are more important because of their role in encouraging and aiding capacity-building. This is relevant because the timing of regulations is very important to their success. Most fisheries follow a roughly similar path of development. Initially, only a venturesome few move on to a new ground or try taking a hitherto unexploited species. If they prosper, word gets out and others follow. If enough others follow, the fishery becomes congested and overfishing is quite likely to result. If, however, managers introduce restrictions relatively early, fishers and their governments start the process of accommodation before they have developed strong interests in maintaining high catch levels. Imposing management early also increases the

71. John R. Beddington and Colin W. Clark, "Allocation Problems between National and Foreign Fisheries with a Fluctuating Fish Resource," *Marine Resource Economics* 1 (1984): 144.

likelihood that quotas will be set sufficiently low that later downward revision can be avoided—though it does not guarantee that result. Downward revision has always inspired the sharpest contentions, with scientific advice routinely set aside to work out quotas that will be minimally satisfactory to all major fishing states. All the pre-1977 commissions faced the problem of catching up to the fishery, either because overfishing had already started, or because the opting-out clauses allowed easy and protracted obstruction. The regional commissions and the Antarctic Commission became active on management questions ahead of the great expansion of fishing on many stocks within their purview. There were, therefore, high hopes that the severe problems of adjustment plaguing the older commissions would be avoided. These hopes have not been entirely borne out, in large part because fisheries issues have remained relatively low on government agendas and have attracted attention from few people outside the circles of those directly involved.

Though still low on national agendas, the importance of fishing is rising in many countries. This pattern was widespread, even after adoption of EEZs. Of the 121 coastal states states in the world, only 30 had lower ocean catches in 1985 through 1987 than in 1975 through 1977,[72] and most were actively expanding their fishing fleets.[73] In many cases, this poses additional problems because enlargement of the fishing industry is likely to increase pressure for avoiding restrictions.

The growth of domestic interest in fishing focuses attention back to the policies of individual governments. Many still treat their EEZs as open-access common pools open to their nationals and any foreigners who can secure authorization. This maintains the pressure for overinvestment as governments attempt to manage fisheries with the same sort of quota regulations that they use internationally. Though eliminating the domestic open access has been discussed among experts for years, only recently have governments begun experimenting with alternatives like limiting the number of boats licensed to fish in particular areas or allocating exclusive fishing rights to individuals or small groups. The enclosure that occurred at the international level with adoption of 200-

72. World Resources Institute, *World Resources 1990–1991*, table 23.2.
73. Compare Lloyd's of London, *Lloyd's Register of Shipping: Statistical Tables*, 1975 and 1985.

mile zones is being repeated at the domestic level wherever such measures have been implemented. Enclosure is happening in another way as well. Both ocean and freshwater fish farming (aquaculture) have been expanding. Statistics remain fragmentary, but Canada, China, Cuba, Ecuador, Egypt, France, Indonesia, Japan, South Korea, New Zealand, Norway, the Philippines, and the United States have all enjoyed growth in this sector.[74] By one estimate, farming and hatchery operations total about 20 million metric tons now, and will equal 25 million by the end of the decade.[75] Such operations involve closing off particular areas or keeping fishes in cages, and create a situation similar to that of settled agriculture on land. Even these changes do not guarantee against overinvestment, but probably keep it at lower levels than occur in an open-access common pool.

## Lessons

Judged by the stricter test of preventing or ending overfishing, the experience with international fisheries management has been discouraging. The failure to achieve much success stems from problems in all three dimensions—concern, contractual environment, and capacity. Concern on the part of governments and other actors has remained low. Fishing issues have seldom become sufficiently salient that governments, the general public, or fishers regarded successful conservation measures as important enough to merit long-term effort. Governments and fishers have also been hobbled by an unfavorable contractual environment. In principle, adoption of 200-mile zones permitted changing this by ending the open-access common pool nature of the resource. In practice, however, many governments have simply treated their EEZs as open areas for their nationals and those foreigners allowed access. National management thus replicates the situation that prevailed globally until 1977. While developing countries have been adding significantly to their national capacity in the past decade, the difficulties of imposing restraint on fishers having little interest in it continue to daunt even the governments of industrial states.

74. World Resources Institute, *World Resources, 1990–1991*, table 23.2.
75. Ken Kelley, "Coming on like Gangbusters," *National Fisherman Yearbook 1991*, 57–59.

Only in a few cases were strong coalitions committed to preventing overfishing forged. In the North Pacific Fur Seal and North Pacific Fisheries cases, coalitions were built around economic rather than environmental concern—fishers and governments wanted to maintain catches and income. In the whaling case, an environmental coalition was formed in the mid-1970s and prevailed not by persuading laggard governments, but by getting leaders to outvote and pressure them. Hence the stubbornness with which Japanese and Icelandic whalers use loopholes to continue taking minke whales (which are not on any endangered species list). In general, however, environmentalists have not become concerned with overfishing, and the fisheries commissions have not been catalysts for bringing them into the policy process.

Both the international and the regional commissions have contributed to a modest rise in concern by encouraging open-ended knowledge creation. All have fostered greater international exchange among fisheries scientists; this is particularly true of those having their own research staff or relying on an existing international scientific body like ICES or the FAO Fisheries Division. In the early years, the scientific exchange led to confidence that the problem of managing stocks to provide steady yields without depletion would be solved. It is a tribute to the commissions' willingess to encourage this that more recent work has forced regulators to acknowledge that their initial goal of providing steady levels of fishing on all stocks was too ambitious. They are still absorbing the implications of more recent work suggesting that many stocks may have to be managed in other ways.

Both the international and the regional fisheries commissions attempted to alter the contractual environment by creating iterated negotiating processes moving from principles to rules. They have been ready to change the rules as greater knowledge accumulated. When the first generation of rules—closed seasons, closed areas, minimum landing size, and minimum net mesh—failed to solve the problem, the international commissions did move to overall quotas. Within a few years most were supplementing those with national allocations, decided either in the commission, or in parallel discussions by the members fishing a particular stock. Neither shift was instantaneous; laggards opposed both, and in some cases commission rules had to be amended first. However, the international commissions display the sort of flexibility in rule-making that is necessary for success in managing changeable situations. While the regional commissions do not adopt rules themselves, they transmit many ideas about possible rules to member governments and encourage coordination of rule-making by states that manage stocks ranging through more than one EEZ. There, too, the advice has reflected the changing scientific consensus about which rules are most likely to be helpful.

The international commissions encouraged development of member state scientific capacity by focusing national attention and efforts on particular species or stocks. The periodic meetings required all members—leaders, followers, and laggards alike—to have enough expertise available to evaluate and react to each other's arguments. Leaders and followers, at least, also had to modify their regulatory and enforcement routines to accommodate joint decisions. That laggards did not is shown in the adoption of joint enforcement schemes, under which the more eager could identify violations, even if prosecution had to be left to the flag state. The regional commissions provide a far clearer example of national capacity building. The FAO-sponsored ones began as technical aid agencies geared to teaching more effective methods of fishing. After adoption of the EEZ, they quickly added transfer of scientific and regulatory skills to their activities.

Yet open-ended knowledge creation, establishing rules, and increasing national capacity were not sufficient. Neither alone nor together did they increase concern enough to focus sustained attention on altering the unfavorable contractual environment in the 1950s or 1960s. Most governments were satisfied with extending national jurisdiction from three to twelve miles from shore, leaving most stocks within the common high seas pool without any real effort to improve how they coordinated management of the common pool. Fisheries regulators were concerned, but there was no way to transmit leader concern to laggards through political pressures or to bribe laggards into better behavior by side-payments. Monitoring systems were so weak that even though aggregate overfishing could be detected, identifying the particular fishers responsible was very difficult. The high likelihood of successful cheating reduced even leader enthusiasm, since self-restraint was obviously not going to be reciprocated by enough others to be worthwhile.

Many governments decided in the mid-1970s to alter the contractual environment by changing the nature of the resource. Some of the governments were reacting to the frustrations of joint management; others had never really liked joint management and were happy that enough others finally agreed on enclosing the resource. Thus, developing country governments desiring to broaden their economic decision-making authority, conservationist governments frustrated with joint management, and coastal fishers desiring to exclude distant-water competitors forged a coalition strong enough to transform the definition of property rights with regard to most fish. The shift from open-access common pool to national enclosure gave individual governments the right to impose their own rules and to monitor others' compliance with them. Leader governments wasted little time taking advantage of the new possibilities. Others moved more slowly, but now laggards could heavily influence the pace and detail of regulations only in their own EEZs or in the remaining areas of high seas.

This shift to national enclosure has not solved all problems. Joint management is still necessary with stocks outside EEZs. Low governmental and public concern still permits laggards to slow the pace beyond what leaders and some followers regard as wise. Second, and far more importantly, most governments have not altered the open-access nature of the national EEZ for their own fishers. Though a few are experimenting with individual allocations of rights, most are still trying to manage the national fishery as a common pool and are encountering at the national level all the problems of overfishing and overinvestment that plagued the international commissions before 1977.

### Appendix: Relevant Treaties

Convention on Fishing and Conservation of the Living Resources in the Baltic Sea. 1973. *International Legal Materials* 12: 1291–97 (1973).

Convention on the Conservation of Antarctic Marine Living Resources. Canberra, 1980. *United States Treaties* 33: 3476–3556.

Convention on the Conservation of the Living Resources of the Southwest Atlantic. 1969. *United Nations Treaty Series* 801: 101–37.

Convention on the Law of the Sea. 1982. *International Legal Materials* 21:1261–1354.

Indo-Pacific Fisheries Council. 1961. *United States Treaties* 13: 2511–19.

Inter-American Tropical Tuna Convention. 1950. *United Nations Treaty Series* 80: 3–13.

International Convention on the Conservation of Atlantic Tunas. 1966. *United Nations Treaty Series* 673: 63–85.

International Convention on the High Seas Fisheries of the North Pacific. 1952. *United Nations Treaty Series* 205: 65–101.

———. Protocol 1978. *United States Treaties* 30: 1095–1166.

General Fisheries Council for the Mediterranean. 1949, as amended 1963. *United Nations Treaty Series* 490: 444–59.

North Atlantic Salmon Conservation Organization. 1982. *Official Journal of the European Community* No. C70.

North Pacific Fur Seal Convention. 1911.

———. 1957. *United Nations Treaty Series* 314: 105–49.

———. 1963 amendments. *United Nations Treaty Series* 494: 303–16.

———. 1969 amendments. *United Nations Treaty Series* 719: 313–18.

———. 1976 amendments. *United States Treaties* 27: 3371–3400.

———. 1980 amendments. *United States Treaties* 32: 5881–98.

Permanent Commission for the South Pacific. 1946. *United Nations Treaty Series* 1006: 331–35.

Treaty on Fisheries between Certain Pacific Island States and the United States of America. 1987. *International Legal Materials* 26: 1053–90.

# III

## Intranational Issues

# 7

## Managing Pesticide Use in Developing Countries

Robert L. Paarlberg

When powerful technologies are transferred to poor countries, the good and bad consequences are hard to control. So it is with pesticides. These chemicals, originally developed by private companies for use in the industrial world, are now being sold in growing quantity to farmers and public health ministries in poor developing countries.

The good they have done is impossible to deny. Tens of millions of human lives have been saved, and hundreds of millions of citizens have enjoyed improved health, thanks to the use of chemical insecticides—including DDT—against vector-borne diseases such as malaria. Pesticides have also become a valuable key to crop protection. Roughly 30 percent of the world's food supply is currently being lost due to pests, plant disease, and rodents, and an *additional* 30 percent might be lost were it not for the use of chemical pesticides.[1] In the tropical countries of the developing world, where pests that attack plants are especially abundant, and where hundreds of millions of poor rural citizens depend upon farming for employment as well as for their food supply, crop protection by chemical pesticides is frequently a matter of life or death.

Serious harm, though, can accompany the use of this powerful chemical technology in developing countries. Pesticides are poisons—designed to kill. Even when used carefully, they often kill more than the intended target population of weeds or insects. Serious environmental damage to fish or wildfowl can result, especially when poisons persist in the food chain, or when they enter the local water supply and then

1. "The Estimation of Pesticide Poisoning: The Need for a Realistic Perspective," International Group of National Associations of Manufacturers of Agrochemical Products (GIFAP), Brussels, April 1986, 1.

move downstream to unprotected locations.[2] Risks to human food consumers are a second concern. Chemical residues on foods produced with pesticides, even in small quantities, can result in chronic as well as acute toxicity.[3] These residues can be an especially serious problem in the tropics, where crops tend to be marketed in rural communities soon after harvest, and often without washing.[4] The use of discarded pesticide tins by poor village dwellers for storage of drinking water often compounds the danger.

The greatest risk, though, is occupational. Millions of poor peasant farmers and agricultural laborers in the developing world risk exposing themselves directly to pesticides whenever they transport, mix, or apply them. Serious poisoning can result from chemical skin contact, swallowing, or inhalation of spray mists. Symptoms can range from nausea and vomiting to convulsions, respiratory failure, and death. The World Health Organization has used several different rough extrapolation methods (accurate data do not exist) to guess that as many as 1.5 million accidental pesticide poisonings occur every year, of which 28,000 result in death.[5] Independent analysts have guessed an even higher annual toll of nearly 3 million cases of poisoning, and about 220,000 deaths.[6] Roughly three-fourths of these annual poisoning deaths take place in the developing countries, though only 20 percent of all pesticides are actually applied there.[7]

All three of these pesticide risks—environmental, consumer, and occupational—are now growing most rapidly in the developing world. This results from a dangerous combination of deficiencies in poor coun-

2. K. Mellanby, "Pesticides, the Environment, and the Balance of Nature," in D. L. Gunn and J. G. R. Stevens, eds., *Pesticides and Human Welfare* (Oxford: Oxford University Press, 1976), 217–27.
3. Doug Campt, "Reducing Dietary Risk," *EPA Journal* 16, 3 (May/June 1990): 18–22.
4. David Bull, *A Growing Problem: Pesticides and the Third World Poor* (Oxford: OXFAM, 1982), 54–62.
5. In some developing countries, suicides represent a significant share of fatal pesticide poisonings. This complicates, considerably, the analysis of exposure risks. World Health Organization, "Assessment of Mortality and Morbidity Due to Unintentional Pesticide Poisonings," WHO/VBC/86.929.
6. J. Jeyaratnam, "Health Problems of Pesticide Usage in the Third World," *British Journal of Industrial Medicine* 42 (1985): 505–6.
7. U.S. Agency for International Development, "Pesticide Use and Poisoning: A Global Review," Report to the United States Congress, September 1990, 7.

tries: in protection available to agricultural workers, in the regulatory capacity of national governments, and in the responsibility and accountability of pesticide manufacturers.

Worker protection is a more difficult problem in the developing world because many of the peasants and rural laborers who handle and apply chemical pesticides are poor and illiterate, and live in remote villages which lack modern medical services. Unable to read warning labels, these rural workers often fail to understand or appreciate chemical risks. Unable to afford protective equipment (or perhaps unwilling to wear that equipment in the tropical heat), they spray their fields barefoot, or not wearing the necessary gloves and masks.

National governments in the developing world are also far behind in the registration and effective regulation of dangerous farm chemicals. While some lack the means, others also lack the motive. Their concern for environmental questions is not well developed, and they may care too little about the welfare of powerless rural farm workers. Three-fourths of developing country governments have now enacted some form of legislation governing the distribution and use of pesticides, but only about 15 percent of these governments, according to a 1988 survey by the United Nations Food and Agriculture Organization (FAO), possess the institutional and technical means (inspection agents, testing laboratories, etc.) to enforce such legislation. Roughly 40 percent of developing countries have not yet created a national registration scheme for the control of pesticide health hazards, and 60 percent do not even know which chemicals are being marketed inside their own country.[8]

Deficiencies in the responsibility and accountability of pesticide manufacturers and formulators are a third source of risk in the developing world. International manufacturers—mostly private companies headquartered in Europe or the United States—are tempted to take advantage of the weak regulatory environment in developing countries by selling products there that they can no longer sell in the developed world. They use aggressive marketing techniques and sometimes fail to provide adequate notification of potential hazards. Private pesticide formulators in the developing world, who sell directly to farmers, fre-

8. UNFAO, "International Code of Conduct on the Distribution and Use of Pesticides: Analysis of Responses to the Questionnaire by Governments," AGP:GC/89/BP.1, January 1989, 6.

quently compound the damage through careless mixing, packaging, and labeling.

What role can international institutions play in addressing these difficulties? Such institutions obviously cannot eradicate, any time soon, the conditions of rural poverty and illiteracy that make pesticide use so dangerous in poor countries. Perhaps they can, however, work to repair the weak regulatory capacity and the inadequate environmentalist motivation of national governments in the developing world. And certainly they should work to reduce irresponsible trade in dangerous pesticide products.

What follows is an assessment of how contemporary international institutions are reacting to this difficult challenge. This assessment will be constructed around the same sequence of actions—agenda setting, international policy, and national policy response—examined by others in this larger study of institutional effectiveness. Several aspects of this assessment, moreover, will reinforce the thrust of our larger study. It will be shown, for example, that the UN Environment Program (UNEP) and FAO have made some of their strongest contributions through the raising of governmental concern and through the creation of an improved contractual environment for the development of international agreements. The visible fruit of this effort is an international Code of Conduct, subscribed to by all parties, which provides environmentalists with an increasingly strict standard for judging and holding to account the behavior of both governments and private industry. If UNEP and FAO had not been available to formulate this code, the goal of safe pesticide use in the developing world would today be even more distant.

The contribution of international institutions to capacity building, however, has so far been quite modest. The efforts made by FAO and UNEP have been well intended, but necessarily limited. On this score we shall in part fault the World Bank, an international institution better designed to perform such tasks, but one which has yet to step in to provide well-funded leadership in the pesticide area.

**Agenda Setting**

The problem of unsafe pesticide use in poor countries is not new. It was becoming known to experts by the 1960s, and rough calculations of the magnitude of the problem were produced in the 1970s. Yet the issue did not become a priority concern for international institutions until the early years of the 1980s. What explains the somewhat belated emergence of this issue as a top international agenda item?

Agricultural pesticides first emerged as a potent political issue in the industrial world following the 1962 publication of Rachel Carson's popular book, *Silent Spring*.[9] Carson, then a civil servant on the public affairs staff of the U.S. Fish and Wildlife Service, framed the issue as one of protecting songbirds from the persistent effects of organochlorine insecticides, such as DDT. The ensuing campaign against DDT, led by private nature protection groups, was an important vanguard to the wider U.S. environmentalist movement in the 1960s.[10] This campaign led eventually to a 1973 ban on DDT by the recently created U.S. Environmental Protection Agency (EPA). Legislative authority to screen pesticides for both acute and chronic human health effects, including cancer risks, had been given to EPA in 1972. The agency soon began using this authority both to register new products with greater care, and to cancel or restrict the domestic use of several dozen existing products.[11] These unilateral U.S. domestic control actions against pesticides were soon mirrored in other industrial countries, including the Scandinavian countries, the member nations of the European Community (EC), and Japan.[12]

The rapid spread of separate national control actions was seen as a threat, however, by the international agrochemical industry—which feared the cost and inconvenience of having to register its products separately in dozens of different countries. U.S. food companies were also worried, since they suspected the EC of planning to use internal pesticide control actions as a disguised form of trade protection. Largely in response to such private industry concerns, the "international harmo-

9. Rachel Carson, *Silent Spring* (Boston: Houghton Mifflin, 1962).

10. Henry P. Caulfield, "The Conservation and Environmental Movements: An Historical Analysis," in James P. Lester, ed., *Environmental Politics and Policy* (Durham: Duke University Press, 1989), 33.

11. Katherine Reichelderfer and Maureen Kuwano Hinkle, "The Evolution of Pesticide Policy," in Carol S. Kramer, ed., *The Political Economy of U.S. Agriculture* (Washington, D.C.: Resources for the Future, 1989), 152.

12. Robert Boardman, *Pesticides in World Agriculture: The Politics of International Regulation* (New York: St. Martin's Press, 1986), 78–97.

nization" of control actions soon emerged as an agenda item within several important international institutions.

The international harmonization of food safety standards was entrusted to a joint body of FAO and the World Health Organization (WHO) named the Codex Alimentarius Commission, in The Hague. Acting on the basis of scientific evaluations submitted by specialists from both FAO and WHO, the commission's Committee on Pesticide Residues (composed of national delegations to FAO and WHO) had begun in 1966 to make judgments on acceptable levels of pesticide residues in selected foods, in hopes that these standards would eventually be incorporated into national regulations. By the early 1980s, this Codex procedure had generated more than 1,600 separate residue tolerance proposals, and a majority of these had been accepted by leading industrial country governments. But the Codex system was intended more to harmonize than to restrict. The tolerances recommended by the Committee on Pesticide Residues were scientifically derived, but usually set high enough to present private industry (which enjoys representation on many national delegations) with a minimum of constraint.

Concerns over the development of EC pesticide controls as a hidden barrier to trade, meanwhile, were mostly addressed in a setting limited exclusively to rich country participation: the Chemicals Group of the Organization for Economic Cooperation and Development (OECD). U.S. officials favored this venue because OECD was an organization that forced EC member states to negotiate as individual governments, rather than as a single powerful community, and because other non-EC industrial countries were also represented there.

On questions of unsafe pesticide use in developing countries, however, international institutions played no significant role until early in the 1980s. It had become clear to some experts and environmental activists, at least by the middle years of the 1960s, that the use of modern pesticides in poor countries would carry unique and potentially acute environmental and occupational safety risks.[13] By the early 1970s, in fact, rough calculations were being made by WHO of the alarming

---

13. The International Union for Conservation of Nature and Natural Resources (IUCN) had highlighted such issues as early as 1966. See Boardman, *Pesticides in World Agriculture*, 116.

number of pesticide poisonings that were probably taking place every year in the developing world. An expert committee from WHO estimated, in 1972, that roughly 500,000 cases of accidental pesticide poisoning were occurring annually, perhaps half of those in the developing world.[14] Not until the early 1980s, though, were activist organizations inclined to use such calculations to put the developing country "safe use" problem squarely on the international agenda.

The international agenda status of this issue was retarded, during the mid-1970s, by what was then being called a world food crisis. Beginning in 1972, and lasting until the end of the decade, international grain prices increased sharply (more than doubling), and agenda-setting agents (including scholars, activists, and the media) in both rich and poor countries became more concerned with ending apparent food shortages in poor countries than with controlling unsafe farm pesticide use. At a highly publicized UN World Food Conference in Rome in 1974, pesticide risks went unmentioned as governments pledged to help boost food production in the developing countries by increasing the delivery of farm chemicals to those countries.[15] This conference made much of the "35 percent of potential yields lost annually" in poor countries due to uncontrolled pests, and it worried about an impending global "pesticide deficit" of 20 to 30 percent.[16]

Such talk was pleasing to a variety of traditionally powerful international actors and institutions. The agrochemical industry was delighted that international leaders were worrying about future "pesticide deficits," rather than planning new regulations. The production-oriented agriculturalists who dominated most national farm ministries, as well as FAO, were likewise pleased to know that boosting output—rather than protecting farm workers, consumers, or the environment—was to remain the major task. Even most nongovernmental organizations (NGOs) were momentarily content to define their purpose as solving the "food crisis."

All this was to change in the 1980s, when world food prices collapsed

14. WHO, "Safe Use of Pesticides," 20th Report of the WHO Expert Committee on Insecticides, Technical Report Series No. 513, Geneva, 1973.
15. Barbara Dinham, "FAO and Pesticides: Promotion or Proscription?" *The Ecologist* 21, 2 (March/April 1991): 62.
16. Boardman, *Pesticides in World Agriculture*, 104.

back to earlier levels, and images of global shortage were replaced (especially in the minds of rich country agenda-setters) by images of food surplus. This turnaround provided a key agenda-setting opportunity to groups more concerned with human health and the environment. One collection of such groups was just then forming into an association called the Pesticides Action Network (PAN). These mostly European-based organizations had highly varied motives. One of the first organizers, the Foundation for Development Alternatives, was a small Dutch group concerned mostly with the damage that pesticide use in Africa might be doing to migratory bird populations in northern Europe. The most important intellectual leadership, however, was provided by OXFAM, a British group with strong Third World antipoverty and rural development credentials. David Bull of OXFAM was then working on an influential book (*A Growing Problem: Pesticides and the Third World Poor*, published by OXFAM in 1982), soon to serve pesticide critics as a valuable reference document. Institutional support was soon offered by the International Organization of Consumers Unions (IOCU), which hosted early meetings in The Hague and in Penang, Malaysia, and which provided the "network" model for political action, adapted to the pesticides issue by PAN. Financial support for some of these early meetings was provided by a grant from the Dutch government.

There was no single, riveting event that galvanized these NGOs into action on pesticides early in the 1980s. The closest thing there has been to such an event—the 1984 disaster at a Union Carbide pesticide plant in Bhopal, India, which killed 2,500 people—occurred several years after PAN had been formed. And the first alarming WHO estimates on pesticide poisonings in the developing world had been released almost a decade *before* PAN was formed.

Part of the glue that originally held PAN together was a strong alienation from the conservative tide then sweeping through several Western governments (Reaganism and Thatcherism), plus a deep mistrust of Western-based multinational corporations. These orientations often made PAN unwelcome inside traditional policy circles in the developed world, but gave it instant credibility among developing world leaders. It was by informing and lobbying sympathetic Third World leaders, especially within the UN system, that PAN was eventually able to put its pesticide concerns squarely on the agenda of international institutions.

PAN discovered several congenial UN settings in which to promote its critical views on pesticides. First was the Governing Council of the United Nations Environment Program, where developing countries (led by Kenya) had been complaining for some time about multinational corporations "dumping" banned hazardous chemicals (not just pesticides) into developing countries. In 1977, the Governing Council had adopted an important resolution affirming that such chemicals should not be exported without the knowledge and "consent" of appropriate authorities in the importing country.[17] PAN groups decided to embrace this concept of "prior informed consent" (the phrase was coined by David Bull), and began encouraging developing country leaders to insist that it be applied specifically to exports of pesticides.

National regulations in some exporting countries had also been moving in the direction of greater restrictions on sales of banned, hazardous chemicals. In 1978, the U.S. Federal Insecticide, Fungicide and Rodenticide Act (FIFRA) had been amended to require more complete labeling of all exported pesticides and to require that when domestically banned pesticides are exported, notification of the sale must be made to officials in the importing country. President Carter signed an executive order in 1981, just before he left office, that would have gone much farther by requiring "consultations" with the governments of importing countries prior to sales of domestically banned products, including some pesticides.[18]

U.S. leadership on this issue soon weakened, however, when President Reagan promptly revoked Carter's executive order. This reopened the door to exports of domestically banned products and galvanized the NGO community into several international actions. Within the UN system, NGOs promoted a 1982 General Assembly resolution (proposed by Venezuela) calling for various forms of official consent by governments in importing countries prior to any sale of domestically banned

17. UNEP, *Report of the Governing Council on the Work of its Fifth Session*, UN Document A/32/25, 1977.
18. David Bull, *A Growing Problem: Pesticides and the Third World Poor*, 151–52.

chemicals.[19] Inside the EC, meanwhile, PAN organizations encouraged the socialist group within the European Parliament to sponsor a resolution calling on the commission to embrace prior informed consent. This resolution passed unanimously in October 1983.[20]

Because of this rapidly building NGO activity early in the 1980s, even FAO was soon obliged to address the issue of safe pesticide use in developing countries. FAO admitted the item to its agenda partly in self-defense; had it left the issue entirely to others, like UNEP or WHO, its traditional agricultural jurisdiction within the UN system might have been reduced. This dynamic of jurisdictional competition and institutional self-defense goes a long way toward explaining the subsequent pace and content of international institutional policies in the pesticide area.

**International Policy**

When FAO examined its traditional pesticide programs to find some way to address the new safe use issue, it discovered at least one ongoing activity that seemed to fit the new imperative: integrated pest management (IPM). The concept of IPM had emerged in the developed world at the end of the 1950s as a reaction among agricultural scientists (not environmentalists) to sole reliance on pesticides for pest control. Sole reliance on chemical pesticides was leading to a number of adverse side effects—including the development of resistance to chemicals in pest populations. Farmers were advised to practice IPM by using a mix of nonchemical as well as chemical pest control techniques (for example, crop rotation), and by using the most powerful chemicals only when pest populations crossed a relatively high threshold of economic injury.

When safe use of pesticides became a top issue for FAO early in the 1980s, it might have seemed logical for the organization to pursue a dramatic expansion of its IPM programs. Some modest expansion did take place, thanks in part to a $1.3 million Netherlands contribution for a cotton project in the Sudan, plus a $4.4 million contribution in 1982 from the Netherlands and several other donor governments for

19. Marc Pallemaerts, "Developments in International Pesticide Regulation," *Environmental Policy and Law*, 18/3, 1988, 65.
20. Marc Pallemaerts, "Export Notification", *E.E.R.* 1, 2 (February 1987): 29.

rice projects in South and Southeast Asia. FAO's IPM programs were also shifted away from pure research, toward field-level training. Yet by the mid-1980s, with the exception of the rice program in Asia (where government support and local extension capacity were both strong), this modest FAO push for IPM had largely peaked.[21]

IPM never quite emerged as FAO's primary answer to the unsafe use problem. This was due in part to IPM's failure to address the two major concerns of the NGO community that had put the issue on the agenda. First, IPM had too little to offer on the matter of occupational safety for Third World applicators, because it promised only indirect benefits through fewer applications. More important, IPM did not address the animating issue of irresponsible corporate behavior in the developing world. Increased regulation of this behavior was what the NGOs (and their friends among the G-77) were most keenly after, and for this purpose IPM was not useful. FAO's joint panel on IPM therefore never became politicized in the early 1980s; it remained dominated by entomologists, and attracted little attention either from the NGO community or from industry.

Regulation of private industry was the battleground, and here FAO's sympathies were clearly with industry. These FAO sympathies grew partly out of a realistic, scientific appraisal of the crop protection problem in poor countries, and partly out of a history of close institutional association. The agrochemical industry, for years, had enjoyed semi-official status within FAO. Beginning in the 1960s, the industry's international lobbying organization in Brussels, GIFAP, had sent representatives to work inside FAO on a joint bureau called the Industry Cooperative Program (ICP), which promoted pesticide use worldwide.[22] Although this direct FAO-industry link was broken in the 1970s, GIFAP continued to enjoy easy access (through the Plant Protection Service) to all FAO activities dealing with pesticides, and was thus in a position to influence the organization's response to the safe use issue.

21. Cotton projects in Latin America were not undertaken for lack of donor support; basic food crop projects in Africa were swamped by the delivery of free chemical pesticides for locust control. G. G. M. Schulten, "Integrated Pest Management in Developing Countries," FAO, Plant Protection Service, Rome, 1991.
22. Dinham, "FAO and Pesticides," 63.

Industry also enjoyed strong support from a number of powerful Western country governments. Neither the U.S. government under Reagan, nor the British government under Thatcher, was eager to see the embrace of any international regulations that might constrain domestic companies from making sales abroad. In most international settings where G-77 or NGO representatives were pushing for tighter restrictions, U.S. and British representatives defended private industry. Other national governments with large, export-oriented agrochemical firms, such as Germany and Japan, often joined in the opposition to tighter regulation.

Despite support from such strong political allies, the agrochemical industry decided to avoid a strategy of outright confrontation. The industry believed it could better protect its interests through careful compromise, co-optation, and delay. Its most important step down this path was to embrace voluntarily what some more moderate NGO leaders had recently started demanding: a new international Code of Conduct to delineate the precise responsibilities of private companies engaged in pesticide sales in the developing world.

GIFAP wanted the code to be voluntary, and wanted it to be drafted by the industry's friends in FAO, rather than by WHO (which had recently drafted a code of conduct for the infant formula industry in poor countries) or by some other institution more hostile to pesticides.[23] FAO had its own institutional interest in this approach, and so the director-general formally proposed the idea in 1981.[24] The motives of both FAO and GIFAP were at first self-serving. FAO hoped to be seen "responding" to the new issue of safe pesticide use in poor countries, just sufficiently to retain its institutional jurisdiction over the issue. GIFAP hoped that its support for a code-drafting process would be enough to preempt NGO charges of corporate irresponsibility, without leading to anything more than a weak and voluntary set of obligations on the industry.

For most of the next six years, this preemptive "Code of Conduct" strategy functioned much as FAO and GIFAP had intended. FAO, for

23. Boardman, *Pesticides in World Agriculture*, 108.
24. FAO, *International Code of Conduct on the Distribution and Use of Pesticides*, Rome, 1990, 1.

its part, used control over the code-drafting process (between 1982 and 1985) to reassert its traditional jurisdiction over pesticide issues, and to demonstrate "responsiveness" to its many critics within the NGO community. To some extent, FAO even managed to co-opt NGO leaders into the process—the job of producing a first draft of the Code was given to David Bull of OXFAM. Much of what Bull originally suggested for the Code—including the key principle of prior informed consent (PIC) by governments in importing countries—was later removed, at GIFAP's and FAO's insistence, in the lengthy revision process that ensued (over a three-year period, the thirty-page code went through ten different drafts).

The original Code of Conduct satisfied GIFAP as well as FAO. Better to accept a strictly voluntary code—and one free of a prior consent provision—than to be faced with mandatory regulation. What the code provided, in fact, was a formal listing of obligations for governments as well as for private industry, thereby restoring some balance to the political debate over who was responsible for safe use in poor countries.[25]

Much of the Code, in fact, describes a fantasy world, in which capable regulatory agents from competent, non-corrupt Third World governments are constantly in the countryside, enjoying the voluntary support and cooperation of private industry, making sure that naturally prudent and self-reliant individual farm workers will have all the information they need to avoid risks from chemical exposure. It has been useful, for industry, to have in hand an official FAO document prescribing this idealized image of safe use in poor countries. Industry representatives promoting pesticide use in poor countries keep copies of the Code of Conduct close at hand, in part to help deflect questions about safety. GIFAP, the industry's international lobbying association, refers to the Code constantly in its public communications, and makes adherence to the Code a formal condition of association membership.

FAO's drafting of a voluntary Code of Conduct was not enough, however, to head off regulatory initiatives in all other settings. Tightened pesticide export regulations were still actively under consideration

---

25. Under Article 5 ("Reducing Health Hazards"), for example, the code lists eleven different things that "governments should do," either alone or in cooperation with industry.

both in UNEP (where prior consent had first been endorsed back in 1977), and in a number of national and regional policy settings in Western Europe. Industry was able, for a time, to protect itself from additional regulation in these settings only with assistance from the U.S. and British governments.

The Reagan and Thatcher governments, early in the 1980s, did not like the concept of prior informed consent (PIC); they did not want restrictions on exports of hazardous chemicals to go beyond the "notification" standard (notification to importing governments) that was already established in the 1978 FIFRA.[26] Sensing that organizations like UNEP wanted much more, the United States and Britain, supported by a number of other industrial, chemical-exporting countries, attempted to create an international consensus for notification only. The institution they used to create this preemptive consensus was OECD.

Meetings of the Chemicals Group at OECD were an attractive setting for this purpose, because the G-77 was not represented, and because NGO participation could be tightly controlled. Only one NGO representative (a Washington attorney for the Natural Resources Defense Council, who had earlier helped create the FIFRA notification procedure) was in attendance. The United States and Britain sought to use these meetings to produce "Guiding Principles" on chemicals trade, which would be limited to one-time-only export notifications plus some simple information exchange. A document was drafted in 1982, and then formally adopted by the OECD Council in 1984, which incorporated these minimal trade control standards.[27]

These minimalist OECD Guiding Principles were then effectively used to dissuade groups such as FAO, the EC, and UNEP from going any farther. Inside FAO, in 1984 and 1985, they were used to hold off de-

26. This U.S. preference for keeping international standards within the bounds already established in U.S. domestic legislation has been described elsewhere as "convenient environmentalism." See Robert L. Paarlberg, "Ecodiplomacy: U.S. Environmental Policy Goes Abroad," in Kenneth A. Oye, Robert J. Lieber, and Donald Rothchild, eds., *Eagle in a New World* (New York: Harper Collins, 1992), 207–32.

27. The notifications required under these OECD Guiding Principles did not have to be given *prior* to export, and "should not be such as to delay or control the export." See Pallemaerts, "Developments in International Pesticide Regulation," 65.

mands from NGO and G-77 activists that the new Code of Conduct include a prior informed consent principle. The Guiding Principles were also used to delay more aggressive EC export control actions, of the kind the European Parliament had unanimously recommended to the EC Commission in its 1983 resolution. Most important of all, the minimalist OECD Guiding Principles were used successfully, for a time, to block more aggressive actions by UNEP.

As a step toward implementing its own 1977 recommendation for PIC, UNEP had decided in 1982 to convene a working group of experts to draft its own "Guidelines for the Exchange of Information on Potentially Harmful Chemicals, in Particular Pesticides, in International Trade." When this working group first met, in 1984, demands for PIC from the G-77 were blocked when the industrial countries rallied around a proposal offered by Great Britain, a weak "Provisional Notification Scheme" which reproduced, verbatim, some of the provisions of the OECD Guiding Principles. A 1985 meeting of the working group, held in the wake of the Bhopal disaster, went no farther.

It was not until the third meeting of the UNEP working group, in London in February 1987, that the dominance of the OECD Guiding Principles finally was broken. By that time, several important developments had occurred. First, in 1985 the OECD itself had finally embraced the concept of prior informed consent, in a somewhat related area of hazardous waste exports. And second, the government of the Netherlands had acted unilaterally in 1985 to authorize PIC restrictions on its own dangerous chemical exports. So when the United States, Britain, and Germany again insisted at the 1987 UNEP working group meeting that the concept of prior informed consent *not* be included in the "London Guidelines" then under debate, the Governing Council of UNEP, which was dominated by a Third World majority, finally lost its patience.

NGOs played a key role in galvanizing Governing Council objections to the exclusion of PIC from the London Guidelines. Representatives from PAN created and circulated to G-77 members of the Governing Council a draft amendment which added PIC to the new guidelines. When the Senegalese representative took up this NGO initiative in June 1987, all other African representatives came on board, and soon it became an issue of G-77 solidarity. To avoid an unseemly North-South conflict, the Governing Council decided to compromise by adopting the proposed London Guidelines without change, but with a pledge that prior informed consent would be added to the guidelines at the next scheduled meeting of the Council, in May 1989.[28]

Once the UNEP Governing Council had provisionally embraced PIC in this fashion, the floodgates were opened for other institutions to do likewise. In November 1987, at the 24th FAO Conference meeting, a resolution was passed by consensus (Resolution 5/87) obliging FAO, at last, to add PIC to its own Code of Conduct.

At this critical juncture two separate risks loomed. First was the risk of an institutional conflict between UNEP and FAO over which would operate the pesticides portion of the new PIC scheme. Second was the risk of a uncooperative rejection of any kind of PIC scheme by the private chemical industry. It is a tribute to the institutions in question that both these risks were overcome.

A critical positive step was taken by the U.S. government, which had been aroused to action by the movement toward PIC. The Office of International Activities at EPA (specifically, the director of the Developing Countries Staff within that office, Edwin Johnson) became convinced in 1987 that some form of international PIC system was now inevitable. He feared it would operate badly if fought over by two separate UN agencies, or if designed without U.S. government and industry participation. Accordingly, EPA persuaded the State Department, Commerce Department, and finally the private chemical industry to accept its role in designing and launching the new PIC scheme. EPA's Johnson then went on to perform this role personally, by participating as an "expert consultant" in a critical series of joint FAO/UNEP meetings between 1988 and 1991. This series of meetings yielded, in June 1991, a coordinated set of guidelines for FAO and UNEP prior informed consent procedures.

Cooperation between FAO and UNEP was not easy to arrange. The first instincts of the FAO secretariat were to try to retain some form of exclusive control over the pesticides portion of the PIC scheme, leaving only the non-pesticide chemicals to UNEP. It is to the credit of the FAO

---

28. Pallemaerts, "Developments in International Pesticide Regulation," 66.

secretariat, and to those (such as EPA's Johnson) who were urging cooperation, that these first instincts did not prevail. UNEP would almost certainly have refused to recognize any limit on its jurisdiction, and the result would have been two separate (and probably incompatible) PIC schemes for pesticides.

In the end, FAO decided to cooperate with UNEP because it sensed its own inability to run a separate and competitive PIC scheme. UNEP had developed an overall advantage in chemicals trade controls, in part because it had earlier embraced the creation of an important international information system—the International Register of Potentially Toxic Chemicals (IRPTC), established in 1976 in Geneva. IRPTC was created to maintain central files on all potentially toxic chemicals, including pesticides, and then to share those files (especially with chemicals managers in the developing world) through a "national correspondent" system. Because of the development of this system, IRPTC was given the job in 1987 of implementing UNEP's new notification system for banned hazardous chemicals in trade—the London Guidelines—and then for overseeing the incorporation of a PIC scheme into those guidelines.[29] Because of such IRPTC activities, UNEP could present itself, in 1988, as ready to implement a PIC scheme for pesticides even without FAO cooperation.

Why, then, did UNEP agree to cooperate on PIC with FAO? UNEP recognized that the first phase of any successful PIC scheme would have to revolve around pesticides—the toxic chemicals that most interested the international NGO community, and those about which the most scientific information had already been collected. (Of all the potentially dangerous man-made chemicals, pesticides are actually the best studied and the most tightly regulated.) To run a successful PIC scheme for pesticides, UNEP knew it would be helpful to have access to FAO's regional and country-level contacts with agricultural ministries in the developing world. UNEP, an organization with only weak in-country contacts (and those, in turn, were mostly with weak environment ministries), knew that a PIC scheme built around pesticides could not function without the strong cooperation of agricultural ministries in

29. UNEP, *IRPTC Bulletin* 10, 1 (March 1990): 4.

the countries that imported pesticides. If these ministries tried to block the PIC scheme (many wanted unlimited access to pesticides imports), or if they simply failed to respond to requests from exporters for consent to sell (a problem encountered by the Netherlands when it tried to launch its own national PIC scheme), the result would be an early failure for PIC.

FAO was also important because of its close ties to industry. Cooperation from private industry, which would be required to share information on chemical specifications, would be essential to the operation of any PIC scheme. UNEP was aware that when WHO and the International Labor Office (ILO) tried to create an International Program on Chemical Safety (IPCS) early in the 1980s, without first securing cooperation from private industry and FAO, the project had encountered resistance and had floundered.[30]

For all these reasons, UNEP needed to cooperate with FAO on PIC almost as much as FAO needed to cooperate with UNEP. Fortunately, both institutions recognized this need. The joint effort that ensued, to create a single coordinated PIC scheme, reveals much about what can be gained when international institutions with different constituencies and differing priorities manage to work together. The first tangible gain was the creation of an inclusive contractual environment, in which both the international NGO community and private industry could participate.

The agrochemical industry, represented by GIFAP, was sufficiently reassured by U.S. government and FAO involvement in PIC to set aside its own opposition and get down to the business of helping design a PIC scheme that would cause minimal inconvenience to chemical exporters. GIFAP sent two representatives to the first expert consultation on PIC in Rome in 1988, and then seven representatives to the second meeting in 1989. GIFAP's major objective (which it achieved) was to restrict the number of pesticides that would initially be subject to PIC, and also to steer FAO and UNEP away from requiring official consent from importing countries on a cumbersome, shipment-by-shipment basis. By 1990, GIFAP was satisfied that these concerns were being taken into account, and while it still had few good words for the PIC, it decided to cooper-

30. Boardman, *Pesticides in World Agriculture*, 126–28.

ate by publishing its own pocket-sized "Guide to the Working of PIC," which it then circulated to its membership.[31]

While the involvement of FAO was bringing GIFAP on board, UNEP's role was enough to ensure parallel participation from the international NGO community. The joint UNEP/FAO meetings that designed PIC were attended by a variety of top-level PAN operatives from IOCU, the Environment Liaison Center (ELC), and the Pesticide Trust. While GIFAP was pushing constantly for fewer restrictions, these NGO representatives were pushing to add chemicals to the PIC list, and to tighten the definition of official consent.

Partly as a result of this active participation by both GIFAP and PAN in the design of the PIC scheme, neither private industry nor the NGO community repudiated the compromise document ("Guidance for Governments") that finally emerged from UNEP and FAO, and which officially launched the scheme, in the summer of 1991.[32] Neither UNEP nor FAO, acting alone, could have brought GIFAP and PAN together for long enough to secure such a broad spectrum of political support for PIC.

Joint action by UNEP and FAO had the further advantage of discouraging other rival international institutions from pursuing uncoordinated and unhelpful actions of their own. Representatives from the Environment Directorate at OECD, which had earlier tried to block PIC, offered money for government training workshops to help ensure successful developing country participation in the new system.[33] Next to fall in line was the EC Commission, which began using the joint UNEP/FAO action on PIC as its means to overcome lingering member country resistance in the EC Council. The Commission was eager to launch PIC in Europe as a new European Community–wide regulation, both to avoid damage to industry from a profusion of differing national regulations, and also to boost its own regulatory authority vis-à-vis member country governments. To this end, it seized upon the new

31. GIFAP, "Prior Informed Consent (PIC): A Guide to Its Working," Brussels, December 1990.
32. UNEP and FAO, "Operation of the Prior Informed Consent Procedure for Banned or Severely Restricted Chemicals in International Trade: Guidance for Governments," Rome and Geneva, 1991.
33. UNEP and FAO, "Report of the Second FAO/UNEP Joint Meeting on Prior Informed Consent," Geneva, 1990.

UNEP/FAO scheme as something the Council, out of a larger international obligation, might feel obliged to endorse.

The UNEP/FAO scheme also helped deflect what might have become a rival initiative inside GATT (General Agreement on Tariffs and Trade). Pressures from African countries had led GATT in 1988 to create a working group tasked with designing a new instrument on trade in "domestically prohibited goods and other hazardous substances." The GATT secretariat supported this initiative, over the objections of the United States, and for a time it appeared that GATT was about to draft its own separate (and legally binding) rules on such things as notification and consent. By 1990, however, GATT representatives were participating more closely in the joint UNEP/FAO initiative on PIC, and coordination improved. When the GATT working group finally issued its draft decision in May 1991, full deference was shown to existing UNEP and FAO schemes such as the London Guidelines and the Code of Conduct.[34]

Coordination with WHO proved somewhat more problematic. FAO and WHO had long been in competition on pesticide issues, and creation of the joint FAO/WHO Codex Alimentarius Commission had not ended that competition. When WHO and ILO tried to use the International Program on Chemical Safety in the early 1980s to dilute FAO's authority over pesticides (UNEP was part of the IPCS, but FAO was not), a serious jurisdictional battle was joined. In hopes that this jurisdictional battle would not scuttle the UNEP/FAO initiative, technical-level representatives from WHO were included in the joint meetings that designed the PIC, and various WHO and IPCS publications (especially WHO's Recommended Classifications of Pesticides by Hazard) were used in constructing the list of chemicals to be included in PIC.[35]

At the political level within WHO, however, a strong preference still remains for someday expanding the competence and reach of IPCS. Such a move would reduce the special status of pesticides alongside other chemicals that can endanger health, and threaten FAO's special

34. GATT, "Decision on Products Banned or Severely Restricted in the Domestic Market," Working Group on Domestically Prohibited Goods and Other Hazardous Substances, 22 May 1991, Geneva.
35. UNEP and FAO, "Report of the Third FAO/UNEP Joint Meeting on Prior Informed Consent," Rome, June 1991.

claim to a lead role in pesticide regulation. If these WHO preferences prevail (for example, as part of the reshuffling of institutional relationships that may occur following the 1992 UN Conference on Environment and Development—UNCED—in Brazil), the newly created joint UNEP/FAO prior informed consent scheme could find itself under challenge.

The joint UNEP/FAO scheme has also failed, so far, to discourage uncoordinated action by the ILO (WHO's principal partner in the IPCS). Although ILO representatives were kept informed and participated in the joint UNEP/FAO meetings, the 77th International Labor Conference in June 1990 nonetheless adopted its own Convention Concerning Safety in the Use of Chemicals in the Workplace, including pesticides. This convention included a number of exporter responsibilities which tended to overlap with measures already specified by UNEP and FAO. By 1991, UNEP and FAO had succeeded in persuading ILO (which was slow in developing its own implementation mechanism for the convention) to coordinate with them, at least on the designation of contact points within importing countries, but the danger of a somewhat redundant and not entirely compatible ILO scheme covering pesticide safety had not been entirely averted.[36]

Still, the development by UNEP and FAO of a jointly operated PIC scheme deserves to be appreciated as a significant institutional achievement. By getting together on the issue of pesticide trade, these two diverse institutions—perhaps the "greenest" and the "brownest" within the entire UN system—created a contractual environment broad enough to engage both NGOs and industry, and strong enough to discourage most rival institutions from any immediate jurisdictional challenge. Part of the strength of this achievement was also its "greening" impact, specifically on FAO. In a ten-year period, FAO had gone from resisting the safe use issue, to drafting a watered-down and voluntary Code of Conduct which contained no prior informed consent provision, to joining with UNEP in the acceptance and design of a PIC scheme. As FAO made this important shift, so to some extent did the international agrochemical industry.

36. UNEP and FAO, "Report of the Third FAO/UNEP Joint Meeting on Prior Informed Consent," Rome, June 1991.

## National Policy Responses

To what extent has national policy or international behavior been altered by these institutional actions? Separate judgments can be made for each of the separate policy thrusts discussed above: FAO's integrated pest management (IPM) programs; FAO's original 1985 Code of Conduct; the limited notification procedures that exporting governments tried to preserve through OECD; and finally the prior informed consent procedure, jointly developed between 1988 and 1991 by UNEP and FAO.

### Integrated Pest Management

Beginning with its Global Program for IPM in 1977, and continuing through the 1980s and into the 1990s, FAO has taken the institutional lead in promoting integrated pest management in the developing world. FAO's purpose is to change the behavior of developing country governments (many of whom ignore IPM and instead subsidize chemical use), and ultimately to change the behavior of individual farmers. To succeed on their own terms, these FAO efforts would require steady financial support from donors in the industrial world as well as strong institutional and political support from governments in the developing world. Only among the Asian rice-growing countries, to date, have they enjoyed both.

Donor support for FAO's IPM program has been narrowly based and inadequate. FAO lacks significant resources of its own to support the costly research and training programs that are needed to develop locally adapted IPM techniques, and then to extend those techniques to adequate numbers of farmers inside poor countries. The largest contributions (of only a few million dollars each) have come from only a few rather small industrial countries—such as the Netherlands (for work in Sudan) and Australia (for work in Southeast Asia). Small institutional contributions have come from UNEP ($830,000 in 1977 to help launch the Global Program) and from the UN Development Program (UNDP) to support IPM in Pakistan and Africa. FAO was unsuccessful in securing $6 million in donor support needed to help fund national projects that it had prepared in Latin America. In some cases, projects were initiated without adequate funding and then failed, leading to further disillusionment.[37]

Higher funding levels may not be a sufficient condition for successful IPM promotion, but they are usually a necessary condition. Training individual farmers in remote rural areas is expensive (IPM experts have recommended weekly visits by extension workers in the first year of training, then visits at two- to three-week intervals in the second year).[38] Effective national programs, even in middle-sized countries without vast numbers of farmers (like Turkey), have been shown to cost at least $25 million each. FAO cannot hope to meet the IPM needs of hundreds of millions of farmers throughout the developing world with a total budget a fraction of that size.

Also, governments in some developing countries provide less than adequate support to FAO's IPM programs. Far from considering pesticides a serious problem, agricultural development bureaucrats and political leaders in many poor countries have continued to promote excessive chemical use, through lavish pesticide subsidies that lower the cost of the chemicals to farmers. Many developing country governments (and farmers) still associate increasing chemical use with modernization, and they tend to become interested in IPM only when a local problem, such as pest resistance to chemicals, makes continued production gains impossible, or when internal budget or foreign exchange constraints make continued import of chemicals too expensive. In response to a 1986 FAO questionnaire, 70 percent of all developing countries that responded said they were not promoting IPM.[39] If these governments eventually do become interested in IPM, they may find themselves without an adequate national agricultural extension service of the kind needed (and used by FAO) to reach individual farmers.

37. In still other cases, IPM projects that were struggling along failed when donors decided to show their generosity by providing excessive quantities of free pesticides as foreign aid.
38. UNEP and FAO, "Integrated Pest Control in Agriculture", Report of the Thirteenth Session of the FAO/UNEP Panel of Experts Meeting, Rome, September 1987, 8.
39. FAO, "International Code of Conduct on the Distribution and Use of Pesticides: Analysis of Responses to the Questionnaire by Governments," AGP: GC/89/BP. 1, January 1989.

To date, only FAO's IPM program for rice in Asia has had the benefit of adequate support from both donors and host governments. This program began at a fortunate time, when governments and farmers—particularly in Southeast Asia—were facing increased costs from a chemicals-only approach to controlling brown plant hoppers on rice. The government of Indonesia finally changed its approach in 1986, by eliminating what had been an 85 percent subsidy on pesticides (this move saved the government $50 million a year), then by banning the use of fifty-seven broad-spectrum pesticides, and finally by embracing IPM.[40] These radical steps were a quick success, as insecticide use in Indonesia promptly fell by 90 percent and average rice yields actually increased.

Once this Indonesian success had been recorded, donor support for FAO's IPM rice program in Asia became somewhat more plentiful, totaling roughly $12 million by 1990. Such funds helped make possible the training of over 500,000 farmers, with annual savings due to de-creased pesticide use on the order of $150 million.[41] Still, even among the Asian rice-growing countries, IPM has yet to make a strong regional mark. Fewer than 4 percent of Asia's irrigated rice farmers are currently believed to be practicing IPM.[42]

### FAO's Code of Conduct
FAO's 1985 "Code of Conduct on the Distribution and Use of Pesticides" was at first a relatively weak document, because it was only voluntary and because it lacked a prior informed consent provision. On the other hand, the conditions of safe pesticide use described by the Code, in its articles on testing, regulation, labeling, packaging, and advertising, were remarkably strict.

40. The Indonesian government dedicated $5 million from its own extension budget for a first wave of IPM training, and, with FAO support, were quickly able to give over 15,000 farmers some IPM exposure. FAO, "Integrated Pest Management in Rice in Indonesia: Status After Three Crop Seasons," Jakarta, May 1988, 7.
41. G. G. M. Schulten, "Needs and Constraints of Integrated Pest Management in Developing Countries," Med. Fac. Landbouww. Rijksuniv. Gent, 55 (2a), 1990, 214.
42. Paul S. Teng, "Irrigated Pest Management in Rice," Department of Plant Pathology, University of Hawaii, Honolulu, January 1990, 20.

Compliance with these strict standards is known to be lacking. When the FAO Conference unanimously approved the code in 1985, it requested that the FAO secretariat cooperate with governments to monitor observance. Accordingly, a questionnaire was circulated one year later to all member nations, designed to collect data on the various issues addressed in the Code. Replying to this questionnaire, many developing country governments acknowledged an inability to meet all the responsibilities given to them under the Code.[43] Responses solicited so soon after promulgation of the Code were not necessarily taken as evidence that the Code was failing. FAO preferred to view these responses as a baseline for judging all future improvements. Still, a significant part of the existing noncompliance by developing country governments will no doubt persist, for reasons of both inadequate motivation and inadequate resources. A block of powerful ministries (agriculture, development, and health) in many poor countries has long favored expanded pesticide use, and will be slow to embrace the safe use issue.[44]

Despite such resistance, FAO is investing considerable energy in strengthening the capacity of developing country governments to comply with the Code of Conduct. In cooperation with other international organizations (such as the Asian Development Bank (ADB) and WHO), as well as donor country national agencies (EPA, (AID), and Germany's

---

43. Thirty-six developing countries (fifteen of which were in Africa) said outright that they were not able to observe the code. Twenty-three of these developing countries had no legislation at all to control the distribution of pesticides; twenty-two had no legislation relating to use; forty-one had no registration scheme to control health hazards; and fifty-seven had not reviewed which pesticides were being marketed within their own borders. Thirty-seven developing countries said they had inadequate treatment facilities for cases of poisoning, and eighty-one had not established the national poison control centers called for by the Code. Fifty-seven developing countries said that stored or marketed pesticides were not being adequately separated from foods. Sixty-two developing countries did not collect use and import statistics. Thirty-eight developing countries said they were not following FAO guidelines on labeling and packaging. FAO, "International Code of Conduct on the Distribution and Use of Pesticides: Analysis of Responses to the Questionnaire by Governments," AGP: GC/89/BP.1, January 1989.
44. This ground-level attachment to pesticides by local developing country officials stands in some contrast to the antipesticide rhetoric so often heard from G-77 representatives posted to UN agencies in Rome and Geneva. Within both private industry and FAO, this considerable gap between UN system rhetoric and home country reality is at times a source of cynicism.

Deutsche Gesellschaft fur Technische Zusammenarbeit) plus some NGOs (including both Greenpeace and GIFAP), FAO organizes training workshops around the world—recently in Thailand, the Philippines, Central America, Africa—at which local officials receive instruction in how to strengthen their own national pesticide regulations. Projects vary from simple training on Code of Conduct implementation to more comprehensive consulting visits designed to assist in the planning of national pesticide registration schemes, development of indigenous regulatory and laboratory capacity, and harmonization of regulations regionally or internationally.

Funding for these field activities is outside FAO's basic budget and usually must be solicited from other donor agencies, such as ADB, or governments. Japan and the Netherlands have been among those most prominent in supporting FAO's code implementation training sessions, but the total dollar value of such support nonetheless remains extremely small, at less than a million dollars a year. FAO's code implementation training activities are in some ways more cost-effective than its IPM activities, because they only have to reach a relatively small cohort of government officials rather than hundreds of thousands of individual farmers.[45] Yet the reach and the value of such training activities cannot be great. Building up the administrative capacity of governments in the developing world by only forty officials at a time (in the training workshops) is a daunting task. And even if well trained, these officials may still lack the physical equipment—expensive laboratory facilities and specialized testing and monitoring equipment—needed to operate the kind of registration and regulation scheme for pesticides described in the Code.

There is no lack of dedication within FAO to making its Code of Conduct a success. FAO is not, however, rich in either the financial resources or the field-level operating capacity needed to ensure that all developing country governments will soon be able to implement the Code. Without a greater commitment to this issue from either the World Bank

---

45. A typical five-week assistance mission by two of FAO's consultant experts will first produce a technical report on a country's specific pesticide regulation needs, then conclude with a one to two-week training workshop for approximately forty government officials, all for a total cost of only about $50,000.

(as we shall advocate below), or from the national assistance ministries of individual donor countries, the capacity of poor country governments to implement the Code of Conduct can be expected to improve only slowly, starting from an extremely low initial level.

Critics of the Code of Conduct focus more often on alleged instances of noncompliance by private industry. When questioned by FAO in 1986 about industry's role in helping to implement the code, developing country governments had few charitable things to say.[46] The extent to which local branches of international companies were the target of these complaints, rather than entirely indigenous formulators or traders, was not made clear.

Informal compliance monitoring is also performed by PAN. The NGO community, even while criticizing the weakness of the Code, has repeatedly used the terms of the Code, in pragmatic fashion, as a standard for imposing greater accountability on the international agrochemical industry. In October 1987, PAN published (through the Environment Liaison Centre in Nairobi) a comprehensive report on Code of Conduct implementation based on information collected by NGOs around the world. This report highlighted numerous Code violations by industry, such as irregular trade practices, reuse of containers, incomplete labeling, and the use of irresponsible advertising and promotional materials. So strong and sweeping was this critique of industry's compliance that GIFAP felt obliged to prepare an extensive rebuttal.[47] GIFAP's rebuttal was based partly on the one-sided nature of the PAN report (PAN gave industry no credit for its lead role in use of pictograms on pesticide labels), partly on a significant number of inaccuracies in the report (growing out of PAN's weak technical understanding of the WHO hazard classification scheme), and partly on an assertion that not enough time had yet passed (only one year since the

---

46. Forty-nine developing countries said industry was not following FAO's guidelines on packaging, storage, and disposal. Forty-nine also said misleading advertising had been encountered from time to time. Thirty-three developing countries judged pesticide traders to be not reputable, and fifteen said traders did not cooperate in the recall of hazardous products. FAO, "International Code of Conduct on the Distribution and Use of Pesticides: Analysis of Responses to the Questionnaire by Governments," AGP:GC/89/BP.1, January 1989.
47. GIFAP, "Implementing the FAO Code of Conduct," Brussels, July 1988.

Code was formally promulgated) to begin holding companies fully to account.

An important public dialogue of accusation and rebuttal between PAN and GIFAP had nonetheless been initiated. The next step was a paper published in 1989 by the Pesticides Trust in London, entitled "The FAO Code: Missing Ingredients."[48] Three years had gone by since formal promulgation of the Code, and PAN was still able to find over 130 examples of advertisements that violated the Code, and numerous examples—especially in Africa—of unsafe use. There is an ironic aspect to this public contretemps between PAN and GIFAP over Code compliance. PAN, which did not initially trust the Code process, is now finding the terms of the Code a convenient device for shaming industry. Industry, meanwhile, so thoroughly embraced the Code of Conduct at the start (making adherence to the Code a condition of GIFAP membership), that it must now take PAN's accusations of noncompliance most seriously. Top leadership at GIFAP is fully aware that the industry's most valuable political asset, its reputation for good citizenship, is at stake. When GIFAP sees a company from one of its member associations criticized by PAN, it investigates not only for the purpose of refuting PAN, but also for the purpose of policing the violation, as best it can, when the report proves to be accurate.

This remains an imperfect mechanism for accountability, since most industry violations of the Code take place at a considerable distance from GIFAP in Brussels, and even at a distance from the national associations which must pledge Code adherence to participate in GIFAP. Most industry Code violations take place in remote rural settings within the developing countries themselves, several layers of management removed from accountability to corporate headquarters.

Defenders of the Code of Conduct, especially within FAO, insist that it was never written as a legal instrument for the purpose of exacting overnight compliance. It was instead written as a consensus view of the direction in which both government and industry should be moving. Its potential contribution, so far, has grown precisely out of its history as a

---

48. "The FAO Code: Missing Ingredients, Prior Informed Consent in the International Code of Conduct on the Distribution and Use of Pesticides, Final Report, October 1989," prepared by the Pesticides Trust for PAN International, London, 1989.

consensual document. Because it is a document originally promoted by industry, evidence of violations, even when gathered by NGOs, must be taken seriously by industry.

## Notification

Official notification, of both chemical exports and control actions, was originally promoted, by private industry and by the rich exporting countries, as a way to protect developing countries from pesticide dangers without unduly constraining trade itself. Notification of this kind became a legal requirement in the United States for pesticides in 1978, and was subsequently embraced in one form or another internationally—first by OECD in its Guiding Principles, then by UNEP in its 1984 Provisional Notification Scheme, which eventually became the 1987 London Guidelines. Compliance, however, has been mixed.

In the United States, procedures have been adopted which somewhat blunt the impact of the law. Section 17(a) of FIFRA requires U.S. companies exporting any pesticides that cannot be used in the United States to first secure a statement of informed permission from the foreign purchaser (often the company's own subsidiary). EPA then transmits this statement, through routine embassy channels, to the government of the importing country. This official notification procedure is relatively convenient for U.S. industry, because the diplomatic channels used seldom touch would-be regulators in importing countries (environment ministries, for example), and also because there is no requirement that EPA's notification reach the importing government before the chemicals are actually shipped.[49]

Rigorous export notification has been even more lacking among some key European governments and chemical firms. In Britain, for example,

49. U.S. notification law also has some significant loopholes. For example, EPA can give U.S. companies something called a "section 3 registration" for domestically banned pesticides, which will then exempt them from any export notification requirement. A U.S. company, Velsicol, received this special category of registration for two of its pesticide exports—chlordane and heptachlor—when those chemicals were banned for domestic use in 1978. Other U.S. companies were then likewise permitted to export these chemicals without notification, under what EPA calls its "me-too" policy. "Exporting Banned Pesticides: Fueling the Circle of Poison," A Greenpeace Report, Washington, D.C., 19 August 1989.

a scheme was introduced in the mid-1980s which provided export notifications on a one-time-only basis, based entirely on the voluntary cooperation of industry. Building upon such relatively weak national schemes, the EC in 1988 finally created its own unified, Community-wide notification procedure—one designed, from the start, for the convenience of European industry. The EC's original list of twenty-one "chemicals subject to notification" was largely restricted to older chemicals that EC companies were no longer manufacturing or holding in stock, and hence were no longer in a position to try to sell abroad. This is part of the reason why a total of only twenty-four notifications were submitted during the first two years the scheme was in effect.

For somewhat different reasons, UNEP's London Guidelines notification scheme also falls short of being a strong success. The notifications originally called for under these guidelines were mostly notifications of domestic "control actions" against chemicals, rather than notifications of actual export. On a strictly voluntary basis, governments were to provide notification of such control actions to IRPTC, which would then relay the notification to the "designated national authorities" (DNAs) of all participating countries. This UNEP procedure for sharing notification of domestic control actions seems to have worked tolerably well, at least at the sending end of the procedure.

Compliance with this UNEP system at the receiving end is more difficult to judge. Under the London Guidelines, the DNAs receiving IRPTC notifications are expected to "assess the risks associated with the chemical, and make timely and informed decisions thereon." Little evidence exists that this has yet happened within developing countries where unsafe pesticide use is a serious problem. Importing country DNAs, in their informal communications with UNEP, have sometimes made joking reference to the "drawer" in which the notifications they have received are piling up.

### Prior Informed Consent

When G-77 members of the Governing Council at UNEP (followed quickly by their counterparts in the FAO Conference) decided in 1987 to embrace prior informed consent, the secretariats of these two organizations were left with the difficult task of deciding how such a scheme could operate. Their instinct was to design a PIC scheme simple enough to be easily implemented, and lax enough to encourage both government and industry compliance. They knew that their own reputation for competence and their own authority would suffer if a complex scheme were to collapse, or if an excessively demanding scheme were to be repudiated and ignored.

The interest of these international civil servants in starting small was shared by private industry, which would have preferred no PIC at all. This same interest was likewise shared, but for very different reasons, by some leaders in the NGO community. PIC had originally been an NGO idea, so representatives from PAN were careful not to push for an overly ambitious scheme that might malfunction. Just as there was a curiously shared interest among these strange bedfellows in creating PIC, so there was a shared interest in creating a modest, workable PIC.

It is not clear at this writing whether the initial design for the PIC officially unveiled in the summer of 1991 will meet the twin requirements of modesty and workability. The procedure will operate in three sequential steps. In *step one*, governments in exporting countries *notify* the DNAs in all importing countries of control actions they have taken to ban or severely restrict a chemical for health or environmental reasons. This is the same fundamental "notification" step required in the original London Guidelines. Under the new PIC procedure, this step will now be taken through IRPTC for industrial chemicals, and through a jointly managed IRPTC/FAO arrangement for pesticides.

In *step two*, governments in all importing countries must respond to the notification, indicating within ninety days whether future imports of the chemical in question will be allowed or not. This response also goes through IRPTC, or, in the case of pesticides, through IRPTC/FAO.

In *step three*, IRPTC or IRPTC/FAO will then disseminate all importing country responses to all exporting country governments, which will be expected to communicate these responses to their exporting industries, and then to ensure that exports do not take place contrary to the decisions of participating importing countries.[50]

50. UNEP and FAO, "Operation of the Prior Informed Consent Procedure for Banned or Severely Restricted Chemicals in International Trade: Guidance for Governments," Rome and Geneva, 1991.

Some of the more demanding features of this scheme are obvious. First, the scheme demands that DNAs in developing countries actually respond—within ninety days—to the notifications from IRPTC or from FAO that they will receive. At the insistence of GIFAP, no response will be taken as tacit consent that new restrictions on products already being imported will not be imposed.

A second demanding feature of this scheme is the requirement that IRPTC and FAO stay abreast of relaying all importing country responses to all other participating governments. Assuming that roughly one hundred countries will participate in PIC, this could mean—for each separate notification of a control action—relaying as many as a hundred separate responses to a hundred separate countries. The administrative burden could quickly grow to exceed IRPTC's still-limited capacity.

This burden will be doubly difficult in the area of pesticides, where IRPTC (in Geneva) will supposedly be administering the PIC jointly with FAO (in Rome). This is an awkward and untested jurisdictional compromise, sure to be strained by the real differences between UNEP and FAO on pesticide issues. Compounding the problem, some countries have now responded to this joint operation of PIC by naming two different DNAs, one of which will presumably communicate with IRPTC, and the other with FAO.[51]

Third, the scheme demands that governments of exporting countries invent a means to relay importing country responses in timely fashion to their own export industries. Industries cannot be asked to honor the consent process without an assurance that they will be notified quickly of who has consented to what.

The difficulties discussed above are those that will have to be surmounted when *new* control actions are reported, after the system is up and running. To get the system running, UNEP and FAO have also devised a scheme for accommodating *old* control actions—those that have been on the books for many years now. The chemicals subject to these earlier actions cannot be ignored, since they are often among the most dangerous, and since some are still traded. Yet including all such earlier

51. As of 31 May 1991, 104 countries had nominated a total of 139 DNAs. FAO, "Report of the Third FAO/UNEP Joint Meeting on Prior Informed Consent," Rome, 3–7 June 1991.

control actions in a first round of notifications would crush the ability of DNAs in importing countries to decide and respond in timely fashion.

To overcome this practical difficulty, UNEP and FAO agreed to start by including past control actions in PIC only when five or more countries have banned or severely restricted the chemical in question. Applying this rule, IRPTC's data base on past control actions was used to generate an initial "PIC list" of twenty-two pesticides, featuring a large number of older insecticides of obvious concern, such as aldrin, chlordane, dieldrin, heptachlor, DDT, endrin, and toxaphene.[52] This start-up procedure temporarily "grandfathered" a number of existing chemicals out of the scheme, but it seemed the best way to ensure workability. All hoped that when DNAs in developing countries finally began receiving "decision guidance documents" for the chemicals on this initial list, they would be able to respond quickly without being overwhelmed.

If this new PIC procedure begins to operate as designed, on the basis of an adequate volume of both notifications and responses through IRPTC and FAO, how much of a constraint is it likely to place on trade? Initially, little or no impact will be anticipated. The initial PIC list contains a number of chemicals so old, and so tightly restricted in the industrial world, as to represent only a small share of international pesticide sales. Many are first-generation organochlorine insecticides, no longer manufactured by the largest chemical companies in industrial countries. Worldwide, organochlorines now account for only about $480 million in yearly sales, or less than 10 percent of the world's $6.2 billion insecticide market, and only about 2 percent of annual world sales of all pesticides.[53] In the United States, the only companies still producing such chemicals for export are relatively small and obscure (Velsicol, Northwest Industries, and Sandoz Crop Protection Corpora-

52. This initial list was first shortened, at the insistence of GIFAP, pending verification of some of the control actions recorded. Then it was reexpanded, at the insistence of NGOs, which presented evidence that three more chemicals— parathion, parathios-methyl, and the herbicide paraquat—should also be included, because of the known hazards associated specifically with their use in the developing world. UNEP and FAO, "Report of the Third FAO/UNEP Joint Meeting on Prior Informed Consent," Rome, 3–7 June 1991.
53. Wood Mackenzie & Co. Ltd., Agrochemical Service, Reference Volume of the Agrochemical Service, May 1990, 2, 33.

tion). In Europe, except for Shell, the largest companies have likewise moved beyond all these chemicals.[54]

Moreover, the inclusion of a chemical in the PIC process does not necessarily mean that exports will have to be constrained. DNAs located in agricultural ministries are likely to say yes to the continued import of any chemicals they are already using. Industry has protected itself, in any case, by insisting that non-responses from DNAs should permit exports to continue as before.

Still, there are several different ways in which this new PIC procedure could eventually have a significant constraining impact on pesticide sales to developing countries. First, a steadily increasing number of chemicals are likely to be made subject to PIC procedures. Under procedures accepted in 1991, a new control action by any *one* participating country will be enough to put a chemical on the list. The result is expected to be a rapid growth in PIC notifications, not only for the older organochlorine insecticides, but also for more of the organophosphates. Eventually the process could cover the newer synthetic pyrethroids (first produced in 1976), which are collectively far more important to the industry.[55]

## Institutional Effectiveness

The effectiveness of these various UNEP and FAO initiatives has so far been quite limited. Still, this is not a case of institutional "failure." The

54. The PIC list—much like the EC's "chemicals subject to notification" list—was built around these older chemicals, in part, because the dollar value of trade that stood to be affected was very small. The only chemicals on the initial list for which there is a large international market are parathion (an organophosphate insecticide) and paraquat (an herbicide).
55. The PIC list of chemicals could expand in other ways as well. PAN has already demonstrated its ability, inside UNEP and FAO, to add chemicals to the list (such as parathion and paraquat) which it considers environmentally or occupationally hazardous in developing country settings. PAN pressure has obliged UNEP/FAO to create a candidate list of chemicals, based on those that WHO considers acutely toxic, and also to send to all DNAs a questionnaire designed to gather more information on such chemicals. So long as NGOs continue to enjoy institutionalized access to the PIC process (through participation in the joint meetings that have developed the process, and through an assured opportunity—along with GIFAP—to review all Decision Guidance Documents before they go to DNAs), they will be in an advantageous position to lobby for a continuous strengthening of the process.

UN special agencies that have taken the lead so far—UNEP and FAO—have each moved the process forward at something close to their own maximum speed, given the weak support available from exporting countries and industries, and given the weak institutional and motivational foundation for action that exists within many societies and governments in the developing world.

The relatively strong performance of UNEP and FAO can be highlighted by noting what did *not* happen once the safe use issue reached the agenda of the UN specialized agencies early in the 1980s. First, FAO (and its friends in the agrochemical industry) did not reject the safe use issue out of hand. Instead, they embraced a "Code of Conduct" approach, which (perhaps unintentionally) implicated both FAO and GIFAP in an emerging consensus that some kinds of industry conduct had to be changed. Meanwhile, UNEP (and its friends among the NGOs) did not reject out of hand the thought of working with FAO. When the moving consensus on pesticides then eventually led both UNEP and FAO to embrace prior informed consent, UNEP agreed to share the PIC for pesticides with FAO. The institutional cooperation that resulted, between the "greenest" and the "brownest" of all the UN special agencies, then led to an unusually cooperative dialogue, as well, among the warring constituencies of these two agencies—PAN and GIFAP. When the PIC procedure was finally launched, in the summer of 1991, it consequently enjoyed the important endorsement of both these essential groups.

Cooperation between UNEP and FAO has not only helped to build consensus between PAN and GIFAP. It has also helped to prevent various other organizations—including WHO, ILO, and GATT—from acting on their earlier inclinations to undertake redundant or uncoordinated actions in the same area. Two of the most frequently observed failings of the UN special agencies—an inability to talk with each other and a tendency to duplicate one another—have thus been avoided in this case.

When we turn from problems avoided to objectives attained, however, the record is not yet as strong. FAO has so far been able to play only a small role in the promotion of integrated pest management in developing countries, due to a lack of its own resources and also due to a lack of adequate (or adequately motivated) national-level institutions in the developing world. Weak institutions in the developing world have likewise frustrated FAO's efforts to promote greater compliance with its Code of Conduct.

UNEP and FAO have devoted enormous energy to the issue of international pesticide trade. This is the issue of greatest political interest to international industry and the NGOs, but it is not main source of unsafe use problems in poor countries. The only achievement here has been slow movement from an imperfectly implemented notification scheme to a far more ambitious experiment with prior informed consent. Even if this PIC experiment succeeds on its own terms, its actual impact on pesticide exports may at first be scarcely noticeable. Compared to the new constraints on exports that some industrial governments might embrace unilaterally in the years ahead (for example, the "circle of poison" legislation in the United States, which would unilaterally halt exports of pesticides either banned or unregistered for domestic use), these international institutional actions seem weak.

What might be done to improve this international institutional performance? One approach, widely favored among the G-77 and some NGOs, is to make the voluntary arrangements that have been developed thus far—such as the PIC in the London Guidelines, and the FAO Code of Conduct—legally binding. In May 1991, UNEP's Governing Council (under the sway of its G77 majority) requested that the ad hoc Working Group on the London Guidelines be reconvened, to consider strengthening the legal basis of the guidelines, including the PIC procedure. Similar pressures to upgrade the "voluntary" status of the Code of Conduct were simultaneously coming from G-77 members of the FAO Conference.

The major exporting states, such as the United States, United Kingdom, Germany, and Japan, have so far opposed transforming the PIC procedure into something legally binding. The EC Commission, which is close to securing Council approval for a legally binding EC prior informed consent scheme to parallel the London Guidelines, is more positively inclined—as are some other industrial countries (like Sweden and Canada) that already have in place national export controls on pesticides that are *tighter* than PIC. The NGOs are divided on the issue, some not wanting the PIC procedure which they helped design to be swamped with too many legal implications before it has had a chance to operate.

The G-77 push to legalize PIC has so far, in any case, been blocked by resistance at the secretariat level within both FAO and UNEP. On two occasions, in 1989 and 1991, the UNEP/FAO joint meeting on PIC advised that upgrading the legal status of PIC was "premature."[56] These working-level international civil servants are fearful that the process of building and maintaining a consensus among divergent groups will be impaired if lawyers start to replace technicians around the tables of decision. The information flow might also dry up, if some participants— particularly private industry, which has the most information—begin to fear self-incrimination. Finally, the healthy process of maintaining a "moving" consensus would be impaired if a legally binding (and hence hard to amend) convention were established. One advantage of the voluntary approach, under the London Guidelines and the Code of Conduct, has been a relative ease of moving forward, toward standards (such as PIC) that are tighter than those that were judged acceptable earlier in the process.

For the purpose of advancing safe use of pesticides within the developing countries themselves, legally binding international instruments may be of less value than the voluntary PIC process now being put in place. What is missing today in many developing countries is an accountable policy process to govern the import and distribution of pesticides. When dangerous pesticides are allowed to be imported and sold (or even subsidized) in circumstances where use will not be safe, it is sometimes difficult to know which government official or agency should be held responsible. One great advantage of the PIC scheme will be the creation of DNAs within developing countries whose official responses can now be scrutinized—by everyone from the local press and political opposition to the international NGOs—when they are asked whether imports will be allowed.

At first, perhaps, these DNAs will come from traditionally pro-pesticide agencies within the importing countries, and will say yes to imports more often than is wise. When they do so, however, it will no

56. UNEP and FAO, "Report of the Third FAO/UNEP Joint Meeting on Prior Informed Consent," Rome, 3–7 June 1991.

longer be a secret. The FAO/IRPTC decision dissemination process will ensure that all DNA responses are centrally available for public scrutiny and comparison. This process of scrutiny and comparison will perhaps help to galvanize stronger opposition by "green" officials inside developing countries to the irresponsible pesticide import and use policies now being pursued by their own "brown" officials. This is a political rather than a legal accountability process; perhaps it will function best without the chilling effects of a legal convention.

Some within UNCED and WHO are also considering a second means for upgrading UN special agency performance in the pesticides/ chemicals area: the creation of a single, centralized "global regime for chemicals." WHO would like to see a dramatically expanded International Program for Chemical Safety (IPCS), which would begin making technical risk assessments, chemical by chemical, that would then be systematically considered and endorsed by national delegates to a single international group (perhaps like the Codex Alimentarius Commission), for subsequent use in risk-benefit assessments at the national policy level. At first, the purpose of such a body would be to assist developing countries in learning about chemical risks, and in developing their own national registration schemes, lest they become dumping grounds for stocks of dangerous chemicals no longer marketable in the industrial world. Eventually, however, it would develop into a legally binding international regime.[57]

The UN agency most obviously threatened by this concept is FAO. If pesticide policy were folded into a larger "chemicals regime" built around IPCS, then FAO (which remains outside IPCS) might be excluded from the picture. There are strong reasons to keep FAO involved in the regulation of pesticides. Confidence would be lost, in the eyes of both private industry and agricultural ministries around the world, if FAO were to be excluded. Without the confidence and constructive par-

57. This plan was very much alive in 1991. Early in the UNCED process, the influential Preparatory Committee (Working Group 2) formally asked the secretary-general of the conference to consider, among other things, strengthening the IPCS; and it has invited WHO and UNEP, among others, to propose "an intergovernmental mechanism for chemical risk assessment and management." UNEP's Governing Council endorsed the idea, and has asked its Executive Director to cooperate in drafting such a proposal.

ticipation of these key constituencies, any pesticides component in this new chemicals regime would be stillborn.

A third option for improving the performance of international institutions in the pesticides area is, unfortunately, the one least talked about. This is the option of mobilizing more industrial country financial and technical resources, and transferring those resources into developing world settings where the capacity to use chemicals safely is still deficient. Remember that unsafe pesticide use grows not so much from an absence of international regulation or cooperation, as from a variety of mostly local deficiencies. So long as rural farm workers in developing countries remain predominantly illiterate, impoverished, and politically or socially marginalized, they will remain vulnerable to the tragedies of unsafe pesticide use. So long as local governments in poor countries lack the capacity to monitor and regulate pesticide use, and to devise and extend alternative crop protection strategies like IPM, pesticide managers in international institutions like UNEP and FAO will have no local partners with whom to cooperate.

The task of repairing local deficiencies (in human resources and institutions) within the rural agricultural sectors of the developing world has traditionally been given over to well-funded international assistance organizations like the World Bank. Under the presidency of Robert S. McNamara (1968–81), the Bank conspicuously dedicated itself to solving rural development problems in poor countries, and Bank lending for this purpose increased in real terms roughly eightfold, to reach a peak of $4.7 billion in 1981.[58] When pesticide issues reached the international agenda in the early 1980s, more of these World Bank resources should have been made available to help address the numerous rural and local deficiencies that were preventing safe use.

Unfortunately, the reaction of the World Bank to the unsafe use problem was *not* to dedicate new resources to such things as national-level agricultural research and extension, IPM, or rural poverty reduction projects. The Bank found itself so sharply attacked in the 1980s for its alleged insensitivity to environmental concerns in poor countries that its first reaction was instead to pull back. Instead of working positively

58. Michael Lipton and Robert Paarlberg, "The Role of the World Bank In Agricultural Development in the 1990s," International Food Policy Research Institute, Washington, D.C., October 1990, 10.

to increase safe use of pesticides in poor countries, the Bank responded defensively—mostly by withdrawing projects from those circumstances where unsafe use might be alleged. The Bank first generated a set of internal "Pesticide Guidelines" in 1985—drawn up in collaboration with AID—which contained a checklist of "operational requirements" and "non-recommended pesticides" for use in future Bank projects.[59]

Beyond such efforts to "green up" existing projects, the Bank did not devote significant new resources to solving unsafe use problems in poor countries. The Bank did agree to serve as "executing agency" for a 1989 regional IPM program in North Africa, but the funding came from UNDP. World Bank projects now contain a larger "sustainable pest management" component, but the costs of this component are "internalized" within the project, rather than paid out of new resources. And Bank lending for agricultural and rural development projects overall, since 1981, has been in a noticeable decline. In fact, it has fallen by roughly 20 percent in real terms.[60]

It is unfortunate that the World Bank has decided to respond to its environmentalist critics not by doing better, but instead by doing less. And it is unfortunate that the NGO community continues to fault the Bank for its occasional sins of commission, rather than for its larger sins of omission in rural environmental protection in developing countries. The World Bank is the only international institution capable of mobilizing financial and technical resources in sufficient quantity, and in a sufficient number of developing country settings, to mount an effective attack on unsafe pesticide use problems.

### Conclusion: What Difference Did International Institutions Make?

International institutions have found the issue of safe pesticide use in poor countries an especially demanding test. The remedies most needed —human resource and institutional development in poor countries,

59. G. J. Jackson, "Pesticides and Pest Management: The Work of the Environment Department—1988–90," World Bank Environment Department, Divisional Working Paper No. 1990-13, Policy Research Division, Washington, D.C., September 1990, 7.
60. Lipton and Paarlberg, "The Role of the World Bank in Agricultural and Rural Development", 10.

governmental capacity building and policy change, plus the shaping and monitoring of private industry behavior, mostly in remote rural locations—are difficult to pursue through traditional intergovernmental institutions.

Part of the difficulty is a narrow understanding of global environmental problems. Since environmental destruction accompanies human activity (especially the process of "development"), we are inclined to assume that the best remedy will always be to "do less" (less fishing, less oil dumping, less CFC production, less sulfur dioxide emissions). International institutions respond to this assumption by promoting agreements (usually among governments) to constrain such damaging actions.

In some cases, however, doing less is not the solution. Especially in the nonwealthy developing societies, environmental destruction can reflect, in many cases, the fact that not enough has yet been done to develop the human and institutional resources needed to protect the environment and make safe use of modern technology.

In the area of safe pesticide use, where rich countries are doing much better than poor countries, international institutions must organize around and act on the objective of doing more, rather than doing less. This will require, most of all, a stronger mobilization of financial and technical resources followed by a more determined extension of those resources into the developing world. We have argued here that one international institution well suited to lead in such an effort—the World Bank—has so far let the opportunity pass. A most important opportunity for international institutions to make a difference is therefore being missed.

This is not to dismiss the valuable steps that traditional intergovernmental institutions have taken in this case. Capacity has been built: Without the informing and coordinating role played by FAO, governments in poor countries would find it noticeably more difficult to promote IPM. The contractual environment has been improved: Without the existence of FAO's consensual Code of Conduct, NGOs and environmentalists would be finding it substantially more difficult to shame industries and governments into taking a concerned and responsible role. And concern has been aroused: Without UNEP's initiative to create a PIC procedure, governments throughout the industrial world might have remained satisfied with a much weaker "notification only" approach to foreign pesticide sales.

Organizations such as FAO and UNEP thus can claim some important achievements in this case. These achievements may even be larger than they appear, because of the expanding pattern of international political action that is now growing up around them. FAO and UNEP, by managing to cooperate with each other, have created a setting in which green NGOs, brown chemical companies, green environmental ministers, brown agricultural ministers, rich exporting country officials, and poor importing country officials can pursue a shared view of their respective international responsibilities. The shared view they are developing, embodied in the FAO Code of Conduct, is of course much weaker than the environmentalist community would prefer. But this has not stopped environmentalists from using the Code to good advantage, to impose greater discipline on private industry. Nor has it stopped the consensus embodied in this Code from moving in a green direction, as evidenced in the recent inclusion of prior informed consent. There is every reason to believe that this process of marginal but constructive change will continue in the years ahead.

# 8

# International Population Institutions: Adaptation to a Changing World Order

Barbara B. Crane

In the mid-1960s, governments joined together to create a series of new international programs whose central purpose was to promote the adoption of national population policies in developing nations and help reduce their high rates of fertility. The programs were the result of initiatives taken primarily by the United States and other Western industrialized nations in the face of widespread skepticism and, in some cases, hostility from developing countries. Prior to 1965, only five developing countries had adopted policies to reduce fertility—China, India, Pakistan, South Korea, and Fiji.

Since that time, international population programs have evolved into a network of semi-autonomous institutions including the United Nations Population Fund (UNFPA); population units of the UN specialized agencies, the World Bank, the U.S. Agency for International Development (USAID), and some other bilateral aid agencies; and the

I would like to express appreciation to the Rockefeller Brothers Fund and the Harvard University Center for International Affairs for helping to support the writing of this chapter under the Center's Project on International Environmental Institutions. I am especially grateful to Jason L. Finkle, Professor of Population Planning at the University of Michigan, for his inspiration, thoughts, and guidance over two decades, which have contributed much to my understanding of international population institutions. This chapter has also benefited immensely from interviews over the years with many policymakers and informed observers, and from their willingness to share ideas as well as relevant information and documents. Finally, I must express appreciation to fellow members of this project, whose comments and questions have been invaluable in the course of preparing this chapter—Peter M. Haas, Robert Keohane, Robert Paarlberg, M. J. Peterson, Ron Mitchell, Ted Parson, and Marc Levy—and to others who reviewed an earlier version—Nazli Choucri, Henry David, Alison McIntosh, and Thomas Merrick.

International Planned Parenthood Federation (IPPF).[1] International population institutions (IPIs) have provided close to $11 billion (1985 dollars) in assistance to developing countries for all phases of their population programs—demographic analysis and contraceptive research; policy development; and training, equipment, and other inputs for the provision of family planning services and related health, communications, and social development programs. Over 90 percent of the assistance is funded by ten major donor governments. IPIs now command wide support among the governments of developing countries as well, although a global consensus on the ends and means of population policies is still elusive.

This paper will seek to describe the political forces that have shaped the agendas and policy formulation of international population institutions (IPIs) as well as their institutional characteristics and outputs. In addition, it will assess the contributions of IPIs to national population policy formulation and implementation.[2]

In the nearly three decades during which IPIs have existed, important exogenous changes have occurred in North-South and East-West relations as well as in the domestic politics of key countries involved in population issues. The population issue has been somewhat insulated from these large-scale changes in the international political and econo-

1. The criteria for inclusion here are that the organizations operate across national boundaries, rely almost entirely on public funds, and play a significant and independent role in international cooperation in the population field. Although IPPF is formally a nongovernmental organization, it receives 90 percent of its funds from donor governments. AID administers the U.S. government bilateral aid program subject to intergovernmental agreements, and, for present purposes, private organizations that rely on AID grants and contracts are treated as part of this program.
   Two key dimensions of population change, other than fertility, are mortality and migration. Mortality has been addressed both nationally and internationally, by a somewhat different set of institutions concerned with public health and medical care. Analysis of the implications of changing population distribution via internal and international migration as well as changing age structures have been absorbed as part of the activities of IPIs in many instances. Beyond some norm creation, however, IPIs have no mandate to help define or implement policy responses.
2. This chapter draws from research and interviews conducted by the author over a number of years on the political and organizational aspects of international cooperation in the population field, much of it in collaboration with Jason L. Finkle of the University of Michigan.

mic order. Nevertheless, the impact of such changes on the preferences and resources of governmental and nongovernmental actors has been evident in the decision-making forums of IPIs. There have also been changes and developments in the relevant science and technology as well as in the institutional structures and procedures of the IPIs themselves, which over time have fed back into the formation of actors' preferences.

For analytical purposes, it is helpful to examine IPIs over three distinct phases of their history, which roughly correspond to some critical turning points in the preferences and resources of major actors: 1965–1974, the period of rapid growth in IPIs under leadership from the United States and other Western donor countries; 1974–1984, a period of greater accommodation to the preferences of developing countries; and 1984–1991, a period marked by conflict over IPIs and a search for new sources of support, especially from the transnational environmental movement. A major challenge for IPIs in the recent period has been adapting to the withdrawal of the U.S. government from participation in the UN Population Fund and the International Planned Parenthood Federation, due to decisions taken in response to domestic political pressure from antiabortion groups.

In comparison with some of the other environmental institutions examined in this volume, IPIs have never produced explicit rules and regulations with regard to population policies, such as quantitative birth rate targets. Instead, a rather weak political consensus has been embodied in a series of resolutions and mandates adopted by governments since the mid-1960s.[3] This consensus has been built around the following principles and norms: (1) Rapid population growth is a major obstacle to economic and social development. (2) Governments should adopt such national population policies as they deem appropriate to their countries' demographic situations. (3) Couples should have the right to determine freely and responsibly the number and spac-

3. See, for example, General Assembly resolutions on "Population Growth and Economic Development," Resolutions 1838 (XVII) adopted in 1962, and 2211 (XXI), adopted in 1966; the World Population Plan of Action, adopted at the UN World Population Conference in Bucharest in 1974; and the Declaration and Recommendations for the Further Implementation of the World Population Plan of Action, adopted at the UN International Conference on Population in Mexico City in 1984.

ing of their children; to this end, governments should assist them in obtaining the information and means to exercise this right. In effect, regardless of their national demographic goals, governments have been encouraged to provide universal access to family planning services.

As will be discussed further, this general consensus papers over significant differences in values and priorities. Still, official policy statements consistent with the consensus have been adopted by major countries in every region of the developing world, a marked change compared with several decades ago. As of 1989, fifty-seven countries, (encompassing about 80 percent of the population of developing regions) had reported to the United Nations that they had formal policies to reduce fertility.[4] Judgments about the effectiveness of these policies and the contribution of IPIs to their effectiveness vary by region and depend greatly on the criteria for evaluation. Researchers have demonstrated the impact of policy and program interventions on both local and national fertility trends in a number of countries, however.[5] By the standards of accomplishment set by other development programs, moreover, the effectiveness of population policies and programs in reducing fertility may be reasonably high. IPIs have played a role in the achievements of these programs by increasing their technical and administrative capacity. The effectiveness of IPIs has been enhanced by their efforts to build coalitions with supporters of family planning in both developed and developing countries, to coordinate their efforts with one another in many phases of national and international programs, and to involve both the commercial and nonprofit private sectors in family planning.

The positive performance of IPIs is unexpected in view of the absence of consensus on explicit policy guidelines and the conflictual politics associated with population and family planning programs, especially in recent years. As this chapter will discuss, a partial explanation for continued IPI vitality can be found in the institutional characteristics and initiatives of IPIs themselves—their ability to provide earmarked funds on easy terms, their decision-making autonomy, and the networks they

4. United Nations, *Trends in Population Policy* (New York: United Nations Population Division Population Studies No. 114).
5. W. Parker Mauldin and John A. Ross, "Family Planning Programs: Efforts and Results, 1982–1989," *Studies in Family Planning* 22 (November/December 1991): 350–367.

have created among themselves and with their counterparts in developing countries.

Another explanation can be found in the efforts over the past five years or so of nongovernmental organizations (NGOs) in the United States and other donor countries to bring together the population and environmental agendas. While environmental concerns have always been linked with population issues, the salience of these considerations has risen to the point that they are frequently advanced now as a leading justification for population programs. Many analysts have argued that population growth exacerbates deforestation, soil erosion, desertification, fossil fuel emissions, and other environmental problems. Although the population-environment coalition has played a role in renewed political and financial support for population programs, it also has some limitations as a source of support for IPIs. The survival and effectiveness of IPIs into the twenty-first century will depend on support and participation from several other key constituencies as well, including women's organizations, planned parenthood advocates, and medical and public health professionals.

These general observations will be developed further in succeeding sections of this chapter, which will address, for the period from roughly 1965 to 1991, agenda setting and policy formulation in IPIs; institutional characteristics, procedures, and outputs of IPIs; and the impact of IPIs on national policies and ultimately on fertility trends.

## Agenda Setting and Policy Formulation in International Population Institutions

After World War II, population specialists became increasingly aware that declining death rates in developing countries, accompanied by continued high birth rates, were resulting in rapid population growth in much of the southern hemisphere.[6] These observations signaled a new phase in a long history of elite concern in both Western and non-Western countries regarding the social implications of population

6. The state of knowledge with regard to population trends at the time is well summarized in a volume prepared by the United Nations, *The Determinants and Consequences of Population Trends* (New York: United Nations Population Division, Population Studies No. 17).

trends.[7] Some early initiatives were taken to bring population policy issues to the attention of governments, and India adopted a national policy to limit population growth as early as 1952. Concern about the consequences of rapid growth and consideration of possible responses did not become a regular feature of the international agenda, however, until major Western governments addressed the issue in the early 1960s. In later phases, international institutions and nongovernmental organizations have also come to play important roles, not only in bringing population policy issues to the agenda but also in shaping the content of policy declarations and guidelines.

**Agenda Setting, 1965–1974**

Until around 1965, a state of deadlock best describes international relations on population issues. Several groups of countries were aligned against the few Scandinavian and Asian countries that were interested in bringing these issues onto the formal agendas of international organizations. In the 1950s, opposition from European and Latin American governments, influenced by Catholic rejection of artificial forms of birth control, precluded the World Health Organization from undertaking even basic research on human reproduction.[8] Socialist governments adhering to Marxist ideologies saw the solution to development problems in the adoption of socialism, and objected to population policies. Nationalism in a number of developing countries, especially in Africa and Latin America, led their governments to reject the idea of population programs as imperialist, racist, or even genocidal. In taking this view, leaders of developing countries also were driven by a traditional understanding of population size and growth as measures of the power and vitality of a nation.

Officially, the U.S. government stayed in the background. American activists, academicians, and even government officials were increasingly

7. See Michael S. Teitelbaum and Jay M. Winter, eds., *Population and Resources in Western Intellectual Traditions* (New York: The Population Council, 1988).
8. Richard Symonds and Michael Carder, *The United Nations and the Population Question, 1945–1970* (New York: McGraw Hill, 1973); Jason Finkle and Barbara Crane, "The World Health Organization and the Population Issue: Organizational Values in the United Nations," *Population and Development Review* 2 (September/December 1976): 367–93.

involved, however, as leaders and participants in a transnational policy coalition promoting new efforts to reduce fertility in developing countries.[9] This coalition had deep historical roots in the earlier birth control and eugenics movements, although by the 1950s and early 1960s, its leaders included scholars specializing in population dynamics and economic development as well as activists and philanthropists such as General William Draper and John D. Rockefeller III. Its members, predominantly in the United States and Europe, also included groups from developing countries, especially in Asia.[10] The coalition had limited success in its objective of mobilizing support for population programs, until it involved the U.S. foreign policy establishment and linked rapid population growth with U.S. security interests and Cold War fears.[11] Other developments facilitated changes in U.S. policy, such as the availability of new contraceptive methods in the early 1960s, which raised hopes that family planning programs could be effective.

9. The concept of a transnational policy coalition refers to coalitions whose memberships transcend national and institutional boundaries. Such coalitions, based on common policy preferences, draw members and supporters from national governments, international organizations, academia, and private associations. The concept derives from previous studies on the importance of networks and coalitions in domestic policy formulation in the United States as well as in international decision-making processes. See Barbara B. Crane and Jason L. Finkle, "Population Policy and World Politics," paper presented to the International Political Science Association, Washington, D. C., September, 1988; Hugh Heclo, "Issue Networks and the Executive Establishment," in *The New American Political System*, ed. Anthony King (Washington, D. C.: American Enterprise Institute), 87–124; and Robert O. Keohane and Joseph S. Nye, "Transgovernmental Relations and International Organizations," *World Politics* 27 (October 1974): 39–62.

10. A number of carefully researched studies provide rich historical background on the early development of IPIs and particularly the U.S. role. See Symonds and Carder, *The United Nations and the Population Question*; Phyllis Piotrow, *World Population Crisis: The United States Response* (New York: Praeger Publishers, 1973); Peter J. Donaldson, *Nature Against Us: The United States and the World Population Crisis, 1965–1980* (Chapel Hill: The University of North Carolina Press, 1990; John Caldwell and Pat Caldwell, *Limiting Population Growth and the Ford Foundation Contribution* (London: Frances Pinter, 1986). See also Jason L. Finkle and Barbara B. Crane, "The Politics of International Population Policy," *International Transmission of Population Policy Experience: Proceedings of the Expert Group Meeting, June 1988* (New York: United Nations, 1990), 167–82; and Dennis Hodgson. "Orthodoxy and Revisionism in American Demography," *Population and Development Review* 14 (December 1985): 541–569.

11. Hodgson, "Orthodoxy and Revisionism in American Demography."

Food shortages in India and other developing countries in 1965 contributed to a sense of crisis.[12] After that year, under the activist administration of President Lyndon Johnson in the United States, the U.S. government put its weight behind the goal of limiting rapid population growth.[13] At that time, the United States not only created a new population program within its own bilateral development assistance effort, but threw its power and influence behind efforts to engage other donor governments and international institutions in assisting developing countries in this area. The focus would be on persuading governments to provide family planning services on as wide a scale as possible, and programs in the UN agencies (including the World Bank), USAID, and IPPF grew rapidly.

From the beginning, IPIs were heavily dominated by the U.S. government and U.S. policy elites. Until the 1980s, the U.S. government provided over half of all population assistance. A number of other donor governments made commitments to population assistance, although for political reasons most preferred to do so through multilateral institutions such as UNFPA and IPPF; only Sweden, Canada, and the United Kingdom were prepared to provide significant amounts on a bilateral basis. U.S.–based nongovernmental organizations such as the Ford Foundation and the Population Council also led the way in providing technical backing for the work of IPIs, supporting academic population centers, and attempting to create a transnational epistemic community around the principles of population growth as an obstacle to economic development and family planning programs as a feasible solution.[14]

In this period, environmental considerations did not play an important role in the agendas of IPIs, although they were certainly recognized by some groups who were concerned with both issue areas.[15] It was the Sierra Club, for example, that commissioned *The Population Bomb* in

12. Piotrow, *World Population Crisis.*
13. Relying on cost-benefit analyses available at the time, Johnson called on members of the United Nations in 1965 to "act on the fact that less than five dollars invested in population control is worth a hundred dollars invested in economic growth" (quoted in Piotrow, *World Population Crisis*, 90).
14. For further background, see Caldwell and Caldwell, *Limiting Population Growth*; and Hodgson, "Orthodoxy and Revisionism in American Demography."
15. National Academy of Sciences, *Rapid Population Growth: Consequences and Policy Implications* (Baltimore, Md.: Johns Hopkins University Press, 1971).

1968, the book which helped give impetus to the "zero population growth" movement in the United States in the late 1960s.[16] A high point in the recognition of population-environment interrelationships was publication of the *Limits to Growth* study in 1972, based on a computer simulation of the processes that could lead to a "global collapse."[17] Significantly, however, *Limits to Growth* and other studies linking global population and environmental phenomena during the 1970s came out after the phase of most rapid institutional development of IPIs had already occurred and thus played no role in early agenda setting on population issues. Moreover, *Limits to Growth* quickly became caught up in controversy and was followed by other studies which highlighted regional differences in population and environmental conditions and which gave more attention to issues of wealth redistribution.

As this phase was coming to an end, it was apparent that the political environment of IPIs would become more complex, primarily because of the way the preferences of actors other than the Western donor governments would be reflected, and even amplified, in the policy-making processes of the IPIs themselves. While a preponderance of power in the international order rested with the United States and other Western industrialized nations, it could not be overlooked that both the problems associated with rapid population growth and control over the solutions resided primarily in the developing countries. By comparison, fertility in the developed countries was already approaching replacement levels in the 1960s and continued to decline. As a result, the preferences of Third World governments and NGOs were bound to carry relatively more weight in establishing the terms of international cooperation in the population field than in other areas of economic development cooperation—where Third World actors were behaving more as supplicants—or in environmental pollution—where they were not the main source of the problem. Early recognition of the need for commitment by developing countries helps account for the heavier emphasis on multilateral cooperation in the population field.[18]

16. Paul Ehrlich, *The Population Bomb* (New York: Ballantine, 1968).
17. Donella Meadows, et al., *The Limits to Growth* (Washington, D.C.: Potomac Associates, 1972).
18. See Richard Gardner, "Toward a World Population Program," in *The Global Partnership*, ed. Richard Gardner and Max Millikan (New York: Frederick A. Praeger, 1968), 332–61.

**Agenda Setting, 1974–1984**

While it was groups in industrialized countries who had been most instrumental in bringing the issue of population growth to the international agenda and in creating international population institutions in the 1960s, these institutions began to take on a life of their own by the early 1970s. The decision-making structures of the institutions, as well as their efforts to carry out their primary tasks, compelled them to become more responsive to the preferences of developing countries. UNFPA, for example, underwent a review in 1972, led by Swedish and Canadian analysts, which resulted in an Economic and Social Council (ECOSOC) resolution making the Fund accountable to the UNDP Governing Council and ECOSOC rather than to the existing advisory board of individuals.[19] The World Bank was reorganized in 1972 to give a greater role to regional and country departments, allowing a stronger voice for borrowers' interests relative to the priorities of donor governments or of the Americans, who remained as top managers.[20] Not surprisingly, decisions about how to program population assistance began to reflect the desires of many developing country governments, for example, the desire to support broader health infrastructure rather than strictly family planning activities. Dialogue in international forums also tended to focus increasingly on whether simply increasing contraceptive services, as stressed by the United States, would succeed in the face of socioeconomic constraints on demand for family planning.

Beyond these institutional decision-making processes of IPIs, however, other exogenous events affected agenda setting and policy formulation. The distribution of bargaining power in the postwar international system was already undergoing change as the economic capabilities of some developing countries increased. Then, several events occurring in rapid sequence in 1973 and 1974 had a galvanizing impact on Third World leaders: the energy crisis, the special UN General Assembly calling for a "new international economic order," and the first intergovernmental worldwide conference on population, held in Bucharest.

19. Stanley Johnson, *World Population and the United Nations: Challenge and Response* (Cambridge: Cambridge University Press, 1987).
20. Barbara B. Crane and Jason L. Finkle, "Organizational Impediments to Development Assistance: The World Bank's Population Program," *World Politics* 33 (July 1981): 516–53.

At Bucharest, the developing countries succeeded in changing the conference agenda designed by IPIs. Third World representatives asserted that population could only be dealt with as part of a comprehensive development strategy, including restructuring the international economic order. The draft World Population Plan of Action was rewritten during the conference to accommodate their position before a final consensus was reached.[21] Developing countries also successfully rejected draft provisions of the plan encouraging governments to adopt quantitative population targets.[22] Addressing itself to all the IPIs, including bilateral and nongovernmental organizations, the plan set out an ambitious agenda, in effect calling on IPIs to be more conscious of the broader socioeconomic setting in which population programs were being undertaken. They were expected to provide more assistance for "integrating" population activities with other programs, for example, by working to broaden economic opportunities for women, reduce infant and child mortality, or alter economic incentives to have children.[23]

The confrontation at Bucharest implied to many observers that developed and developing countries continued to be at an impasse on population issues. Yet some of the apparent conflict at Bucharest was an artifact of the timing, structure, and dynamics of the conference itself.[24] Moreover, the revised agenda at Bucharest held some strong initial appeal for IPIs: First, it was consistent with the broad agenda of "redistribution with growth" and "basic needs" that was taking hold in development institutions at that time and thus potentially broadened the coalition supporting the work of IPIs. By implying that both population control and structural change could be accomplished simultaneously, the new agenda helped to break the earlier deadlock.[25] Second, it

21. Jason L. Finkle and Barbara B. Crane, "The Politics of Bucharest: Population, Development, and the New International Economic Order," *Population and Development Review* 2 (September/December 1976): 87–114.
22. Johnson, *World Population and the United Nations*.
23. See Margaret Wolfson, *Changing Approaches to Population Problems* (Paris: Development Center, Organization for Economic Cooperation and Development, 1978).
24. Finkle and Crane, "The Politics of Bucharest."
25. Clarity in formal statements of policy goals may be dysfunctional, whereas ambiguity may reduce conflict and allow for desirable learning and experimentation in policy implementation. See Richard E. Matland, "Synthesizing the

implied a more diffuse and perhaps less exacting set of performance criteria than the criterion of fertility decline.

Relatively soon after Bucharest, it became apparent that neither the development nor population institutions would have the resources, capacity, or leverage with developing countries to effectively implement the full Bucharest agenda. The narrower agenda, focused on family planning and related activities, continued to be more feasible and more likely to attract increases in earmarked donor contributions for the work of IPIs. Many governments, even those which had been vocal at Bucharest, proceeded to cooperate with IPIs in domestic implementation of conventional family planning programs.

In this period, population-environment linkages, while addressed in periodic international meetings and scientific gatherings, receded into the background of population debates. A large-scale study intended to go beyond previous global models was begun under the administration of President Carter, but was not published until late in his term, as the *Global 2000 Report*.[26] In 1983, a UN-sponsored expert meeting on the subject found little consensus.[27]

As this phase drew to a close, support for population-related activities from Western donor countries seemed to be lagging, especially when measured in constant dollars, and even more so in relation to the growing demand for family planning. The executive director of the UN Population Fund successfully sought endorsement from developing countries, in the face of donor skepticism, for a second world population conference, in the hope that such a conference could reignite enthusiasm and regenerate donor commitment.

## Agenda Setting, 1984–1991

As had occurred with the Bucharest conference ten years earlier, forces that were beginning to stir below the visible surface of political events

Implementation Literature: The Ambiguity-Conflict Model of Policy Implementation," paper prepared for the American Political Science Association, Washington, D.C., 1991.

26. G. O. Barney, ed., *The Global 2000 Report to the President of the United States* (Elmsford, New York: Pergamon, 1980).

27. United Nations, *Population, Resources, Environment and Development, Proceedings of the Expert Group* (New York: United Nations Population Division Population Studies No. 90, 1984).

came to the top on the occasion of a global meeting, the UN-sponsored International Conference on Population in Mexico City in 1984. And, as before, political dynamics beyond the control of the conference organizers helped shape its agenda and outcome.[28] By this time, as noted above, the governments of the developing countries were supportive of international dialogue and cooperation on population issues, even if they had not yet assembled the ingredients for successful domestic programs. Third World governments no longer saw international population programs as threatening to their national interests; many had benefited from IPI assistance, and many had been persuaded that far from enhancing their national power, rapid population growth was interfering with their development goals. Moreover, what had been the Third World bloc in the UN system was less unified in 1984. Why, then, did problems arise for IPIs during and after the Mexico City conference?

Throughout the period from 1965 to the early 1980s, IPI founders and leaders had identified with a public goods rationale for seeking to limit fertility. This rationale had strong support in the governments of both donor and recipient countries, but it had also weakened IPIs both from an intellectual and a political standpoint. The drive to limit fertility rested mainly on the proposition that slowing population growth would reduce the negative externalities of childbearing for society as a whole by providing savings that would be released as capital for economic growth. From an intellectual standpoint, economists and others questioned the empirical basis for this rationale, and it came under increasing pressure by the end of the 1970s.[29] Politically, the emphasis of IPI founders on population programs as public goods skirted the issue of how the benefits of any resulting economic growth would be distributed. Further, this rationale dictated the specification of policy alternatives: The focus was on expediting the provision of subsidized, modern contraceptives to as many couples as possible.

An important consequence of this focus was to weaken the appeal of family planning programs to other potential constituencies, especially nongovernmental groups concerned with other health and humanitarian

28. For further background, see Jason L. Finkle and Barbara B. Crane, "Ideology and Politics at Mexico City: The United States at the 1984 International Conference on Population," *Population and Development Review* 11, 1 (March 1985): 1–28.
29. Hogdson, "Orthodoxy and Revisionism in American Demography."

concerns and with the reproductive health and overall status of women. Yet these constituencies could not be dismissed. Population and family planning programs are not simply public goods; they are also private goods in that individuals and families may perceive benefits (or damages) to themselves from limiting or spacing births, regardless of the broader macroeconomic or societal-level impact of the programs. Moreover, despite efforts by professionals specializing in population and family planning to contain the issues in a technical framework, knowledge about the practice of family planning and even about the provision of services, is relatively diffuse. There is inevitable resistance to these issues' becoming the exclusive domain of any epistemic community. Thus, by the late 1970s and early 1980s, negative perceptions of family planning programs increasingly led to strong attacks from affected constituencies. Many of these attacks were expressed more at the international level than in national policy making; although in countries as diverse as India, the Philippines, Brazil, and Kenya, family planning issues became swept up in increasingly competitive domestic politics.[30]

To begin with, the international women's movement had gained strength, and within it were a growing number of women's health advocates who feared that women's rights and safety were being ignored in family planning programs.[31] Women's rights supporters also argued that family planning would not make much progress until women's education, employment, and health status improved. In addition, the international health community had grown stronger as a result of new donor initiatives, and its leaders questioned disproportionate spending for family planning when health needs were still relatively neglected. Perceiving that family planning programs were often organized separately from health services, the director-general of WHO accused such

30. A good example of the impact of new political actors on family planning programs is the women's movement in Brazil during the 1980s. See Sonia E. Alvarez, *Engendering Democracy in Brazil: Women's Movements in Transition* (Princeton, N.J.: Princeton University Press, 1990).
31. For background on the development of an organized transnational feminist response to IPIs, see Betsy Hartmann, *Reproductive Rights and Wrongs: The Global Politics of Population Control and Contraceptive Choice* (New York: Harper and Row, 1987).

programs of "imposing a vertical structure which has nothing to do with people's understanding."[32] Each of these groups in effect challenged both the policy ends and means associated with the creation of IPIs in the late 1960s. They objected to treatment of population stabilization as an urgent policy goal; but most of their criticisms focused on the means by which population programs were being implemented, and on the need for a higher quality of care and for mechanisms to assure voluntarism in the delivery of family planning services. Because these groups accepted the basic value of family planning for individuals, their stance was more reformist than oppositional. Both groups had adherents in positions of influence in developing countries. The minister of health in Nigeria, for example, who shared these views, played a dominant role in shaping his government's approach to implementing its family planning program, resisting pressures both from AID and from others within the Nigerian government for a more vertical program.

In the same period, another set of actors was also coalescing which would be much more radical in its aims and tactics—a transnational antiabortion movement, endorsed, if not actively supported, by the Vatican. This movement was as opposed to international population and family planning programs as to abortion itself.[33] After Pope John Paul II assumed office in 1978, the Vatican became more politically active on a global scale on many issues, extending its outreach efforts into Catholic communities in both developed and developing countries.[34] On reproductive issues, the pope expressed strong convictions. In his words: "The experiences and trends of recent years clearly emphasize the profoundly negative effects of contraceptive programmes. These programmes have increased sexual permissiveness and promoted irresponsible conduct.... Moreover, from contraceptive programmes a

32. International Planned Parenthood Federation, "Rescue Mission for Tomorrow's Health: Interview with Dr. Halfdan Mahler," *People* 6, 2 (1979): 25–28.
33. Jacqueline Kasun, "The International Politics of Contraception," *Policy Review*, 19 (Winter 1981): 135–52; Monsignor James T. McHugh, "Population Strategies and the United States," in *Demographic Policies from a Christian Viewpoint: Proceedings of the Symposium, Rio de Janeiro, 27–30 September 1982*, ed. Franco Biffi. (Rome: International Federation of Catholic Universities 1984), 409–25.
34. Samuel Huntington, "Religion and the Third Wave," *The National Interest* 24 (Summer 1991): 29–42.

transition has in fact often been made to the practice of sterilization and abortion, financed by governments and international organizations."[35]

Ironically, just as the transnational policy coalition concerned with population control had benefited from U.S. government support in the mid-1960s, so did the antiabortion movement after President Ronald Reagan took office in 1981. From the beginning of his term, administration leaders openly expressed their lack of enthusiasm for population assistance and for international institutions in general, often portraying both as instances of unwanted "social engineering." Some were so opposed to the USAID population program that, in 1982, they sought without success to eliminate it from the federal budget. The program nevertheless was retained, although with mounting harassment from antiabortion elements in the administration. In 1984, with an election campaign impending, these elements succeeded in dominating preparations for U.S. participation in the Mexico City conference, controlling selection of the U.S. delegation and preparation of the U.S. position paper in the White House.[36] At the conference itself, the U.S. delegation sparked controversy by declaring population growth to be a "neutral phenomenon." In addition, delegation leaders supported the Vatican in an amendment to the draft recommendations, which was then adopted as part of the final consensus, affirming that abortion should not be "promoted as a method of family planning." The U.S. delegation also announced a new policy by the United States to withhold support for international and private organizations involved in abortion-related activities even with their own funds (subsequently known as "the Mexico City policy").

In the year following the conference, the U.S. government implemented the Mexico City policy by terminating funding to UNFPA and IPPF and introducing new restrictions on its bilateral assistance. In the case of UNFPA, antiabortion groups argued that the United States should disassociate itself from an organization which was assisting China's family planning program, because of what they alleged to be

35. Pope John Paul II, "Address to Dr. Rafael M. Salas, Vatican City, June 7, 1984," (Washington, D.C.: National Conference of Catholic Bishops, Committee for Pro-Life Activities, 1984). The whole of the pope's statement, made to the head of the UN Population Fund, was printed by the American bishops and widely distributed at the Mexico City conference.
36. Finkle and Crane, "Ideology and Politics at Mexico City."

government-mandated, coercive abortions. In the case of IPPF, anti-abortion groups perceived the organization as an advocate for abortion and objected to the involvement of a few local IPPF affiliates in providing abortion services. The World Bank was not so directly susceptible to White House influence, although abortion considerations were introduced in U.S. voting on World Bank loans.

The U.S. actions have been disruptive for IPIs and have nearly succeeded, until recently, in eliminating abortion altogether from the agendas of IPIs. The impact of the political conflicts over IPIs described above has been further reflected in changes in their agendas, away from an emphasis on integrating population programs into comprehensive government-administered development programs, and toward a new emphasis on the provision of family planning services, often through the private sector. This new emphasis has been accompanied by new initiatives to involve both profit-making and nonprofit organizations in distributing contraceptives. New attention is also being given to the role and attitudes of women and to their broader reproductive health needs; to ways and means of ensuring informed choice by individuals using contraceptives; to the role of health systems in providing follow-up care; and to the role of breast-feeding and natural family planning methods in limiting fertility. These changes, reflected in the agendas of IPI policy-making forums as well as of more technical decision-making bodies, are not just a function of political pressures. New knowledge, new technologies, and a natural learning process from almost three decades of experience, often at the grassroots level, have also had effects on IPIs and even on those of their original founders who are still involved. IPI leaders have demonstrated a growing appreciation of what is required to achieve the sustained attitudinal and behavioral changes required for effective family planning.

The most dramatic and visible changes in the agendas of IPI policy-making forums have arisen from the coalition that has been built since 1984 between supporters of IPIs and supporters of international cooperation to protect the natural environment.[37] Several factors account

37. The political history of the alliance between supporters of international population and environmental programs is yet to be written and is far more complex in both its global and national manifestations than can possibly be captured here. In addition to other works specifically cited, this account draws

for this coalition. To begin with, in the early 1980s, the environmental movement itself was growing stronger and more transnational in character, uniting groups from different countries. This process gained new impetus with the 1982 UN conference on the environment in Nairobi. The founding in 1982 of the World Resources Institute, based in Washington, did much to bring together environmental expertise and activism in the United States with the global environmental and development agendas.[38]

In addition, new research had been undertaken on environmental trends in developing areas, providing mounting evidence of deforestation, soil erosion, and desertification.[39] To many analysts, population growth was a leading cause.[40] Reducing population growth was readily incorporated into the concept of "sustainable development," which became the common aspiration of the environmental and development communities during the 1980s.[41] Population policies were increasingly portrayed as a low-cost way to "buy critical time" to solve environmental problems.[42] In the last few years, heightened fears concerning global

on interviews; a handbook prepared by the National Audubon Society and the Population Crisis Committee, *Why Population Matters: A Handbook for the Environmental Activist* (Washington, D.C.: NAS and PCC, 1991); and an excellent paper by Chantal Worzala, "Conservation Through Contraception: The Environmental Lobby for International Population Assistance," *Journal of Public and International Affairs* (forthcoming).

38. Robert Repetto, ed., *The Global Possible* (New Haven: Yale University Press, 1985).

39. See, for example, Norman Myers, "The Exhausted Earth," *Foreign Policy* 42 (1981): 141–55; Prabha Pingali and Hans B. Binswanger, "Population Density and Farming Systems: The Changing Locus of Innovations and Technical Change," Washington, D.C.: working paper no. ARV24, World Bank, 1984.

40. For a moderate view of the interrelationship, see Robert Repetto, "Population, Resources, Environment: An Uncertain Future," *Population Bulletin* 42 (April 1989): 1–43.

41. Repetto, *The Global Possible*; World Commission for Environment and Development (the Brundtland Commission), *Our Common Future* (Oxford: Oxford University Press, 1987); World Bank/IMF Development Committee, *Environment, Growth and Development* (World Bank: Washington, D.C., 1987); and Lester Brown, et al., *State of the World 1986: A Worldwatch Institute Report on Progress Toward A Sustainable Society* (New York: W.W. Norton, 1986).

42. R. Paul Shaw, "Rapid Population Growth and Environmental Deterioration: Ultimate versus Proximate Factors," *Environmental Conservation* 16, 3 (1989): 199–208.

climate change have drawn new attention to the environmental agenda, and to population growth as a cause of deforestation and increasing fossil fuel consumption, leading to increasing emissions of "greenhouse gases."[43]

Most important in precipitating a closer political alliance between supporters of international environmental and population programs, however, was the threat to population programs posed by the Reagan administration and New Right opponents of these programs.[44] The developing alliance was fostered by Americans who had facilitated cross-fertilization between the two movements for some years, such as Russell Peterson, president of the National Audubon Society (NAS). NAS strengthened its work in population after 1985, eventually followed by other leading environmental organizations in the United States such as the Sierra Club and the National Wildlife Federation.[45] In 1990, population and environmental groups created the Campaign on Population and Environment (COPE), formalizing the joint educational and lobbying activities that had been developing in Washington for several years.

43. See World Resources Institute, *World Resources 1990–91* (New York: Oxford University Press, 1990); and National Academy of Sciences, *Policy Implications of Greenhouse Warming* (Washington, D.C.: National Academy Press, 1991). On the other hand, a recent study by researchers at the University of North Carolina highlights the complexities of the relationships between population growth and deforestation and the inadequacy of currently available data. Martha Geores and Richard Bilsborrow, "Population and the Environment: A Cross-Country Exploration of Deforestation in Low Income Countries," paper presented at the Population Association of America, Washington, D.C., 1991.
44. The New Right also opposed strong policy interventions to protect the environment, and leading officials under the Reagan administration rejected most of the conclusions of the *Global 2000 Report*. See, for example, an address by Danny J. Boggs, then Deputy Secretary of the U.S. Department of Energy, "An Optimistic Global Future: Facts and Processes," address to the American Association for the Advancement of Science (Washington, D.C.: U.S. Department of Energy, mimeographed, 1984). Members of the New Right agreed with optimists who argued that free markets and technological change would accommodate population growth and resolve environmental problems. Julian Simon and Herman Kahn, *The Resourceful Earth: A Response to Global 2000* (New York: Basil Blackwell, 1984).
45. Mark Haskell, "New Ties: Population and the Environment," *Population Today* 18 (1990); and United States NGO Steering Committee on Development, Environment, and Population, *Making Common Cause: A Statement and Action Plan by U.S.–Based Development, Environment and Population NGOs* Washington, D.C.: World Resources Institute, 1985.

During this period, others outside the United States were also recognizing the value of closer cooperation among agencies with population and environmental responsibilities. For example, the International Planned Parenthood Federation undertook joint activities with the World Conservation Union (IUCN), and UNFPA with the UN Environment Program (UNEP).[46] More recently, population-environment relationships have been featured in numerous meetings and reports of UNFPA, the World Bank, IPPF, and other IPIs, and UNFPA has been closely involved in preparations for the 1992 UN Conference on Environment and Development.

While cooperative activities have raised the political visibility of population-environment relationships, links between the two movements are more problematic than anticipated by those who promoted them in the aftermath of the 1984 Mexico City conference, for several reason. First, the environmental community itself is divided on the degree of significance that should be accorded population and family planning issues. This division corresponds roughly with the broader ideological split in the environmental movement between those willing to work within the existing political and economic structures and those who believe fundamental social change is required, especially on the part of the industrialized countries. For the latter group, reducing population growth is no solution to environmental problems; others are simply skeptical of the more extreme or simplistic formulations of population-environment relationships.[47]

Second, even members of the environmental movement who support IPIs may be forced to reassess how much attention they want to give to population issues. Economic recession has interfered with financial support for the environmental cause and has made it more vulnerable to threats that support may be withdrawn. In the United States in particu-

46. A British planned parenthood leader interviewed by the author in 1986 suggested that there was a need to look again at the population-environment relationship and "get away from sex."
47. See, for example, Barry Commoner, "Rapid Population Growth and Environmental Stress," paper presented to the United Nations Expert Group on Consequences of Rapid Population Growth, 24–26 August, 1988 (New York: United Nations, 1988); and Robert Repetto and Thomas Holmes, "The Role of Population in Resource Depletion," *Population and Development Review* 9, 4 (1983): 609–32.

lar, some organizations have found it difficult in recent years to support the population community on issues such as the Mexico City policy and funding for UNFPA. The National Audubon Society, the National Wildlife Federation, and others have been publicly attacked by anti-abortion groups for their support of international population programs.[48] Even if involvement in population issues is not seen as a liability, environmentalists have less incentive to work with IPI supporters than vice versa. IPI supporters are not prepared to take on the broader environmental agenda, and, lacking significant grassroots support among voters, would not be strong allies if they did. As a result, the relationship is rather one-sided, particularly in the United States, where the emphasis of recent joint efforts has simply been on raising funding levels for population assistance.

Third, although environmentalism has substantial local-level support compared with population programs, and has broadened and deepened its base of support over the years, its origin as a white middle-class movement is still a liability in trying to appeal to disadvantaged groups. On the international level, environmentalists have had to work hard to convince developing countries that environmental protection measures will not impede their economic growth. Considerable progress has been made in this regard since 1972, but including population control on the agenda adds to the challenge for environmentalists in promoting their own goals. Some leaders of developing countries are concerned about population growth and their "environmental security."[49] Yet other representatives of developing countries are still highly resistant to giving too much attention to population issues—and countries often speak with different voices in different forums. In preparations for the United Nations Conference on Environment and Development (UNCED) in 1992, Third World delegates have again expressed fears, first raised twenty years ago at the Stockholm conference, that global environmental problems would be attributed more to rapid population growth in poor countries than to excess consumption in rich countries. Some social scientists and transnational women's networks are also suspicious of propositions linking population and the environment, par-

48. *The Washington Post*, 10 September 1989.
49. Julius K. Nyerere, *The Challenge to the South: Report of the South Commission* (New York: Oxford University Press, 1990).

ticularly those concerning the centrality of women to "sustainable development." Women, it is suggested, are being blamed for everything
from having too many babies to consuming too much firewood. These
critics posit that the responsibility belongs much more with the work-
ings of exploitative social institutions and international markets.[50]

IPIs will undoubtedly benefit to some degree from the support of environmentalists, just as they benefited in the 1960s and 1970s from the
endorsement of Western foreign policy elites who were primarily concerned with the role of population stabilization and economic development in global stability and security. Indeed, the links these elites
frequently draw between population, sustainable development, and
security are evidence of the continuity in their interests over time. The
American chairman of the Development Assistance Committee of the
Organization for Economic Cooperation and Development (OECD) recently called on planners for UNCED "to bring together the strands of
national and international policy—relating the development, environmental, and population aspects of what is a single issue. . . . I hope the
United States will seize this opportunity for leadership on what is surely
the most important security issue we have ever faced."[51]

The role of elite groups expressing public goods rationales for
population programs is especially important in placing these programs
on national and global policy agendas and in determining how much resources and attention IPIs and their programs receive in relation to
other sectors. Indications are that IPIs currently are receiving relatively
generous financial support and are renewing their focus on family
planning—trends which can be attributed in large measure to the favorable climate generated by the population-environment coalition. The
extent to which population programs make a difference in the achievement of collective environmental goals will always be controversial,
however, and, as suggested above, there is a limit to the influence even a
strong environmental movement is likely to have on IPIs. Moreover, the

50. Women's International Policy Action Committee, *Official Report: World
Women's Congress for a Healthy Planet, 8–12 November 1991, Miami, Florida
USA* (New York: Women's Environment and Development Organization,
1992).
51. Joseph C. Wheeler, "Unsustainability: A Security Issue," remarks to the
International Development Conference, Washington, D.C., 24 January 1991,
mimeographed.

world has changed since the 1960s, when the pre-Vietnam U.S. foreign policy establishment embraced the case for international population programs; this establishment has diminished both in its unity and in its capacity to influence U.S. and international policies.

This analysis of the influences on agenda setting and policy formulation in international population institutions has demonstrated the impact of changes over recent decades in the preferences and resources of the major state actors—the United States and other Western governments as well as the developing countries. Transnational policy coalitions also have risen in importance and have been able to gain greater access to the policy-making structures of IPIs. Changes in knowledge and technology have played a decidedly secondary, although not irrelevant, role. To explain how IPIs have managed to develop relatively effective programs in a highly politicized environment, it is essential to know more about the critical features of their institutional structures and procedures as well as their interorganizational relationships.

## Institutional Characteristics, Procedures, and Outputs

The initiation and implementation of family planning programs on a large scale has relied heavily on North-South resource transfers and on extensive bureaucratic structures and networks, unlike some environmental policy interventions that are more regulatory in character. While this discussion will highlight some similarities in the structures of the various IPIs, it will also attempt to reveal some of the important differences among them through each of the major phases—both in the ways they experience the impact of external political pressures and in their relations with counterparts in developing countries.

### Institutional Characteristics, 1965–1974

This period was primarily one of institution-building, mainly following from the initiatives of members of the transnational policy coalition interested in reducing population growth. Coalition members lobbied the U.S. Congress to earmark funds in foreign assistance appropriations for population and family planning programs. In addition, they saw the distinct advantages of creating multilateral programs which could elicit the support of other donors who were unprepared for both political and technical reasons to mount bilateral programs, and which could serve countries for which bilateral assistance would be unavailable or unacceptable. Leading members of this coalition—mostly Americans such as General Draper and others affiliated with the newly formed Population Crisis Committee in Washington, D.C.—solicited contributions from various donor governments to the International Planned Parenthood Federation (IPPF). The effect was to transform IPPF from a small, essentially volunteer organization into a major channel of public assistance to private family planning associations in developing countries. Coalition members also persuaded the UN secretary-general to move what had been a small trust fund administered by the demographic unit of the UN Secretariat into the UN Development Program (UNDP). They wanted the fund, now known as the UN Population Fund (UNFPA), to become a channel for significant financial support for the work of UN specialized agencies as well as for direct assistance to governments. As an incentive to other donors, U.S. government contributions to UNFPA were provided on a fifty-fifty matching basis. Finally, coalition members were instrumental in the decision of the World Bank, soon after Robert McNamara its became its president in 1968, to encourage population policies and create a unit in the Bank devoted to lending for projects to help reduce fertility.[52]

All of the IPIs except IPPF were nested in institutions already engaged in development assistance activities, although in almost every case population programs were endowed with an unusual degree of financial and organizational autonomy—or their leaders wrested such autonomy for them. Moreover, while each IPI has developed a bureaucracy to manage programs, all have tended to remain small relative to the amount of funds they commit, acting more as catalysts for larger networks—for example, the UN specialized agencies which often help

52. Significantly, in the mid-1960s, some coalition members had hoped that the World Health Organization (WHO) would take the lead in multilateral assistance for family planning programs. This alternative may have been precluded because of the voting power of developing country members of WHO that were opposed to these programs. On the other hand, a strong case can be made that a more favorable attitude by the WHO secretariat and its powerful director-general at the time could have led to a different configuration of IPIs and, probably, to a more health-oriented international effort. See Finkle and Crane, "The World Health Organization and the Population Issue."

execute UNFPA-funded projects and nongovernmental agencies that have grants and contracts from USAID.

The reasons that population programs as were designed separate entities are found in an unusual convergence of interests among developed and developing countries which, paradoxically, grew out of their initial political deadlock over the role of population programs in international development assistance. From the standpoint of the coalition supporting new international population programs, it was important to start these programs with a sense of urgency and to ensure that they would have visibility and be as free as possible from excessive bureaucratic constraints. In the institutional environment of development assistance, it was desirable that they not have to compete directly with other activities that were less politically sensitive or for which it was easier to demonstrate immediate returns. The coalition also recognized that the commitment of recipient governments would be needed for effective international cooperation in the population field, but would be harder to attain than in other areas of development. Conversely, from the standpoint of most leaders of developing countries, creating separate programs was preferable, as it was important that new population activities not divert resources from other development activities.

A similar convergence of interests often led to the provision of international population assistance on different terms than development assistance in other sectors—a situation which still applies. There was a larger proportion of grant funding and more funding for local costs and for recurrent costs, including contraceptives and salaries of family planning managers and workers. There was also more funding through intermediary organizations such as NGOs and universities based in the United States and other industrialized countries. Fewer requirements were placed on governments for matching funds. Initially, the World Bank made the fewest exceptions to its usual project lending procedures and conditions; these eventually had to be eased to overcome difficulties in getting countries to accept loans for population activities. The cumulative impact of these relatively easy terms for population assistance was to provide incentives for recipient governments and NGOs to accept IPI assistance, with considerable flexibility in how they would implement it.

During this period, the funds available for population assistance exceeded what most governments were prepared to spend, particularly on family planning services. Under these conditions, IPIs provided much assistance for purposes often only indirectly connected to increasing contraceptive use: USAID for biomedical research; the World Bank for buildings and equipment; UNFPA for censuses and maternal and child health programs; and IPPF for building awareness of family planning. IPIs were often in competition with one another to influence the structures and priorities of national programs, and coordination among them was weak. Each IPI tended to develop its own connections within any given country—for example, UNFPA with population program leaders, the World Bank with finance and development planning ministries, WHO with health ministries, and IPPF with private family planning associations. This situation often made it more difficult for countries to develop a coherent policy and exacerbated the tendency of governments to speak with different voices.

## Institutional Characteristics, 1974–1984

In the first five years or so after Bucharest, the growth of IPIs, measured in financial terms, slowed down. Consistent with the Bucharest message of integrating population and development activities, IPI leaders moved to link population activities more closely to the overall structures and priorities of development assistance donors. UNFPA field representatives were assigned to work more closely with UNDP resident country representatives. The U.S. Agency for International Development was reorganized to give a greater role in decision making to regional and country offices and to limit the authority and personnel of its central Office of Population.[53] The World Bank decided it should pursue a more integrated approach to lending for population programs and associate them more closely with initiatives in health and nutrition, by redesignating its Population Projects Department as the Population, Health, and Nutrition Department.[54] The Bank also sought to integrate family planning components into projects in other sectors such as education and urban development. These reorganizations had their

53. See Donaldson, *Nature Against Us.*
54. Crane and Finkle, "Organizational Impediments to Development Assistance."

greatest impact on the activities of UNFPA and the World Bank, although even in these organizations, "integration" was hard to put into practice. USAID's policy coordination division (not in the Office of Population) began to support a new research program concerned with socioeconomic determinants of fertility. The Office of Population retained considerable funds and personnel of its own, however, which enabled it to continue to emphasize family planning services and to dominate program development and implementation within USAID.

In each of these IPIs, especially UNFPA and the World Bank population unit, leaders were constantly pressed to subordinate the objective of expanding access to family planning to other institutional and policy objectives—a situation which was desirable or not depending on how one viewed these various objectives. UNFPA needed to have recipient countries' support in UN policy-making bodies in order to gain status in the UN system and operate at the field level. Moreover, UNFPA provided assistance in the form of grants, which governments did not need to repay. For these reasons, UNFPA was not in a strong position to set conditions on its assistance, nor could it demand strict accountability. The then executive director of UNFPA took this fundamental reality and made it into a selling point for UNFPA, touting UNFPA's flexibility and willingness to trust countries as means of building the countries' self-reliance and commitment to their own programs.[55] In contrast, the World Bank, dominated by donors and offering countries loans, which they would have to repay (usually for buildings and equipment), sought to demand much greater accountability and to condition its population loans on policy and organizational reforms that the Bank felt would be consistent with its fertility-reduction objectives.[56]

Both agencies encountered difficulties in adhering to their own philosophies. In practice, much of the decision making on UNFPA expenditures was centralized in New York where individual projects were approved. And while the World Bank might seek to monitor expenditures more closely, it had only limited capacity to hold countries

55. See the book by Rafael M. Salas, then executive director of UNFPA, *People: An International Choice—The Multilateral Approach to Population* (Oxford: Pergamon, 1976).
56. Crane and Finkle, "Organizational Impediments to Development Assistance."

accountable for program performance or to condition additional loans on previous achievement.

The model for an effective national program in this period was probably Indonesia, which was able to benefit from assistance from all three major IPIs—the World Bank, UNFPA, and USAID—by virtue of the government's strong commitment to fertility reduction and its ability to coordinate and manage the assistance itself. An ineffective program was that of Egypt, which, although it too was assisted by IPIs, was poorly implemented and in the mid-1970s was diverted by the appeal of the Bucharest agenda toward experimenting with integrated population and development projects. Overall, the experience of this period demonstrated that neither governments nor IPIs were institutionally well equipped to implement a comprehensive development-oriented strategy.

**Institutional Characteristics, 1984–1991**
During this phase, following the International Conference on Population in Mexico City, IPIs were challenged to respond to new adversities in their political environment. Apart from the political fireworks generated by the Reagan administration during the 1984 conference in Mexico City, and the termination of direct support to UNFPA and IPPF, there has been considerable continuity in the funding and implementation of U.S. international population assistance. Congress has continued to provide earmarked funding for population programs at increasing levels, and the Office of Population maintains its leadership and autonomy within USAID, having escaped threats that it would disappear under an agency reorganization plan adopted in 1991. Moreover, the program remains focused on supporting family planning services and closely related research, education, and policy development work. Recently, leaders of the Office have indicated a new determination to give priority in its assistance to the most demographically significant countries, an approach consistent with the desire of those who originally supported its creation as an instrument to help stabilize world population growth.[57] The World Bank's population program, which lost focus and momentum during the Reagan years, has recently increased its

57. Interviews with staff members of the USAID Office of Population, June and September 1991.

lending, including more support for the recurrent costs of contraceptives. UNFPA, similarly, is voicing renewed commitment to family planning.[58] These developments have been happening while major donors such as the World Bank and USAID have been undergoing a fundamental reorientation away from supporting technical inputs in such functional areas of development as agriculture, education, and health, and toward support for structural adjustment programs aimed at macroeconomic objectives. Under these circumstances, the strengthening of the network of IPIs since 1984 has been particularly noteworthy.

Most significant during the period since 1984 have been developments in the network of international population institutions. In order to respond to external challenges, IPIs have worked more cooperatively together to build political support, co-opt opponents, and increase program efficiency. Other important factors for cooperation have been greater demand for population assistance in developing countries compared with earlier years, and better coordination within governments. Both political and financial considerations have led IPIs to improve their division of labor and capitalize more on their different areas of comparative advantage. Cooperative relationships have also been fostered by frequent formal and informal meetings that bring different IPI leaders together, close working level contacts, mobility of personnel among IPIs, common professional training and publications, and the autonomy of IPIs within their broader institutional settings. One example of the network's ability to adapt has been its response to the Reagan administration's decision not to contribute to IPPF. USAID and the World Bank have provided funds directly to IPPF regional offices and to individual IPPF-affiliated national family planning associations, rather than to the central IPPF secretariat.[59]

Further indications of how IPIs are adapting to their more difficult task environment can be found in a number of mutually reinforcing trends and events of the last five years: *UNFPA* held a major meeting in Europe (the Amsterdam Forum in 1989) and gained additional financial

58. Nafis Sadik, *The State of the World Population 1991* (New York: United Nations Population Fund, 1991).
59. See International Planned Parenthood Federation, *Annual Report 1990–91* (London: IPPF, 1991).

support from European donors; planned for a new global fund for contraceptives with participation from AID and other donors; and joined
UNDP in gaining intergovernmental approval to increase financial and
technical support for country programs directly, rather than through
UN specialized agencies. *IPIs in general* have collaborated more with
the private nonprofit and commercial sectors to expand the channels
through which family planning services are made available; upgraded
their management procedures; worked with women's groups, health
advocates, and even Catholic Church–affiliated natural family planning
groups; and developed guidelines and measures to help ensure a higher
quality of care in delivery of family planning services.

## The Impact of International Population Institutions: National Policy Responses and Fertility Trends

From the time IPIs were created, their leaders have attached great importance to the task of monitoring the impact of IPI programs—on governments' official policies and family planning programs as well as on
fertility behavior and, ultimately, on population size and growth rates.
The results of these monitoring activities have helped to justify donor
support for population programs, encourage lagging developing countries to participate, and provide information for program planning. The
monitoring apparatus which has evolved over the years is organiza-
tionally decentralized, and yet has involved considerable interorganizational cooperation among the IPIs. The Population Council, a private
organization in New York receiving close to half of its funds from
USAID and other IPIs, has probably been the single most important
supporter of policy and program research. The United Nations Population Division also produces authoritative reports on all phases of
population policies and demographic change. The World Bank,
UNFPA, and IPPF support a variety of publications to disseminate information to policymakers around the world, as do such private organizations as the Population Reference Bureau and the Population Crisis
Committee, both based in Washington. Advocates of population and
family planning programs in developing countries—usually government
officials, parliamentarians, or academic leaders—are therefore able to
base their arguments on relatively extensive documentation about

national and international policies, quantitative demographic analyses, and survey findings.

Despite the plethora of information available, evaluating the effectiveness of IPIs is conceptually a complicated task. First, not all can agree on the criteria against which they should be evaluated. Since the time when IPIs were founded, conflict over their specific goals and objectives has remained high, as the earlier discussion of agenda setting and policy formulation has revealed. While most analysts would recognize that fertility reduction alone is an insufficient criterion, few can agree on how to introduce other criteria of social welfare. Second, assessments of individual IPIs will yield a different conclusion than assessments of them as a group. Each institution functions with a different set of constraints; together, they can be seen as more effective in advancing national policies and programs than if they are examined individually.[60]

Third, and most important, it is extremely difficult to isolate the impact of external assistance and other IPI activities from other influences on the formulation and implementation of national population policies. The role of IPIs in fertility reduction, if that is accepted as the ultimate criterion of their effectiveness, is even more a matter of subjective judgment. This judgment is more problematic because some IPI activities, such as providing contraceptive supplies, have—or appear to have—immediate effects, while other activities are more likely to have long-term payoffs. It may take ten to twenty years, for example, for population and family life education programs aimed at young people, or training programs for demographers and health professionals, to be put in place and show results in increased use of contraception. The impact of IPIs, taking these complications into account, will be discussed below at greater length, with attention to changes over time.

## The Impact of IPIs, 1965–1974

The easy terms on which international population assistance was provided in these early years, and the large volume of funds relative to demand for assistance, meant that positive incentives were present for

60. For a fuller elaboration of the need to examine systems of international organizations, using the population case, see Gayl D. Ness and Steven R. Brechin, "Bridging the Gap: International Organizations as Organizations," *International Organization* 42, 2 (1988): 245–73.

the governments of developed and developing countries as well as UN agencies to become involved in international population programs. Conformity with the principles of international resolutions appeared to increase rapidly as other Western donor countries made contributions to the UN Population Fund and IPPF, and as developing countries announced the adoption of national policies and programs to reduce population growth. Between 1965 and 1974, some twenty-seven countries came forward, including some countries—such as Egypt, Kenya, Colombia, and the Philippines—whose governments have vacillated in their commitments to implementing the policies since then. On the whole, however, the effectiveness of IPIs in this period was fairly high; they gained attention for the problem of rapid population growth and, through their initial investments in research, training, and equipment, helped launch national programs in a number of countries.

**Table 8.1**  Countries with national policies to reduce fertility

| Total fertility rate (est. 1990)[a] | Year of policy adoption | | | |
|---|---|---|---|---|
| | Pre–1965 | 1965–1973 | 1974–1983 | 1984–1992 |
| 4.5–8.1 | **Pakistan (6.6)** | **Kenya (6.7)** | Senegal (6.5) | Rwanda (8.1) |
| | | Ghana (6.3) | Haiti (6.4) | Yemen (7.4) |
| | | **Iran (6.2)**[b] | Guatemala (5.3) | Uganda (7.4) |
| | | Nepal (6.1) | El Salvador | Zambia (7.2) |
| | | **Bangladesh (4.9)** | (4.6) | Niger (7.1) |
| | | Botswana (4.9) | | **Tanzania (7.1)** |
| | | | | Liberia (6.8) |
| | | | | Gambia (6.5) |
| | | | | Sierra Leone (6.5) |
| | | | | Swaziland (6.2) |
| | | | | **Nigeria (6.2)** |
| | | | | Zimbabwe (5.6) |
| | | | | **Algeria (5.4)** |
| | | | | Papua New Guinea (5.3) |
| | | | | Honduras (5.3) |

**Table 8.1**   (*continued*)

| Total fertility rate (est. 1990)[a] | Year of policy adoption | | | |
| --- | --- | --- | --- | --- |
| | Pre–1965 | 1965–1973 | 1974–1983 | 1984–1992 |
| 3.0–4.5 | India (3.9) | Egypt (4.5) | Vietnam (4.0) | South Africa (4.5) |
| | | Morocco (4.5) | Mexico (3.8) | Peru (4.0) |
| | | Tunisia (4.1) | | |
| | | Philippines (4.1) | | |
| | | Turkey (3.7) | | |
| | | Malaysia (3.6)[b] | | |
| | | Dominican Republic (3.6) | | |
| | | Indonesia (3.0) | | |
| 1.2–2.9 | Fiji (2.7) | Colombia (2.9) | | |
| | China (2.3) | Jamaica (2.6) | | |
| | South Korea (1.6) | Sri Lanka (2.5) | | |
| | | Trinidad and Tobago (2.4) | | |
| | | Thailand (2.2) | | |
| | | Mauritius (2.0) | | |
| | | Singapore (1.8)[b] | | |
| | | Barbados (1.8) | | |
| | | Taiwan (1.7)[b] | | |
| | | Hong Kong (1.2)[b] | | |

Sources:  United Nations Department of International Economic and Social Affairs, *World Population Policies*, Vols. I–III (New York: United Nations, 1987–1990); Population Reference Bureau, *1991 World Population Data Sheet*, Washington, D.C.: Population Reference Bureau, 1991); Dorothy L. Nortman, *Population and Family Planning Programs: A Compendium of Data through 1981* (New York: The Population Council, 11th edition, 1982); author's interviews.

Note: Countries over 500,000 population; countries with population over 20 million listed in **boldface**.

[a] The total fertility rate represents the average number of children a woman will have assuming that the current age-specific birth rates will remain constant throughout her childbearing years. Replacement level fertility is a total fertility rate of about 2.1.

[b] Fertility reduction policy substantially revised since first adopted due to political or demographic reasons.

## The Impact of IPIs, 1974–1984

An assessment of the overall effectiveness of IPIs in their assistance to developing countries during this decade should keep in mind that the Bucharest conference broadened the agenda—implying much more complex tasks for IPIs—at a time when the overall system of Western-supported development assistance was weakening. Moreover, many countries were less responsive than they had been earlier to public aid donors promoting policy reforms, because now the countries were able to do more borrowing on relatively easy terms on the private capital markets.[61] Overall, although the various IPIs made some programmatic accommodations to the Bucharest "message," there was more continuity than change in actual resource allocations after the 1974 conference. The accomplishments of IPIs seem small when measured against the broader agenda of Bucharest, but considerably greater with respect to more immediate family planning objectives.

The effectiveness of individual IPIs in assisting national programs was variable, of course, and often governed by country-specific factors. In general, however, UNFPA probably benefited from efforts by USAID and the World Bank to influence countries to strengthen national population policies and programs, sometimes as an implicit or explicit condition for other kinds of development assistance. At the same time, countries could turn to UNFPA to support some of the program management, training, and research activities in which other IPIs were less interested. As time went on, the increasing demand for population-related aid had the effect of reducing competition among IPIs in providing assistance, and the institutions learned from experience. Positive coordination was still difficult to achieve, however, because of different institutional priorities and decision-making procedures.

The roles and effectiveness of IPIs varied by region. In Asia, where there were more mature population programs with the capacity to absorb large sums of aid, USAID and the World Bank were relatively more influential and effective than other donors, the former because of its focus on family planning, and the latter because of its ability to pro-

---

61. Robert E. Wood, *From Marshall Plan to Debt Crisis: Foreign Aid and Development Choices in the World Economy* (Berkeley: University of California Press, 1986).

vide relatively large loans for program infrastructure. In Latin America as well, USAID, along with IPPF, was able to do more than other IPIs in the area of family planning, not only because of its focus on that objective, but because of its ability to fund relatively strong nongovernmental agencies in a region where few governments wanted to commit themselves overtly to fertility reduction or to be directly involved in services. Thus, although UNFPA was active in the Latin American region, it had to spend a great deal on activities unrelated to fertility reduction, and there was almost no role for the World Bank. In Africa, progress made by all donors prior to 1984 was extremely slow, but USAID may have led the way in assistance to family planning by fostering NGO involvement. Both USAID and the World Bank, because of their role in economic reform in Africa, were also relatively influential in policy development. UNFPA was appreciated by African countries for its willingness to support broader population activities such as census-taking, creation of population units in development planning agencies, and development of health infrastructure, which might have long-run benefits for making and implementing population policies. Relying mainly on WHO to provide technical assistance for family planning, however, UNFPA accomplished little in this area.

### The Impact of IPIs, 1984–1991

By the time of the Mexico City conference, all but a few major governments of developing countries had articulated official population policies, covering some 90 percent of their combined population; they had also participated actively in IPIs and supported intergovernmental resolutions. In addition, although they approached family planning in a variety of ways, they were all receiving some external assistance.

A major development since 1984 has been the adoption of population policies by sub-Saharan African countries. Many of these countries were previously laggards in adhering to IPI programs, and some were even pronatalist in their policies. Apart from general offers of assistance, IPIs used a combination of specific strategies to bring about policy change in African governments, including presentations of quantitative models of the impact of population growth; support for leaders' participation in international workshops and conferences; demonstration projects; and, in a few cases, conditions on structural adjustment loans. Now, African countries have greatly expanded their role as recipients of international population assistance.[62] What remains unclear is how much of African behavior reflects commitment to the principles and norms of IPIs and how much is an expression of a desperate need for external resources. Past experience suggests, however, that assistance from IPIs may help create the constituencies for stronger implementation in the future.

An even more recent development is the increasing participation in IPIs of the countries of Eastern Europe and the former Soviet Union. To some extent, these countries will be competing with developing countries of Asia, Africa, and Latin America for attention and assistance. This situation will require some IPIs to reevaluate their priorities. Because of low fertility rates in Eastern Europe and many of the former Soviet republics, the population control rationale initially underlying IPIs does not apply, although the need for improved reproductive health and family planning services is compelling.

Since 1984, a tougher standard against which to assess the impact of IPIs might seem appropriate, such as the extent to which governments are willing to commit their own resources to fertility-related programs. In recent years, governments of developing countries, excluding China, have increased their contributions to about 60 percent of the resources for their national population programs, or close to $1 billion in 1988.[63] As for donor governments other than the United States, support for IPIs since 1984 has been mixed, and has been greatly affected by overall aid-weariness. Currently, however, all of the OECD donors contribute to international population programs, with eight directing more than one percent of their aid to these programs, and three (the United States, Norway, and Finland), more than 2 percent.[64] France, a major development aid donor in other areas, contributes negligible amounts.

To assess the effectiveness of IPIs, one must go beyond profiles of government policies and programs to consider what difference IPIs have

62. United Nations Population Fund, *Global Population Assistance Report, 1982–1989* (New York: UNFPA, 1991).
63. Family Health International, *A Penny a Day* (Research Triangle Park, N. C.: Family Health International, 1990).
64. United Nations Population Fund, *Global Population Assistance Report.*

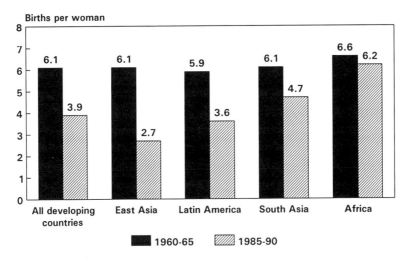

**Figure 8.1**
Fertility trends in the developing world by region
Source: United Nations, 1991.

made to program outcomes, especially to fertility decline. Initially, however, one must consider what is known about the causes of fertility decline and the impact of national programs on fertility.[65] A brief look at fertility trends themselves may be the best place to start. Fertility has come down rapidly in some countries, such as those of East Asia and Latin America, and scarcely at all in others, such as the poorest countries of Africa (See figure 8.1).

It is not easy to disentangle the programmatic factors influencing fertility behavior from socioeconomic factors such as changes in women's education and employment. Yet a number of expert analyses—some cross-national and some focused longitudinally on particular countries—

65. The analysis here focuses on lower fertility as the measure of population program effectiveness; however, it should also be remembered that it takes time for changes in fertility to be translated into lower rates of population growth, which may remain high due to declining mortality and large numbers of people entering the reproductive age groups. John Bongaarts and his colleagues at the Population Council nevertheless estimate that "past programs have already produced a population reduction of 412 million through 1990. . . ." "The Demographic Impact of Family Planning Programs," *Studies in Family Planning* 21 (1990): 305. The impact of such a reduction on environmental deterioriation, scattered across many locales, would be difficult to measure.

conclude that organized family planning programs account for a substantial portion of those declines that have occurred.[66] According to a recent study by researchers at the Population Council in New York, "in the absence of family planning programs fertility in the Third World would have been 5.4 births per woman rather than the actual 4.2 for 1980–85."[67] The impact would have been much smaller, however, if China had been excluded from this assessment. The compulsory nature of the Chinese program, and its independence from IPIs until relatively recently, suggests a more qualified assessment of IPI influence on overall Third World fertility declines.[68] Further questions are raised by the experience of Brazil, which suggests that under some circumstances at least, fertility can come down significantly without an explicit national population policy or large-scale external assistance.[69]

Still, studies in a number of individual countries substantiate the conclusion that national family planning programs have helped to accelerate the pace of fertility decline, an effect which is likely to increase over time.[70] By the criterion of fertility decline, Indonesia, Mexico, Thailand, South Korea, and Tunisia might be counted among the successes, with Ghana and Pakistan among the failures. For other countries, such as India, Bangladesh, and Egypt, the picture is more mixed, and for still others, such as Nigeria and Tanzania, it is too early to judge the impact of recently adopted policies (see table 8.1).

66. See Robert J. Lapham and George B. Simmons, eds., *Organizing for Effective Family Planning Programs* (Washington, D.C.: National Academy Press, 1987).
67. Bongaarts, et al., "The Demographic Impact of Family Planning Programs."
68. For an authoritative analysis of China's population policy, see Judith Banister, *China's Changing Population* (Stanford, Calif.: Stanford University Press, 1987).
69. See Thomas Merrick, "The Evolution and Impact of Policies on Fertility and Family Planning: Brazil, Colombia, and Mexico," in *Population Policy: Contemporary Issues*, ed. Godfrey Roberts (New York: Praeger, 1990), 147–66.
70. See, for example, Francisco Alba and Joseph E. Potter, "Population and Development in Mexico Since 1940: An Interpretation," *Population and Development Review* 12 (March, 1986): 47–76; Donald Warwick, "The Indonesian Family Planning Program: Government Influence and Client Choice," *Population and Development Review* 12 (September 1986): 453–90; and John Knodel and Nibhon Debavalya, "Thailand's Reproductive Revolution," *International Family Planning Perspectives* 4 (Summer 1978): 34–49.

**IPI Effectiveness: Summary and Discussion**

Based on the available evidence, it is reasonable to suggest that IPIs have made a major contribution to the achievements of national programs in those countries they have assisted.[71] In the Introduction to this volume, Keohane, Haas, and Levy have presented a basic framework which can help to account for changes in national policies and programs. They posit three major sources of explanation (the "three Cs"): changes in governmental *concern* and policy preferences attributable to the influence of international institutions; changes in the *contractual environment* due to the ability of international institutions to reduce transaction costs, improve the flow of information, and monitor the behavior of governments; and changes in the *capacity* of governments to follow through on their policy commitments where international institutions have provided financial and technical incentives.

*Concern at the national level.* As described in this paper, IPIs have played an important role in bringing about changes in national awareness and concern about population issues, and have successfully portrayed population programs as compatible with the interests of individual nations and the world as a whole, not just with those of the rich, industrialized nations. Thus IPIs have been instrumental in legitimizing such programs in the eyes of Third World governments. In most developing countries, external sources of influence working in association with receptive national leaders have been more important than domestic pressure groups. Every developing country with a national family planning program has received external assistance in some measure, ranging from one percent or less in the case of China to 90 percent or more of program expenditure in the case of Bangladesh and some other poor countries. Implicit and occasionally explicit links to other forms of development assistance have augmented this incentive effect. It has therefore been important that IPIs are closely associated with the broader development missions of the UN system, the World Bank, and

---

71. One researcher conducted a quantitative analysis and found a positive correlation between population aid levels and contraceptive prevalence, but candidly acknowledges that "foreign support is both attracted to and solicited by the more effective family planning programs." Donaldson, *Nature Against Us*, 171.

USAID and other bilateral aid agencies. At the same time, IPIs have been able to sustain at least a minimal level of concern in donor governments, even through tough political times. When the administrations of Ronald Reagan and Margaret Thatcher lost enthusiasm for population programs during the 1980s, the impact of their actions on developing countries was greatly mitigated by the relative autonomy of IPIs and their close networks with one another and with population policy advocates in the countries.

*The contractual environment.* Significantly, major actors in the population field are not pursuing a specific set of rules and regulations for countries regarding fertility and population growth rates. In general, however, IPIs have helped to reduce the transaction costs involved in building a wide consensus on the desirability of limiting population growth. The visibility they give to population programs helps to strengthen adherents of these programs in national debates. IPI communication activities accelerate the diffusion of ideas among policymakers and individual citizens. IPIs have further reduced transaction costs for governments by supporting relevant research on contraceptive methods and on fertility attitudes and behavior; procuring necessary commodities and equipment on a bulk purchase basis; and coordinating resources and skills to enhance the ability of a number of countries—including small European donors as well as some developing countries—to provide assistance. In addition, by monitoring government policy changes and evaluating their impact, IPIs provide a constant reminder of what has been accomplished as well as what more can be done by governments, individually and collectively.

*Capacity-building.* Finally, IPIs have had their most direct effects in two areas, although the second uses the most resources: (1) helping to build national scientific and technological capacity to collect data, better understand population-development interrelationships, and develop and adapt new contraceptive technologies; and (2) helping to provide the resources necessary to carry out programs, even supporting their recurrent as well as capital costs. Categories of activity that have been supported include training programs; facilities, vehicles, and contraceptives; research and evaluation activities; and materials for use in promoting family planning through mass media and educational channels. Capacity-building has also been aimed at the private sector.

Assessing the short- and long-term impact of different forms of assistance on national capacity is a complex endeavor, especially when it comes to determining areas in which external assistance may actually substitute for or interfere with indigenous capacity-building. What is certain, however, is that family planning activities, perhaps like some environmental measures that developing countries may be encouraged to adopt, often hold few immmediate payoffs for political leaders who invest political or financial capital in them. Thus, international assistance is usually a critical element of the political economy of these programs. IPIs also help provide the impetus for South-South cooperation and capacity-building, a kind of "second generation" impact. Institutions in Indonesia and Thailand, for example, are now serving as sources of technical assistance and as training sites for other countries in the region.

What would have happened if population assistance had been provided entirely on a bilateral basis, without the special funding arrangements and intergovernmental consensus documents associated with IPIs? Most likely, the total amounts spent for population programs would have been much less, as all but a few donors have been unprepared, for political and technical reasons, to undertake bilateral programs of their own. In addition, fewer governments of developing countries would have made large-scale commitments, and national programs would have had to undertake on their own some of the research, training, and purchasing functions that have been coordinated and supported by IPIs.

On the other hand, are there different institutional arrangements that could have led to more effective assistance and stronger population policies? Answering this question requires some heroic assumptions about what kinds of population policies would be optimal and what other arrangements that could have been undertaken in the 1960s would have yielded dramatically different results, yet been politically and economically feasible. The most sensible response seems to be that, given the constraints of the times, no fundamentally different institutional arrangements could be envisioned, nor was it possible to make fundamental changes once institutions were in place. Still, some modest reforms within the existing framework might have been initiated by IPI executives. For example, UNFPA might have hired a higher proportion of technically trained staff; the World Bank could have relaxed its project lending procedures and placed more staff in the field; and USAID might have built a stronger policy research capability into the Office of Population, to balance its heavy emphasis on delivery of family planning services.

## Conclusion

The creation of IPIs in the late 1960s was facilitated by a transnational policy coalition whose members believed that population control would promote economic development and political stability in Third World nations. Backed by the power and influence of the U.S. government, IPIs emerged as a semi-autonomous set of institutions whose primary purpose was to help reduce fertility and population growth through the promotion of family planning. Certain institutional characteristics of population programs—their nesting within the larger interorganizational system of development assistance and, in the case of UNFPA and the World Bank, within the UN system—compelled the programs to accommodate their family planning mission to the preferences of other development aid units and implementing agencies in the developing countries. Yet, other characteristics of IPIs—earmarked funding, separate administrative units, and relaxation of some of the conditions normally attached to development assistance—enabled them to survive and become increasingly effective despite pressures to accommodate to other objectives. In effect, all of these fundamental characteristics allowed IPIs to grow and adapt through the 1980s, even as the economic development rationale for population control lost intellectual ground, and as controversies over the implementation of family planning programs increased in a world where power was becoming more diffuse. In addition, despite its limitations, the linkage with the environmental movement appears to have helped in restoring focus and momentum to IPIs. Whether the coalition helps IPIs in the future may depend on the progress and direction of the environmental movement itself, both in the United States and transnationally.

Ultimately, much of the future growth, vitality, and effectiveness of IPIs is likely to derive from the participation of those motivated by the more immediate and individual benefits of family planning programs, such as women's groups, health professionals, and planned parenthood advocates. It is the struggles among these groups, along with religious opponents of family planning and abortion, that will drive important choices concerning how population programs are organized in relation to health services or other social programs, what methods of contraception are used, and whether abortion services are made available. Of necessity, decisions on these questions will be made at the national level in developing countries, and will reflect the increasing social and economic differences among them.

The absence of clear, internationally agreed-upon rules—for example, concerning optimal fertility or population growth rates or the best measures to achieve fertility goals—is, if anything, an advantage. Yet broader norms and guidelines formulated at the international level will continue to play a role in national policy making. Through their publications, conferences, and other communication activities, IPIs have a contribution to make in ensuring that diverse viewpoints are represented in both national and international debates. IPIs can also help ensure that the resources and technology are available to implement national decisions. The continued autonomy of the system of IPIs—its freedom from domination by any single set of actors—is an essential organizational prerequisite to performing these functions well, as is a willingness by the executive heads of IPI to assume a greater burden of leadership in an increasingly challenging political environment.

# IV
## Conclusion

# 9

# Improving the Effectiveness of International Environmental Institutions

Marc A. Levy, Robert O. Keohane, and Peter M. Haas

Our analysis of international environmental institutions has focused on the activities of international organizations. We have looked for sources of institutional effectiveness, recognizing that international institutions could, in the worst case, have negative effects on environmental quality. Our study is limited by the short time during which international activity with regard to protection of the environment has been intense, and by the limited repertoire of international responses. We look for institutional effectiveness, therefore, by seeking impacts on political processes as an intermediary step toward improving environmental quality. This is not just a case of looking where the light is brighter. For international institutions to make a difference environmentally, they must spawn political change, and therefore it is appropriate to judge them according to how well they do so.[1] Environmental protection is a political activity.

Based on our examination of the political consequences of international environmental institutions, we have formulated some tentative general propositions and some specific lessons for leaders and designers of international institutions who wish to use international organizations

The authors are grateful to Antonia Chayes, David Fairman, Ronald Mitchell, Robert Paarlberg, and Raymond Vernon for comments on earlier versions of this chapter, and to participants at seminars presented by Robert Keohane at the Stanford University Department of Political Science, the John F. Kennedy School of Government at Harvard University, the International Institutions Program of the Center for International Affairs at Harvard, and to the committee on the environment of the Social Science Research Council.
1. For a useful discussion of issues involved in choosing whether to evaluate policy outcomes or policy processes, see Giandomenico Majone, *Evidence, Argument, and Persuasion in the Policy Process* (New Haven: Yale University Press, 1989), 172–78.

and regulations to improve the quality of the natural and human environment. Our case studies reveal three distinctive functions of international environmental institutions: They enhance the ability to make and keep agreements, they promote concern among governments, and they build national political and adminstrative capacity. We find little evidence that international organizations enforce rules; indeed, in our case studies, monitoring of environmental quality and national policy measures was a far more important institutional activity than direct enforcement, and promoting reevaluation of state interests was more important than forcing behavior against a state's interest.[2]

## The Effects of International Environmental Institutions

Governments establish international environmental institutions in order to respond collectively to problems that they have not been able to solve without institutional support. Effective governmental responses are inhibited principally by three major factors: low levels of concern about the environmental threat, lack of capacity to manage it, and the inability to overcome problems of collective action. The first two problems apply to both commons and national environmental problems. The third applies primarily to commons issues, although it may be of some relevance in national problems if facilitation of regulatory rules is demanded.

Institutions that helped improve the quality of efforts to protect the environment—effective institutions—helped to overcome each of these obstacles. Each role or function proved to be significant for advancing international movement and forcing action at each stage of the policy process: agenda setting, international policy formulation, and national policy response. We evaluate the effectiveness of international environmental institutions according to the degree to which they help to ameliorate problems of concern, capacity, and the contractual environment at each of the three stages.

2. This judgment is in accord with the conclusions of Abram Chayes and Antonia Handler Chayes, "Compliance without Enforcement: State Behavior Under Regulatory Treaties," *Negotiation Journal*, July 1991, 311–30.

## Increasing Governmental Concern

During the phase of formulating an international policy response (including agenda setting), some states might not feel sufficient concern regarding the environmental threat, and thus may be unwilling to devote scarce resources toward alleviating it. In each of our cases, there were periods when some actors were motivated to solve an environmental problem, but were unable to overcome the central bottleneck created by the fact that their concern was not shared by other governments. In such a case it is unrealistic to expect institutions to promulgate effective regulatory rules; the states showing low concern (or laggard states) will either block rules or insist on weak rules. When strong rules are blocked, institutional responses are merely symbolic, as in the early oil pollution case and some fisheries. It is also unrealistic to expect adjustment of national policies in accord with institutionally expressed norms and principles where concern is lacking.

Institutions are not powerless in such settings. We have identified several ways in which they can boost concern within states. Where laggard states' lack of concern is due to a misunderstanding of their own interests, normative pronouncements (reduce transborder air pollution, stop destroying the ozone layer) accompanied by collaborative scientific reviews can contribute to a shift from low to high concern. The collaborative reviews of scientific evidence under the Vienna Convention and Montreal Protocol clearly played a major role in the increased concern within several governments about the problem of stratospheric ozone depletion.

Institutions can also serve as magnifiers of public pressure, when they foster competition among governments to be more pro-environment, as is seen in the Baltic and North Sea ministerial meetings, successive ozone talks after 1987, and acid rain "tote-board diplomacy." International institutions play a key role as sounding boards in a competitive game among politicians to impress publics. Although intergovernmental organizations are almost always extremely reticent in criticizing governments, nongovernmental organizations (NGOs) do not face such constraints. They play an active role, using information gained at formal international meetings, as well as public statements made by governmental officials, to embarrass governments and criticize national policy.

Under these conditions, international institutions are part of a complex network of governments, international institutions, nonprofit NGOs, the mass media, and industry groups, in which public pressure may overwhelm industry and government resistance.

International institutions can focus normative pressure on states as well. When international principles and norms have been agreed upon, they may acquire a certain legitimacy and come to be regarded as premises, or as intrinsically valuable, rather than as contestable reflections of interest-based compromises. Just as UNESCO in the 1970s offered many resolutions whose theme was "the collective legitimation of the world's doers of good or the delegitimation of its doers of evil," international environmental institutions can seek to legitimize or delegitimize, state practices.[3] Yet as the example of UNESCO suggests, such efforts are not necessarily successful.

Institutions can also have an impact on how states express their concern at the international level. International institutions with open procedures for agenda setting may enable weak states, or groups of states, to put issues on the international agenda in ways that cannot be ignored by others. Furthermore, international organizational arrangements may give proponents of action greater influence, through established leadership roles, than they would have in an anarchic international system. Thus domestic concern about environmental issues may be magnified at the international level, and it may, due to the institution, be more feasible to mobilize coalitions for policy change. The acid rain regime is a good example of this—the Nordic states used the Long-Range Transboundary Air Pollution Convention (LRTAP), originally agreed on for other reasons, to create significant international environmental policies.

Institutions can also increase concern by linking issues. A laggard state may have low concern over an environmental problem, but if an institution helps link the environmental issue to other issues which are of concern, then laggards may reevaluate their reluctance. Such linkage is direct in the case of material incentives (financial aid and technology

3. James P. Sewell, "UNESCO: Pluralism Rampant," in Robert W. Cox and Harold K. Jacobson, eds., *The Anatomy of Influence: Decision Making in International Organization* (New Haven: Yale University Press, 1973), 149. The concept of collective legitimation was first developed by Inis L. Claude. See his *The Changing United Nations* (New York: Random House, 1967), chap. 4.

transfer to developing countries and Eastern Europe; trade sanctions in the Montreal Protocol). It is also present in a less direct form when governments exert diplomatic pressure within the context of an environmental institution, raising the prospect that life may be made difficult for the laggard in other areas if the laggard does not come around. Institutions help increase such diplomatic pressure, both by making a laggard's opposition public, and by creating the opportunity to form interstate coalitions explicitly designed to put pressure on laggards. In the stratospheric ozone and acid rain cases, environmentalist "clubs" explicitly exerted pressure on opponents of emerging institutional rules. Other cases saw less formal international coalitions emerge, as in the pesticide trade and North and Baltic Sea cases.

International institutions are not always successful in enhancing concern about environmental problems, as the cases of intentional oil pollution (until the 1970s) and fisheries demonstrate. International institutions do not provide a magic formula for success, since they are typically weak unless other forces—notably, domestic environmental movements—create conditions for their effective operation. Indeed, the key events bolstering concern are often not associated with international institutions: Crises or shocks can have substantial impact, and changes in ruling parties or government personnel can have similarly profound effects. Nevertheless, we have shown that international institutions can increase concern about environmental policy, when conditions are right.

### Enhancing the Contractual Environment

The degree of concern that governments express about an international environmental problem reflects not only their views on the issues, but their calculations about both the feasibility of such action and its costs and benefits to them. Thus, expressed concern is in part a function of our other two crucial factors: the nature of the contractual environment and state capacity. If levels of effective communication among states and their ability to make credible commitments to one another are low, it may seem futile to raise new issues for international agendas. Environmental institutions, however, can enhance the quality of the contractual environment, thus facilitating the development and maintenance of international agreements. Institutions create bargaining forums in which information is shared, thereby reducing the transaction costs of negotiating agreements. Institutions that create ongoing negotiating processes help make commitments more credible by ensuring regular interaction among participants on the same set of issues.

Another way institutions can make it easier to strike agreements is to provide monitoring and verification services. It is a commonplace that uncertainty regarding others' future actions can restrain otherwise willing countries from accepting mutual constraints. Monitoring can help overcome this obstacle in three ways: by measuring aspects of environmental quality, by observing potential sources of pollution (such as oil tankers), and by monitoring national policy. Institutions can also serve as scapegoats, enabling governments to transfer blame for costly adjustment measures.

Every institution we studied monitored aspects of environmental quality, either directly or in conjunction with independent scientific laboratories. Although many institutions also gathered data on the activities of potential sources of pollution, only the acid rain monitoring program and the world fertility survey were able to validate national reports more or less independently; every other such program relied solely on national reports of behavior. In spite of governments' ability to falsify national reports (secretariats never dare to challenge them) we find that other governments value them. Where public interest is high, NGOs and domestic bureaucracies that want more effective action can take this information and apply public or intragovernmental pressure for the government in question to live up to its promises. With respect to national policies, international institutions are also dependent on national reporting. Yet in this arena as well, misrepresentation seems to be the exception rather than the rule. Governments value the exchange of information regarding national policies for its role in reducing uncertainty regarding future actions.

Where concern is very high, the ability to monitor violations may not be essential for cooperation. States undertook significant new policy measures in the North Sea and Baltic despite the lack of well-funded and integrated systems for monitoring either compliance or environmental quality. Monitoring arrangements for compliance with the ozone protocols still have loopholes, are based on awkward economic proxies for actual environmental emissions, and do not generate prompt identification of violations. With respect to ozone, the major industrialized countries appear to have such strong incentives to reduce production of ozone-depleting chemicals that they find these weak verification measures satisfactory, and their concern about cheating is low.

Sometimes, however, international environmental problems generate what Arthur Stein has called games of "collaboration," in which noncooperative equilibria are suboptimal.[4] To maintain cooperative patterns of action more beneficial for all participants, they must be assured that their partners are not cheating; thus in these situations, effective monitoring is a condition for sustained cooperation. Since systematic monitoring of oil tankers at sea was impractical, controls on vessel-source pollution only became effective when equipment regulations (which could be easily monitored) replaced discharge rules as the principal means of regulation. Prior to the adoption of exclusive economic zones (EEZs) in the late 1970s, the ability of fishing fleets to escape detection created a climate of distrust which contributed to the failure of collective efforts to manage fish stocks.

Enhancing the contractual environment is most relevant for commons problems, where regulatory rules specifying mutual restraints are the dominant focus of bargaining. The case studies above have shown repeatedly that international institutions can facilitate the making and keeping of international agreements by improving the contractual environment. Without institutional provision of a locus for bargaining and information-gathering, collective behavior would have been characterized more often by inaction or least-common-denominator outcomes.

Perhaps more surprisingly, actions that appear aimed at improving the contractual environment are also relevant for the politics of dealing with national-level environmental problems. The prior informed consent rules associated with pesticide trade, for example, are not intended as solutions to a commons problem, but as a means to assist national responses to the problem in developing countries. They provide points

4. Arthur A. Stein, "Coordination and Collaboration: Regimes in an Anarchic World," in Stephen D. Krasner, ed., *International Regimes* (Ithaca, N.Y.: Cornell University Press, 1983), 115–40. For a particularly clear discussion, see Lisa L. Martin, "Interests, Power and Multilateralism," *International Organization* (Autumn, 1992) Vol 46 No 4.

of accountability within national governments, which may enable concerned groups, within society and within governments of pesticide importing countries, to make exact commitments, to pressure for more effective controls on pesticide availability and use, to monitor compliance, and to apply strategies of reciprocity. In general, institutional activities that enhance the contractual environment can facilitate the negotiation of norms and principles governing national problems, as well as those operating at an international level for commons problems.

This dual role of regulatory rules explains our striking finding that so many international institutional responses to environmental problems have been regulatory in form. With the exception of population, regulatory standards were set in each case we investigated (though not always formally enshrined in international law), even when it was clearly impossible or unrealistic for many states to apply them.[5] Such a pattern is explicable, since regulations do more than regulate—they help generate political concern, they set normative standards, they communicate intensity of preferences, and they legitimate financial transfers (such as the international fund established at Montreal to promote compliance with regulations designed to protect the ozone layer) that might otherwise be termed bribes or even blackmail.

## Increasing National Capacity

For collective principles, norms and rules to be promulgated and implemented, it is not sufficient for governments to be concerned about environmental problems and for the contractual environment to be reasonably benign. Governments must also have the technical capacity to negotiate meaningful regulations that take cognizance of both the environmental realities and the political and economic incentives facing governments, firms, and other organizations that can affect outcomes. After such regulations have been specified and agreed upon, the burden of action shifts to national responses, which are often inhibited by low political, legal and administrative capacity. Leaders of weakly institutionalized states may genuinely want to conform to international norms

---

5. Whether reliance on command-and-control regulations rather than market-based incentives is somehow necessitated by the nature of international politics or whether it represents a failure of policy imagination, is an issue that we have not explored here.

and principles and comply with regime rules, but may lack the political legitimacy, or the loyalty of competent and honest bureaucracies, necessary to develop and implement domestic initiatives. International regulations create an external demand for effective domestic action, and international coalitions, including NGOs, may prompt increasing internal demand; but severe constraints may exist on the ability of the state to supply effective policy. When this problem is serious, international institutions can play an important role in helping to increase domestic capacity, sometimes by transferring resources to weak governments in the form of technical assistance or outright aid, in other instances by creating interorganizational networks that serve as catalysts and facilitators.

Capacity-building is particularly important for less developed countries and for the new East European democracies, whose administrative and political abilities are often limited by lack of resources. Technical assistance and aid by international institutions are familiar. Training programs, the provision of policy-relevant information, and research grants, can help weak governments create stronger policy programs. Often such programs are staffed mainly by national experts from strong states, under the auspices of the international institution. In many of our cases such programs helped states to improve their own ability to develop and implement effective measures to protect the environment. For instance, the ozone fund enables less developed countries to find alternatives to CFCs, population assistance helps governments implement family planning programs, technical assistance from the Food and Agriculture Organization (FAO) helps national pesticide registrars and promotes integrated pest management, and fishery commissions train national fisheries managers. Institutions contributed to building private sector capacity as well. Fisheries commissions trained private fishers as well as state managers. The International Maritime Organization's World Maritime University and other training seminars help educate ship captains in applying international and national environmental measures to their day-to-day operations.

Although international environmental institutions have built national capacity in significant ways, it would be too much to claim that the impact has been impressive by the standards of what would be needed to ensure environmental protection. Resources are often meager, so that

the familiar aid activities described hardly transform the abilities of
governments to cope effectively with environmental problems. Since
international environmental organizations typically have small bureaucracies (a pattern of which we approve), to promote national capacity
they have to develop networks with other agencies with related operational programs, such as the World Bank, the UN Development Program, and various regional development banks. Such interorganizational
coalitions helped to promote capacity-building on issues concerning
ozone depletion, the North and Baltic seas, acid rain in Europe, pesticide trade, and population, and to some extent on fisheries. It is sugges-
tive that in the one case where coalitions with operational organizations
were absent, marine oil pollution, we find virtually no increase in the
national capacities of less developed countries. The "paths to effectiveness" of international environmental institutions are indicated in table
9.1, which specifies some representative institutional activities falling

**Table 9.1** Paths to effectiveness: How international environmental institutions
boost the three Cs

| Role of institutions | Representative institutional activities |
| --- | --- |
| Increase governmental concern | Facilitate direct and indirect linkage of issues |
| | Create, collect, and disseminate scientific knowledge |
| | Create opportunities to magnify domestic public pressure |
| Enhance contractual environment | Provide bargaining forums that<br>• reduce transaction costs<br>• create an iterated decision-making process |
| | Conduct monitoring of<br>• environmental quality<br>• national environmental performance<br>• national environmental policies |
| | Increase national and international accountability |
| Build national capacity | Create interorganizational networks with operational organizations to transfer technical and management expertise |
| | Transfer financial assistance |
| | Transfer policy-relevant information and expertise |
| | Boost bureaucratic power of domestic allies |

under each of our three main rubrics: increasing concern, enhancing the contractual environment, and building national capacity.

Increasing governmental concern, enhancing the contractual environment, and building state capacity are not strictly sequential activities, but interact with one another synergistically. Reinforcing one is likely to strengthen the others, while weakness on one front may spill over onto another. Effective institutions will address these interactions with sophisticated strategies operating at multiple levels, in a dynamic process. A good international political process is not necessarily one that reaches "the best policies" at a given point in time, but rather is one that generates creative solutions on a continuing basis.

Weak technical capacity on the part of participating states, for example, may also inhibit expressions of concern, because governments that are technically ignorant are likely to take vague positions or stress principled positions, being reluctant to discuss specific costs and benefits for fear of being unable to evaluate others' arguments. And during the phase of national policy responses, it is entirely possible that problems of low concern will reemerge. It may turn out that some regime members had enough concern to accept mututal commitments, but not enough to make the necessary domestic adjustments. Or it may be that domestic political opponents who had been uninvolved during the negotiation of international rules loom as more formidable obstacles once domestic adjustment measures are deliberated. If problems of low concern emerge during this phase, the networks formed by international environmental institutions can increase the influence of their domestic allies by providing them with information or by mobilizing transnational coalitions to influence their governments.

Monitoring programs, to take another example, often did more than generate useful information. They were often promoted to build national capacity in order to help a broad base of governments participate in an informed manner in international environmental negotiations. Laggard countries often supported monitoring programs, hoping to build their own indigenous capacity.

These synergies are revealed in the case of pesticide trade. The ultimate goal is the development of effective national programs to protect farm workers from hazardous materials. Clearly, an effective institutional response will have to increase political and administrative capacity in developing countries. But to achieve this goal, international norms, principles and rules may be required, calling for agreement-enhancing roles. (Such international commitments may provide the necessary ammunition against domestic opponents to guarantee bureaucratic survival.) And during periods of domestic struggle over the terms of adjustment, an institution may be useful in magnifying public pressure (therefore increasing concern). Although in this chapter we have isolated these three roles of international environmental institutions for the purpose of explication, we acknowledge that in reality the linkages are interactive and often complex.

Furthermore, as we have stressed, the degree to which international environmental institutions have succeeded in these roles has varied across issue areas. In fisheries, institutions did not increase governmental concern and played only a marginal role in improving the contractual environment; the key change on the latter dimension was the shift to 200-mile national zones in 1977. The salience to domestic publics in the West of the issues of ozone and acid rain has been much greater than that of intentional oil pollution and pesticide trade, giving more scope for "tote-board diplomacy" on the former issues. The role of international institutions in improving the contractual environment through fostering negotiations and monitoring activity has been greater on issues of ozone, acid rain and Baltic–North Sea pollution than with respect to fisheries or population. Efforts by international institutions to build state capacity have been most marked with respect to developing countries or former members of the Soviet bloc; they are less significant toward developed pluralist countries in the West. Generally, the more an issue engages the attention of publics within democracies, the more significant the institutional role of increasing concern; the more an issue involves policy implementation in less developed countries, the more important is national capacity building. Effective institutions affected each of the three Cs. We summarize the patterns identified in our case studies in table 9.2.

### Lessons for International Environmental Institutionalists

What are the implications of these findings for those who wish to build effective international environmental institutions? Because we have stu-

Table 9.2 Range of effects of international institutions in case studies

| Case | Concern | Contractual environment | Capacity | Comments |
|---|---|---|---|---|
| Ozone | Yes | Yes | Yes | Possibly too late |
| Baltic and North seas | Yes | Yes | Yes | |
| Acid rain | Yes | Yes | Yes | |
| Oil pollution | No | Yes | Some | |
| Fisheries | No | No | No | |
| Pesticide trade | Some | Not applicable | Some | Recent case |
| Population | Yes | Not applicable | Yes | |

died only a small sample of cases, which were not scientifically chosen, we are not able to offer definitive judgments on the entire range of practical questions being debated in the context of the U.N. Conference on Environment and Development (UNCED). Nonetheless, certain conclusions emerge quite strongly, and we present them here as our modest advice to architects of international environmental institutions.

**Build Environment-Centered Coalitions**
The most general lesson to be drawn from our case studies is that the most significant roles of international institutions—as magnifiers of concern, facilitators of agreement, and builders of capacity—do not require large administrative bureaucracies. Indeed, running such a bureaucracy may distract leaders of international organizations from their most important tasks, which are quintessentially political: to create and manipulate dynamic processes by which governments change conceptions of their interests; and to mobilize and coordinate complex policy networks involving governments, NGOs, subunits of governments, and industry groups, as well as a variety of international organizations having different priorities and political styles. Insofar as capacity needs to be built, international environmental organizations should seek first to make operational arrangements with other inter-

national organizations, thus building mutually reinforcing networks and coalitions rather than establishing competing bureaucracies. Indeed, keeping the size of secretariats small forces them to build bridges to other groups and develop networks rather than hierarchies. A reputation for competent professionalism may induce others to cooperate as well.

Our cases reveal that a variety of environment-centered coalitions can be effective. Institutions can help create and nurture coalitions among like-minded governments, action-oriented groups within other institutions and organizations, supportive NGOs, environmental protection ministries, and other international organizations. Institutions commonly perform better when environment ministries serve as lead agencies in their deliberations. Although some coalitional responses are beyond an institution's control, institutional architects may have some influence over the shape of supporting coalitions.[6]

The only apparent exception to this rule, the highly effective rule-making capability of the European Community, in fact supports the general conclusion. Though the EC now contains a large bureaucracy with substantial resources for promoting environmental protection, its environmental decision-making capabilities grew very slowly at first. Environmental decisionmakers relied crucially at first, and still rely significantly, on allies within member state governments and among private actors.[7]

### Foster Open-ended Knowledge Creation

Environmental institutions are typically constructed to deal with problems that are not well understood. The only reliable knowledge is that current understandings of the problem will be obsolete in ten or twenty years. In this respect they are different from many (though not all) other international institutions. Hence the policies and organizations that comprise institutions should not codify existing knowledge in rules that

6. For a useful discussion, see James K. Sebenius, "Negotiating a Regime to Control Global Warming," in Richard Elliot Benedick et al., *Greenhouse Warming: Negotiating a Global Regime* (Washington, D.C., World Resources Institute, 1991), 69–98.
7. Stanley P. Johnson and Guy Corcelle, *The Environmental Policy of the European Communities* (London: Graham and Trotman, 1989).

are difficult to change, but should, on the contrary, foster an openended process of knowledge creation.

Such a process would require regular scientific monitoring of the environment. The universal circulation of information should be encouraged. Such science should be nonpartisan and untainted by national concerns, to offset suspicions that monitoring activities constitute political control by another means, or are a disingenuous way to promote the economic advantages of selected groups. Monitoring should be done in laboratories, through direct contracts with international organizations, to guarantee its insulation from national policy agendas. But actual work should be done by national scientists, since governments typically pay closer attention to the findings of their own nationals. The provision of information should be indirect rather than formal and institutionalized, in order to eliminate distributional bargaining over the provision of information, government censorship and control, and myopia in reporting.[8] It should also be made available frequently and promptly. The UN Environment Program (UNEP) could serve as a clearinghouse for such information. A particularly timely and effective means of diffusion is through the annual State of the Environment Report by the executive director to UNEP's Governing Council.

Institutions should also monitor and publicize state environmental policies. Secretariats should be authorized to gather and disseminate information regarding governments' actual environmental protection measures. In addition to providing information for NGOs and other domestic groups, such activity would provide information about programs that less developed countries and governments with weaker capabilities could emulate. This function, combined with its environmental monitoring role, would be a useful function for UNEP in the post-UNCED order. The Organization for Economic Cooperation and Development (OECD) is already providing this policy-review role among advanced industrial countries, and is seeking to extend it to the new regimes of Eastern Europe.

8. Mostafa K. Tolba, "Building an Environmental Institutional Framework for the Future," *Environmental Conservation* 17, 2 (Summer 1990); Edward L. Miles, "Science, Politics and International Ocean Management," *Policy Papers in International Affairs* No. 33 (Berkeley: Institute of International Studies, 1987); James K. Sebenius "Designing Negotiations Toward a New Regime," *International Security* 15 (Spring 1991), pp. 110–148.

In addition to monitoring, institutions can help promote the widespread development of scientific knowledge concerning the various causes of environmental damage, and the various consequences of suspected pollutants, thus providing feedback for more accurate agenda specification over time. Without institutional intervention, knowledge that is relevant to policy making remains trapped within those nations active in scientific research. Knowledge that is so generated commonly diffuses quite slowly, especially to countries of low concern, where it is often most needed. Institutions can help speed up the diffusion process by forming multinational assessment panels, working groups, and collaborative research programs. Such international knowledge-based exercises can often make effective use of innovative and expert transnational organizations, such as the International Institute for Applied Systems Analysis (IIASA), International Council of Scientific Unions (ICSU), and International Union for the Conservation of Nature (IUCN), in ways that national efforts cannot.

Agendas should be structured around environmental harm rather than particular pollutants. The fact that the Vienna Convention does not even mention CFCs by name was considered by activists to represent a failure, but in fact the opposite is true. Agendas that focus on harm rather than pollutants encourage broadening knowledge rather than limiting it. This makes possible a broadening regulatory scope, which, as the ozone layer case indicates, can be a matter of human survival. Although the acid rain regime was prompted by concern over acidified lakes and dying forests, it had an agenda that encouraged consideration of any environmental harm having some connection to a pollutant which crossed borders. It has fostered considerable creation and spread of knowledge about a variety of pollutants, some of which have no role in acidification or forest death. The agendas of most fishery commissions, by contrast, remained very limited, and the International Convention for the Prevention of Pollution by Ships (MARPOL) never included land-based sources of pollution within its purview, even though they were at least as threatening as ship-based sources.

### Create a Dynamic Process That Moves from Norms to Rules

None of the institutions we studied began life as successes, though some have become so. In fact, most international environmental institutions were first considered deep disappointments by those who had worked to create them. Our studies show that there is cause for optimism even following inauspicious starts, and that effective institutions seize opportunities to expand the consequences of their activity.

Effective institutions begin with commitments "merely" to norms and principles, and either lack regulatory rules or possess only very weak ones. This is exactly as it should be. If states waited to form institutions until there was enough concern and scientific understanding to adopt strong rules, they would wait much too long. Institutions are needed early on to help create the conditions that make strong rules possible (except in the population case, where many consider regulatory rules undesirable).[9]

In order to move from norms to rules, institutions must create a dynamic process of negotiation in which interests are discussed, possibilities for joint regulations are explored, and reasons for concern investigated. Such a process serves as a focal point for action, and permits the various coalition-building processes we highlighted above to bear fruit at their own rates. It puts into place, piece by piece, the elements of an effective institutional response. For example, a monitoring program may be agreed to early, as part of an information-gathering exercise (as occurred in the acid rain and ozone cases). If rules are later adopted, such a program will foster cooperative behavior by reducing uncertainties as to how much cheating is going on. Likewise, reporting of national policy measures may be undertaken first with reference only to norms and principles; such a process will likely have more effect after rules are adopted, when reviews of national policies threaten to reveal noncompliance.

Many of the mechanisms that facilitate adoption of effective rules and meaningful national implementation of joint rules are time-consuming to create. A major advantage of an ongoing negotiation process that strives to move from norms to rules is that it helps lay the groundwork for effective rule-making when the moment becomes ripe. When major crises or shocks occur, an institution that has laid the groundwork with

9. A similar point is made by Abram Chayes in "Managing the Transition to a Global Warming Regime or What to Do'til the Treaty Comes," in Benedick et al., *Greenhouse Warming*, 61–68.

facilitating mechanisms will be much better positioned to seize the opportunity to lock in strong rules than an institution waiting to put together a comprehensive package. The ozone hole, and the discovery of its cause in 1987, would not have galvanized the rapid response it did were it not for the procedural mechanisms put in place by the Vienna Convention and Montreal Protocol. Nor would the international response to the crisis sparked by the German forest death in 1981 and 1982 have been as swift if LRTAP had not been in place.

Our evaluation of policy measures must be sensitive to the political process of moving from norms to rules, as well as to issues of economic efficiency and ethical sensitivity. For example, on economic and ethical grounds it is easy to be critical of across-the-board percentage reductions from a common baseline, which are commonly employed at an early stage in international regulation of the environment. Such across-the-board cuts are unlikely to be economically efficient, since they do not target the worst polluters, for which the greatest improvements could be attained at the lowest cost. They are not fair, since they discriminate against governments that have already taken environmentally sound measures. And expectations of similar across-the-board cuts in the future could lead governments to refrain from taking early unilateral action to reduce environmental damage. Yet the great political virtue of such rules is that the severity of required reductions is likely to correlate with the intensity of domestic support for actions to protect the environment, since it is precisely those countries that have reduced emissions most where political support for pollution control is greatest. And countries where domestic concern is less developed tend to be those where less severe reduction are required under across-the-board rules. Thus, for all their drawbacks, across-the-board cuts may facilitate building initial coalitions to support policy regulation, which more efficient or fair rules could foreclose.

## Build National Capacity

Finally, our research has led us to appreciate the often central importance of building political and administrative capacity both within the state and in civil society. International environmental institutions, when they are effective, are not merely rule-making bodies. They are also vehicles for transferring skills and expertise, and for empowering domestic actors who are motivated to solve domestic problems of international importance.

Institutions should self-consciously attempt to foster capacity-building by providing policy-relevant information in a form that is readily usable. Such information can be used by environmentalist allies within governments to develop better programs and to justify their actions to domestic opponents. It can also be used by private actors, such as NGOs, to put pressure on governments to adopt improved regulatory practices. Capacity-building is often a necessary condition for effectiveness, which is another reason for environmental institutions to begin with norms and principles and move toward rules. Often the initial norms and principles, even though they fail to directly alter state behavior through binding rules, set in motion a process that builds domestic capacity in member governments. When conditions become ripe for binding rules, the capacity is in place to implement them effectively. In the acid rain regime, the governments of Eastern Europe emerged from the Cold War with a more sophisticated air pollution policy infrastructure than they would have had they not been members of the regime. This is a striking effect, given the antipathy of the Communist regimes to environmental protection. Today, now that conditions permit more serious consideration of these countries' compliance, such compliance is more likely because capacity (though admittedly weaker than the new governments would like) is in place.

### Implications for State Sovereignty

Environmental interdependence restricts the ability of governments to attain their objectives unilaterally, and it is often asserted that such interdependence threatens state sovereignty. Conversely, one sometimes hears that state sovereignty makes effective international environmental action impossible. Since sovereignty is a contested and complex concept, it may be worthwhile to examine these arguments with some care.[10]

---

10. Much of this discussion follows a more general, and thorough, discussion of sovereignty in Robert O. Keohane, "Sovereignty, Interdependence and International Institutions," Working Paper No. 1, Center for International Affairs, Harvard University, February 1991.

Sovereignty is essentially a legal term, meaning that a state "is subject to no other state and has full and exclusive powers within its jurisdiction without prejudice to the limits set by applicable law.[11] Formal sovereignty refers to a state's legal supremacy and independence, and is threatened neither by international environmental interdependence nor by the agreements that states make to regulate it. Indeed, the formal sovereignty of states that might not otherwise be recognized as independent may be validated by their participation in international organizations such as the United Nations, and by their signatures on international agreements.

However, formal sovereignty does not prevent the ozone layer from being depleted or reduce the incidence of acid rain. States find that to take effective collective action, they have to limit their own legal freedom of action, so that their partners will do the same. Thus they permit their *operational sovereignty*—their legal freedom of action under international law—to be eroded. They agree to "modification of their asserted freedom to act as they please in relation to their natural resources, industrial practices, and the environment."[12] Thus interdependence changes the relationship between operational sovereignty and effectiveness. In a world of genuinely independent states, legal freedom of action may be a precondition for effectiveness in goal attainment; but under conditions of high interdependence, maintaining such operational sovereignty may prevent effective action by anyone. Thus, international environmental interdependence and negotiations about it reinforce formal sovereignty while limiting operational sovereignty.

This combination of persistent formal sovereignty and eroding operational sovereignty makes international environmental action politically complex and conceptually confusing. International negotiations are laborious and time-consuming. Laggards often determine the overall pace of change. Effective enforcement of regulations on enterprises and governments requires the consent of the states involved. It is important

11. Stanley Hoffmann, "International Systems and International Law," in Hoffmann, *Janus and Minerva: Essays in the Theory and Practice of International Politics* (Boulder: Westview, 1987), 172–3, citing Permanent Court of International Justice, Series A., No. 1 (1923).
12. Lynton Keith Caldwell, *International Environmental Policy: Emergence and Dimensions*, second edition (Durham: Duke University Press, 1990), 311.

to recognize, however, that these difficulties are the result of the under-lying structure of world politics rather than of deficiencies of organizational design. A new international environmental organization within the UN bureaucracy would almost surely be equally cumbersome, albeit in different ways. The likely effect of establishing such a new international organization would not be to reduce the impact of state sovereignty. Rather, interstate political struggles would be encompassed within the organization—governments would seek to appoint to high office officials sympathetic to their arguments or blandishments, and even the empty pronouncements of the organization would require time-consuming meetings to negotiate. Public pronouncements of principle and prejudice would predominate over constructive private negotiations. Groups and individuals concerned about the environment might eventually turn away in disillusionment and disgust.

Operational sovereignty is eroded by international environmental interdependence. The persistence of the core of sovereignty creates difficulties for collective action. But neither sovereignty nor interdependence is about to disappear. Those of us who study international environmental institutions have a value-laden purpose: to improve the quality of the planetary environment. With this commitment in mind, we seek to analyze how the legal concept of state sovereignty and the practical fact of substantial state autonomy coexist with global interdependence, and how, subject to political constraints, the world's environment can be improved. We cannot wish away state sovereignty, any more than nationalists can dispel the reality of international environmental interdependence.

## Directions for Future Research

The research reported in this volume has focused on the effects of international institutions on specific environmental problems. Since in order to provide a subject matter for the study, we have chosen issues in which international institutions have been active, we do not pretend to explain the origins of such institutions. Were that our task, we would have a faulty research design, because we did not compare our cases to instances in which institutions could have been established but were not. It might be that the issues we examined are among those for which the conditions were most propitious for the formation and operation of international institutions.

A broader study would ask about the implications for effective environmental policy making of both the characteristics shared by environmental issues in general, and the distinctive attributes of particular issues, whether they concern fisheries, ozone, or acid rain. Such a study would choose issue areas without respect to institutional development, and seek to explain variations in institutionalization and cooperation over time. It would compare them on the basis of features hypothesized to make environmental cooperation more or less difficult.[13] Our focus has been on institutions, since these can be affected by policy, and much of our purpose has been descriptive and practical. For a deeper social scientific study capable of reaching valid causal inferences, comparative analysis of environmental issues, on the basis of an analysis of characteristics that make cooperation more or less difficult, would be essential.

A more ambitious study along those lines would require cooperation among scholars. We have made a modest gesture in this direction, in this volume, by adopting a definition of effectiveness that emphasizes political effects on member states more than environmental quality per se. In addition to facilitating our own analysis, this definition has the advantage of being compatible with those used in other contemporary research efforts, so that our findings can be compared with those of others.[14] Those research efforts that evaluate alternative plausible paths

13. For one such effort, see Oran R. Young and Gail Osherenko, eds., *The Politics of International Regime Formation: Lessons from Arctic Cases* (Ithaca, N.Y.: Cornell University Press, 1993).
14. A research project based at Dartmouth College defines an institution's effectiveness according to two dimensions: success in "solving the problem that motivated its establishment," and changing "the behavior of those whose actions are relevant to the problem" (Marc A. Levy, Gail Osherenko, Oran R. Young, "The Effectiveness of International Regimes: A Design for Large-Scale Collaborative Research," Institute for Arctic Studies, Dartmouth College, 4 December 1991, 15. A joint research project based between the Fridtjof Nansen Institute, the University of Oslo and the Institute at Marine studies, University of Washington, defines effectiveness according to three dimensions, which diverge from our definition and that of the Dartmouth group: achievement of declared goals, degree of correspondence between institutional outputs and expert advice, and improvement in environmental quality over the hypothetical state of affairs in the absence of international cooperation. Jørgen Wettestad and Steinar Andresen, "The Effectiveness of International Resource Cooperation: Some Preliminary Findings," Fridtjof Nansen Institute, Norway, 1991, 2.

to institutional effectiveness, by looking within the decision-making processes of the actors, are most likely to generate cumulative knowledge. Such research must be sensitive to the possibility that international institutions may have different effects on the policy processes of different countries. Since such work is time-consuming, enough knowledge to support valid generalizations will only be generated if many researchers, using similar concepts and methods, work simultaneously in different parts of the world.

Even within the constraints set by our focus on institutions rather than issue areas, and our emphasis on institutional effectiveness, our findings are preliminary. International environmental cooperation has only become widespread during the last decade or so. Continuing evaluation of new patterns of political behavior, relevant to the environment, will surely be essential to reach more broadly based judgments about which types of institutions have been most effective. In particular, research by political scientists could undertake three tasks: (1) pay more attention to the activities of developing countries, nongovernmental organizations, and business firms; (2) analyze issues of institutional overload, which may become increasingly important; and (3) inquire about how institutions "learn."

**More Actors**

We began this project by focusing on intergovernmental institutions dealing with environmental problems of concern to people in Europe and North America. After all, it is on such issues, including ozone and acid rain, that institutional innovation has been most visible; most of our evidence about effectiveness comes from the experience of advanced industrialized countries. Yet many international environmental problems cannot be managed successfully without effective action by developing countries, which implies changes in their politics and national capacity. We need studies of environmental policy making in the South that look systematically for evidence as to whether, and in which ways, international environmental institutions make a difference.[15]

15. For a study that argues that international environmental institutions in the Mediterannean have raised concern in North African countries, see Peter M. Haas, *Saving the Mediterranean: The Politics of International Environmental Cooperation* (New York: Columbia University Press, 1990).

Our analysis has admittedly been state-centric. As we have argued, this emphasis is appropriate given the central role states must play in any effective responses to international environmental problems. But as our empirical analysis makes clear, non-state actors are often important. For example, environmental NGOs clearly interact with international environmental institutions in complex ways. NGOs are often the source of policy innovation at the international level, the instruments of diffusion of international norms and practices, and sources of national-level information at the international level. NGOs operate on a complex playing field with multiple loyalties and blurred jurisdictions, often wielding greater influence than students of international politics have come to expect from actors who are weaker, according to conventional criteria, than their corporate and state adversaries.

More systematic research on the relationships between non-state actors and international institutions would be valuable. A first step would be to conduct an inductive mapping of NGOs as they affect environmental politics: Which NGOs are active on which issues? Are NGOs more relevant to issues of increasing concern about environmental policies than to issues of the contractual environment or capacity-building? Are intergovernmental institutions more effective when energetic NGOs exist to prod them, to publicize their activities, and to galvanize support for them within societies? Most broadly, what strategies do states and intergovernmental organizations follow with regard to NGOs on environmental policies? Under what conditions do states and intergovernmental organizations seek to exclude NGOs, or to co-opt them? Answers to such questions could be fascinating and revealing.[16]

Business firms also interact with international environmental organizations, and help to shape international rules. Enterprises are especially significant in determining the range of technological solutions to environmental problems, hence in affecting institutional effectiveness.

16. We are grateful for comments along these lines by Joseph S. Nye and other members of the International Institutions Program at the Center for International Affairs, 12 March 1992. See "Policies and Institutions: Nongovernmental Institutions," in World Resources Institute, *World Resources 1992–93* (New York: Oxford University Press, 1992), 215–34; and Paul Wapner, "Making States Biodegradable: Environmental Activism and World Politics," unpublished Ph.D. dissertation, Princeton University, 1991.

More energetic international actions for ozone protection, acid rain, regional seas protection, and controlling oil pollution from tanker operations were all facilitated by the availability of technological options which made such objectives appear feasible. However, technological change is in part a function of institutional influences, and in part autonomous. Technology has been both a contributing cause and a consequence of institutional effectiveness. Corporate decisions to invest in new technologies are driven in part by signals from institutions regarding future market opportunities. For instance, while progress in the ozone case after the Montreal Protocol was made easier by virtue of possible CFC substitutes, the availability of such commercial substitutes was itself the consequence of prior research and development decisions by the major producers. In the United States, the major producers accurately perceived in the early 1980s that little domestic CFC regulation was likely to occur, and reduced their research on alternative chemicals. It was only after the pace of international efforts resumed after 1986 that corporate research into alternatives responded, as companies began to search for new products that might become marketable if CFCs were banned worldwide.

In the course of this study, we have become increasingly aware of the effects that international negotiations and the evolution of international institutions can have on the availability of new technologies relevant to environmental problems. Technology does not simply exist or not exist. It arises in response to anticipated economic demands, conditional on the state of scientific knowledge and underlying technical capabilities. Anticipated economic demand, as in the CFC case, is to a considerable extent the result of anticipated environmental regulation. An important issue in considering international environmental regulation is the degree of elasticity of the underlying technology. If increased demand, fostered by regulation, is likely to bring a valuable new technology into being, the case for regulation is strengthened; conversely, if no such technology seems feasible, the costs of regulation may be very high.

### Institutional Overload

Another line of research is warranted to deal with what can be called the problems of success. International environmental institutions are proliferating rapidly. And the more successful ones, because they influence governments' decision making, place growing demands on governments' already crowded agendas. It follows that continued success at building effective international environmental institutions will soon place intolerable burdens on national administrative capacity, even for states with advanced regulatory apparatuses. A recent study in Sweden found 180 international environmental bodies which had some claim to the active involvement of the Swedish government. The UNCED negotiations, barring the unlikely event of a complete failure, will only accelerate the proliferation of international environmental agreements. This will make life difficult for national regulators.

In trade politics, similar problems were avoided (or mitigated) by the convention of most-favored nation (MFN) status, in which privileges granted to one nation through negotiated agreements were automatically extended to other nations that played by the same rules. This simplified politics by obviating the need to negotiate hundreds of treaties at a time, while also reducing the need for conference diplomacy. Security politics are simplified in part by the formation of alliances that aggregate political bargaining among manageable numbers of more or less like-minded countries. International monetary politics are simplified by the practice of pegging currencies, formally or informally, to a common currency, a basket of currencies, or gold. It is not clear what sort of techniques can be adopted to make international environmental politics more manageable. There are no clear analogues to MFN, alliances, or pegged currencies. In preparation for the Earth Summit, UNCED considered several dozen proposals for reforming international environmental decision making. None attracted widespread support, and most were either plainly unworkable or plainly inadequate.[17] Good studies of how governments are coping with the institutional overlaps and high demands they already face, especially in the institutionally dense region of Europe, would shed new light on institutional effectiveness and inform the current debate on institutional reform.

### Institutional Learning
All international institutions, because they are under human control, are capable of becoming more effective over time as a result of learning. Yet

17. Many of the proposals are reviewed in A/CONF.151/PC 102 (13 December 1991).

we lack a rigorous understanding of how they do so, of what strategies of learning work better than others, and of what conditions are most conducive to learning. The realm of international environmental institutions provides a useful laboratory for asking these questions.

Do institutional innovations (such as the use of the "ozone-depletion potential" to regulate a widening basket of CFCs, or "critical loads" to regulate acid rain) tend to come from similar sources? How can institutions promote more innovation? Many institutions, in particular UNEP, are becoming involved in a wide variety of environmental issues. To what extent are lessons transmitted from one area of activity to another? For instance, the political techniques of a convention followed by protocols, and concurrent assessment and regulatory activities, were first developed by UNEP's Regional Seas Program for the Mediterranean in 1975, and subsequently applied in UNEP's nine other regional seas efforts as well as for protecting stratospheric ozone and reducing acid rain. To what extent are substantive linkages being drawn between issues as institutions gain experience in their management and become familiar with the technical interlinkages?[18]

## Conclusions

Efforts to control international environmental problems have been carried out incrementally rather than holistically. Each set of issues has been considered separately, independently of possible common underlying causes such as population growth, patterns of consumer demand, and practices of modern industrial production. No attempts have been made systematically to reform a global political system that inhibits countries from experiencing the full costs of transboundary pollution

18. For a study of how UNEP drew lessons from the Mediterranean Action Plan and applied them to other regional seas programs see Peter M. Haas, "Save the Seas: UNEP's Regional Seas Programme and the Coordination of Regional Pollution Control Efforts," in Elisabeth Mann Borgese et al., eds., *Ocean Yearbook 9* (Chicago: University of Chicago Press, 1991). For other studies of international learning, see Ernst B. Haas, *When Knowledge is Power: Three Models of Change in International Organizations* (Berkeley: University of California Press, 1990); Joseph S. Nye, Jr., "Nuclear Learning and U.S.–Soviet Security Regimes," *International Organization* 41 (Summer 1987): 371–402; and George W. Breslauer and Philip E. Tetlock, eds., *Learning in U.S. and Soviet Foreign Policy* (Boulder: Westview Press, 1991).

and confers legal authority and responsibility on states, which often lack the resources and administrative skills to exercise effective domestic governance. The skeptic might ask: Is it possible to mitigate environmental problems without abrogating state sovereignty?

Rather surprisingly, the answer seems to be a cautious yes. Reformist institutionalist measures have facilitated international cooperation on several of the issues we have studied. In acid rain, oil pollution from tankers, Baltic and North Sea pollution, and stratospheric ozone depletion, agenda setting was reasonably prompt and accurate, international decisions were taken, and national policies implementing those decisions have been carried out. Although international institutions have not been integrated with one another in a systematic way, their efforts have complemented one another better than we would have expected. For instance, while the International Maritime Organization (IMO) started out with an exclusive focus on oil pollution from ships, it has expanded the types of pollution it addressed from that source, and other institutions were designed to deal with additional sources of marine pollution: land-based sources of pollution and non-vessel sources of coastal pollution were treated by UNEP and by Baltic and North Sea institutions. UNEP and the Food and Agriculture Organization (FAO) worked together remarkably well on issues having to do with chemical pesticides. However, the first half-century of efforts to control intentional oil pollution of the oceans is a story of failure; fisheries regulation has been notably ineffective; and until very recently, the World Bank has resisted environmentalists' attempts to make it "green". Our arguments for the virtues of incrementalism should not be misunderstood as briefs for complacency.

If judged by standards of budgets and authority, intergovernmental organizations and rules are extremely weak. The impact of international institutions lies in their performance of three catalytic functions: increasing governmental concern, enhancing the contractual environment, and increasing national political and administrative capacity. International organizations led by politically savvy executives, who tailor their actions to political obstacles, can design political arrangements that increase the probability of achieving effective results in accord with the "art of the possible." The success of these arrangements will depend in part, as do all international cooperative activities, on the support of governments and on the underlying conditions that make such support forthcoming. But they will also depend on human choice and human action.

On a more speculative and optimistic note, it is worthwhile to ask whether even the nascent international environmental institutions that we now observe are contributing to a new world environmental order. While the nation-state remains the principal legitimate source of public policy, environmental norms promulgated at the international level have in many cases been accepted by states. Indeed, sometimes normative pressures, bolstered by political incentives, seem to have led to regulations—reducing emissions to zero or imposing costly equipment requirements—even when such measures may not be justified on cost-benefit grounds. Actions taken to reduce Baltic and North Sea pollution, to require segregated ballast tanks, and to achieve critical loads of acidic deposition provide examples of the effects of such normative pressures. Such patterns of normative convergence could be significant in the long run, if publics are willing to sacrifice other values, such as maximizing economic growth, in order to save the environment. Yet, since action for environmental protection has been only marginal so far, the test of such commitment is still to come.

Whether a new world environmental order emerges or not, there is likely to be more international environmental cooperation in future years, and therefore more conflict over its terms. Across issue areas, we will observe variation in the nature and strength of international rules and the size, autonomy, and dynamism of intergovernmental organizations. These institutional variations will be explicable partly on the basis of underlying characteristics of world politics, including the actors involved in the issue and their capabilities; whether costs and benefits are diffuse or concentrated; and the resulting patterns of state and non-state interests. In a world of states, the views of powerful laggards will be particularly important. But patterns of cooperation will also depend, in part, on the objectives that intergovernmental organizations and leading governments pursue, on the strategies they devise, and on the cumulative effects of institutions.

The patterns are certain to vary, and they are sure to be fascinating to social scientists as well as activists. All we hope to have shown in this book is that even weak and young international institutions, such as those described here, have proved that they can to some extent facilitate international environmental cooperation. When they work effectively, international environmental institutions sow the seeds of political concern, they enable motivated actors to garner the capacity to manage domestic adjustment, and they overcome uncertainty and mistrust to make cooperation possible.

# Index

Abortion, 366–367

Access, to fisheries, 249, 250, 257, 289

Acid rain, 6, 8, 9, 10, 11, 12, 15, 16, 17, 22, 76, 82, 399, 400, 402, 408, 424. *See also* Long-Range Transboundary Air Pollution (LRTAP) Convention

causes of, 78–81

institutional response to, 21, 406

protocols on, 91–100

reduction of, 118–127

research on, 111, 113, 115–116, 120–121, 130–131(table)

ACOPS. See United Kingdom Advisory Committee on the Prevention of Pollution of the Sea

ADB. *See* Asian Development Bank

Aden, Gulf of, 216, 221

Advisory Committee on Marine Pollution (ICES), 150

Aerosol sprays, 34–35, 36–37, 39

Africa, 52, 259, 330, 387. *See also various countries; regions*

pesticide issues in, 316, 319n21, 328, 334, 336

population programs in, 385–386

Agenda setting, 11–13, 180

in CFCs, 28–34

in fisheries commissions, 265–272

in LRTAP, 109–113

in marine pollution, 146–150

in oil pollution issues, 188, 222–225

in pesticide use, 312–318

in population policies, 355–373

Agricultural Ministry (Denmark), 166

Agriculture

integrated pest management in, 318–319, 330–332

pesticide use, 309–311

pollution from, 148, 152, 165–167

World Bank role in, 347–348

Agrochemical industry, 315

Code of Conduct and, 336–337

pesticides in, 313–314, 335–336, 343

power of, 319–320

prior informed consent schemes, 324, 326–327, 339

AID. *See* United States Agency for International Development

Air pollution, 75, 415. *See also* Acid rain

critical load and, 101, 102–103, 104(table)

long-range transport of, 79–80, 81

in marine environments, 142, 143, 145

Air Pollution Unit (ECE), 84

Air Quality Agreement, 82–83n11

Aktionsconferenz Nordsee, 154

Alkali industry, 78–79

Alliance for Responsible CFC Policy, 36, 41, 46

American Tunaboat Association, 273

*Amoco Cadiz*, 217, 224

Investment, 16–17, 52, 70, 161–162
IOCU. *See* International Organization of Consumers Unions
IOFC. *See* Indian Ocean Fisheries Commission
IOPP. *See* International Oil Pollution Prevention Certificate
IPCS. *See* International Program on Chemical Safety
IPFC. *See* Indo-Pacific Fisheries Commission
IPIs. *See* International population institutions
IPM. *See* Integrated pest management
IPPF. *See* International Planned Parenthood Federation
Ireland, 141, 151, 217n106
IRPTC. *See* International Register of Potentially Toxic Chemicals
Italy, 209, 211
  CFC production in, 29, 53
  nitrogen oxide protocol in, 95, 108
  oil pollution in, 198, 217n106
  sulfur dioxide emissions in, 119–120
IUCN. *See* International Union for the Conservation of Nature; World Conservation Union
IWC. *See* International Whaling Commission

Japan, 37, 211, 231, 301, 313, 320, 334
  CFC production in, 42, 56, 70
  fisheries issues in, 259, 260, 261, 262–263, 276, 282, 284, 287, 289, 290, 294, 302
  Montreal Protocol and, 50n75, 55
  oil pollution, 198, 204, 217, 231
John Paul II, 365–366
Johnson, Edwin, 324
Johnson, Lyndon, 358
Joint Monitoring Program (OSPAR-COM), 169

Kenya, 54, 317, 364, 382
Krill fishery, 290–291

Large Combustion Plant Directive (LCPD), 107, 108
Latin America, 319n21, 387. *See also various countries*
  fisheries issues in, 260, 284, 290
  population issues in, 356, 385, 386
Law of the Sea negotiations, 186, 193, 228
Laws, 20. *See also conventions; protocols*
  fisheries access, 257, 263
  international, 17, 186, 193, 228, 257
  marine environment, 135, 143, 145
LCPD. *See* Large Combustion Plant Directive
LDCs. *See* Less developed countries
Lead, 151, 158
League Committee of Experts, 198
League of Nations, 197
Leesburg workshop, 40–41
Less developed countries (LDCs), and CFCs, 60, 61, 63–64. *See also* Developing countries; Third World
Licensing, 175–176, 272
  marine dumping and incineration, 151–152, 160, 165, 169, 170
*Limits to Growth*, 359
Load on top (LOT), 205–206, 209, 237, 240, 243
  enforcement of, 218–219, 227
  promotion of, 207, 233–234
London Dumping Convention, 143, 208
London Guidelines, 323, 325, 328, 337, 338, 339, 344, 345
Long-Range Transboundary Air Pollution (LRTAP) Convention, 75, 128–129(table), 145, 400
  compliance with, 113, 115
  creation of, 81–83
  critical loads in, 100, 102–103
  decision making in, 86–87
  and emissions reduction, 114(table), 116–127
  Executive Body (EB) of, 84–85, 90, 100, 105